gender

 Other titles in this series include:

gender

A READER *for* WRITERS

Megan L. Titus
Rider University

Wendy L. Walker
Texas A&M University–Corpus Christi

New York   Oxford
Oxford University Press

Oxford University Press is a department of the University of Oxford.
It furthers the University's objective of excellence in research,
scholarship, and education by publishing worldwide.

Oxford   New York
Auckland   Cape Town   Dar es Salaam   Hong Kong   Karachi
Kuala Lumpur   Madrid   Melbourne   Mexico City   Nairobi
New Delhi   Shanghai   Taipei   Toronto

With offices in
Argentina   Austria   Brazil   Chile   Czech Republic   France   Greece
Guatemala   Hungary   Italy   Japan   Poland   Portugal   Singapore
South Korea   Switzerland   Thailand   Turkey   Ukraine   Vietnam

For titles covered by Section 112 of the US Higher Education
Opportunity Act, please visit www.oup.com/us/he for the
latest information about pricing and alternate formats.

Published by Oxford University Press
198 Madison Avenue, New York, New York 10016
http://www.oup.com

Oxford is a registered trademark of Oxford University Press

Library of Congress Cataloging-in-Publication Data

Names: Titus, Megan, author.
Title: Gender : a reader for writers / Megan Titus, Rider University, Wendy
    Walker, Texas A&M University.
Description: 1 Edition. | New York : Oxford University Press, 2016.
Identifiers: LCCN 2015037609| ISBN 9780190298852 | ISBN 9780190298876
Subjects: LCSH: Gender expression. | Sex role. | Identity (Psychology)
Classification: LCC HQ1075 .T598 2016 | DDC 305.3--dc23 LC record available
    at http://lccn.loc.gov/2015037609

Printing number: 9 8 7 6 5 4 3 2 1

Printed in the United States of America
on acid-free paper

brief table of contents

Table of Contents

Adrienne Rich, **"What Does a Woman Need to Know?"**   76

"Women have lived and continue to live in ignorance of our collective context, vulnerable to the projections of men's fantasies about us as they appear in art, in literature, in sciences, in the media, the so-called humanistic studies. I suggest that not anatomy, but enforced ignorance, has been a crucial key to our powerlessness."

Sandra Cisneros, **"Guadalupe the Sex Goddess"**   85

"I was angry for so many years every time I saw *la Virgen de Guadalupe*, my culture's role model for brown women like me. She was damn dangerous, an ideal so lofty and unrealistic it was laughable. Did boys have to aspire to be Jesus?"

Zachary Pullin, **"Two Spirit: The Story of a Movement Unfolds"**   91

"Two-spirit—the movement, the societies, and the term itself—marks a return to a tradition that historically recognized more than two genders. It's meant to honor Native American languages and traditions that were nearly forgotten in some cases."

Julia R. Johnson, **"Cisgender Privilege, Intersectionality, and the Criminalization of CeCe McDonald: Why Intercultural Communication Needs Transgender Studies"**   96

"The treatment of McDonald illustrates the layers of violence often imposed on persons who are transgender, particularly trans* persons of color who are (or are perceived to be) working class or poor."

Tommi Avicolli Mecca, **"He Defies You Still: The Memoirs of a Sissy"**   109

"What did being a sissy really mean? It was a way of walking (from the hips rather than the shoulders); it was a way of talking (often with a lisp or a in high-pitched voice); it was a way of relating to others (gently, not wanting to fight, or hurt anybody's feelings)."

Vanessa Vitiello Urquhart, **"Why I'm Still a Butch Lesbian"**   119

"In our culture, the impulse to distance oneself from negatives associated with women and femininity is endemic. When we insult men, we do it by comparing them to women. When we compare women to men, we're generally praising them."

"Cut. Shredded. Jacked. Those are violent straight-boy adjectives that mean 'beautiful.' But we straight boys aren't supposed to think of other men as beautiful. We're supposed to think of the most physically gifted men as warrior soldiers, as dangerous demigods."

5 Gender and Popular Culture 229

"Yes, it is a princess movie. Yes, it's about love. But it is not restrictive about what love is and what being a princess means. There is a greater focus on women's relationships and journeys and how girls can save the day—Anna, through her sacrifice, and Elsa, by being herself."

"Bringing in a Strong Female Character™ isn't actually a feminist statement, or an inclusionary statement, or even a basic equality statement, if the character doesn't have any reason to be in the story except to let filmmakers point at her on the poster and say 'See? This film totally respects strong women!'"

"By riding for white female rappers to the exclusion of Black women, Black men collude with the system against Black women, by demonstrating that our needs, aspirations and feelings do not matter and are not worthy of having a hearing."

"But something tells me Kim probably has no clue about the cultural and historic significance of what she's done. Instead, she probably just thought it would be cool to do an edgy photo shoot with a famous photographer. And many of you have fallen for that oversimplified stance as well."

"According to *Orange Is the New Black* . . . men in prison are 'super-predators' while women in prison are, often, innocent victims, doomed by circumstances and their own painful but touching character flaws."

"At times, [*Kimmy Schmidt*] resembles a Nickelodeon tween show—which is just how its heroine might imagine her own life. Yet, without any contradiction, it's also a sitcom about a rape survivor."

6   Gender and Work   265

"I want a wife who takes care of the children when they are sick, a wife who arranges to be around when the children need special care, because, of course, I cannot miss classes at school. My wife must arrange to lose time at work and not lose the job. It may mean a small cut in my wife's income from time to time, but I guess I can tolerate that."

"I still strongly believe that women can 'have it all' (and that men can too). I believe that we can 'have it all at the same time.' But not today, not with the way America's economy and society are currently structured."

"Feminism insists on women's right to make choices—about whether to marry, whether to have children, whether to combine work and family or to focus on one over the other. It also urges men and women to share the joys and burdens of family life and calls on society to place a higher priority on supporting caregiving work."

"Movies and television, of course, aren't always the truest representations of real life, and sometimes give viewers extreme portrayals of the Stay-At-Home dad. He is often made to be a bumbling goof who runs around the house putting out small fires while wearing his wife's apron. . . . Things are, of course, different from the movies, not so comical, and most of the time, not so dramatic."

"Banning women from combat does not ensure military effectiveness. It only perpetuates counterproductive gender stereotypes and biases. It is time for the U.S. military to get over its hang-ups and acknowledge women's rightful place on the battlefield."

"The gender differences in the world of work are striking, extensive, and enduring. They exist in multiple dimensions. Although the most obvious gap is in labor force participation rates, there are other persistent gender gaps . . . that affect the extent to which paid work expands well-being, agency, and future economic opportunities."

7   Gender and Globalization   325

"The principle of women's equality is a simple, self-evident truth, but the work of turning that principle into practice is rarely simple. It takes years and even generations of patient, persistent work, not only to change a country's laws, but to change its people's minds, to weave throughout culture and tradition in public discourse and private views the unassailable fact of women's worth and women's rights."

"'These will probably be the poorest people you ever meet. But still, they're just *girls*. Some are popular. Some are socially awkward. I even have class clowns. . . . When anyone from the outside comes in to try to teach them anything, those are some of the few moments in their lives that they actually have hope. And some of the few times that they can simply be themselves. *Girls*.'"

"It is well established that female genital mutilation (FGM) is not required in Muslim law. It is an ancient cultural practice that existed before Islam, Christianity and Judaism. It is also agreed across large swathes of the world that it is barbaric."

"In recent years, in part due to the one-child policy, filial roles have changed dramatically. In imperial China women occupied an inferior position in society. During the Maoist era they were largely emancipated into the work-force. . . . Women's education and rights continued to improve in the three decades following China's opening-up and reform."

"The peculiar practices of Islam with respect to women had always formed part of the Western narrative of the quintessential otherness and inferiority of Islam."

Contents by Genre

academic

journalism

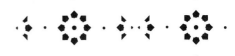

preface

When we are born into this world, the first thing the doctor usually says is, "It's a boy!" or "It's a girl!" From the moment we take our first breaths, we are marked by our gender.

But actually, our gender identity begins even earlier than that.

While we're still in the womb, our mothers can make the decision to find out our sex. So even before we're born and the doctor proclaims our gender, an ultrasound technician may tell our mothers that we are a boy or a girl. Of course, the technicians are known to make mistakes—boy parts can sometimes be hidden from the tech's eyes.

But, if our sex is revealed before we're born, people will inundate us with tiny baby clothes that mark our gender: blue overalls and sports-themed gear for boys, pink dresses and headbands for girls. Even our bedrooms become gendered: boys' rooms have dinosaurs, sports, or cars; girls' rooms have ballerinas, Hello Kitty, or fairy tales.

So, imagine what would happen if our room was all ready, all decked out in pink and white and lace, and when we were born, the doctor exclaimed, "It's a boy!"

As this anecdote demonstrates, gender is imbued into our psyche, sometimes even while we're still in the womb. It not only helps define us, but also informs how we construct the identity of others. It is a lens through which we see the world; the more we understand our own gender identity, the more we can see how our identity fits into society. A large part of the way we interact with the world is, in fact, determined by our gender.

We chose the readings in this book to serve as a guide to introduce you to the theoretical concepts of gender, as well as to provoke you into thinking about how your own gender serves as a lens through which you view the world and through which the world views you. Even if the author or the subject(s) of the readings is a different gender than you, we hope that you imagine your own gendered position in relation to the position of the subject of the text. For example, if you are of a different gender, we invite you to recognize how your reading of that particular text could be informed by your gender. If you are the same gender, we invite you to ponder how this story resonates with you and why. We also invite you to read these texts together, observe which can be read with each other and which should be read against each other, and why.

Because gender studies is by nature an interdisciplinary field, so too are the texts we've chosen. Our authors hail from fields as diverse as political science, communication, law, film, and biology. They are professors, filmmakers, lawyers, scientists, and human rights activists. The texts are scholarly, informative, and creative. We chose pieces that we love, that we feel strongly about as being integral to the field of gender studies, that highlight underrepresented voices, and that present opposing points of view.

One note about the organization of this book: you will note that we do not go in chronological order of the date the texts were published. Instead, we decided to present the texts thematically, even within the chapters. In some cases, such as Chapter 1, chronology made sense because Aristotle sets the standard for gender roles for hundreds of years to come. At other times, such as in Chapter 3, we made a conscious decision to begin with the theme—in that case, stereotypes of masculinity—and then move into critiques of those stereotypes. So, although Steinem's essay is the oldest in the chapter (having been published in 1978), it's actually the third in sequence.

We also included the original date and place of publication in the introduction to each text. This context will be of great importance as you enter into a critical analysis of these readings. A good reader will make note of where and when a text was written because these facts give contextual clues to the original audience of a text and, thus, the author's intent. As you read these texts, analyze the tone with which the author writes and the evidence the author uses, and assess the strength (or weakness) of the author's argument. Each piece in this book has a distinctive, strong point of view and is rife with the opportunity for deep analysis. That's part of what makes gender such an ample topic for this Oxford Reader Series.

Gender: A Reader for Writers is part of a series of brief single-topic readers from Oxford University Press designed for today's college writing courses. Each reader in this series approaches a contemporary conversation from multiple perspectives:

- **Timely** Most selections were originally published in 2010 or later.
- **Global** Sources and voices from around the world are included.
- **Diverse** Selections come from a range of nontraditional and alternate print and online media, as well as representative mainstream sources.
- **Curated** Every author of a volume in this series is a teacher-scholar whose expertise in the writing classroom as well as in a volume's specific subject informs his or her choice of readings.

In addition to the rich array of perspectives on topical (even urgent) issues addressed in each reader, each volume features an abundance of different genres and styles—from the academic research paper to the pithy Twitter argument. Useful but nonintrusive pedagogy includes the following:

- **Chapter introductions** that provide a brief overview of the chapter's theme and a sense of how the chapter's selections relate both to the overarching theme and to each other.
- **Headnotes** introduce each reading by providing concise information about its original publication and encourage students to explore their prior knowledge of (or opinions about) some aspect of the selection's content.
- **"Analyze" and "Explore"** questions after each reading scaffold and support student reading for comprehension as well as rhetorical considerations, providing prompts for reflection, classroom discussion, and brief writing assignments.
- **"Forging Connections" and "Looking Forward" prompts** after each chapter encourage critical thinking by asking students to compare perspectives and strategies among readings both within the chapter and with readings in other chapters, suggesting writing assignments (many of which are multimodal) that engage students with larger conversations in the academy, the community, and the media.
- **An appendix on "Researching and Writing about Gender"** guides student inquiry and research in a digital environment. Coauthored by a research librarian and a writing program director, this appendix provides real-world, transferable strategies for locating, assessing, synthesizing, and citing sources in support of an argument.

about the authors

Megan L. Titus directs the composition program at Rider University, where she is an assistant professor of English. In the English Department, she teaches a variety of courses, ranging from first-year to advanced writing and rhetoric. She is also on the faculty for the gender and sexuality studies program, where she regularly teaches the gender and sexuality studies senior seminar and for whom she developed the course Popular Constructions of Gender and Sexuality. She holds degrees in English and creative writing from Muhlenberg College (BA), English and writing studies from Montclair State University (MA), and English and rhetoric and composition from Ohio University (PhD). She also holds a certificate in women's and gender studies from Ohio University. Her research interests include writing program administration and gender as well as gender and popular culture. Her work has appeared in *WPA: Writing Program Administration* and *Praxis: A Writing Center Journal*.

Wendy L. Walker is a professional assistant professor of English at Texas A & M University–Corpus Christi, where she teaches first-year writing and rhetoric as well as introductory 20th- and 21st-century American literature classes that emphasize multiethnic, minority, and women writers. She holds degrees in English from Otterbein University (BA), gender, literature, and modernity from the University of Warwick (MA), and English and literature from Ohio University (PhD). She also holds a certificate in women's and gender studies from Ohio University. Her research interests include feminist literary theory, Chicana feminist theory, and Chicana literature.

acknowledgments

This project has its roots in two composition classes at Ohio University. ENG 153A: Writing about Gender was a dedicated special-topics class. Students who signed up for the course knew that the readings and writing assignments would have a focus on gender. Similarly, ENG 306J: Women and Writing was a course that, although instructors were allowed to shape their own focus, emphasized women's writing. Many of the readings in this book have their origins in these two classes. Later, we taught versions of these classes at Rider University and Texas A&M University–Corpus Christi, adding and cutting readings and developing discussion questions and writing assignments. The success of these courses over the years suggested to us that we had something special. There is no way that what began as parts of two syllabi almost ten years ago would have come to fruition without the support, the feedback, and the interest of those we would like to thank.

First, our students, who, through their responses to our readings and writing assignments over the years, provided substantial feedback and advice on the crafting of our course syllabi and, later, this book.

As we put this book together, we received feedback and advice from our friends and colleagues. In particular, we thank Laurel Harris, Nowell Marshall, Mary Morse, and Vanita Neelakanta at Rider University; Robin Carstensen at Texas A&M University–Corpus Christi; Caitlin Hawes; Lydia McDermott at Whitman College; and Talinn Phillips at Ohio University for the perspectives they brought to the shaping of this text and the support they offered as we constructed the table of contents and the apparatus.

At Oxford, we worked with a stellar team that, over and over, demonstrated its commitment to excellence in the production of textbooks. Our editor, Garon Scott, has been always accessible, always open to suggestions, and always supportive of our project. He helmed this ship with a steadfast hand, and for that we are forever grateful. Lisa Black, our permissions editor, had to track down a number of texts for us and did so with a patience and persistence to be much admired. Michael Kopf, our production editor, offered feedback as we embarked on the copyediting process and guided us through the particulars of readying this manuscript for publication.

Above all, we'd like to thank our families. In particular, Megan says thank you to Matt Schario, who took over many of the household and childcare duties as this project developed and who unfailingly offered his time as an early reader of a full draft of the manuscript. She also thanks Luke for his hugs and his love, even when Mommy had to type with one hand and play catch with the other. Wendy thanks Judy Walker and Liberty Welsh, who patiently listened to frequent and detailed accounts of our progress on this project and who always had encouraging words.

1 Introduction to Gender

Imagine that you've arrived at a friend's party. Your friend is excited for you to meet Chris, someone who is visiting from your friend's hometown. On meeting you, Chris shakes your hand vigorously and says, "It's so great to finally meet you!" After shaking hands, you look Chris over carefully. Chris has dark hair and eyes, and a medium build. Chris is wearing a black t-shirt, jeans, and sneakers.

Based on what you've learned about Chris, would you say that Chris is male or female? What clues in the text suggest this to you?

Every day, gender is shaping the way that we see the world. It impacts the way that we look at ourselves and the way we look at others. In a way, it tells us what to think.

If you said that Chris is a male, why was that your conclusion? If you believe Chris is female, again, why did you think so? Our notions of what makes a "man" and what makes a "woman" would have helped you see

Chris as one gender over another, although we have presented a gender-neutral name, appearance, and attitude.

In the readings that follow, you will begin to investigate the origins of our preconceived notions of gender. As you will see, these notions are rooted in our understandings of gender as biological, as social, as psychological, as political, and as historical. We begin with a selection from Aristotle's *Politics*. Although Aristotle is a well-known philosopher and rhetorician, he also has some clear ideas on men's and women's roles that still resonate in today's society. "Declaration of Sentiments and Resolutions," written by women including Elizabeth Cady Stanton and Lucretia Mott at the Seneca Falls conference in 1848, is a statement of women's rights that uses the Declaration of Independence as a model. Lois Gould's story "X: A Fabulous Child's Story" asks us to challenge the gender roles set forth by theorists like Aristotle and to consider what a child raised without gender might be like and why. Judith Lorber argues that gender is a social construction in " 'Night to His Day': The Social Construction of Gender." Finally, in "The Five Sexes: Why Male and Female Are Not Enough," Anne Fausto-Sterling uses biology to demonstrate that our bodies are not so easily pigeonholed into one of two gender categories. As you work your way through the introductory readings, think about what ideas about gender they are highlighting for you and how they might work to set up the rest of the textbook.

Aristotle
From *Politics*

The Greek philosopher **Aristotle** (c. 384 BCE–322 BCE) was a teacher, playwright, scientist, and prolific writer. The philosopher Plato was his own teacher, and among Aristotle's students were King Philip of Macedonia and Alexander the Great. Today, Aristotle's writings help form the foundations of philosophy and rhetoric. What follows is a selection from Book I of Aristotle's text *Politics*. In this section of *Politics*, Aristotle expounds on the idea of the city (*polis*) and "political community" in contrast to communities such as the household. Our specific interest in this text is the way in which Aristotle presents the hierarchy of the family and the roles of men and women in the family and household. As you read, consider how Aristotle presents human nature and how that relates to his representation of gender.

Book First

I Every state is a community of some kind, and every community is established with a view to some good; for mankind always act in order to obtain that which they think good. But, if all communities aim at some good, the state or political community, which is the highest of all, and which embraces all the rest, aims at good in a greater degree than any other, and at the highest good.

Some people think[1] that the qualifications of a statesman, king, householder, and master are the same, and that they differ, not in kind, but only in the number of their subjects. For example, the ruler over a few is called a master; over more, the manager of a household; over a still larger number, a statesman or king, as if there were no difference between a great household and a small state. The distinction which is made between the king and the statesman is as follows: When the government is personal, the ruler is a king; when, according to the rules of the political science, the citizens rule and are ruled in turn, then he is called a statesman.

But all this is a mistake; for governments differ in kind, as will be evident to any one who considers the matter according to the method[2] which has hitherto guided us. As in other departments of science, so in politics, the compound should always be resolved into the simple elements or least parts of the whole. We must therefore look at the elements of which the state is composed, in order that we may see in what the different kinds of rule differ from one another, and whether any scientific result can be attained about each one of them.

II He who thus considers things in their first growth and origin, whether a state or anything else, will obtain the clearest view of them. In the first place there must be a union of those who cannot exist without each other; namely, of male and female, that the race may continue (and this is a union which is formed, not of deliberate purpose, but because, in common with other animals and with plants, mankind have a natural desire to leave behind them an image of themselves), and of natural ruler and subject, that both may be preserved. For that which can foresee by the exercise of mind is by nature intended to be lord and master, and that which can with its body give effect to such foresight is a subject, and by nature a slave; hence master and slave have the same interest. Now nature has distinguished between the female and the slave. For she is not niggardly, like the smith who fashions the Delphian knife for many uses; she makes each thing for a single use, and every instrument is best made when intended for one and not for many uses. But among barbarians no distinction is made between women and slaves, because there is no natural ruler among them: they are a community of slaves, male and female. Wherefore the poets say—

"It is meet that Hellenes should rule over barbarians";

as if they thought that the barbarian and the slave were by nature one.

Out of these two relationships between man and woman, master and slave, the first thing to arise is the family, and Hesiod is right when he says—

"First house and wife and an ox for the plough,"

for the ox is the poor man's slave. The family is the association established by nature for the supply of men's everyday wants, and the members of it are called by Charondas "companions of the cupboard," and by Epimenides the Cretan, "companions of the manger." But when several families are united, and the association aims at something more than the supply of daily needs, the first society to be formed is the village. And the most natural form of the village appears to be that of a colony from the family, composed of the children and grandchildren, who are said to be suckled "with the same milk." And this is the reason why Hellenic states were originally governed by kings; because the Hellenes were under royal rule before they came together, as the barbarians still are. Every family is ruled by the eldest, and therefore in the colonies of the family the kingly form of government prevailed because they were of the same blood. As Homer says[3]:

"Each one gives law to his children and to his wives."

For they lived dispersedly, as was the manner in ancient times. Wherefore men say that the Gods have a king, because they themselves either are or were in ancient times under the rule of a king. For they imagine, not only the forms of the Gods, but their ways of life to be like their own.

When several villages are united in a single complete community, large enough to be nearly or quite self-sufficing, the state comes into existence, originating in the bare needs of life, and continuing in existence for the sake of a good life. And therefore, if the earlier forms of society are natural, so is the state, for it is the end of them, and the nature of a thing is its end. For what each thing is when fully developed, we call its nature, whether we are speaking of a man, a horse, or a family. Besides, the final cause and end of a thing is the best, and to be self-sufficing is the end and the best.

Hence it is evident that the state is a creation of nature, and that man is by nature a political animal. And he who by nature and not by mere accident is without a state, is either a bad man or above humanity; he is like the

"Tribeless, lawless, hearthless one,"

whom Homer[4] denounces—the natural outcast is forthwith a lover of war; he may be compared to an isolated piece at draughts.

Now, that man is more of a political animal than bees or any other gregarious animals is evident. Nature, as we often say, makes nothing in vain,[5] and man is the only animal whom she has endowed with the gift of speech.[6] And whereas mere voice is but an indication of pleasure or pain, and is therefore found in other animals (for their nature attains to the perception of pleasure and pain and the intimation of them to one another, and no further), the power of speech is intended to set forth the expedient and inexpedient, and therefore likewise the just and the unjust. And it is a characteristic of man that he alone has any sense of good and evil, of just and unjust, and the like, and the association of living beings who have this sense makes a family and a state.

Further, the state is by nature clearly prior to the family and to the individual, since the whole is of necessity prior to the part; for example, if the whole body be destroyed, there will be no foot or hand, except in an equivocal sense, as we might speak of a stone hand; for when destroyed the hand will be no better than that. But things are defined by their working and power; and we ought not to say that they are the same when they no longer have their proper quality, but only that they have the same name. The proof that the state is a creation of nature and prior to the individual is that the individual, when isolated, is not self-sufficing; and therefore he is like a part in relation to the whole. But he who is unable to live in society, or who has no need because he is sufficient for himself, must be either a beast or a god:

he is no part of a state. A social instinct is implanted in all men by nature, and yet he who first founded the state was the greatest of benefactors. For man, when perfected, is the best of animals, but, when separated from law and justice, he is the worst of all; since armed injustice is the more dangerous, and he is equipped at birth with arms, meant to be used by intelligence and virtue, which he may use for the worst ends. Wherefore, if he have not virtue, he is the most unholy and the most savage of animals, and the most full of lust and gluttony. But justice is the bond of men in states, for the administration of justice, which is the determination of what is just,[7] is the principle of order in political society. [. . .]

V But is there any one thus intended by nature to be a slave, and for whom such a condition is expedient and right, or rather is not all slavery a violation of nature?

There is no difficulty in answering this question, on grounds both of reason and of fact. For that some should rule and others be ruled is a thing not only necessary, but expedient; from the hour of their birth, some are marked out for subjection, others for rule.

And there are many kinds both of rulers and subjects (and that rule is the better which is exercised over better subjects—for example, to rule over men is better than to rule over wild beasts; for the work is better which is executed by better workmen, and where one man rules and another is ruled, they may be said to have a work); for in all things which form a composite whole and which are made up of parts, whether continuous or discrete, a distinction between the ruling and the subject element comes to light. Such a duality exists in living creatures, but not in them only; it originates in the constitution of the universe; even in things which have no life there is a ruling principle, as in a musical mode. But we are wandering from the subject. We will therefore restrict ourselves to the living creature, which, in the first place, consists of soul and body: and of these two, the one is by nature the ruler, and the other the subject. But then we must look for the intentions of nature in things which retain their nature, and not in things which are corrupted. And therefore we must study the man who is in the most perfect state both of body and soul, for in him we shall see the true relation of the two; although in bad or corrupted natures the body will often appear to rule over the soul, because they are in an evil and unnatural condition. At all events we may firstly observe in living creatures both a despotical and a constitutional rule; for the soul rules the body with a despotical rule, whereas the intellect rules the appetites with a constitutional and royal rule. And it is clear that the rule of the soul over the body, and of the mind and the rational element over the passionate, is natural and expedient; whereas the equality of the two or the rule of the inferior is always hurtful. The same holds good of animals in relation to men; for tame animals have a better nature than wild, and all tame animals are better off when they are ruled by man; for then they are preserved. Again, the male is by nature superior, and the female inferior; and the one rules, and the other is ruled; this principle, of necessity, extends to all mankind. Where then there is such a difference as that between soul and body, or between men and animals (as in the case of those whose business is to use their body, and who can do nothing better), the lower sort are by nature slaves, and it is better for them as for all inferiors that they should be under the rule of a master. For he who can be, and therefore is, another's and he who participates in rational principle enough to apprehend, but not to have, such a principle, is a slave by nature. Whereas the lower animals cannot even apprehend a principle; they obey their instincts. And indeed the use made of slaves and of tame animals is not very different; for both with their bodies minister to the needs of life. Nature would like to distinguish between the bodies of freemen and slaves, making the one strong for servile labour, the other upright, and although useless for such services, useful for political life in the arts both of war and peace. But the opposite often happens—that some have the souls and others have the bodies of freemen. And doubtless if men differed from one another in the mere forms of their bodies as much as the statues of the Gods do from men, all would acknowledge that the inferior class should be slaves of the superior. And if this is true of the body, how much more just that a similar distinction should exist in the soul? But the beauty of the body is seen, whereas the beauty of the soul is not seen. It is clear, then, that some men are by nature free, and others slaves, and that for these latter slavery is both expedient and right. [. . .]

XII Of household management we have seen[8] that there are three parts—one is the rule of a master over slaves, which has been discussed already,[9] another of a father, and the third of a husband. A husband and father, we saw, rules over wife and children, both free, but the rule differs, the rule over his children being a royal, over his wife a constitutional rule. For although there may be exceptions to the order of nature, the male is by nature

fitter for command than the female, just as the elder and full-grown is superior to the younger and more immature. But in most constitutional states
the citizens rule and are ruled by turns, for the idea of a constitutional state
implies that the natures of the citizens are equal, and do not differ at all.[10]
Nevertheless, when one rules and the other is ruled we endeavour to create
a difference of outward forms and names and titles of respect, which may be
illustrated by the saying of Amasis about his foot-pan.[11] The relation of the
male to the female is of this kind, but there the inequality is permanent.
The rule of a father over his children is royal, for he rules by virtue both of
love and of the respect due to age, exercising a kind of royal power. And
therefore Homer has appropriately called Zeus "father of Gods and men,"
because he is the king of them all. For a king is the natural superior of his
subjects, but he should be of the same kin or kind with them, and such is
the relation of elder and younger, of father and son.

XIII Thus it is clear that household management attends more to men
than to the acquisition of inanimate things, and to human excellence more
than to the excellence of property which we call wealth, and to the virtue
of freemen more than to the virtue of slaves. A question may indeed be
raised, whether there is any excellence at all in a slave beyond and higher
than merely instrumental and ministerial qualities—whether he can have
the virtues of temperance, courage, justice, and the like; or whether slaves
possess only bodily and ministerial qualities. And, whichever way we
answer the question, a difficulty arises; for, if they have virtue, in what will
they differ from freemen? On the other hand, since they are men and share
in rational principle, it seems absurd to say that they have no virtue. A similar question may be raised about women and children, whether they too
have virtues: ought a woman to be temperate and brave and just, and is a
child to be called temperate, and intemperate, or not? So in general we may
ask about the natural ruler, and the natural subject, whether they have the
same or different virtues. For if a noble nature is equally required in both,
why should one of them always rule, and the other always be ruled? Nor
can we say that this is a question of degree, for the difference between ruler
and subject is a difference of kind, which the difference of more and less
never is. Yet how strange is the supposition that the one ought, and that
the other ought not, to have virtue! For if the ruler is intemperate and
unjust, how can he rule well? If the subject, how can he obey well? If he
be licentious and cowardly, he will certainly not do his duty. It is evident,

therefore, that both of them must have a share of virtue, but varying as natural subjects also vary among themselves. Here the very constitution of the soul has shown us the way; in it one part naturally rules, and the other is subject, and the virtue of the ruler we maintain to be different from that of the subject;—the one being the virtue of the rational, and the other of the irrational part. Now, it is obvious that the same principle applies generally, and therefore almost all things rule and are ruled according to nature. But the kind of rule differs;—the freeman rules over the slave after another manner from that in which the male rules over the female, or the man over the child; although the parts of the soul are present in all of them, they are present in different degrees. For the slave has no deliberative faculty at all; the woman has, but it is without authority; and the child has, but it is immature. So it must necessarily be supposed to be with the moral virtues also; all should partake of them, but only in such manner and degree as is required by each for the fulfilment of his duty. Hence the ruler ought to have moral virtue in perfection, for his function, taken absolutely, demands a master artificer, and rational principle is such an artificer; the subjects, on the other hand, require only that measure of virtue which is proper to each of them. Clearly, then, moral virtue belongs to all of them; but the temperance of a man and of a woman, or the courage and justice of a man and of a woman, are not, as Socrates maintained,[12] the same; the courage of a man is shown in commanding, of a woman in obeying. And this holds of all other virtues, as will be more clearly seen if we look at them in detail, for those who say generally that virtue consists in a good disposition of the soul, or in doing rightly, or the like, only deceive themselves. Far better than such definitions is their mode of speaking, who, like Gorgias,[13] enumerate the virtues. All classes must be deemed to have their special attributes; as the poet says of women,

> "Silence is a woman's glory,"

but this is not equally the glory of man. The child is imperfect, and therefore obviously his virtue is not relative to himself alone, but to the perfect man and to his teacher, and in like manner the virtue of the slave is relative

> "The courage of a man is shown in commanding, of a woman in obeying."

to a master. Now we determined[14] that a slave is useful for the wants of life, and therefore he will obviously require only so much virtue as will prevent him from failing in his duty through cowardice or lack of self-control. Some one will ask whether, if what we are saying is true, virtue will not be required also in the artisans, for they often fail in their work through the lack of self-control? But is there not a great difference in the two cases? For the slave shares in his master's life; the artisan is less closely connected with him, and only attains excellence in proportion as he becomes a slave. The meaner sort of mechanic has a special and separate slavery; and whereas the slave exists by nature, not so the shoemaker or other artisan. It is manifest, then, that the master ought to be the source of such excellence in the slave, and not a mere possessor of the art of mastership which trains the slave in his duties.[15] Wherefore they are mistaken who forbid us to converse with slaves and say that we should employ command only,[16] for slaves stand even more in need of admonition than children.

So much for this subject; the relations of husband and wife, parent and child, their several virtues, what in their intercourse with one another is good, and what is evil, and how we may pursue the good and escape the evil, will have to be discussed when we speak of the different forms of government.[17] For, inasmuch as every family is a part of a state, and these relationships are the parts of a family, and the virtue of the part must have regard to the virtue of the whole, women and children must be trained by education with an eye to the constitution,[18] if the virtues of either of them are supposed to make any difference in the virtues of the state. And they must make a difference: for the children grow up to be citizens, and half the free persons in a state are women.[19]

Of these matters, enough has been said; of what remains, let us speak at another time. Regarding, then, our present inquiry as complete, we will make a new beginning. And, first, let us examine the various theories of a perfect state.

NOTES

1. Cp. Plato, *Politicus*, 258 E–259 D.
2. Cp. Bk. 1, VIII.
3. *Od.* ix. 114, quoted by Plato, *Laws*, iii. 680 B, and in *N. Eth.* x. 1180[a] 28.
4. *Il.* ix. 63.
5. Cp. Bk. 1, VIII.
6. Cp. Bk. 7, XIV.

7. Cp. *Nic. Eth.* v. 1134ᵃ 31.

8. Bk. 1, IV.

9. Bk. 1, IV–VII.

10. Cp. Bk. 2, I; Bk. 3, XVII.

11. Herod. ii. 172.

12. Plato, *Meno*, 72 A–73 C.

13. *Meno*, 71 E, 72 A.

14. Bk. 1, V, cf. Bk. 1, XII.

15. Cp. Bk. 1, VII.

16. Plato, *Laws*, vi. 777 E.

17. The question is not actually discussed in the *Politics*.

18. Cp. Bk. 5, IX; Bk. 8, II.

19. Plato, *Laws*, vi. 781 A.

Analyze

1. According to Aristotle, what is a common misconception that people tend to have about the "qualifications" of different heads of state? Why do people hold this misconception?

2. What does Aristotle see as the main difference between men and animals? Why is this difference significant?

3. How does Aristotle delineate what are male and female "roles" and "virtues"?

4. Why does Aristotle believe that men are "by nature fitter for command than" women?

Explore

1. Return to Aristotle's definition of male and female roles. How do these compare to current notions of gender?

2. Why does Aristotle believe that a father is akin to royalty? What comparisons does he draw on to make this argument? Are there counterarguments that you might present to challenge Aristotle's point of view?

3. In Chapter 13, Aristotle writes that "silence is a woman's glory," but not a man's or a child's. Why does he make this statement? To what extent do you agree or disagree with this sentiment, and why?

Seneca Falls Convention
"Declaration of Sentiments and Resolutions"

The "Declaration of Sentiments" was presented at the 1848 **Seneca Falls Convention** in Seneca Falls, New York, the first convention to address women's rights in the United States. The declaration was coauthored by Elizabeth Cady Stanton, Lucretia Coffin Mott, Matilda Gage, Martha Coffin Wright, and Mary Ann McClintock. It ends with twelve resolutions demanding that women have "immediate admission to all the rights and privileges which belong to them as citizens of the United States." As you read, consider how the authors' rewording of aspects of the Declaration of Independence helps to underscore their argument.

When, in the course of human events, it becomes necessary for one portion of the family of man to assume among the people of the earth a position different from that which they have hitherto occupied, but one to which the laws of nature and of nature's God entitle them, a decent respect to the opinions of mankind requires that they should declare the causes that impel them to such a course.

We hold these truths to be self-evident: that all men and women are created equal; that they are endowed by their Creator with certain inalienable rights; that among these are life, liberty, and the pursuit of happiness; that to secure these rights governments are instituted, deriving their just powers from the consent of the governed. Whenever any form of government becomes destructive of these ends, it is the right of those who suffer from it to refuse allegiance to it, and to insist upon the institution of a new government, laying its foundation on such principles, and organizing its powers in such form, as to them shall seem most likely to effect their safety and happiness. Prudence, indeed, will dictate that governments long established should not be changed for light and transient causes; and accordingly all experience hath shown that mankind are more disposed to suffer, while evils are sufferable, than to right themselves by abolishing the forms to which they were accustomed. But when a long train of abuses and usurpations, pursuing invariably the same object evinces a design to reduce them under absolute despotism, it is their duty to throw off such government, and to provide new guards for their future security. Such has been the patient sufferance of the women under this government, and such is now the necessity which constrains them to demand the equal station to which they are entitled.

The history of mankind is a history of repeated injuries and usurpations on the part of man toward woman, having in direct object the establishment of an absolute tyranny over her. To prove this, let facts be submitted to a candid world.

He has never permitted her to exercise her inalienable right to the elective franchise.

He has compelled her to submit to laws, in the formation of which she had no voice.

He has withheld from her rights which are given to the most ignorant and degraded men—both natives and foreigners.

Having deprived her of this first right of a citizen, the elective franchise, thereby leaving her without representation in the halls of legislation, he has oppressed her on all sides.

He has made her, if married, in the eye of the law, civilly dead.

He has taken from her all right in property, even to the wages she earns.

He has made her, morally, an irresponsible being, as she can commit many crimes with impunity, provided they be done in the presence of her husband. In the covenant of marriage, she is compelled to promise obedience to her husband, he becoming, to all intents and purposes, her master—the law giving him power to deprive her of her liberty, and to administer chastisement.

He has so framed the laws of divorce, as to what shall be the proper causes, and in case of separation, to whom the guardianship of the children shall be given, as to be wholly regardless of the happiness of women—the law, in all cases, going upon a false supposition of the supremacy of man, and giving all power into his hands.

After depriving her of all rights as a married woman, if single, and the owner of property, he has taxed her to support a government which recognizes her only when her property can be made profitable to it.

He has monopolized nearly all the profitable employments, and from those she is permitted to follow, she receives but a scanty remuneration. He closes against her all the avenues to wealth and distinction which he considers most honorable to himself. As a teacher of theology, medicine, or law, she is not known.

He has denied her the facilities for obtaining a thorough education, all colleges being closed against her.

He allows her in Church, as well as State, but a subordinate position, claiming Apostolic authority for her exclusion from the ministry, and, with some exceptions, from any public participation in the affairs of the Church.

He has created a false public sentiment by giving to the world a different code of morals for men and women, by which moral delinquencies which exclude women from society, are not only tolerated, but deemed of little account in man.

He has usurped the prerogative of Jehovah himself, claiming it as his right to assign for her a sphere of action, when that belongs to her conscience and to her God.

He has endeavored, in every way that he could, to destroy her confidence in her own powers, to lessen her self-respect, and to make her willing to lead a dependent and abject life.

Now, in view of this entire disfranchisement of one-half the people of this country, their social and religious degradation—in view of the unjust laws above mentioned, and because women do feel themselves aggrieved, oppressed, and fraudulently deprived of their most sacred rights, we insist that they have immediate admission to all the rights and privileges which belong to them as citizens of the United States.

In entering upon the great work before us, we anticipate no small amount of misconception, misrepresentation, and ridicule; but we shall use every instrumentality within our power to effect our object. We shall employ agents, circulate tracts, petition the State and National legislatures, and endeavor to enlist the pulpit and the press in our behalf. We hope this Convention will be followed by a series of Conventions embracing every part of the country.

Resolutions

Whereas, the great precept of nature is conceded to be, that "man shall pursue his own true and substantial happiness." Blackstone in his Commentaries remarks, that this law of Nature being coeval with mankind, and dictated by God himself, is of course superior in obligation to any other. It is binding over all the globe, in all countries and at all times; no human laws are of any validity if contrary to this, and such of them as are valid, derive all their force, and all their validity, and all their authority, mediately and immediately, from this original; therefore,

Resolved, That such laws as conflict, in any way, with the true and substantial happiness of woman, are contrary to the great precept of nature and of no validity, for this is "superior in obligation to any other."

Resolved, That all laws which prevent woman from occupying such a station in society as her conscience shall dictate, or which place her in a position inferior to that of man, are contrary to the great precept of nature, and therefore of no force or authority.

Resolved, That woman is man's equal—was intended to be so by the Creator, and the highest good of the race demands that she should be recognized as such.

Resolved, That the women of this country ought to be enlightened in regard to the laws under which they live, that they may no longer publish their degradation by declaring themselves satisfied with their present position, nor their ignorance, by asserting that they have all the rights they want.

Resolved, That inasmuch as man, while claiming for himself intellectual superiority, does accord to woman moral superiority, it is pre-eminently his duty to encourage her to speak and teach, as she has an opportunity, in all religious assemblies.

Resolved, That the same amount of virtue, delicacy, and refinement of behavior that is required of woman in the social state, should also be required of man, and the same transgressions should be visited with equal severity on both man and woman.

Resolved, That the objection of indelicacy and impropriety, which is so often brought against woman when she addresses a public audience, comes with a very ill-grace from those who encourage, by their attendance, her appearance on the stage, in the concert, or in feats of the circus.

Resolved, That woman has too long rested satisfied in the circumscribed limits which corrupt customs and a perverted application of the Scriptures have marked out for her, and that it is time she should move in the enlarged sphere which her great Creator has assigned her.

Resolved, That it is the duty of the women of this country to secure to themselves their sacred right to the elective franchise.

Resolved, That the equality of human rights results necessarily from the fact of the identity of the race in capabilities and responsibilities.

Resolved, therefore, That, being invested by the Creator with the same capabilities, and the same consciousness of responsibility for their exercise,

it is demonstrably the right and duty of woman, equally with man, to promote every righteous cause by every righteous means; and especially in
regard to the great subjects of morals and religion, it is self-evidently her
right to participate with her brother in teaching them, both in private and
in public, by writing and by speaking, by any instrumentalities proper to be
used, and in any assemblies proper to be held; and this being a self-evident
truth growing out of the divinely implanted principles of human nature,
any custom or authority adverse to it, whether modern or wearing the
hoary sanction of antiquity, is to be regarded as a self-evident falsehood,
and at war with mankind.

[At the last session Lucretia Mott offered and spoke to the following
resolution:]

Resolved, That the speedy success of our cause depends upon the zealous
and untiring efforts of both men and women, for the overthrow of the monopoly of the pulpit, and for the securing to woman an equal participation
with men in the various trades, professions, and commerce.

Analyze

1. The mimicry of the Declaration of Independence is meant to appeal to
   the audience's sense of patriotism. Is this an effective approach on the
   authors' part? Why or why not? In what other ways do the authors
   evoke patriotism?
2. Within the resolutions, the authors repeat the phrase "the great precept of nature." What is the great precept of nature, and how is the lack
   of women's rights "contrary" to this?
3. Why do the authors assert that the success of their cause includes "the
   overthrow of the monopoly of the pulpit"?

Explore

1. The "Declaration of Sentiments" was hugely controversial, with opposition to it coming from the public and the press. Why do you think this is?
2. It is widely acknowledged that the women's rights movement stemmed
   from the antislavery movement. In fact, most of the authors of the
   "Declaration of Sentiments" were active abolitionists, and Frederick
   Douglass, former slave and noted abolitionist, attended and addressed

the Seneca Falls Convention. Do some digging on this and then write an essay in which you show how these two movements developed and how they were related to one another.

3. In addition to the early women's movement's link to the antislavery movement, Native American scholars such as Wilma Mankiller and Paula Gunn Allen argue that American Indian matrilineal and matriarchal tribal structures also had an important influence on the feminist ideas that were emerging in the 19th century. How would you find out more about this influence? Create a list of keywords that you would use as a starting point. What does your initial research reveal? Does this research reveal additional keywords that are helpful? Continue your research, noting how and why your list of keywords changes.

Lois Gould
"X: A Fabulous Child's Story"

Lois Gould was known for her keen portrayals of the complexities of women's inner lives. Her novel *Such Good Friends* was a best seller. She also wrote *The New York Times* "Hers" column and served as editor at both *The Ladies Home Journal* and *McCall's*. "X: A Fabulous Child's Story" was originally published in *Ms.* magazine in 1972 before being revised and published as a book in 1978. It is Gould's sole children's story, but consider how it might have been written with a broader audience in mind.

Once upon a time, a Baby named X was born. This Baby was named X so that nobody could tell whether it was a boy or a girl.

Its parents could tell, of course, but they couldn't tell anybody else. They couldn't even tell Baby X—at least not until much, much later.

You see, it was all part of a very important Secret Scientific Xperiment, known officially as Project Baby X.

The smartest scientists had set up this Xperiment at a cost of Xactly 23 billion dollars and 72 cents. This might seem like a lot for one Baby, even if it was an important Secret Scientific Xperimental Baby.

But when you remember the cost of strained carrots and stuffed bunnies, and popcorn for the movies and booster shots for camp, let alone 28 shiny quarters from the tooth fairy, you begin to see how it adds up.

Besides, long before Baby X was born, the smart scientists had to be paid to work out the secret details of the Xperiment, and to write the *Official Instruction Manual*, in secret code, for Baby X's parents, whoever they were.

These parents had to be selected very carefully. Thousands of mothers and fathers volunteered. But then the scientists made them take thousands of tests and answer thousands of tricky questions.

Almost everybody failed because, it turned out, almost everybody really wanted either a baby boy or a baby girl, and not a Baby X at all.

Also, almost everybody was afraid that a Baby X would be a lot more trouble than a boy or a girl. (They were right, too.)

There were families with grandparents named Milton and Agatha, who didn't see why the baby couldn't be named Milton or Agatha instead of X, even if it *was* an X.

There were families with aunts who insisted on knitting tiny dresses and uncles who insisted on sending tiny baseball mitts.

Worst of all, there were families that already had other children who couldn't be trusted to keep the secret. Certainly not if they knew the secret was worth 23 billion dollars and 72 cents—and all you had to do was to take one little peek at Baby X in the bathtub to know what it was.

But, finally, the scientists found the Joneses, who really wanted to raise an X more than any other kind of baby—no matter how much trouble it would be.

Ms. and Mr. Jones had to promise they would take equal turns caring for X, and feeding it, and singing it lullabies.

And they had to promise never to hire any baby-sitters. The government scientists knew perfectly well that a baby-sitter would probably peek at X in the bathtub, too.

The day the Joneses brought their baby home, lots of friends and relatives came over to see it. None of them knew about the secret Xperiment, though. So the first thing they asked was what kind of a baby X was.

When the Joneses smiled and said, "It's an X!" nobody knew what to say. They couldn't say, "Look at her cute little dimples!"

On the other hand, they couldn't say, "Look at his husky little biceps!"

And they didn't feel right about saying just plain "kitchy-coo." In fact, all they could say was that the Joneses were very rude to play such a silly joke on their friends and relatives.

But, of course, the Joneses were not joking. "It's an X" was absolutely all they would tell anyone. And that made the friends and relatives very angry.

The relatives all felt embarrassed about having an X in the family.

"People will think there's something wrong with it!" some of them whispered.

"There is something wrong with it!" others whispered back.

"Nonsense!" the Joneses told them all cheerfully. "What could possibly be wrong with this perfectly adorable X?"

Nobody could answer that, except Baby X, who had just finished its bottle. Baby X's answer was a loud, satisfied burp.

Clearly, nothing at all was wrong. Nevertheless, nobody they knew felt comfortable about buying a present for a Baby X. The cousins who had sent a tiny football helmet would not come and visit any more. And the neighbors who sent a pink-flowered romper suit pulled their shades down when the Joneses passed their house.

The Official Instruction Manual had warned the new parents that this would happen, so they didn't fret about it. Besides, they were too busy with Baby X and the hundreds of different Xercises for treating it properly.

Ms. and Mr. Jones had to be Xtra careful about how they played with little X. They knew that if they kept bouncing it up in the air and saying how *strong* and *active* it was, they'd be treating it more like a boy than an X. But if all they did was cuddle it and kiss it and tell it how *sweet* and *dainty* it was, they'd be treating it more like a girl than an X.

On page 1654 of the *Official Instruction Manual*, the scientists prescribed: "plenty of bouncing and plenty of cuddling, *both*. X ought to be strong and sweet and active. Forget about *dainty* altogether."

There were other problems, too. Toys, for instance. And clothes. On his first shopping trip, Mr. Jones told the store clerk, "I need some clothes and toys for my new baby." The clerk smiled and said, "Well, now, is it a boy or a girl?" "It's an X," Mr. Jones said, smiling back. But the clerk got all red in the face and said huffily, "In *that* case, I'm afraid I can't help you, sir."

So Mr. Jones wandered helplessly up and down the aisles trying to find what X needed. But everything in the store was piled up in sections marked BOYS or GIRLS.

There were "Boys' Pajamas" and "Girls' Underwear" and "Boys' Fire Engines" and "Girls' Housekeeping Sets." Mr. Jones went home without buying anything for X.

That night he and Ms. Jones consulted page 2326 of the *Official Instruction Manual*. It said firmly: "Buy plenty of everything!"

So they bought plenty of sturdy blue pajamas in the Boys' Department and cheerful flowered underwear in the Girls' Department.

And they bought all kinds of toys. A boy doll that made pee-pee and cried, "Pa-Pa." And a girl doll that talked in three languages and said, "I am the Pres-i-dent of Gen-er-al Mo-tors."

They also bought a storybook about a brave princess who rescued a handsome prince from his ivory tower, and another one about a sister and brother who grew up to be a baseball star and a ballet star, and you had to guess which was which.

The head scientists of Project Baby X checked all their purchases and told them to keep up the good work. They also reminded the Joneses to see page 4629 of the *Manual*, where it said, "Never make Baby X feel *embarrassed* or *ashamed* about what it wants to play with. And if X gets dirty climbing rocks, never say, 'Nice little Xes don't get dirty climbing rocks.'"

Likewise, it said, "If X falls down and cries, never say, 'Brave little Xes don't cry.' Because, of course, nice little Xes *do* get dirty, and brave little Xes *do* cry. No matter how dirty X gets, or how hard it cries, don't worry. It's all part of the Xperiment."

Whenever the Joneses pushed Baby X's stroller in the park, smiling strangers would come over and coo: "Is that a boy or a girl?" The Joneses would smile back and say, "It's an X." The strangers would stop smiling then, and often snarl something nasty—as if the Joneses had said something nasty to *them*.

By the time X grew big enough to play with other children, the Joneses' troubles had grown bigger, too. Once a little girl grabbed X's shovel in the sandbox, and zonked X on the head with it. "Now, now, Tracy," the little girl's mother began to scold, "little girls mustn't hit little—" and she turned to ask X, "Are you a little boy or a little girl, dear?"

Mr. Jones, who was sitting near the sandbox, held his breath and crossed his fingers.

X smiled politely at the lady, even though X's head had never been zonked so hard in its life. "I'm a little X," said X.

"You're a *what*?" the lady exclaimed angrily. "You're a little b-r-a-t, you mean!"

"But little girls mustn't hit little Xes, either!" said X, retrieving the shovel with another polite smile. "What good does hitting do, anyway?"

X's father, who was still holding his breath, finally let it out, uncrossed his fingers, and grinned back at X.

And at their next secret Project Baby X meeting, the scientists grinned, too. Baby X was doing fine.

But then it was time for X to start school. The Joneses were really worried about this, because school was even more full of rules for boys and girls, and there were no rules for Xes.

The teacher would tell boys to form one line, and girls to form another line.

There would be boys' games and girls' games, and boys' secrets and girls' secrets.

The school library would have a list of recommended books for girls, and a different list of recommended books for boys.

There would even be a bathroom marked BOYS and another one marked GIRLS.

Pretty soon boys and girls would hardly talk to each other. What would happen to poor little X?

The Joneses spent weeks consulting their *Instruction Manual.*

There were 249½ pages of advice under "First Day of School." Then they were all summoned to an Urgent Xtra Special Conference with the smart scientists of Project Baby X.

The scientists had to make sure that X's mother had taught X how to throw and catch a ball properly, and that X's father had been sure to teach X what to serve at a doll's tea party.

X had to know how to shoot marbles and how to jump rope and, most of all, what to say when the Other Children asked whether X was a Boy or a Girl.

Finally, X was ready. The Joneses helped X button on a nice new pair of red and white checked overalls, and sharpened six pencils for X's nice new pencil box, and marked X's name clearly on all the books in its nice new book bag.

X brushed its teeth and combed its hair, which just about covered its ears, and remembered to put a napkin in its lunch box.

The Joneses had asked X's teacher if the class could line up alphabetically, instead of forming separate lines for boys and girls. And they had asked if X could use the principal's bathroom, because it wasn't marked anything except BATHROOM. X's teacher promised to take care of all those problems. But nobody could help X with the biggest problem of all—Other Children.

Nobody in X's class had ever known an X before. Nobody had even heard their parents say, "Some of my best friends are Xes."

What would other children think? Would they make Xist jokes? Or would they make friends?

You couldn't tell what X was by studying its clothes—overalls don't even button right to left, like girls' clothes, or left to right, like boys' clothes.

And you couldn't guess whether X had a girl's short haircut or a boy's long haircut.

And it was very hard to tell by the games X liked to play. Either X played ball very well for a girl, or else X played house very well for a boy.

Some of the children tried to find out by asking X tricky questions, like, "Who's your favorite sports star?" That was easy. X had two favorite sports stars: a girl jockey named Robyn Smith and a boy archery champion named Robin Hood.

Then they asked, "What's your favorite TV program?" And that was even easier. X's favorite TV program was "Lassie," which stars a girl dog played by a boy dog.

When X said its favorite toy was a doll, everyone decided that X must be a girl. But then X said that the doll was really a robot, and that X had computerized it, and that it was programmed to bake fudge brownies and then clean up the kitchen.

After X told them that, the other children gave up guessing what X was. All they knew was they'd sure like to see X's doll.

After school, X wanted to play with the other children. "How about shooting some baskets in the gym?" X asked the girls. But all they did was make faces and giggle behind X's back.

"Boy, is *he* weird," whispered Jim to Joe.

"How about weaving some baskets in the arts and crafts room?" X asked the boys. But they all made faces and giggled behind X's back, too.

"Boy, is *she* weird," whispered Susie to Peggy.

That night, Ms. and Mr. Jones asked X how things had gone at school.

X tried to smile, but there were two big tears in its eyes. "The lessons are okay," X began, "but . . ."

"But?" said Ms. Jones.

"The Other Children hate me," X whispered. "Hate you?" said Mr. Jones.

X nodded, which made the two big tears roll down and splash on its overalls.

Ms. and Mr. Jones just looked at X, and then at each other. "Other Children," said Ms. Jones thoughtfully.

"Other Children," echoed Mr. Jones sadly.

Once more, the Joneses reached for their *Instruction Manual.* Under "Other Children," they found the following message:

"What did you Xpect? Other Children have to obey all the silly boy–girl rules, because their parents taught them to. Lucky X—you don't have to stick to the rules at all! All you have to do is be yourself.

"P.S. We're not saying it'll be easy."

X liked being itself. But X cried a lot that night, partly because it felt afraid.

So X's father held X tight, and cuddled it, and couldn't help crying a little, too.

And X's mother cheered them both up by reading an Xciting story about an enchanted prince called Sleeping Handsome, who woke up when Princess Charming kissed him.

The next morning, they all felt much better, and little X went back to school with a brave smile and a clean pair of red and white checked overalls.

There was a seven-letter-word spelling bee in class that day. And a seven-lap boys' relay race in the gym. And a seven-layer-cake baking contest in the girls' kitchen corner.

X won the spelling bee. X also won the relay race.

And X almost won the baking contest, except it forgot to light the oven. Which only proves that nobody's perfect.

One of the Other Children noticed something else, too. He said: "X don't care about winning. And X don't care about losing. X just thinks it's fun playing—boys' stuff *and* girls' stuff."

"Come to think of it," said another one of the Other Children, "maybe X is having twice as much fun as we are!"

So after school that day, the girl who beat X at the baking contest gave X a big slice of her prize-winning cake.

And the boy X beat in the relay race asked X to race him home.

From then on, some really funny things began to happen.

Susie, who sat next to X in class, suddenly refused to wear pink dresses to school any more. She insisted on wearing red and white checked overalls—just like X's.

Overalls, she told her parents, were much better for climbing monkey bars.

Then Jim, the class football nut, started wheeling his little sister's doll carriage around the football field.

He'd put on his entire football uniform, except for the helmet.

Then he'd put the helmet *in* the carriage, lovingly tucked under an old set of shoulder pads.

Then he'd start jogging around the field, pushing the carriage and singing "Rockabye Baby" to his football helmet.

He told his family that X did the same thing, so it must be okay. After all, X was now the team's star quarterback.

Susie's parents were horrified by her behavior, and Jim's parents were worried sick about his.

But the worst came when the twins, Joe and Peggy, decided to share everything with each other.

Peggy used Joe's hockey skates, and his microscope, and took half his newspaper route.

Joe used Peggy's needlepoint kit, and her cookbooks, and took two of her three baby-sitting jobs.

Peggy started running the lawn mower, and Joe started running the vacuum cleaner.

Their parents weren't one bit pleased with Peggy's wonderful biology experiments, or with Joe's terrific needlepoint pillows.

They didn't care that Peggy mowed the lawn better, and that Joe vacuumed the carpet better.

In fact, they were furious. It's all that little X's fault, they agreed. Just because X doesn't know what it is, or what it's supposed to be, it wants to get everybody *else* mixed up, too!

Peggy and Joe were forbidden to play with X any more. So was Susie, and then Jim, and then *all* the Other Children.

But it was too late: the Other Children stayed mixed up and happy and free, and refused to go back to the way they'd been before X.

Finally, Joe and Peggy's parents decided to call an emergency meeting of the school's Parents' Association, to discuss "The X Problem."

They sent a report to the principal stating that X was a "disruptive influence," and demanding immediate action.

The Joneses, they said, should be *forced* to tell whether X was a boy or a girl. And then X should be *forced* to behave like whichever it was.

If the Joneses refused to tell, the Parents' Association said, then X must take an Xamination. An Impartial Team of Xperts must Xamine it physically and mentally, and issue a full report. If X's test showed it was a boy, it would have to start obeying all the boys' rules. If it proved to be a girl, X would have to obey all the girls' rules.

And if X turned out to be some kind of mixed-up misfit, then X must be Xpelled from school. Immediately! And a new rule must be passed, so that no little Xes would ever come to school again.

The principal was very upset. Disruptive influence? Mixed-up misfit?

But X was an Xcellent student! All the teachers said it was a delight to have X in their classes!

X was president of the student council. X had won first prize in the talent show, and second prize in the art show, and honorable mention in the science fair, and won six athletic events on field day, including the potato race.

Nevertheless, insisted the Parents' Association, X is a Problem Child. X is the Biggest Problem Child we have ever seen!

So the principal reluctantly notified X's parents that numerous complaints about X's behavior had come to the school's attention.

And that after the Impartial Team of Xperts' Xamination, the school would decide what to do about X.

The Joneses reported this at once to the Project X scientists, who referred them to page 85769 of the *Instruction Manual*. "Sooner or later," it said, "X will have to be Xamined, physically and mentally, by an Impartial Team of Xperts.

"This may be the only way any of us will know for sure whether X is mixed up—or whether everyone else is."

The night before X was to be Xamined, the Joneses tried not to let X see how worried they were.

"What if—?" Mr. Jones would say. And Ms. Jones would reply, "No use worrying."

Then a few minutes later, Ms. Jones would say, "What if—?" and Mr. Jones would reply, "No use worrying."

X just smiled at them both, and hugged them hard and didn't say much of anything. X was thinking: What if—? And then X thought: No use worrying.

At Xactly 9 o'clock the next day, X reported to the school health office.

The principal, along with a committee from the Parents' Association, X's teacher, X's classmates, and Ms. and Mr. Jones, waited in the hall outside.

Inside, the Impartial Team of Xperts had set up their famous testing machine: the Superpsychiamedicosocioculturometer.

Nobody knew Xactly how the machine worked, or the details of the tests X was to be given, but everybody knew they'd be *very* hard, and that when it was all over, the Xperts would reveal Xactly what everyone wanted to know about X, but were afraid to ask.

It was terribly quiet in the hall. Almost spooky. Once in a while, they would hear a strange noise inside the room.

There were buzzes.

And a beep or two.

And several bells.

An occasional light would flash under the door. (The Joneses thought it was a white light, but the principal thought it was blue. Two or three children swore it was either yellow or green. And the Parents' Committee missed it completely.)

Through it all, you could hear the Impartial Team of Xperts' voices, asking hundreds of questions, and X's voice, answering hundreds of answers.

The whole thing took so long that everyone knew it must be the most complete Xamination anyone had ever had to take.

Poor X, the Joneses thought.

Serves X right, the Parents' Committee thought.

I wouldn't like to be in X's overalls right now, the children thought.

At last, the door opened. Everyone crowded around to hear the results. X didn't look any different; in fact, X was smiling. But the Impartial Team of Xperts looked terrible. They looked as if they were crying!

"What happened?" everyone began shouting. Had X done something disgraceful? "I wouldn't be a bit surprised!" muttered Peggy and Joe's parents.

"Did X flunk the *whole* test?" cried Susie's parents.

"Or just the most important part?" yelled Jim's parents.

"Oh, dear," sighed Mr. Jones.

"Oh, dear," sighed Ms. Jones.

"*Sssh,*" ssshed the principal. "The Xperts are trying to speak."

Wiping his eyes and clearing his throat, one Xpert began, in a hoarse whisper. "In our opinion," he whispered—you could tell he must be very upset—"in our opinion, young X here—"

"Yes? Yes?" shouted a parent impatiently.

"*Sssh!*" ssshed the principal.

"Young *Sssh* here, I mean young X," said the other Xpert, frowning, "is just about—"

"Just about *what*? Let's have it!" shouted another parent.

". . . just about the *least* mixed-up child we've ever Xamined!" Xclaimed the two Xperts, together. Behind the closed door, the Superpsychiamedicosocioculturometer made a noise that sounded like a contented hum.

"Yay for X!" yelled one of the children. And then the others began yelling, too. Clapping and cheering and jumping up and down.

"*SSSH!*" Ssshed the principal, but nobody did.

The Parents' Committee was angry and bewildered.

How *could* X have passed the whole Xamination?

Didn't X have an *identity* problem? Wasn't X mixed up at *all*?

Wasn't X *any* kind of a misfit?

How could it *not* be, when it didn't even *know* what it was? And why was the Impartial Team of Xperts crying?

Actually, they had stopped crying and were smiling politely through their tears. "Don't you see?" they said. "We're crying because it's wonderful! X has absolutely no identity problem! X isn't one bit mixed up! As for being a misfit—ridiculous! X knows perfectly well what it is! Don't you, X?" The Xperts winked. X winked back.

"But what *is* X?" shrieked Peggy and Joe's parents.

"*We* still want to know what it is!"

"Ah, yes," said the Xperts, winking again. "Well, don't worry. You'll all know one of these days. And you won't need us to tell you."

"What? What do they mean?" some of the parents grumbled suspiciously.

Susie and Peggy and Joe all answered at once. "They mean that by the time it matters which sex X is, it won't be a secret any more!"

With that, the Xperts began to push through the crowd toward X's parents. "How do you do," they said, somewhat stiffly. And then they both reached out to hug Ms. and Mr. Jones. "If we ever have an X of our own," they whispered, "we sure hope you'll lend us your instruction manual."

Needless to say, the Joneses were very happy. The Project Baby X scientists were rather pleased, too. So were Susie, Jim, Peggy, Joe, and all the Other Children. The Parents' Association wasn't, but they had promised to accept the Xperts' report, and not make any more trouble. They even invited Ms. and Mr. Jones to become honorary members, which they did.

Later that day, all X's friends put on their red and white checked overalls and went over to see X.

They found X in the back yard, playing with a very tiny baby that none of them had ever seen before.

The baby was wearing very tiny red and white checked overalls.

"How do you like our new baby?" X asked the Other Children proudly.

"It's got cute dimples," said Jim.

"It's got husky biceps, too," said Susie.

"What kind of baby is it?" asked Joe and Peggy.

X frowned at them. "Can't you tell?" Then X broke into a big, mischievous grin. "*It's a Y!*"

Analyze

1. Why do you think the "Secret Scientific Xperiment known as Project Baby X" was going to cost "Xactly 23 billion dollars and 72 cents"?

2. When the Joneses bring Baby X home and show it to their friends and relatives, why do you think the first question they ask is, "What kind of baby X was"? Why does "having an X in the family" create embarrassment, and why do the Joneses' family worry that others "will think there's something wrong with it"?

3. Why are there "249½ pages of advice given under 'First Day of School'"? What does this tell us about how school reinforces traditional gender roles in boys and girls?

4. Although the "Other Children" are initially wary of X, they come to accept it and even follow its lead: Susie refuses to wear pink dresses and tells her parents that overalls are more suitable for climbing monkey bars; Peggy begins mowing the lawn and Joe runs the vacuum cleaner. Do you think this is a typical response? Why or why not? Why do the Other Children's parents see X as a "bad influence"?

5. What argument is Gould making when she ends the story with the Xperts' exclamation that "X isn't one bit mixed up! As for being a misfit—ridiculous! X knows perfectly well what it is"?

Explore

1. Ms. and Mr. Jones worry about how to bring up Baby X: "If they kept bouncing it up in the air and saying how strong and active it was, they'd

be treating it more like a boy than an X. But if all they did was cuddle it and kiss it and tell it how sweet and dainty it was, they'd be treating it more like a girl than an X." What does their anxiety reveal about gender norms for boys and girls? Make a list of behaviors that are "normal" for little boys and a list of what is "normal" for little girls. Compare your lists with a classmate and discuss why these behaviors are considered normal.

2. In the story, Gould says that Baby X's parents "had to be selected very carefully. Thousands of people volunteered to take thousands of tests with thousands of tricky questions. Almost everyone failed because it turned out almost everybody wanted a boy or a girl and not a Baby X at all." What kind of "tricky questions" do you think these volunteers were asked? Create a list of five tricky questions that you believe would reveal a parent's desire for a Baby X, a baby girl, or a baby boy. Share your questions with a peer and discuss which questions might reveal a parent's specific desire and how the questions work to show this bias.

3. Mr. Jones frets when he goes shopping for Baby X and finds that "everything was in sections marked BOYS or GIRLS: 'Boys' Pajamas' and 'Girls' Underwear' and 'Boys' Fire Engines' and 'Girls' Housekeeping Sets.'" Go to a store in your area that sells both children's clothes and toys, such as Babies-R-Us or Target. Would Mr. Jones experience the same trauma if he were shopping today? Which items seem to be specifically marketed for boys and which items for girls? What about unisex items? Are these difficult or easy to find? Based on your finding, write an essay that argues what normative gender behaviors these items encourage, using examples of specific items as evidence.

Judith Lorber
"'Night to His Day': The Social Construction of Gender"

Judith Lorber is a professor emerita of sociology and women's studies at the CUNY Graduate Center and Brooklyn College of the City University of New York. Her book, *Paradoxes of Gender*, from which this reading is taken, was published in 1994. In the chapter republished here, "'Night to His Day': The

Social Construction of Gender," Lorber contends that sex, sexuality, and gender are socially constructed, but that gender is the main concept by which we structure our lives and that gender sets "society's entire set of values." As you read, think about the extent to which Lorber establishes her claim that gender is a social construction and what that means for us as individuals.

Talking about gender for most people is the equivalent of fish talking about water. Gender is so much the routine ground of everyday activities that questioning its taken-for-granted assumptions and presuppositions is like thinking about whether the sun will come up.[1] Gender is so pervasive that in our society we assume it is bred into our genes. Most people find it hard to believe that gender is constantly created and re-created out of human interaction, out of social life, and is the texture and order of that social life. Yet gender, like culture, is a human production that depends on everyone constantly "doing gender" (West and Zimmerman 1987).

And everyone "does gender" without thinking about it. Today, on the subway, I saw a well-dressed man with a year-old child in a stroller. Yesterday, on a bus, I saw a man with a tiny baby in a carrier on his chest. Seeing men taking care of small children in public is increasingly common—at least in New York City. But both men were quite obviously stared at—and smiled at, approvingly. Everyone was doing gender—the men who were changing the role of fathers and the other passengers, who were applauding them silently. But there was more gendering going on that probably fewer people noticed. The baby was wearing a white crocheted cap and white clothes. You couldn't tell if it was a boy or a girl. The child in the stroller was wearing a dark blue T-shirt and dark print pants. As they started to leave the train, the father put a Yankee baseball cap on the child's head. Ah, a boy, I thought. Then I noticed the gleam of tiny earrings in the child's ears, and as they got off, I saw the little flowered sneakers and lace-trimmed socks. Not a boy after all. Gender done.

Gender is such a familiar part of daily life that it usually takes a deliberate disruption of our expectations of how women and men are supposed to act to pay attention to how it is produced. Gender signs and signals are so ubiquitous that we usually fail to note them—unless they are missing or ambiguous. Then we are uncomfortable until we have successfully placed the other person in a gender status; otherwise, we feel socially dislocated.

In our society, in addition to man and woman, the status can be *transvestite* (a person who dresses in opposite-gender clothes) and *transsexual* (a person who has had sex-change surgery). Transvestites and transsexuals carefully construct their gender status by dressing, speaking, walking, gesturing in the ways prescribed for women or men—whichever they want to be taken for—and so does any "normal" person.

For the individual, gender construction starts with assignment to a sex category on the basis of what the genitalia look like at birth.[2] Then babies are dressed or adorned in a way that displays the category because parents don't want to be constantly asked whether their baby is a girl or a boy. A sex category becomes a gender status through naming, dress, and the use of other gender markers. Once a child's gender is evident, others treat those in one gender differently from those in the other, and the children respond to the different treatment by feeling different and behaving differently. As soon as they can talk, they start to refer to themselves as members of their gender. Sex doesn't come into play again until puberty, but by that time, sexual feelings and desires and practices have been shaped by gendered norms and expectations. Adolescent boys and girls approach and avoid each other in an elaborately scripted and gendered mating dance. Parenting is gendered, with different expectations for mothers and for fathers, and people of different genders work at different kinds of jobs. The work adults do as mothers and fathers and as low-level workers and high-level bosses shapes women's and men's life experiences, and these experiences produce different feelings, consciousness, relationships, skills—ways of being that we call feminine or masculine.[3] All of these processes constitute the social construction of gender.

Gendered roles change—today fathers are taking care of little children, girls and boys are wearing unisex clothing and getting the same education, women and men are working at the same jobs. Although many traditional social groups are quite strict about maintaining gender differences, in other social groups they seem to be blurring. Then why the one-year-old's earrings? Why is it still so important to mark a child as a girl or a boy, to make sure she is not taken for a boy or he for a girl? What would happen if they were? They would, quite literally, have changed places in their social world.

To explain why gendering is done from birth, constantly and by everyone, we have to look not only at the way individuals experience gender but at gender as a social institution. As a social institution, gender is one of the major ways that human beings organize their lives. Human society depends on a predictable division of labor, a designated allocation of scarce goods, assigned responsibility for children and others who cannot care for themselves, common values and their systematic transmission to new members, legitimate leadership, music, art, stories, games, and other symbolic productions. One way of choosing people for the different tasks of society is on the basis of their talents, motivations, and competence—their demonstrated achievements. The other way is on the basis of gender, race, ethnicity—ascribed membership in a category of people. Although societies vary in the extent to which they use one or the other of these ways of allocating people to work and to carry out other responsibilities, every society uses gender and age grades. Every society classifies people as "girl and boy children," "girls and boys ready to be married," and "fully adult women and men," constructs similarities among them and differences between them, and assigns them to different roles and responsibilities. Personality characteristics, feelings, motivations, and ambitions flow from these different life experiences so that the members of these different groups become different kinds of people. The process of gendering and its outcome are legitimated by religion, law, science, and the society's entire set of values.

In order to understand gender as a social institution, it is important to distinguish human action from animal behavior. Animals feed themselves and their young until their young can feed themselves. Humans have to produce not only food but shelter and clothing. They also, if the group is going to continue as a social group, have to teach the children how their particular group does these tasks. In the process, humans reproduce gender, family, kinship, and a division of labor—social institutions that do not exist among animals. Primate social groups have been referred to as families, and their mating patterns as monogamy, adultery, and harems. Primate behavior has been used to prove the universality of sex differences—as built into our evolutionary inheritance (Haraway 1978a). But animals' sex differences are not at all the same as humans' gender differences; animals' bonding is not kinship; animals' mating is not ordered by marriage; and animals' dominance hierarchies are not the equivalent of human stratification systems. Animals group on sex and age, relational categories that are physiologically, not socially, different. Humans create gender and age-group categories that are socially, and not necessarily physiologically, different.[4]

For animals, physiological maturity means being able to impregnate or conceive; its markers are coming into heat (estrus) and sexual attraction. For humans, puberty means being available for marriage; it is marked by rites that demonstrate this marital eligibility. Although the onset of physiological puberty is signaled by secondary sex characteristics (menstruation, breast development, sperm ejaculation, pubic and underarm hair), the onset of social adulthood is ritualized by the coming-out party or desert walkabout or bar mitzvah or graduation from college or first successful hunt or dreaming or inheritance of property. Humans have rituals that mark the passage from childhood into puberty and puberty into full adult status, as well as for marriage, childbirth, and death; animals do not (van Gennep 1960). To the extent that infants and the dead are differentiated by whether they are male or female, there are different birth rituals for girls and boys, and different funeral rituals for men and women (Biersack 1984, 132–33). Rituals of puberty, marriage, and becoming a parent are gendered, creating a "woman," a "man," a "bride," a "groom," a "mother," a "father." Animals have no equivalents for these statuses.

Among animals, siblings mate and so do parents and children; humans have incest taboos and rules that encourage or forbid mating between members of different kin groups (Lévi-Strauss 1956, [1949] 1969). Any animal of the same species may feed another's young (or may not, depending on the species). Humans designate responsibility for particular children by kinship; humans frequently limit responsibility for children to the members of their kinship group or make them into members of their kinship group with adoption rituals.

Animals have dominance hierarchies based on size or on successful threat gestures and signals. These hierarchies are usually sexed, and in some species, moving to the top of the hierarchy physically changes the sex (Austad 1986). Humans have stratification patterns based on control of surplus food, ownership of property, legitimate demands on others' work and sexual services, enforced determinations of who marries whom, and approved use of violence. If a woman replaces a man at the top of a stratification hierarchy, her social status may be that of a man, but her sex does not change.

Mating, feeding, and nurturant behavior in animals is determined by instinct and imitative learning and ordered by physiological sex and age (Lancaster 1974). In humans, these behaviors are taught and symbolically reinforced and ordered by socially constructed gender and age grades. Social gender and age statuses sometimes ignore or override physiological sex and age completely. Male and female animals (unless they physiologically change) are not interchangeable; infant animals cannot take the place of adult animals. Human females can become husbands and fathers, and human males can become wives and mothers, without sex-change surgery (Blackwood 1984). Human infants can reign as kings or queens.

Western society's values legitimate gendering by claiming that it all comes from physiology—female and male procreative differences. But gender and sex are not equivalent, and gender as a social construction does not flow automatically from genitalia and reproductive organs, the main physiological differences of females and males. In the construction of ascribed social statuses, physiological differences such as sex, stage of development, color of skin, and size are crude markers. They are not the source of the social statuses of gender, age, grade, and race. Social statuses are carefully constructed through prescribed processes of teaching, learning, emulation, and enforcement. Whatever genes, hormones, and biological evolution contribute to human social institutions is materially as well as qualitatively transformed by social practices. Every social institution has a material base, but culture and social practices transform that base into something with qualitatively different patterns and constraints. The economy is much more than producing food and goods and distributing them to eaters and users; family and kinship are not the equivalent of having sex and procreating; morals and religions cannot be equated with the fears and ecstasies of the brain; language goes far beyond the sounds produced by tongue and larynx. No one eats "money" or "credit"; the concepts of "god" and "angels" are the subjects of theological disquisitions; not only words but objects, such as their flag, "speak" to the citizens of a country.

Similarly, gender cannot be equated with biological and physiological differences between human females and males. The building blocks of gender are *socially constructed statuses*. Western societies have only two genders, "man" and "woman." Some societies have three genders—men, women, and *berdaches* or *hijras* or *xaniths*. Berdaches, hijras, and xaniths are biological males who behave, dress, work, and are treated in most respects as social women; they are therefore not men, nor are they female women; they are, in our language, "male women."[5] There are African and American Indian societies that have a gender status called *manly hearted women*—biological females who work, marry, and parent as men; their social status is "female men" (Amadiume 1987; Blackwood 1984). They do not have to behave or dress as men to have the social responsibilities and prerogatives of husbands and fathers; what makes them men is enough wealth to buy a wife.

Modern Western societies' *transsexuals* and *transvestites* are the nearest equivalent of these crossover genders, but they are not institutionalized as third genders (Bolin 1987). Transsexuals are biological males and females who have sex-change operations to alter their genitalia. They do so in order to bring their physical anatomy in congruence with the way they want to live and with their own sense of gender identity. They do not become a third gender; they change genders. Transvestites are males who live as women and females who live as men but do not intend to have sex-change surgery. Their dress, appearance, and mannerisms fall within the range of what is expected from members of the opposite gender, so that they "pass." They also change genders, sometimes temporarily, some for most of their lives. Transvestite women have fought in wars as men soldiers as recently as the nineteenth century; some married women, and others went back to being women and married men once the war was over.[6] Some were discovered when their wounds were treated; others not until they died. In order to work as a jazz musician, a man's occupation, Billy Tipton, a woman, lived most of her life as a man. She died recently at seventy-four, leaving a wife and three adopted sons for whom she was husband and father, and musicians with whom she had played and traveled, for whom she was "one of the boys" (*New York Times* 1989a).[7] There have been many other such occurrences of women passing as men to do more prestigious or lucrative men's work (Matthaei 1982, 192–93).[8]

Genders, therefore, are not attached to a biological substratum. Gender boundaries are breachable, and individual and socially organized shifts from one gender to another call attention to "cultural, social, or aesthetic dissonances" (Garber 1992, 16). These odd or deviant or third genders show us what we ordinarily take for granted—that people have to learn to be women and men. Men who cross-dress for performances or for pleasure often learn from women's magazines how to "do femininity" convincingly (Garber 1992, 41–51). Because transvestism is direct evidence of how gender is constructed, Marjorie Garber claims it has "extraordinary power . . . to disrupt, expose, and challenge, putting in question the very notion of the 'original' and of stable identity" (1992, 16).

Gender Bending

It is difficult to see how gender is constructed because we take it for granted that it's all biology, or hormones, or human nature. The differences between women and men seem to be self-evident, and we think they would occur no matter what society did. But in actuality, human females and males are physiologically more similar in appearance than are the two sexes of many species of animals and are more alike than different in traits and behavior (C. F. Epstein 1988). Without the deliberate use of gendered clothing, hairstyles, jewelry, and cosmetics, women and men would look far more alike.[9] Even societies that do not cover women's breasts have gender-identifying clothing, scarification, jewelry, and hairstyles.

The ease with which many transvestite women pass as men and transvestite men as women is corroborated by the common gender misidentification in Westernized societies of people in jeans, T-shirts, and sneakers. Men with long hair may be addressed as "miss," and women with short hair are often taken for men unless they offset the potential ambiguity with deliberate gender markers (Devor 1987, 1989). Jan Morris, in *Conundrum*, an autobiographical account of events just before and just after a sex-change operation, described how easy it was to shift back and forth from being a man to being a woman when testing how it would feel to change gender status. During this time, Morris still had a penis and wore more or less unisex clothing; the context alone made the man and the woman:

> Sometimes the arena of my ambivalence was uncomfortably small. At the Travellers' Club, for example, I was obviously known as a man of sorts—women were only allowed on the premises at all during a few hours of the day, and even then were hidden away as far as possible in lesser rooms or alcoves. But I had another club, only a few hundred yards away, where I was known only as a woman, and often I went directly from one to the other, imperceptibly changing roles on the way—"Cheerio, sir," the porter would say at one club, and "Hello, madam," the porter would greet me at the other. (1975, 132)

Gender shifts are actually a common phenomenon in public roles as well. Queen Elizabeth II of England bore children, but when she went to Saudi Arabia on a state visit, she was considered an honorary man so that she could confer and dine with the men who were heads of a state that forbids unrelated men and women to have face-to-unveiled-face contact. In contemporary Egypt, lower-class women who run restaurants or shops dress in men's clothing and engage in unfeminine aggressive behavior, and middle-class educated women of professional or managerial status can take positions of authority (Rugh 1986, 131). In these situations, there is an important status change: These women are treated by the others in the situation as if they are men. From their own point of view, they are still women. From the social perspective, however, they are men.[10]

In many cultures, gender bending is prevalent in theater or dance—the Japanese kabuki are men actors who play both women and men; in Shakespeare's theater company, there were no actresses—Juliet and Lady Macbeth were played by boys. Shakespeare's comedies are full of witty comments on gender shifts. Women characters frequently masquerade as young men, and other women characters fall in love with them; the boys playing these masquerading women, meanwhile, are acting out pining for the love of men characters.[11] In *As You Like It*, when Rosalind justifies her protective cross-dressing, Shakespeare also comments on manliness:

> *Were it not better,*
> *Because that I am more than common tall,*
> *That I did suit me all points like a man:*
> *A gallant curtle-axe upon my thigh,*
> *A boar-spear in my hand, and in my heart*
> *Lie there what hidden women's fear there will,*
> *We'll have a swashing and martial outside,*
> *As many other mannish cowards have*
> *That do outface it with their semblances.*   (I, i, 115–22)

Shakespeare's audience could appreciate the double subtext: Rosalind, a woman character, was a boy dressed in girl's clothing who then dressed as a boy; like bravery, masculinity and femininity can be put on and taken off with changes of costume and role (Howard 1988, 435).[12]

M Butterfly is a modern play of gender ambiguities, which David Hwang (1989) based on a real person. Shi Peipu, a male Chinese opera singer who sang women's roles, was a spy as a man and the lover as a woman of a Frenchman, Gallimard, a diplomat (Bernstein 1986). The relationship lasted twenty years, and Shi Peipu even pretended to be the mother of a child by Gallimard. "She" also pretended to be too shy to undress completely. As "Butterfly," Shi Peipu portrayed a fantasy Oriental woman who made the lover a "real man" (Kondo 1990b). In Gallimard's words, the fantasy was "of slender women in chong sams and kimonos who die for the love of unworthy foreign devils. Who are born and raised to be perfect women. Who take whatever punishment we give them, and bounce back, strengthened by love, unconditionally" (D. H. Hwang 1989, 91). When the fantasy woman betrayed him by turning out to be the more powerful "real man," Gallimard assumed the role of Butterfly and, dressed in a geisha's robes, killed himself: "because 'man' and 'woman' are oppositionally defined terms, reversals . . . are possible" (Kondo 1990b, 18).[13]

But despite the ease with which gender boundaries can be traversed in work, in social relationships, and in cultural productions, gender statuses remain. Transvestites and transsexuals do not challenge the social construction of gender. Their goal is to be feminine women and masculine men (Kando 1973). Those who do not want to change their anatomy but do want to change their gender behavior fare less well in establishing their social identity. The women Holly Devor called "gender blenders" wore their hair short, dressed in unisex pants, shirts, and comfortable shoes, and did not wear jewelry or makeup. They described their everyday dress as women's clothing: One said, "I wore jeans all the time, but I didn't wear men's clothes" (Devor 1989, 100). Their gender identity was women, but because they refused to "do femininity," they were constantly taken for men (1987, 1989, 107–42). Devor said of them: "The most common area of complaint was with public washrooms. They repeatedly spoke of the humiliation of being challenged or ejected from women's washrooms. Similarly, they found public change rooms to be dangerous territory and the buying of undergarments to be a difficult feat to accomplish" (1987, 29). In an ultimate ironic twist, some of these women said "they would feel like transvestites if they were to wear dresses, and two women said that they had been called transvestites when they had done so" (1987, 31). They resolved the ambiguity of their gender status by identifying as women in private and passing as men in public to avoid harassment on the street, to get men's jobs, and, if they were lesbians, to make it easier to display affection publicly with their lovers (Devor 1989, 107–42). Sometimes they even used men's bathrooms. When they had gender-neutral names, like Leslie, they could avoid the bureaucratic hassles that arose when they had to present their passports or other proof of identity, but because most had names associated with women, their appearance and their cards of identity were not conventionally congruent, and their gender status was in constant jeopardy.[14] When they could, they found it easier to pass as men than to try to change the stereotyped notions of what women should look like.

Paradoxically, then, bending gender rules and passing between genders does not erode but rather preserves gender boundaries. In societies with only two genders, the gender dichotomy is not disturbed by transvestites, because others feel that a transvestite is only transitorily ambiguous—is "really a man or woman underneath." After sex-change surgery, transsexuals end up in a conventional gender status—a "man" or a "woman" with the appropriate genitals (Eichler 1989). When women dress as men for business reasons, they are indicating that in that situation, they want to be treated the way men are treated; when they dress as women, they want to be treated as women:

> By their male dress, female entrepreneurs signal their desire to sus-
> pend the expectations of accepted feminine conduct without losing
> respect and reputation. By wearing what is "unattractive" they sig-
> nify that they are not intending to display their physical charms
> while engaging in public activity. Their loud, aggressive banter con-
> trasts with the modest demeanor that attracts men. . . . Overt sig-
> nalling of a suspension of the rules preserves normal conduct from
> eroding expectations. (Rugh 1986, 131)

For Individuals, Gender Means Sameness

Although the possible combinations of genitalia, body shapes, clothing, mannerisms, sexuality, and roles could produce infinite varieties in human beings, the social institution of gender depends on the production and maintenance of a limited number of gender statuses and of making the members of these statuses similar to each other. Individuals are born sexed but not gendered, and they have to be taught to be masculine or feminine.[15] As Simone de Beauvoir said: "One is not born, but rather becomes, a woman . . . ; it is civilization as a whole that produces this creature . . . which is described as feminine" (1953, 267).

Children learn to walk, talk, and gesture the way their social group says girls and boys should. Ray Birdwhistell, in his analysis of body motion as human communication, calls these learned gender displays *tertiary* sex characteristics and argues that they are needed to distinguish genders be-cause humans are a weakly dimorphic species—their only sex markers are genitalia (1970, 39–46). Clothing, paradoxically, often hides the sex but displays the gender.

In early childhood, humans develop gendered personality structures and sexual orientations through their interactions with parents of the same and opposite gender. As adolescents, they conduct their sexual behavior according to gendered scripts. Schools, parents, peers, and the mass media guide young people into gendered work and family roles. As adults, they take on a gendered social status in their society's stratification system. Gender is thus both ascribed and achieved (West and Zimmerman 1987).

The achievement of gender was most dramatically revealed in a case of an accidental transsexual—a baby boy whose penis was destroyed in the course of a botched circumcision when he was seven months old (Money and Ehrhardt 1972, 118–23). The child's sex category was changed to "female," and a vagina was surgically constructed when the child was seventeen months old. The parents were advised that they could successfully raise the child, one of identical twins, as a girl. Physicians assured them that the child was too young to have formed a gender identity. Children's sense of which gender they belong to usually develops around the age of three, at the time that they start to group objects and recognize that the people around them also fit into categories—big, little; pink-skinned, brown-skinned; boys, girls. Three has also been the age when children's appearance is ritually gendered, usually by cutting a boy's hair or dressing him in distinctively masculine clothing. In Victorian times, English boys wore dresses up to the age of three, when they were put into short pants (Garber 1992, 1–2).

The parents of the accidental transsexual bent over backward to feminize the child—and succeeded. Frilly dresses, hair ribbons, and jewelry created a pride in looks, neatness, and "daintiness." More significant, the child's dominance was also feminized:

> The girl had many tomboyish traits, such as abundant physical energy, a high level of activity, stubbornness, and being often the dominant one in a girls' group. Her mother tried to modify her tomboyishness: ". . . I teach her to be more polite and quiet. I always wanted those virtues. I never did manage, but I'm going to try to manage them to—my daughter—to be more quiet and ladylike." From the beginning the girl had been the dominant twin. By the age of three, her dominance over her brother was, as her mother described it, that of a mother hen. The boy in turn took up for his sister, if anyone threatened her. (Money and Ehrhardt 1972, 122)

This child was not a tomboy because of male genes or hormones; according to her mother, she herself had also been a tomboy. What the mother had learned poorly while growing up as a "natural" female she insisted that her physically reconstructed son-daughter learn well. For both mother and child, the social construction of gender overrode any possibly inborn traits.

People go along with the imposition of gender norms because the weight of morality as well as immediate social pressure enforces them. Consider how many instructions for properly gendered behavior are packed into this mother's admonition to her daughter: "This is how to hem a dress when you see the hem coming down and so to prevent yourself from looking like the slut I know you are so bent on becoming" (Kincaid 1978).

Gender norms are inscribed in the way people move, gesture, and even eat. In one African society, men were supposed to eat with their "whole mouth, wholeheartedly, and not, like women, just with the lips, that is half-heartedly, with reservation and restraint" (Bourdieu [1980] 1990, 70). Men and women in this society learned to walk in ways that proclaimed their different positions in the society:

> The manly man . . . stands up straight into the face of the person he approaches, or wishes to welcome. Ever on the alert, because ever threatened, he misses nothing of what happens around him. . . . Conversely, a well brought-up woman . . . is expected to walk with a slight stoop, avoiding every misplaced movement of her body, her head or her arms, looking down, keeping her eyes on the spot where she will next put her foot, especially if she happens to have to walk past the men's assembly. (70)

Many cultures go beyond clothing, gestures, and demeanor in gendering children. They inscribe gender directly into bodies. In traditional Chinese society, mothers bound their daughters' feet into three-inch stumps to enhance their sexual attractiveness. Jewish fathers circumcise their infant sons to show their covenant with God. Women in African societies remove the clitoris of prepubescent girls, scrape their labia, and make the lips grow together to preserve their chastity and ensure their marriageability. In Western societies, women augment their breast size with silicone and reconstruct their faces with cosmetic surgery to conform to cultural ideals of feminine beauty. Hanna Papanek (1990) notes that these practices reinforce the sense of superiority or inferiority in the adults who carry them out as well as in the children on whom they are done: The genitals of Jewish fathers and sons are physical and psychological evidence of their common dominant religious and familial status; the genitals of African mothers and daughters are physical and psychological evidence of their joint subordination.[16]

Sandra Bem (1981, 1983) argues that because gender is a powerful "schema" that orders the cognitive world, one must wage a constant, active battle for a child not to fall into typical gendered attitudes and behavior. In 1972, *Ms. Magazine* published Lois Gould's fantasy of how to raise a child free of gender-typing. The experiment calls for hiding the child's anatomy from all eyes except the parents' and treating the child as neither a girl nor a boy. The child, called X, gets to do all the things boys *and* girls do. The experiment is so successful that all the children in X's class at school want to look and behave like X. At the end of the story, the creators of the experiment are asked what will happen when X grows up. The scientists' answer is that by then it will be quite clear what X is, implying that its hormones will kick in and it will be revealed as a female or male. That ambiguous, and somewhat contradictory, ending lets Gould off the hook; neither she nor we have any idea what someone brought up totally androgynously would be like sexually or socially as an adult. The hormonal input will not create gender or sexuality but will only establish secondary sex characteristics; breasts, beards, and menstruation alone do not produce social manhood or womanhood. Indeed, it is at puberty, when sex characteristics become evident, that most societies put pubescent children through their most important rites of passage, the rituals that officially mark them as fully gendered—that is, ready to marry and become adults.

Most parents create a gendered world for their newborn by naming, birth announcements, and dress. Children's relationships with same-gendered and different-gendered caretakers structure their self-identifications and personalities. Through cognitive development, children extract and apply to their own actions the appropriate behavior for those who belong in their own gender, as well as race, religion, ethnic group, and social class, rejecting what is not appropriate. If their social categories are highly valued, they value themselves highly; if their social categories are low status, they lose self-esteem (Chodorow 1974). Many feminist parents who want to raise androgynous children soon lose their children to the pull of gendered norms (T. Gordon 1990, 87–90). My son attended a carefully nonsexist elementary school, which didn't even have girls' and boys' bathrooms. When he was seven or eight years old, I attended a class play about "squares" and "circles" and their need for each other and noticed that all the girl squares and circles wore makeup, but none of the boy squares and circles did.

I asked the teacher about it after the play, and she said, "Bobby said he was not going to wear makeup, and he is a powerful child, so none of the boys would either." In a long discussion about conformity, my son confronted me with the question of who the conformists were, the boys who followed their leader or the girls who listened to the woman teacher. In actuality, they both were, because they both followed same-gender leaders and acted in gender-appropriate ways. (Actors may wear makeup, but real boys don't.)

For human beings there is no essential femaleness or maleness, femininity or masculinity, womanhood or manhood, but once gender is ascribed, the social order constructs and holds individuals to strongly gendered norms and expectations. Individuals may vary on many of the components of gender and may shift genders temporarily or permanently, but they must fit into the limited number of gender statuses their society recognizes. In the process, they re-create their society's version of women and men: "If we do gender appropriately, we simultaneously sustain, reproduce, and render legitimate the institutional arrangements. . . . If we fail to do gender appropriately, we as individuals—not the institutional arrangements—may be called to account (for our character, motives, and predispositions)" (West and Zimmerman 1987, 146).

The gendered practices of everyday life reproduce a society's view of how women and men should act (Bourdieu [1980] 1990). Gendered social arrangements are justified by religion and cultural productions and backed by law, but the most powerful means of sustaining the moral hegemony of the dominant gender ideology is that the process is made invisible; any possible alternatives are virtually unthinkable (Foucault 1972; Gramsci 1971).[17]

For Society, Gender Means Difference

The pervasiveness of gender as a way of structuring social life demands that gender statuses be clearly differentiated. Varied talents, sexual preferences, identities, personalities, interests, and ways of interacting fragment the individual's bodily and social experiences. Nonetheless, these are organized in Western cultures into two and only two socially and legally recognized gender statuses, "man" and "woman."[18] In the social construction of gender, it does not matter what men and women actually do; it does not even matter if they do exactly the same thing. The social institution of gender insists only that what they do is *perceived* as different.

If men and women are doing the same tasks, they are usually spatially segregated to maintain gender separation, and often the tasks are given different job titles as well, such as executive secretary and administrative assistant (Reskin 1988). If the differences between women and men begin to blur, society's "sameness taboo" goes into action (G. Rubin 1975, 178). At a rock and roll dance at West Point in 1976, the year women were admitted to the prestigious military academy for the first time, the school's administrators "were reportedly perturbed by the sight of mirror-image couples dancing in short hair and dress gray trousers," and a rule was established that women cadets could dance at these events only if they wore skirts (Barkalow and Raab 1990, 53).[19] Women recruits in the U.S. Marine Corps are required to wear makeup—at a minimum, lipstick and eye shadow—and they have to take classes in makeup, hair care, poise, and etiquette. This feminization is part of a deliberate policy of making them clearly distinguishable from men Marines. Christine Williams quotes a twenty-five-year-old woman drill instructor as saying: "A lot of the recruits who come here don't wear makeup; they're tomboyish or athletic. A lot of them have the preconceived idea that going into the military means they can still be a tomboy. They don't realize that you are a *Woman* Marine" (1989, 76–77).[20]

If gender differences were genetic, physiological, or hormonal, gender bending and gender ambiguity would occur only in hermaphrodites, who are born with chromosomes and genitalia that are not clearly female or male. Since gender differences are socially constructed, all men and all women can enact the behavior of the other, because they know the other's social script: " 'Man' and 'woman' are at once empty and overflowing categories. Empty because they have no ultimate, transcendental meaning. Overflowing because even when they appear to be fixed, they still contain within them alternative, denied, or suppressed definitions" (J. W. Scott 1988a, 49). Nonetheless, though individuals may be able to shift gender statuses, the gender boundaries have to hold, or the whole gendered social order will come crashing down.

Paradoxically, it is the social importance of gender statuses and their external markers—clothing, mannerisms, and spatial segregation—that makes gender bending or gender crossing possible—or even necessary. The social viability of differentiated gender statuses produces the need or desire to shift statuses. Without gender differentiation, transvestism and transsexuality would be meaningless. You couldn't dress in the opposite gender's clothing if all clothing were unisex. There would be no need to reconstruct genitalia to match identity if interests and life-styles were not gendered. There would be no need for women to pass as men to do certain kinds of work if jobs were not typed as "women's work" and "men's work." Women would not have to dress as men in public life in order to give orders or aggressively bargain with customers.

Gender boundaries are preserved when transsexuals create congruous autobiographies of always having felt like what they are now. The transvestite's story also "recuperates social and sexual norms" (Garber 1992, 69). In the transvestite's normalized narrative, he or she "is 'compelled' by social and economic forces to disguise himself or herself in order to get a job, escape repression, or gain artistic or political 'freedom'" (Garber 1992, 70). The "true identity," when revealed, causes amazement over how easily and successfully the person passed as a member of the opposite gender, not a suspicion that gender itself is something of a put-on.

Gender Ranking

Most societies rank genders according to prestige and power and construct them to be unequal, so that moving from one to another also means moving up or down the social scale. Among some North American Indian cultures, the hierarchy was male men, male women, female men, female women. Women produced significant durable goods (basketry, textiles, pottery, decorated leather goods), which could be traded. Women also controlled what they produced and any profit or wealth they earned. Since women's occupational realm could lead to prosperity and prestige, it was fair game for young men—but only if they became women in gender status. Similarly, women in other societies who amassed a great deal of wealth were allowed to become men—"manly hearts." According to Harriet Whitehead (1981):

> Both reactions reveal an unwillingness or inability to distinguish the sources of prestige—wealth, skill, personal efficacy (among other things)—from masculinity. Rather there is the innuendo that if a person performing female tasks can attain excellence, prosperity, or social power, it must be because that person is, at some level, a man.... A woman who could succeed at doing the things men did was honored as a man would be.... What seems to have been more disturbing to the culture—which means, for all intents and

purposes, to the men—was the possibility that women, within their own department, might be onto a good thing. It was into this unsettling breach that the berdache institution was hurled. In their social aspect, women were complimented by the berdache's imitation. In their anatomic aspect, they were subtly insulted by his vaunted superiority. (108)

In American society, men-to-women transsexuals tend to earn less after surgery if they change occupations; women-to-men transsexuals tend to increase their income (Bolin 1988, 153–60; Brody 1979). Men who go into women's fields, like nursing, have less prestige than women who go into men's fields, like physics. Janice Raymond, a radical feminist, feels that transsexual men-to-women have advantages over female women because they were not socialized to be subordinate or oppressed throughout life. She says:

> We know that we are women who are born with female chromosomes and anatomy, and that whether or not we were socialized to be so-called normal women, patriarchy has treated and will treat us like women. Transsexuals have not had this same history. No man can have the history of being born and located in this culture as a woman. He can have the history of *wishing* to be a woman and of *acting* like a woman, but this gender experience is that of a transsexual, not of a woman. Surgery may confer the artifacts of outward and inward female organs but it cannot confer the history of being born a woman in this society. (1979, 114)

Because women who become men rise in the world and men who become women fall, Elaine Showalter (1987) was very critical of the movie *Tootsie*, in which Dustin Hoffman plays an actor who passes as a woman in order to be able to get work. "Dorothy" becomes a feminist "woman of the year" for standing up for women's rights not to be demeaned or sexually harassed. Showalter feels that the message of the movie is double-edged: "Dorothy's 'feminist' speeches . . . are less a response to the oppression of women than an instinctive situational male reaction to being treated like a woman. The implication is that women must be taught by men how to win their rights. . . . It says that feminist ideas are much less threatening when they come from a man" (123). Like Raymond, Showalter feels that being or having been a man gives a transsexual man-to-woman or a man cross-dressed as a woman a social advantage over those whose gender status was always "woman."[21] The implication here is that there is an experiential superiority that doesn't disappear with the gender shift.

For one transsexual man-to-woman, however, the experience of living as a woman changed his/her whole personality. As James, Morris had been a soldier, foreign correspondent, and mountain climber; as Jan, Morris is a successful travel writer. But socially, James was far superior to Jan, and so Jan developed the "learned helplessness" that is supposed to characterize women in Western society:

> We are told that the social gap between the sexes is narrowing, but I can only report that having, in the second half of the twentieth century, experienced life in both roles, there seems to me no aspect of existence, no moment of the day, no contact, no arrangement, no response, which is not different for men and for women. The very tone of voice in which I was now addressed, the very posture of the person next in the queue, the very feel in the air when I entered a room or sat at a restaurant table, constantly emphasized my change of status.
>
> And if others' responses shifted, so did my own. The more I was treated as woman, the more woman I became. I adapted willy-nilly. If I was assumed to be incompetent at reversing cars, or opening bottles, oddly incompetent I found myself becoming. If a case was thought too heavy for me, inexplicably I found it so myself. . . . Women treated me with a frankness which, while it was one of the happiest discoveries of my metamorphosis, did imply membership of a camp, a faction, or at least a school of thought; so I found myself gravitating always towards the female, whether in sharing a railway compartment or supporting a political cause. Men treated me more and more as junior, . . . and so, addressed every day of my life as an inferior, involuntarily, month by month I accepted the condition. I discovered that even now men prefer women to be less informed, less able, less talkative, and certainly less self-centered than they are themselves; so I generally obliged them. (1975, 165–66)[22]

Components of Gender

By now, it should be clear that gender is not a unitary essence but has many components as a social institution and as an individual status.[23]

As a social institution, gender is composed of:

Gender statuses, the socially recognized genders in a society and the norms and expectations for their enactment behaviorally, gesturally, linguistically, emotionally, and physically. How gender statuses are evaluated depends on historical development in any particular society.

Gendered division of labor, the assignment of productive and domestic work to members of different gender statuses. The work assigned to those of different gender statuses strengthens the society's evaluation of those statuses— the higher the status, the more prestigious and valued the work and the greater its rewards.

Gendered kinship, the family rights and responsibilities for each gender status. Kinship statuses reflect and reinforce the prestige and power differences of the different genders.

Gendered sexual scripts, the normative patterns of sexual desire and sexual behavior, as prescribed for the different gender statuses. Members of the dominant gender have more sexual prerogatives; members of a subordinate gender may be sexually exploited.

Gendered personalities, the combinations of traits patterned by gender norms of how members of different gender statuses are supposed to feel and behave. Social expectations of others in face-to-face interaction constantly bolster these norms.

Gendered social control, the formal and informal approval and reward of conforming behavior and the stigmatization, social isolation, punishment, and medical treatment of nonconforming behavior.

Gender ideology, the justification of gender statuses, particularly, their differential evaluation. The dominant ideology tends to suppress criticism by making these evaluations seem natural.

Gender imagery, the cultural representations of gender and embodiment of gender in symbolic language and artistic productions that reproduce and legitimate gender statuses. Culture is one of the main supports of the dominant gender ideology.

For an individual, gender is composed of:

Sex category to which the infant is assigned at birth based on appearance of genitalia. With prenatal testing and sex-typing, categorization is prenatal. Sex category may be changed later through surgery or reinspection of ambiguous genitalia.

Gender identity, the individual's sense of gendered self as a worker and family member.

Gendered marital and procreative status, fulfillment or nonfulfillment of allowed or disallowed mating, impregnation, childbearing, kinship roles.

Gendered sexual orientation, socially and individually patterned sexual desires, feelings, practices, and identification.

Gendered personality, internalized patterns of socially normative emotions as organized by family structure and parenting.

Gendered processes, the social practices of learning, being taught, picking up cues, enacting behavior already learned to be gender-appropriate (or inappropriate, if rebelling, testing), developing a gender identity, "doing gender" as a member of a gender status in relationships with gendered others, acting deferent or dominant.

Gender beliefs, incorporation of or resistance to gender ideology.

Gender display, presentation of self as a certain kind of gendered person through dress, cosmetics, adornments, and permanent and reversible body markers.

For an individual, all the social components are supposed to be consistent and congruent with perceived physiology. The actual combination of genes and genitalia, prenatal, adolescent, and adult hormonal input, and procreative capacity may or may not be congruous with each other and with sex-category assignment, gender identity, gendered sexual orientation and procreative status, gender display, personality, and work and family roles. At any one time, an individual's identity is a combination of the major ascribed statuses of gender, race, ethnicity, religion, and social class, and the individual's achieved statuses, such as education level, occupation or profession, marital status, parenthood, prestige, authority, and wealth. The ascribed statuses substantially limit or create opportunities for individual achievements and also diminish or enhance the luster of those achievements.

Gender as Process, Stratification, and Structure

As a social institution, gender is a process of creating distinguishable social statuses for the assignment of rights and responsibilities. As part of a stratification system that ranks these statuses unequally, gender is a major building block in the social structures built on these unequal statuses.

As a *process*, gender creates the social differences that define "woman" and "man." In social interaction throughout their lives, individuals learn what is expected, see what is expected, act and react in expected ways, and thus simultaneously construct and maintain the gender order: "The very injunction to be a given gender takes place through discursive routes: to be a good mother, to be a heterosexually desirable object, to be a fit worker, in sum, to signify a multiplicity of guarantees in response to a variety of different demands all at once" (J. Butler 1990, 145). Members of a social group neither make up gender as they go along nor exactly replicate in rote fashion what was done before. In almost every encounter, human beings produce gender, behaving in the ways they learned were appropriate for their gender status, or resisting or rebelling against these norms. Resistance and rebellion have altered gender norms, but so far they have rarely eroded the statuses.

Gendered patterns of interaction acquire additional layers of gendered sexuality, parenting, and work behaviors in childhood, adolescence, and adulthood. Gendered norms and expectations are enforced through informal sanctions of gender-inappropriate behavior by peers and by formal punishment or threat of punishment by those in authority should behavior deviate too far from socially imposed standards for women and men.

Everyday gendered interactions build gender into the family, the work process, and other organizations and institutions, which in turn reinforce gender expectations for individuals.[24] Because gender is a process, there is room not only for modification and variation by individuals and small groups but also for institutionalized change (J. W. Scott 1988a, 7).

As part of a *stratification* system, gender ranks men above women of the same race and class. Women and men could be different but equal. In practice, the process of creating difference depends to a great extent on differential evaluation. As Nancy Jay (1981) says: "That which is defined, separated out, isolated from all else is A and pure. Not-A is necessarily impure, a random catchall, to which nothing is external except A and the principle of order that separates it from Not-A" (45). From the individual's point of view, whichever gender is A, the other is Not-A; gender boundaries tell the individual who is like him or her, and all the rest are unlike. From society's point of view, however, one gender is usually the touchstone, the normal, the dominant, and the other is different, deviant, and subordinate. In Western society, "man" is A, "wo-man" is Not-A. (Consider what a society would be like where woman was A and man Not-A.)

The further dichotomization by race and class constructs the gradations of a heterogeneous society's stratification scheme. Thus, in the United States, white is A, African American is Not-A; middle class is A, working class is Not-A, and "African-American women occupy a position whereby the inferior half of a series of these dichotomies converge" (P. H. Collins 1990, 70). The dominant categories are the hegemonic ideals, taken so for granted as the way things should be that white is not ordinarily thought of as a race, middle class as a class, or men as a gender. The characteristics of these categories define the Other as that which lacks the valuable qualities the dominants exhibit.

In a gender-stratified society, what men do is usually valued more highly than what women do because men do it, even when their activities are very similar or the same. In different regions of southern India, for example, harvesting rice is men's work, shared work, or women's work: "Wherever a task is done by women it is considered easy, and where it is done by [men] it is considered difficult" (Mencher 1988, 104). A gathering and hunting society's survival usually depends on the nuts, grubs, and small animals brought in by the women's foraging trips, but when the men's hunt is successful, it is the occasion for a celebration. Conversely, because they are the superior group, white men do not have to do the "dirty work," such as housework; the most inferior group does it, usually poor women of color (Palmer 1989).

Freudian psychoanalytic theory claims that boys must reject their mothers and deny the feminine in themselves in order to become men: "For boys the major goal is the achievement of personal masculine identification with their father and sense of secure masculine self, achieved through superego formation and disparagement of women" (Chodorow 1978, 165). Masculinity may be the outcome of boys' intrapsychic struggles to separate their identity from that of their mothers, but the proofs of masculinity are culturally shaped and usually ritualistic and symbolic (Gilmore 1990).

The Marxist feminist explanation for gender inequality is that by demeaning women's abilities and keeping them from learning valuable technological skills, bosses preserve them as a cheap and exploitable reserve army of labor. Unionized men who could be easily replaced by women collude in this process because it allows them to monopolize the better paid, more interesting, and more autonomous jobs: "Two factors emerge as helping men maintain their separation from women and their control of technological occupations. One is the active gendering of jobs and people. The second is the continual creation of sub-divisions in the work processes, and levels in work hierarchies, into which men can move in order to keep their distance from women" (Cockburn 1985, 13).

Societies vary in the extent of the inequality in social status of their women and men members, but where there is inequality, the status "woman" (and its attendant behavior and role allocations) is usually held in lesser esteem than the status "man." Since gender is also intertwined with a society's other constructed statuses of differential evaluation—race, religion, occupation, class, country of origin, and so on—men and women members of the favored groups command more power, more prestige, and more property than the members of the disfavored groups. Within many social groups, however, men are advantaged over women. The more economic resources, such as education and job opportunities, are available to a group, the more they tend to be monopolized by men. In poorer groups that have few resources (such as working-class African Americans in the United States), women and men are more nearly equal, and the women may even outstrip the men in education and occupational status (Almquist 1987).

As a *structure*, gender divides work in the home and in economic production, legitimates those in authority, and organizes sexuality and emotional life (Connell 1987, 91–142). As primary parents, women significantly influence children's psychological development and emotional attachments, in the process reproducing gender. Emergent sexuality is shaped by heterosexual, homosexual, bisexual, and sadomasochistic patterns that are gendered—different for girls and boys, and for women and men—so that sexual statuses reflect gender statuses.

When gender is a major component of structured inequality, the devalued genders have less power, prestige, and economic rewards than the valued genders. In countries that discourage gender discrimination, many major roles are still gendered; women still do most of the domestic labor and child rearing, even while doing full-time paid work; women and men are segregated on the job and each does work considered "appropriate";

women's work is usually paid less than men's work. Men dominate the positions of authority and leadership in government, the military, and the law; cultural productions, religions, and sports reflect men's interests.

In societies that create the greatest gender difference, such as Saudi Arabia, women are kept out of sight behind walls or veils, have no civil rights, and often create a cultural and emotional world of their own (Bernard 1981). But even in societies with less rigid gender boundaries, women and men spend much of their time with people of their own gender because of the way work and family are organized. This spatial separation of women and men reinforces gendered differentness, identity, and ways of thinking and behaving (Coser 1986).

Gender inequality—the devaluation of "women" and the social domination of "men"—has social functions and a social history. It is not the result of sex, procreation, physiology, anatomy, hormones, or genetic predispositions. It is produced and maintained by identifiable social processes and built into the general social structure and individual identities deliberately and purposefully. The social order as we know it in Western societies is organized around racial, ethnic, class, and gender inequality. I contend, therefore, that the continuing purpose of gender as a modern social institution is to construct women as a group to be the subordinates of men as a group. The life of everyone placed in the status "woman" is "night to his day—that has forever been the fantasy. Black to his white. Shut out of his system's space, she is the repressed that ensures the system's functioning" (Cixous and Clément [1975] 1986, 67).

The Paradox of Human Nature

To say that sex, sexuality, and gender are all socially constructed is not to minimize their social power. These categorical imperatives govern our lives in the most profound and pervasive ways, through the social experiences and social practices of what Dorothy Smith calls the "everyday/ everynight world" (1990, 31–57). The paradox of human nature is that it is *always* a manifestation of cultural meanings, social relationships, and power politics; "not biology, but culture, becomes destiny" (J. Butler 1990, 8). Gendered people emerge not from physiology or sexual orientation but from the exigencies of the social order, mostly, from the need for a reliable division of the work of food production and the social (not physical) reproduction of new members. The moral imperatives of religion and cultural representations guard the boundary lines among genders and ensure that what is demanded, what is permitted, and what is tabooed for the people in each gender is well known and followed by most (C. Davies 1982). Political power, control of scarce resources, and, if necessary, violence uphold the gendered social order in the face of resistance and rebellion. Most people, however, voluntarily go along with their society's prescriptions for those of their gender status, because the norms and expectations get built into their sense of worth and identity as a certain kind of human being and because they believe their society's way is the natural way. These beliefs emerge from the imagery that pervades the way we think, the way we see and hear and speak, the way we fantasize, and the way we feel.

There is no core or bedrock human nature below these endlessly looping processes of the social production of sex and gender, self and other, identity and psyche, each of which is a "complex cultural construction" (J. Butler 1990, 36). *For humans, the social is the natural.* Therefore, "in its feminist senses, gender cannot mean simply the cultural appropriation of biological sexual difference. Sexual difference is itself a fundamental—and scientifically contested—construction. Both 'sex' and 'gender' are woven of multiple, asymmetrical strands of difference, charged with multifaceted dramatic narratives of domination and struggle" (Haraway 1990, 140).

NOTES

1. Gender is, in Erving Goffman's words, an aspect of *Felicity's Condition*: "any arrangement which leads us to judge an individual's . . . acts not to be a manifestation of strangeness. Behind Felicity's Condition is our sense of what it is to be sane" (1983, 27). Also see Bem 1993; Frye 1983, 17–40; Goffman 1977.
2. In cases of ambiguity in countries with modern medicine, surgery is usually performed to make the genitalia more clearly male or female.
3. See J. Butler 1990 for an analysis of how doing gender *is* gender identity.
4. Douglas 1973; MacCormack 1980; Ortner 1974; Ortner and Whitehead 1981a; Yanagisako and Collier 1987. On the social construction of childhood, see Ariès 1962; Zelizer 1985.
5. On the hijras of India, see Nanda 1990; on the xaniths of Oman, Wikan 1982, 168–86; on the American Indian berdaches, W. L. Williams 1986. Other societies that have similar institutionalized third-gender men are the Konaig of Alaska, the Tanala of Madagascar, the Mesakin of Nuba, and the Chukchee of Siberia (Wikan 1982, 170).
6. Durova 1989; Freeman and Bond 1992; Wheelwright 1989.
7. Gender segregation of work in popular music still has not changed very much, according to Groce and Cooper 1990, despite considerable androgyny in some very popular figures. See Garber 1992 on androgyny. She discusses Tipton on pp. 67–70.

8. In the nineteenth century, not only did these women get men's wages, but they also "had male privileges and could do all manner of things other women could not: open a bank account, write checks, own property, go anywhere unaccompanied, vote in elections" (Faderman 1991, 44).

9. When unisex clothing and men wearing long hair came into vogue in the United States in the mid-1960s, beards and mustaches for men also came into style again as gender identifications.

10. For other accounts of women being treated as men in Islamic countries, as well as accounts of women and men cross-dressing in these countries, see Garber 1992, 304–52.

11. Dollimore 1986; Garber 1992, 32–400; Greenblatt 1987, 66–93; Howard 1988. For Renaissance accounts of sexual relations with women and men of ambiguous sex, see Laqueur 1990a, 134–39. For modern accounts of women passing as men that other women find sexually attractive, see Devor 1989, 136–36; Wheelwright 1989, 53–59.

12. Females who passed as men soldiers had to "do masculinity," not just dress in a uniform (Wheelwright 1989, 50–78). On the triple entendres and gender resonances of Rosalind-type characters, see Garber 1992, 71–77.

13. Also see Garber 1992, 234–66.

14. Bolin also describes how many documents have to be changed by transsexuals to provide a legitimizing "paper trail" (1988, 145–47). Note that only members of the same social group know which names are women's and which men's in their culture, but many documents list "sex."

15. For an account for how a potential man-to-woman transsexual learned to be feminine, see Garfinkel 1967, 116–85, 285–88. For a gloss on this account that points out how, throughout his encounters with Agnes, Garfinkel failed to see how he himself was constructing his own masculinity, see Rogers 1992.

16. Paige and Paige (1981, 147–49) argue that circumcision ceremonies indicate a father's loyalty to his lineage elders—"visible public evidence that the head of a family unit of their lineage is willing to trust others with his and his family's most valuable political asset, his son's penis" (147). On female circumcision, see El Dareer 1982; Lightfoot-Klein 1989; van der Kwaak 1992; Walker 1992. There is a form of female circumcision that removes only the prepuce of the clitoris and is similar to male circumcision, but most forms of female circumcision are far more extensive, mutilating, and spiritually and psychologically shocking than the usual form of male circumcision. However, among the Australian aborigines, boys' penises are slit and kept open, so that they urinate and bleed the way women do (Bettelheim 1962, 165–206).

17. The concepts of moral hegemony, the effects of everyday activities (praxis) on thought and personality, and the necessity of consciousness of these processes before political change can occur are all based on Marx's analysis of class relations.

18. Other societies recognize more than two categories, but usually no more than three or four (Jacobs and Roberts 1989).

19. Carol Barkalow's book has a photograph of eleven first-year West Pointers in a math class, who are dressed in regulation pants, shirts, and sweaters, with short haircuts. The caption challenges the reader to locate the only woman in the room.

20. The taboo on males and females looking alike reflects the U.S. military's homophobia (Bérubé 1989). If you can't tell those with a penis from those with a vagina, how are you going to determine whether their sexual interest is heterosexual or homosexual unless you watch them having sexual relations?

21. Garber feels that *Tootsie* is not about feminism but about transvestism and its possibilities for disturbing the gender order (1992, 5–9).

22. See Bolin 1988, 149–50, for transsexual men-to-women's discovery of the dangers of rape and sexual harassment. Devor's "gender blenders" went in the opposite direction. Because they found that it was an advantage to be taken for men, they did not deliberately cross-dress, but they did not feminize themselves either (1989, 126–40).

23. See West and Zimmerman 1987 for a similar set of gender components.

24. On the "logic of practice," or how the experience of gender is embedded in the norms of everyday interaction and the structure of formal organizations, see Acker 1990; Bourdieu [1980] 1990; Connell 1987; Smith 1987a.

REFERENCES

Acker, Joan. 1990. Hierarchies, jobs, and bodies: A theory of gendered organizations. *Gender & Society* 5: 390–407.

Almquist, Elizabeth M. 1987. Labor market gendered inequality in minority groups. *Gender & Society* 1: 400–14.

Amadiume, Ifi. 1987. *Male daughters, female husbands: Gender and sex in an African society.* London: Zed Books.

Ariès, Philippe. 1962. *Centuries of childhood: A social history of family life,* translated by Robert Baldick. New York: Vintage.

Austad, Steven N. 1986. Changing sex nature's way. *International Wildlife,* May–June, 29.

Barkalow, Carol, with Andrea Raab. 1990. *In the men's house.* New York: Poseidon Press.

Bem, Sandra Lipsitz. 1981. Gender schema theory: A cognitive account of sex typing. *Psychological Review* 88: 354–64.

———. 1983. Gender schema theory and its implications for child development: Raising gender-aschematic children in a gender schematic society. *Signs* 8: 598–616.

———. 1993. *The lenses of gender: Transforming the debate on sexual inequality.* New Haven: Yale University Press.

Bernard, Jessie. 1981. *The female world.* New York: Free Press.

Bernstein, Richard. 1986. France jails 2 in odd case of espionage. *New York Times*, 11 May.

Bérubé, Allan. 1989. Marching to a different drummer: Gay and lesbian GIs in World War II. In *Hidden from history: Reclaiming the gay and lesbian past*, edited by Martin Bauml Duberman, Martha Vicinus, and George Chauncey, Jr. New York: New American Library.

Bettelheim, Bruno. 1962. *Symbolic wounds: Puberty rites and the envious male*. London: Thames and Hudson.

Biersack, Aletta. 1984. Paiela "women-men": The reflexive foundations of gender ideology. *American Ethnologist* 11: 118–38.

Birdwhistell, Ray L. 1970. *Kinesics and context: Essays on body motion communication*. Philadelphia: University of Pennsylvania Press.

Blackwood, Evelyn. 1984. Sexuality and gender in certain Native American tribes: The case of cross-gender families. *Signs* 10: 27–42.

Bolin, Anne. 1987. Transsexualism and the limits of traditional analysis. *American Behavioral Scientist* 31: 41–65.

———. 1988. *In search of Eve: Transsexual rites of passage*. South Hadley, Mass.: Bergin & Garvey.

Bourdieu, Pierre. [1980] 1990. *The logic of practice*. Stanford, Calif.: Stanford University Press.

Brody, Jane E. 1979. Benefits of transsexual surgery disputed as leading hospital halts the procedure. *New York Times*, 2 October.

Butler, Judith. 1990. *Gender trouble; Feminism and the subversion of identity*. New York and London: Routledge.

Chodorow, Nancy. 1974. Family structure and feminine personality. In *Women, culture, and society*, edited by Michelle Zimbalist Rosaldo and Louise Lamphere. Stanford, Calif.: Stanford University Press.

———. 1978. *The reproduction of mothering*. Berkeley: University of California Press.

Cixous, Hélène, and Catherine Clément. [1975] 1986. *The newly born woman*, translated by Betsy Wing. Minneapolis: University of Minnesota Press.

Cockburn, Cynthia. 1985. *Machinery of dominance: Women, men and the technical know-how*. London: Pluto Press.

Collins, Patricia Hill. 1990. *Black feminist thought: Knowledge, consciousness, and the politics of empowerment*. Boston: Unwin Hyman.

Connell, R. [Robert] W. 1987. *Gender and power: Society, the person, and sexual politics*. Stanford, Calif.: Stanford University Press.

Coser, Rose Laub. 1986. Cognitive structure and the use of social space. *Sociological Forum* 1: 1–26.

Davies, Christie. 1982. Sexual taboos and social boundaries. *American Journal of Sociology* 87: 1032–63.

De Beauvoir, Simone. 1953. *The second sex*, translated by H. M. Parshley. New York: Knopf.

Devor, Holly. 1987. Gender blending females: Women and sometimes men. *American Behavioral Scientist* 31: 12–40.

———. 1989. *Gender blending: Confronting the limits of duality.* Bloomington: Indiana University Press.

Dollimore, Jonathan. 1986. Subjectivity, sexuality, and transgression: The Jacobean connection. *Renaissance Drama,* n.s 17: 53–81.

Douglas, Mary. 1973. *Natural symbols.* New York: Vintage.

Durova, Nadezhda. 1989. *The cavalry maiden: Journals of a Russian officer in the Napoleonic Wars,* translated by Mary Flemin Zirin. Bloomington: Indiana University Press.

Eichler, Margit. 1989. Sex change operations: The last bulwark of the double standard. In *Feminist frontiers II,* edited by Laurel Richardson and Verta Taylor. New York: Random House.

El Dareer, Asma. 1982. *Woman, why do you weep? Circumcision and its consequences.* London: Zed Books.

Epstein, Cynthia Fuchs. 1988. *Deceptive distinctions: Sex, gender and the social order.* New Haven: Yale University Press.

Faderman, Lillian. 1991. *Odd girls and twilight lovers: A history of lesbian life in twentieth-century America.* New York: Columbia University Press.

Foucault, Michel. 1972. *The archeology of knowledge and the discourse on language,* translated by A. M. Sheridan Smith. New York: Pantheon.

Freeman, Lucy, and Alma Halbert Bond. 1992. *America's first woman warrior: The courage of Deborah Sampson.* New York: Paragon.

Frye, Marilyn. 1983. *The politics of reality: Essays in feminist theory.* Trumansburg, N.Y.: Crossing Press.

Garber, Marjorie. 1992. *Vested interests: Cross-dressing and cultural anxiety.* New York and London: Routledge.

Garfinkel, Harold. 1967. *Studies in ethnomethodology.* Englewood Cliffs, N.J.: Prentice Hall.

Gilmore, David D. 1990. *Manhood in the making: Cultural concepts of masculinity.* New Haven: Yale University Press.

Goffman, Erving. 1977. The arrangement between the sexes. *Theory and Society* 4: 301–33.

———. 1983. Felicity's condition. *American Journal of Sociology* 89: 1–53.

Gordon, Tuula. 1990. *Feminist mothers.* New York: New York University Press.

Gould, Lois. 1972. X: A fabulous child's story. *Ms. Magazine,* December, 74–76, 105–106.

Gramsci, Antonio. 1971. *Selections from the prison notebooks,* translated by Quintin Hoare and Geoffrey Nowell Smith. New York: International Publishers.

Greenblatt, Stephen. 1987. *Shakespearean negotiations: The circulation of social energy in Renaissance England.* Berkeley: University of California Press.

Groce, Stephen B., and Margaret Cooper. 1990. Just me and the boys? Women in local-level rock and roll. *Gender & Society* 4: 200–29.

Haraway, Donna. 1978. Animal sociology and a natural economy of the body politic. Part I: A political physiology of dominance. *Signs* 4: 21–36.

———. 1990. Investment strategies for the evolving portfolio of primate females. In *Body-politics: Women and the discourses of science*, edited by Mary Jacobus, Evelyn Fox Keller, and Sally Shuttleworth. New York and London: Routledge.

Howard, Jean E. 1988. Crossdressing, the theater, and gender struggle in early modern England. *Shakespeare Quarterly* 39: 418–41.

Hwang, David Henry. 1989. *M. Butterfly*. New York: New American Library.

Jacobs, Sue-Ellen, and Christine Roberts. 1989. Sex, sexuality, and gender variance. In *Gender and anthropology*, edited by Sandra Morgen. Washington, D.C.: American Anthropological Association.

Jay, Nancy. 1981. Gender and dichotomy. *Feminist Studies* 7: 38–56.

Kando, Thomas. 1973. *Sex change: The achievement of gender identity among feminized transsexuals*. Springfield, Ill.: Charles C Thomas.

Kincaid, Jamaica. 1978. Girl. *The New Yorker*, 26 June.

Kondo, Dorinne K. 1990. *M. Butterfly*: Orientalism, gender, and a critique of essentialist identity. *Cultural Critique*, no. 16 (Fall): 5–29.

Lancaster, Jane Beckman. 1974. *Primate behavior and the emergence of human culture*. New York: Holt, Rinehart, and Winston.

Laqueur, Thomas. 1990. *Making sex: Body and gender from the Greeks to the Freud*. Cambridge, Mass.: Harvard University Press.

Lévi-Strauss, Claude. 1956. The family. In *Man, culture, and society*, edited by Harry L. Shapiro. New York: Oxford.

———. [1949] 1969. *The elementary structures of kinship*, translated by J. H. Bell and J. R. von Sturmer. Boston: Beacon Press.

Lightfoot-Klein, Hanny. 1989. *Prisoners of ritual: An odyssey into female circumcision in Africa*. New York: Harrington Park Press.

MacCormack, Carol P. 1980. Nature, culture and gender: A critique. In *Nature, culture, and gender*, edited by Carol P. MacCormack and Marilyn Strathern. Cambridge, England: Cambridge University Press.

Matthaei, Julie A. 1982. *An economic history of women's work in America*. New York: Schocken.

Mencher, Joan. 1988. Women's work and poverty: Women's contribution to household maintenance in South India. In *A home divided: Women and income in the third world*, edited by Daisy Dwyer and Judith Bruce. Palo Alto, Calif.: Stanford University Press.

Money, John and Anke A. Ehrhardt. 1972. *Man & woman, boy & girl*. Baltimore, Md.: Johns Hopkins University Press.

Morris, Jan. 1975. *Conundrum*. New York: Signet.

Nanda, Serena. 1990. *Neither man nor woman: The hijiras of India*. Belmont, Calif.: Wadsworth.

New York Times. 1989. Musician's death at 74 reveals he was a woman. 2 February.

Orntner, Sherry B. 1974. Is male to female as nature to culture? In *Woman Culture, and Society*, edited by Michelle Zimbalist Rosaldo and Louise Lamphere. Stanford, CA: Stanford University Press.

Ortner, Sherry B., and Harriet Whitehead. 1981a. Introduction: Accounting for sexual meanings. In Ortner and Whitehead (eds.).

———. (eds.). 1981b. *Sexual meanings: The cultural construction of gender and sexuality*. Cambridge, England: Cambridge University Press.

Paige, Karen Erickson, and Jeffrey M. Paige. 1981. *The politics of reproductive ritual*. Berkeley: University of California Press.

Palmer, Phyllis. 1989. *Domesticity and dirt: Housewives and domestic servants in the United States, 1920–1945*. Philadelphia: Temple University Press.

Papanek, Hanna. 1979. Family status production: The "work" and "non-work" of women. *Signs* 4: 775–81.

Raymond, Janice G. 1979. *The transsexual empire: The making of the she-male*. Boston: Beacon Press.

Reskin, Barbara F. 1988. Bringing the men back in: Sex differentiation and the devaluation of women's work. *Gender & Society* 2: 58–81.

Rogers, Mary F. 1992. They were all passing: Agnes, Garfinkel, and company. *Gender & Society* 6: 169–91.

Rubin, Gayle. 1975. The traffic in women: Notes on the political economy of sex. In *Toward an anthropology of women*, edited by Rayna R[app] Reiter. New York: Monthly Review Press.

Rugh, Andrea B. 1986. *Reveal and conceal: Dress in contemporary Egypt*. Syracuse, N.Y.: Syracuse University Press.

Scott, Joan Wallach. 1988. *Gender and the politics of history*. New York: Columbia University Press.

Showalter, Elaine. 1987. Critical cross-dressing: Male feminists and the woman of the year. In *Men in feminism*, edited by Alice Jardine and Paul Smith. New York: Methuen.

Smith, Dorothy E. 1987. *The everyday world as problematic: A feminist sociology*. Toronto: University of Toronto Press.

———. 1990. *The conceptual practices of power: A feminist sociology of knowledge*. Toronto: University of Toronto Press.

van der Kwaak, Anke. 1992. Female circumcision and gender identity: A questionable alliance? *Social Science and Medicine* 35: 777–87.

Van Gennep, Arnold. 1960. *The rites of passage*, translated by Monika B. Vizedom and Gabrielle L. Caffee. Chicago: University of Chicago Press.

Walker, Molly K. 1992. Maternal reactions to fetal sex. *Health Care for Women International* 13: 293–302.

West, Candace, and Don Zimmerman. 1987. Doing gender. *Gender & Society* 1: 125–51.

Wheelwright, Julie. 1989. *Amazons and military maids: Women who cross-dressed in pursuit of life, liberty and happiness.* London: Pandora Press.

Whitehead, Harriet. 1981. The bow and the burden strap: A new look at institutionalized homosexuality in native North America. In Ortner and Whitehead (eds.).

Wikan, Unni. 1982. *Behind the veil in Arabia: Women in Oman.* Baltimore, Md.: Johns Hopkins University Press.

Williams, Christine L. 1989. *Gender differences at work: Women and men in nontraditional occupations.* Berkeley: University of California Press.

Williams, Walter L. 1986. *The spirit and the flesh: Sexual diversity in American Indian culture.* Boston: Beacon Press.

Yanagisako, Sylvia Junko, and Jane Fishburne Collier. 1987. Toward a unified analysis of gender and kinship. In *Gender and kinship: Essays toward a unified analysis,* edited by Jane Fishburne Collier and Sylvia Junko Yanagisako. Berkeley: University of California Press.

Zelizer, Viviana A. 1985. *Pricing the priceless child: The changing social value of children.* New York: Basic Books.

Analyze

1. How does Lorber use a comparison of humans and animals to demonstrate that gender in humans is "not attached to a biological substratum"?

2. Why does Lorber believe that gender bending "does not erode but rather preserves gender boundaries?"

3. What are some of the ways that societies use gender to mark difference? What impact do those methods have on individuals marked as different (such as women or transsexuals)?

Explore

1. Read the Wikipedia entries for "sex" and "gender." Make a list of attributes for each. To what extent do these attributes reflect Lorber's argument that sex is biological and gender is socially constructed?

2. In the section "For Individuals, Gender Means Sameness," Lorber cites Lois Gould's story "X: A Fabulous Child's Story." How does Lorber address Gould's representation of a genderless child? What's your take on Lorber's point of view, and why?

3. In this essay, Lorber argues that gender creates social stratifications that enhance the gap between the status of men and women. Why? What are some current ways that contemporary society continues to create (or support) these stratifications? Are there ways that society has begun to challenge them? Write an essay in which you explore contemporary gender structures and consider the extent to which Lorber's ideas still hold true today.

Anne Fausto-Sterling
"The Five Sexes: Why Male and Female Are Not Enough"

Dr. Anne Fausto-Sterling is the Nancy Duke Lewis Professor Emerita of Biology and Gender Studies in the Department of Molecular and Cell Biology and Biochemistry at Brown University. She is one of the leading experts in the field of biology and gender development and is the author of several acclaimed books that have sought to reshape the way we think about the connections among feminism, gender identity, and science. In this essay, "The Five Sexes: Why Male and Female Are Not Enough," Fausto-Sterling makes an argument for the importance of envisioning gender on a scale from "male" to "female," with those ranging somewhere in between falling into a range of intersex categories. Although this is a highly scientific article, Fausto-Sterling presents the information in this essay in fairly straightforward terms. How does she manage to accomplish this?

In 1843 Levi Suydam, a twenty-three-year-old resident of Salisbury, Connecticut, asked the town board of selectmen to validate his right to vote as a Whig in a hotly contested local election. The request raised a flurry of objections from the opposition party, for reasons that must be rare in the annals of American democracy: it was said that Suydam was more female than male and thus (some eighty years before suffrage was extended to women) could not be allowed to cast a ballot. To settle the dispute a physician, one William James Barry, was brought in to examine Suydam. And, presumably upon encountering a phallus, the good doctor declared the prospective voter male. With Suydam safely in their column the Whigs won the election by a majority of one.

Barry's diagnosis, however, turned out to be somewhat premature. Within a few days he discovered that, phallus notwithstanding, Suydam menstruated regularly and had a vaginal opening. Both his/her physique and his/her mental predispositions were more complex than was first suspected. S/he had narrow shoulders and broad hips and felt occasional sexual yearnings for women. Suydam's "feminine propensities, such as a fondness for gay colors, for pieces of calico, comparing and placing them together, and an aversion for bodily labor, and an inability to perform the same, were remarked by many," Barry later wrote. It is not clear whether Suydam lost or retained the vote, or whether the election results were reversed.

Western culture is deeply committed to the idea that there are only two sexes. Even language refuses other possibilities; thus to write about Levi Suydam I have had to invent conventions—*s/he* and *his/her*—to denote someone who is clearly neither male nor female or who is perhaps both sexes at once. Legally, too, every adult is either man or woman, and the difference, of course, is not trivial. For Suydam it meant the franchise; today it means being available for, or exempt from, draft registration, as well as being subject, in various ways, to a number of laws governing marriage, the family and human intimacy. In many parts of the United States, for instance, two people legally registered as men cannot have sexual relations without violating anti-sodomy statutes.

But if the state and the legal system have an interest in maintaining a two-party sexual system, they are in defiance of nature. For biologically speaking, there are many gradations running from female to male; and depending on how one calls the shots, one can argue that along that spectrum lie at least five sexes—and perhaps even more.

For some time medical investigators have recognized the concept of the intersexual body. But the standard medical literature uses the term *intersex* as a catch-all for three major subgroups with some mixture of male and female characteristics: the so-called true hermaphrodites, whom I call herms, who possess one testis and one ovary (the sperm- and egg-producing vessels, or gonads); the male pseudohermaphrodites (the "merms"), who have testes and some aspects of the female genitalia but no ovaries; and the female pseudohermaphrodites (the "ferms"), who have ovaries and some aspects of the male genitalia but lack testes. Each of those categories is in itself complex; the percentage of male and female characteristics, for instance, can vary enormously among members of the same subgroup. Moreover, the inner lives of the people in each subgroup—their special needs and their problems, attractions and repulsions—have gone unexplored by science. But on the basis of what is known about them I suggest that the three intersexes, herm, merm and ferm, deserve to be considered additional sexes each in its own right. Indeed, I would argue further that sex is a vast, infinitely malleable continuum that defies the constraints of even five categories.

Not surprisingly, it is extremely difficult to estimate the frequency of intersexuality, much less the frequency of each of the three additional sexes: it is not the sort of information one volunteers on a job application. The psychologist John Money of Johns Hopkins University, a specialist in the study of congenital sexual-organ defects, suggests intersexuals may constitute as many as 4 percent of births. As I point out to my students at Brown University, in a student body of about 6,000 that fraction, if correct, implies there may be as many as 240 intersexuals on campus—surely enough to form a minority caucus of some kind.

In reality though, few such students would make it as far as Brown in sexually diverse form. Recent advances in physiology and surgical technology now enable physicians to catch most intersexuals at the moment of birth. Almost at once such infants are entered into a program of hormonal and surgical management so that they can slip quietly into society as "normal" heterosexual males or females. I emphasize that the motive is in no way conspiratorial. The aims of the policy are genuinely humanitarian, reflecting the wish that people be able to "fit in" both physically and psychologically. In the medical community, however, the assumptions behind that wish—that there be only two sexes, that heterosexuality alone is normal, that there is one true model of psychological health—have gone virtually unexamined.

The word *hermaphrodite* comes from the Greek names Hermes, variously known as the messenger of the gods, the patron of music, the controller of dreams or the protector of livestock, and Aphrodite, the goddess of sexual love and beauty. According to Greek mythology, those two gods parented Hermaphroditus, who at age fifteen became half male and half female when his body fused with the body of a nymph he fell in love with. In some true hermaphrodites the testis and the ovary grow separately but bilaterally; in others they grow together within the same organ, forming an ovo-testis. Not infrequently, at least one of the gonads functions quite well, producing either sperm cells or eggs, as well as functional levels of the sex hormones—androgens or estrogens. Although in theory it might be possible for a true hermaphrodite to become both father and mother to a child, in practice the appropriate ducts and tubes are not configured so that egg and sperm can meet.

In contrast with the true hermaphrodites, the pseudo-hermaphrodites possess two gonads of the same kind along with the usual male (XY) or female (XX) chromosomal makeup. But their external genitalia and secondary sex characteristics do not match their chromosomes. Thus merms have testes and XY chromosomes, yet they also have a vagina and a clitoris, and at puberty they often develop breasts. They do not menstruate, however. Ferms have ovaries, two X chromosomes and sometimes a uterus, but they also have at least partly masculine external genitalia. Without medical intervention they can develop beards, deep voices and adult-size penises.

No classification scheme could more than suggest the variety of sexual anatomy encountered in clinical practice. In 1969, for example, two French investigators, Paul Guinet of the Endocrine Clinic in Lyons and Jacques Decourt of the Endocrine Clinic in Paris, described ninety-eight cases of true hermaphroditism—again, signifying people with both ovarian and testicular tissue—solely according to the appearance of the external genitalia and the accompanying ducts. In some cases the people exhibited strongly feminine development. They had separate openings for the vagina and the urethra, a cleft vulva defined by both the large and the small labia, or vaginal lips, and at puberty they developed breasts and usually began to menstruate. It was the oversize and sexually alert clitoris, which threatened sometimes at puberty to grow into a penis, that usually impelled them to seek medical attention. Members of another group also had breasts and a feminine body type, and they menstruated. But their labia were at least partly fused, forming an incomplete scrotum. The phallus (here an embryological term for a structure that during usual development goes on to form either a clitoris or a penis) was between 1.5 and 2.8 inches long; nevertheless, they urinated through a urethra that opened into or near the vagina.

By far the most frequent form of true hermaphrodite encountered by Guinet and Decourt—55 percent—appeared to have a more masculine physique. In such people the urethra runs either through or near the phallus, which looks more like a penis than a clitoris. Any menstrual blood exits periodically during urination. But in spite of the relatively male appearance of the genitalia, breasts appear at puberty. It is possible that a sample larger than ninety-eight so-called true hermaphrodites would yield even more contrasts and subtleties. Suffice it to say that the varieties are so diverse that it is possible to know which parts are present and what is attached to what only after exploratory surgery.

The embryological origins of human hermaphrodites clearly fit what is known about male and female sexual development. The embryonic gonad generally chooses early in development to follow either a male or a female sexual pathway; for the ovo-testis, however, that choice is fudged. Similarly, the embryonic phallus most often ends up as a clitoris or a penis, but the existence of intermediate states comes as no surprise to the embryologist. There are also uro-genital swellings in the embryo that usually either stay open and become the vaginal labia or fuse and become a scrotum. In some hermaphrodites, though, the choice of opening or closing is ambivalent. Finally, all mammalian embryos have structures that can become the female uterus and the fallopian tubes, as well as structures that can become part of the male sperm-transport system. Typically either the male or the female set of those primordial genital organs degenerates, and the remaining structures achieve their sex-appropriate future. In hermaphrodites both sets of organs develop to varying degrees.

Intersexuality itself is old news. Hermaphrodites, for instance, are often featured in stories about human origins. Early biblical scholars believed Adam began life as a hermaphrodite and later divided into two people—a male and a female—after falling from grace. According to Plato there once were three sexes—male, female and hermaphrodite—but the third sex was lost with time.

Both the Talmud and the Tosefta, the Jewish books of law, list extensive regulations for people of mixed sex. The Tosefta expressly forbids hermaphrodites to inherit their fathers' estates (like daughters), to seclude themselves with women (like sons) or to shave (like men). When hermaphrodites menstruate they must be isolated from men (like women); they are disqualified from serving as witnesses or as priests (like women), but the laws of pederasty apply to them.

In Europe a pattern emerged by the end of the Middle Ages that, in a sense, has lasted to the present day: hermaphrodites were compelled to choose an established gender role and stick with it. The penalty for transgression was often death. Thus in the 1600s a Scottish hermaphrodite living as a woman was buried alive after impregnating his/her master's daughter.

For questions of inheritance, legitimacy, paternity, succession to title and eligibility for certain professions to be determined, modern Anglo-Saxon legal systems require that newborns be registered as either male or female. In the U.S. today sex determination is governed by state laws. Illinois permits adults to change the sex recorded on their birth certificates should a physician attest to having performed the appropriate surgery. The New York Academy of Medicine, on the other hand, has taken an opposite view. In spite of surgical alterations of the external genitalia, the academy argued in 1966, the chromosomal sex remains the same. By that measure a person's wish to conceal his or her original sex cannot outweigh the public interest in protection against fraud.

During this century the medical community has completed what the legal world began—the complete erasure of any form of embodied sex that does not conform to a male–female, heterosexual pattern. Ironically, a more sophisticated knowledge of the complexity of sexual systems has led to the repression of such intricacy.

In 1937 the urologist Hugh H. Young of Johns Hopkins University published a volume titled *Genital Abnormalities, Hermaphroditism and Related Adrenal Diseases*. The book is remarkable for its erudition, scientific insight and open-mindedness. In it Young drew together a wealth of carefully documented case histories to demonstrate and study the medical treatment of such "accidents of birth." Young did not pass judgment on the people he studied, nor did he attempt to coerce into treatment those intersexuals who rejected that option. And he showed unusual even-handedness in referring to those people who had had sexual experiences as both men and women as "practicing hermaphrodites."

One of Young's more interesting cases was a hermaphrodite named Emma who had grown up as a female. Emma had both a penis-size clitoris and a vagina, which made it possible for him/her to have "normal" heterosexual sex with both men and women. As a teenager Emma had had sex with a number of girls to whom s/he was deeply attracted; but at the age of nineteen s/he had married a man. Unfortunately, he had given Emma little sexual pleasure (though *he* had had no complaints), and so throughout that marriage and subsequent ones Emma had kept girlfriends on the side. With some frequency s/he had pleasurable sex with them. Voting describes his subject as appearing "to be quite content and even happy." In conversation Emma occasionally told him of his/her wish to be a man, a circumstance Young said would be relatively easy to bring about. But Emma's reply strikes a heroic blow for self-interest:

> Would you have to remove that vagina? I don't know about that because that's my meal ticket. If you did that, I would have to quit my husband and go to work, so I think I'll keep it and stay as I am. My husband supports me well, and even though I don't have any sexual pleasure with him, I do have lots with my girlfriends.

Yet even as Young was illuminating intersexuality with the light of scientific reason, he was beginning its suppression. For his book is also an extended treatise on the most modern surgical and hormonal methods of changing intersexuals into either males or females. Young may have differed from his successors in being less judgmental and controlling of the patients and their families, but he nonetheless supplied the foundation on which current intervention practices were built.

By 1969, when the English physicians Christopher J. Dewhurst and Ronald R. Gordon wrote *The Intersexual Disorders*, medical and surgical approaches to intersexuality had neared a state of rigid uniformity. It is hardly surprising that such a hardening of opinion took place in the era of the feminine mystique—of the post–Second World War flight to the suburbs and the strict division of family roles according to sex. That the medical consensus was not quite universal (or perhaps that it seemed poised to break apart again) can be gleaned from the near-hysterical tone of Dewhurst and Gordon's book, which contrasts markedly with the calm reason of Young's founding work. Consider their opening description of an intersexual newborn:

> One can only attempt to imagine the anguish of the parents. That a newborn should have a deformity ... [affecting] so fundamental an issue as the very sex of the child ... is a tragic event which immediately conjures up visions of a hopeless psychological misfit doomed to live always as a sexual freak in loneliness and frustration.

Dewhurst and Gordon warned that such a miserable fate would, indeed, be a baby's lot should the case be improperly managed; "but fortunately," they wrote, "with correct management the outlook is infinitely better than the poor parents—emotionally stunned by the event—or indeed anyone without special knowledge could ever imagine."

Scientific dogma has held fast to the assumption that without medical care hermaphrodites are doomed to a life of misery. Yet there are few empirical studies to back up that assumption, and some of the same research gathered to build a case for medical treatment contradicts it. Francies Benton, another of Young's practicing hermaphrodites, "had not worried over his condition, did not wish to be changed, and was enjoying life." The same could be said of Emma, the opportunistic hausfrau. Even Dewhurst and Gordon, adamant about the psychological importance of treating intersexuals at the infant stage, acknowledged great success in "changing the sex" of older patients. They reported on twenty cases of children reclassified into a different sex after the supposedly critical age of eighteen months. They asserted that all the reclassifications were "successful," and they wondered then whether reregistration could be "recommended more readily than [had] been suggested so far."

The treatment of intersexuality in this century provides a clear example of what the French historian Michel Foucault has called biopower. The knowledge developed in biochemistry, embryology, endocrinology, psychology and surgery has enabled physicians to control the very sex of the human body. The multiple contradictions in that kind of power call for some scrutiny. On the one hand, the medical "management" of intersexuality certainly developed as part of an attempt to free people from perceived psychological pain (though whether the pain was the patient's, the parents' or the physician's is unclear). And if one accepts the assumption that in a sex-divided culture people can realize their greatest potential for happiness and productivity only if they are sure they belong to one of only two acknowledged sexes, modern medicine has been extremely successful.

On the other hand, the same medical accomplishments can be read not as progress but as a mode of discipline. Hermaphrodites have unruly bodies. They do not fall naturally into a binary classification; only a surgical shoehorn can put them there. But why should we care if a "woman," defined as one who has breasts, a vagina, a uterus and ovaries and who menstruates, also has a clitoris large enough to penetrate the vagina of another woman? Why should we care if there are people whose biological equipment enables them to have sex "naturally" with both men and women? The answers seem to lie in a cultural need to maintain clear distinctions between the sexes. Society mandates the control of intersexual bodies because they blur and bridge the great divide. Inasmuch as hermaphrodites literally embody both sexes, they challenge traditional beliefs about sexual difference: they possess the irritating ability to live sometimes as one sex and sometimes the other, and they raise the specter of homosexuality.

But what if things were altogether different? Imagine a world in which the same knowledge that has enabled medicine to intervene in the management of intersexual patients has been placed at the service of multiple sexualities. Imagine that the sexes have multiplied beyond currently imaginable limits. It would have to be a world of shared powers. Patient and physician, parent and child, male and female, heterosexual and homosexual—all those oppositions and others would have to be dissolved as sources of division. A new ethic of medical treatment would arise, one that would permit ambiguity in a culture that had overcome sexual division. The central mission of medical treatment would be to preserve life. Thus hermaphrodites would be concerned primarily not about whether they can conform to society but about whether they might develop potentially life-threatening conditions—hernias, gonadal tumors, salt imbalance caused by adrenal malfunction—that sometimes accompany hermaphroditic development. In my ideal world medical intervention for intersexuals would take place only rarely before the age of reason; subsequent treatment would be a cooperative venture between physician, patient and other advisers trained in issues of gender multiplicity.

I do not pretend that the transition to my utopia would be smooth. Sex, even the supposedly "normal," heterosexual kind, continues to cause untold anxieties in Western society. And certainly a culture that has yet to come to grips—religiously and, in some states, legally—with the ancient and relatively uncomplicated reality of homosexual love will not readily embrace intersexuality. No doubt the most troublesome arena by far would be the rearing of children. Parents, at least since the Victorian era, have fretted, sometimes to the point of outright denial, over the fact that their children are sexual beings.

All that and more amply explains why intersexual children are generally squeezed into one of the two prevailing sexual categories. But what would be the psychological consequences of taking the alternative road—raising children as unabashed intersexuals? On the surface that tack seems fraught with peril. What, for example, would happen to the intersexual child amid the unrelenting cruelty of the school yard? When the time came to shower in gym class, what horrors and humiliations would await the intersexual as his/her anatomy was displayed in all its non-traditional glory? In whose gym class would s/he register to begin with? What bathroom would s/he use? And how on earth would Mom and Dad help shepherd him/her through the mine field of puberty?

In the past thirty years those questions have been ignored, as the scientific community has, with remarkable unanimity, avoided contemplating the alternative route of unimpeded intersexuality. But modern investigators tend to overlook a substantial body of case histories, most of them compiled between 1930 and 1960, before surgical intervention became rampant. Almost without exception, those reports describe children who grew up knowing they were intersexual (though they did not advertise it) and adjusted to their unusual status. Some of the studies are richly detailed—described at the level of gym-class showering (which most intersexuals avoided without incident); in any event, there is not a psychotic or a suicide in the lot.

Still, the nuances of socialization among intersexuals cry out for more sophisticated analysis. Clearly, before my vision of sexual multiplicity can be realized, the first openly intersexual children and their parents will have to be brave pioneers who will bear the brunt of society's growing pains. But in the long view—though it could take generations to achieve—the prize might be a society in which sexuality is something to be celebrated for its subtleties and not something to be feared or ridiculed.

Analyze

1. Fausto-Sterling opens her essay with the story of Levi Suydam. Why does she decide to do this? How does Suydam's story set up the context of the essay—and help establish Fausto-Sterling's argument?

2. What are the "five sexes" Fausto-Sterling advocates for in this essay? How does she use the concept of the five sexes to make a broader argument about sex and gender?

3. How does Fausto-Sterling use the story of Hermaphroditus to explain to readers the definition of a hermaphrodite?

4. According to Fausto-Sterling, how has the "medical management" of intersexuality developed alongside concerns for intersex individuals' psychological well-being?
5. Does Fausto-Sterling believe that her vision of sexuality is one that can be realized in our time? Why or why not?

Explore

1. Do a quick Internet search of the term "intersex"—for example, you might look at the Wikipedia page on intersex, as well as the website for the Intersex Society of North America. What did you learn about intersexuality as a concept and about intersex individuals? To what extent does Fausto-Sterling's argument fit into that conversation?
2. To get a sense of the struggles that intersex individuals face, watch the promotional video for the documentary *Born Between* (available online). In this documentary, intersex individuals talk about the issues Fausto-Sterling raises in her essay, such as gender reassignment surgery and marriage. After reading Fausto-Sterling's essay and watching the documentary, to what extent do you agree with Fausto-Sterling that we need a refining of our biological understanding of sex and gender?
3. How do Fausto-Sterling's ideas regarding the impact of social structures on our understanding of biological sex speak to Judith Lorber's discussion of gender as a social construct? In what ways does Lorber's essay support Fausto-Sterling's argument, and why?

Forging Connections

1. In "Night to His Day," Judith Lorber contends, "For human beings there is no essential femaleness or maleness, femininity or masculinity, womanhood or manhood, but once gender is ascribed, the social order constructs and holds individuals to strongly gendered norms and expectations." Do you think the other authors we have read in this chapter would agree with this statement? Why or why not? Cite specific passages from the authors you discuss to support your answer.
2. Think about this chapter in relation to your expectations for the textbook. How do the selections set up what you think the textbook will be about? Skim through the readings in subsequent chapters. What concepts from this chapter do you think you'll need to carry with you to future readings, and why?

Looking Further

1. Early in "The Five Sexes: Why Male and Female Are Not Enough,"
   Anne Fausto-Sterling states, "In the medical community, however, the
   assumptions behind that wish [to have each child born into the world
   fit into one of two gender categories]—that there be only two sexes,
   that heterosexuality alone is normal, that there is one true model of
   psychological health—have gone virtually unexamined." Later in the
   essay she points to Paul Guinet and Jacques Decourt, Hugh H. Young,
   and Christopher J. Dewhurst and Ronald R. Gordon as medical experts who have importantly contributed to this conversation. How
   would you attempt to find out how the conversation has continued
   since Fausto-Sterling's essay was published in 1993 as well as what additional terms/phrases have been addressed (Young describes "practicing
   hermaphrodites," whereas Dewhurst and Gordon refer to intersexuals
   as "hopeless psychological misfits," and so on)? Create a researchable
   question that considers how this scholarship has evolved and write an
   essay about how the conversation has continued in the decades since
   Fausto-Sterling's work was published. Integrate summary and paraphrase from Fausto-Sterling's text, and include quotations from your
   research to show how this conversation has evolved over time.

2. In this chapter, we hope you have discovered that gender is something
   that cannot be confined to two boxes: male or female. Instead, gender
   is something that is fluid and is not easily contained. In her TED talk,
   "Why I Must Come Out" (available online at the TED website), fashion model Geena Rocero discusses her upbringing as a boy and her
   path to self-discovery. As you watch Rocero's talk, think about her
   path to having her biological sex match her gender performance. To
   what extent do biological sex and gender performance *have* to match,
   as opposed to being fluid, and why or why not?

2 Gender and Identity

In the first chapter, we introduced you to Chris and asked you to identify Chris as "male" or "female" and to consider the cues that led you to your conclusion. Basically, we asked you to think about what makes Chris, well, "Chris."

Now we ask you to turn that gaze on yourself. What makes you you?

When we think about identity, there are several markers that we automatically define ourselves by. Gender, sex, race, and ethnicity are three of the most common ways to establish one's identity. However, even within one's gender, there are subcategories that may become important aspects of one's identity. For instance, one may say, "I am a woman," but what does that mean? What does it mean to be a woman, or a man, or hijra (the Indian term for those who identify as neither male nor female), or two spirit (the Native American term for a third gender)? What qualities does society associate with these identities, and to what extent do we choose to embody them? If one is born a woman, for instance, does one have to identify as a woman? If one is born a woman, does one have to adopt the qualities of a woman that society deems necessary to identify as a woman?

The choices that gender identity presents us with will be explored in the following chapter. As you move through the readings, think about the way in which identity is presented and how that identity is fraught with tension, both on an individual and on a social level. A commencement address to the students of Smith College (a women's college), Adrienne Rich's "What Does a Woman Need to Know?" encourages the new female graduates to interrogate the way society defines them as women—and attempts to redefine feminism. Sandra Cisneros's essay "Guadalupe the Sex Goddess" examines the connection between one's religious identity and sexuality. In "Two Spirit: The Story of a Movement Unfolds," Zachary Pullin discusses the Native American identity of two spirit that embraces both masculine and feminine qualities. In "Cisgender Privilege, Intersectionality, and the Criminalization of CeCe McDonald," Julia R. Johnson argues for the importance of transgender identity in communication studies. Tommi Avicolli Mecca's essay "He Defies You Still: The Memoirs of a Sissy" explores the pain one feels having an identity—in this case, "sissy"—forced on him/her by others. Vanessa Vitiello Urquhart's essay "Why I'm Still a Butch Lesbian" argues why she continues to embrace her identity as a butch lesbian instead of turning to an identity that would be called more masculine.

Adrienne Rich
"What Does a Woman Need to Know?"

Author and women's rights activist **Adrienne Rich** was born in Baltimore, Maryland, and published her first book of poetry in 1951, the same year she graduated from Radcliffe College, a women's college in Cambridge, Massachusetts. Over her lifetime she won numerous awards for her poetry and prose. She was also a dedicated women's and LGBT rights activist and wrote about the tension many women face between their own identities and the expectations society places on them to fulfill traditional "feminine" roles.

"What Does a Woman Need to Know?" was the commencement address for the Smith College Class of 1979. As a women's college, Smith is dedicated to forwarding women's education and intellectualism. Commencement speeches typically both look backward and forward to provide the new graduates with guidance for their future lives. As you read, think about the audience—graduating (female) college seniors. How does Rich offer guidance for these students, and why?

I have been very much moved that you, the class of 1979, chose me for your commencement speaker. It is important to me to be here, in part because Smith is one of the original colleges for women, but also because she has chosen to continue identifying herself as a women's college. We are at a point in history where this fact has enormous potential, even if that potential is as yet unrealized. The possibilities for the future education of women that haunt these buildings and grounds are enormous, when we think of what an independent women's college might be: a college dedicated both to teaching women what women need to know and, by the same token, to changing the landscape of knowledge itself. The germ of those possibilities lies symbolically in The Sophia Smith Collection, an archive much in need of expansion and increase, but which by its very existence makes the statement that women's lives and work are valued here and that our foresisters, buried and diminished in male-centered scholarship, are a living presence, necessary and precious to us.

Suppose we were to ask ourselves simply: What does a woman need to know to become a self-conscious, self-defining human being? Doesn't she need a knowledge of her own history, of her much-politicized female body, of the creative genius of women of the past—the skills and crafts and techniques and visions possessed by women in other times and cultures, and how they have been rendered anonymous, censored, interrupted, devalued? Doesn't she, as one of that majority who are still denied equal rights as citizens, enslaved as sexual prey, unpaid or underpaid as workers, withheld from her own power—doesn't she need an analysis of her condition, a knowledge of the women thinkers of the past who have reflected on it, a knowledge, too, of women's world-wide individual rebellions and organized movements against economic and social injustice, and how these have been fragmented and silenced?

Doesn't she need to know how seemingly natural states of being, like heterosexuality, like motherhood, have been enforced and institutionalized to deprive her of power? Without such education, women have lived and continue to live in ignorance of our collective context, vulnerable to the projections of men's fantasies about us as they appear in art, in literature, in the sciences, in the media, in the so-called humanistic studies. I suggest that not anatomy, but enforced ignorance, has been a crucial key to our powerlessness.

There is—and I say this with sorrow—there is no women's college today which is providing young women with the education they need for survival as whole persons in a world which denies women wholeness— that knowledge which, in the words of Coleridge, "returns again as power." The existence of Women's Studies courses offers at least some kind of life line. But even Women's Studies can amount simply to compensatory history; too often they fail to challenge the intellectual and political structures that must be challenged if women as a group are ever to come into collective, nonexclusionary freedom. The belief that established science and scholarship—which have so relentlessly excluded women from their making—are "objective" and "value-free" and that feminist studies are "unscholarly," "biased," and "ideological" dies hard. Yet the fact is that all science, and all scholarship, and all art are ideological; there is no neutrality in culture. And the ideology of the education you have just spent four years acquiring in a women's college has been largely, if not entirely, the ideology of white male supremacy, a construct of male subjectivity. The silences, the empty spaces, the language itself, with its excision of the female, the methods of discourse tell us as much as the content, once we learn to watch for what is left out, to listen for the unspoken, to study the patterns of established science and scholarship with an outsider's eye. One of the dangers of a privileged education for women is that we may lose the eye of the outsider and come to believe that those patterns hold for humanity, for the universal, and that they include us.

And so I want to talk today about privilege and about tokenism and about power. Everything I can say to you on this subject comes hard-won, from the lips of a woman privileged by class and skin color, a father's favorite daughter, educated at Radcliffe, which was then casually referred to as the Harvard "Annex." Much of the first four decades of my life was spent in a continuous tension between the world the Fathers taught me to see, and had rewarded me for seeing, and the flashes of insight that came through the eye of the outsider. Gradually those flashes of insight, which at times could seem like brushes with madness, began to demand that I struggle to connect them with each other, to insist that I take them seriously. It was only when I could finally affirm the outsider's eye as the source of a legitimate and coherent vision, that I began to be able to do the work I truly wanted to do, live the kind of life I truly wanted to live, instead of carrying out the assignments I had been given as a privileged woman and a token.

For women, all privilege is relative. Some of you were not born with class or skin-color privilege; but you all have the privilege of education, even if it is an education which has largely denied you knowledge of yourselves as women. You have, to begin with, the privilege of literacy; and it is well for us to remember that, in an age of increasing illiteracy, 60 percent of the world's illiterates are women. Between 1960 and 1970, the number of illiterate men in the world rose by 8 million, while the number of illiterate women rose by 40 million.[1] And the number of illiterate women is increasing. Beyond literacy, you have the privilege of training and tools which can allow you to go beyond the content of your education and re-educate yourselves—to debrief yourselves, we might call it, of the false messages of your education in this culture, the messages telling you that women have not really cared about power or learning or creative opportunities because of a psycho-biological need to serve men and produce children; that only a few atypical women have been exceptions to this rule; the messages telling you that woman's experience is neither normative nor central to human experience. You have the training and the tools to do independent research, to evaluate data, to criticize, and to express in language and visual forms what you discover. This is a privilege, yes, but only if you do not give up in exchange for it the deep knowledge of the unprivileged, the knowledge that, as a woman, you have historically been viewed and still are viewed as existing, not in your own right, but in the service of men. And only if you refuse to give up your capacity to think as a woman, even though in the graduate schools and professions to which many of you will be going you will be praised and rewarded for "thinking like a man."

The word *power* is highly charged for women. It has been long associated for us with the use of force, with rape, with the stockpiling of weapons, with the ruthless accrual of wealth and the hoarding of resources, with the power that acts only in its own interest, despising and exploiting the powerless—including women and children. The effects of this kind of power are all around us, even literally in the water we drink and the air we breathe, in the form of carcinogens and radioactive wastes. But for a long time now, feminists have been talking about redefining power, about that meaning of power which returns to the root—*posse, potere, pouvoir*: to be able, to have the potential, to possess and use one's energy of creation—*transforming power*. An early objection to feminism—in both the nineteenth and twentieth centuries—was that it would make women behave like men—ruthlessly, exploitatively, oppressively. In fact, radical feminism looks to a transformation of human relationships and structures in which power, instead of a thing to be hoarded by a few, would be released to and from within the many, shared in the form of knowledge, expertise, decision making, access to tools, as well as in the basic forms of food and shelter and health care and literacy. Feminists—and many nonfeminists—are, and rightly so, still concerned with what power would mean in such a society, and with the relative differences in power among and between women here and now.

Which brings me to a third meaning of power where women are concerned: the false power which masculine society offers to a few women, on condition that they use it to maintain things as they are, and that they essentially "think like men." This is the meaning of female tokenism: that power withheld from the vast majority of women is offered to a few, so that it appears that any "truly qualified" woman can gain access to leadership, recognition, and reward; hence, that justice based on merit actually prevails. The token woman is encouraged to see herself as different from most other women, as exceptionally talented and deserving, and to separate herself from the wider female condition; and she is perceived by "ordinary" women as separate also, perhaps even as stronger than themselves.

Because you are, within the limits of all women's ultimate outsiderhood, a privileged group of women, it is extremely important for your future sanity that you understand the way tokenism functions. Its most immediate contradiction is that, while it seems to offer the individual token woman a means to realize her creativity, to influence the course of events, it also, by exacting of her certain kinds of behavior and style, acts to blur her outsider's eye, which could be her real source of power and vision. Losing her outsider's vision, she loses the insight which both binds her to other women and affirms her in herself. Tokenism essentially demands that the token deny her identification with women as a group, especially with women less privileged than she: if she is a lesbian, that she deny her relationships with individual women; that she perpetuate rules and structures and criteria and methodologies which have functioned to exclude women; that she renounce or leave undeveloped the critical perspective of her female consciousness. Women unlike herself—poor women, women of color, waitresses, secretaries, housewives in the supermarket, prostitutes, old women—become invisible to her; they may represent too acutely what she has escaped or wished to flee.

President Conway tells me that ever-increasing numbers of you are going on from Smith to medical and law schools. The news, on the face of it, is good: that, thanks to the feminist struggle of the past decade, more doors into these two powerful professions are open to women. I would like to believe that any profession would be better for having more women practicing it, and that any woman practicing law or medicine would use her knowledge and skill to work to transform the realm of health care and the interpretations of the law, to make them responsive to the needs of all those—women, people of color, children, the aged, the dispossessed—for whom they function today as repressive controls. I would like to believe this, but it will not happen even if 50 percent of the members of these professions are women, unless those women refuse to be made into token insiders, unless they zealously preserve the outsider's view and the outsider's consciousness.

For no woman is really an insider in the institutions fathered by masculine consciousness. When we allow ourselves to believe we are, we lose touch with parts of ourselves defined as unacceptable by that consciousness; with the vital toughness and visionary strength of the angry grandmothers, the shamanesses, the fierce marketwomen of the Ibo Women's War, the marriage-resisting women silkworkers of prerevolutionary China, the millions of widows, midwives, and women healers tortured and burned as witches for three centuries in Europe, the Beguines of the twelfth century, who formed independent women's orders outside the domination of the Church, the women of the Paris Commune who marched on Versailles, the uneducated housewives of the Women's Cooperative Guild in England who memorized poetry over the washtub and organized against their oppression as mothers, the women thinkers discredited as "strident," "shrill," "crazy," or "deviant" whose courage to be heretical, to speak their truths, we so badly need to draw upon in our own lives. I believe that every woman's soul is haunted by the spirits of earlier women who fought for their unmet needs and those of their children and

> "No woman is really an insider in the institutions fathered by masculine consciousness."

their tribes and their peoples, who refused to accept the prescriptions of a male church and state, who took risks and resisted, as women today—like Inez Garcia, Yvonne Wanrow, Joan Little, Cassandra Peten—are fighting their rapists and batterers. Those spirits dwell in us, trying to speak to us. But we can choose to be deaf; and tokenism, the myth of the "special" woman, the unmothered Athena sprung from her father's brow, can deafen us to their voices.

In this decade now ending, as more women are entering the professions (though still suffering sexual harassment in the workplace, though still, if they have children, carrying two full-time jobs, though still vastly outnumbered by men in upper-level and decision-making jobs), we need most profoundly to remember that early insight of the feminist movement as it evolved in the late sixties: *that no woman is liberated until we all are liberated*. The media flood us with messages to the contrary, telling us that we live in an era when "alternate life styles" are freely accepted, when "marriage contracts" and "the new intimacy" are revolutionizing heterosexual relationships, that shared parenting and the "new fatherhood" will change the world. And we live in a society leeched upon by the "personal growth" and "human potential" industry, by the delusion that individual self-fulfillment can be found in thirteen weeks or a weekend, that the alienation and injustice experienced by women, by Black and Third World people, by the poor, in a world ruled by white males, in a society which fails to meet the most basic needs and which is slowly poisoning itself, can be mitigated or dispersed by Transcendental Meditation. Perhaps the most succinct expression of this message I have seen is the appearance of a magazine for women called *Self*. The insistence of the feminist movement, that each woman's selfhood is precious, that the feminine ethic of self-denial and self-sacrifice must give way to a true woman identification, which would affirm our connectedness with all women, is perverted into a commercially profitable and politically debilitating narcissism. It is important for each of you, toward whom many of these messages are especially directed, to discriminate clearly between "liberated life style" and feminist struggle, and to make a conscious choice.

It's a cliché of commencement speeches that the speaker ends with a peroration telling the new graduates that however badly past generations have behaved, their generation must save the world. I would rather say to you, women of the class of 1979: Try to be worthy of your foresisters, learn from your history, look for inspiration to your ancestresses. If this history has been poorly taught to you, if you do not know it, then use your educational privilege to learn it. Learn how some women of privilege have compromised the greater liberation of women, how others have risked their privileges to further it; learn how brilliant and successful women have failed to create a more just and caring society, precisely because they have tried to do so on terms that the powerful men around them would accept and tolerate. Learn to be worthy of the women of every class, culture, and historical age who did otherwise, who spoke boldly when women were jeered and physically harassed for speaking in public, who—like Anne Hutchinson, Mary Wollstonecraft, the Grimké sisters, Abby Kelley, Ida B. Wells-Barnett, Susan B. Anthony, Lillian Smith, Fannie Lou Hamer—broke taboos, who resisted slavery—their own and other people's. To become a token woman—whether you win the Nobel prize or merely get tenure at the cost of denying your sisters—is to become something less than a man indeed, since men are loyal at least to their own world view, their laws of brotherhood and male self-interest. I am not suggesting that you imitate male loyalties; with the philosopher Mary Daly, I believe that the bonding of women must be utterly different and for an utterly different end: not the misering of resources and power, but the release, in each other, of the yet unexplored resources and transformative power of women, so long despised, confined, and wasted. Get all the knowledge and skill you can in whatever professions you enter; but remember that most of your education must be self-education, in learning the things women need to know and in calling up the voices we need to hear within ourselves.

NOTE

1. United Nations, Department of International Economic and Social Affairs, Statistical Office, *1977 Compendium of Social Statistics* (New York: United Nations, 1980).

Analyze

1. Despite the emergence of women's studies programs, why does Rich believe that college does not prepare women for the kind of education they need? What kind of education is that?
2. How does Rich's description of the term "power" demonstrate the ways in which women have been denied power? How do she and other feminists want to reconsider that definition, and why?

3. How does Rich define the term "tokenism," and why is it important that women understand that they are not "token insiders," either in academia or in their chosen professions?

4. Consider Rich's tone as a commencement speaker. How might you describe Rich's tone in this piece? What language does she use that would support your description, and why? How does Rich's own experience as a graduate of a women's college contribute to your understanding of her tone?

5. Rich states that a commencement speech typically ends with "a peroration telling the new graduates that however badly past generations have behaved, their generation must save the world." First, if you're unsure, look up "peroration." What does it mean? Then, how does Rich put a different spin on the idea of the peroration of a commencement? What is her message to the graduates of Smith College, and why is she making this particular message?

Explore

1. Rich describes the current state of women in the United States as those who are "still denied equal rights as citizens, enslaved as sexual prey, unpaid or underpaid workers, withheld from [their] own power." To what extent do these conditions still apply to American women today? Write an essay that looks at each of these issues and compares Rich's descriptions to the current state of U.S. women.

2. Watch "The Girl Effect: The Clock Is Ticking" (YouTube). Both "The Girl Effect" and "What Does a Woman Need to Know?" are making specific claims about the value of education to women. Write an essay in which you compare and contrast the messages in both pieces regarding the value of a woman's education.

3. First, as a class, in groups, or on your own, develop a list of questions you might ask a woman about her experience with education. You might think about her educational background, how she was perceived both while she was completing her education and after, and her own perceptions of the value of education. Then, interview a woman in your family who is older than you about her educational experience and ask her these questions. Write a narrative of that woman's educational experience that makes an argument for the value of education for women.

Sandra Cisneros
"Guadalupe the Sex Goddess"

Sandra Cisneros is a key figure in Chicana literature; she is the first female Mexican American author to have her work published by a mainstream publisher, known best for her novel *The House on Mango Street* (1984). She grew up migrating back and forth between Chicago and Mexico City with her family, and in her novels, poems, short stories, and essays, she explores feeling caught between U.S. and Mexican cultures while belonging to neither, the deeply embedded patriarchal values of both, and the formation of a Chicana identity. In "Guadalupe the Sex Goddess," published by *Ms.* magazine in 1996, she describes a Latina sexuality heavily influenced by Roman Catholicism. As you read, consider how religion shapes our attitudes about sex and how, for Cisneros, the personal is political.

In high school I marveled at how white women strutted around the locker room, nude as pearls, as unashamed of their brilliant bodies as the Nike of Samothrace. Maybe they were hiding terrible secrets like bulimia or anorexia, but, to my naive eye then, I thought of them as women comfortable in their skin.

You could always tell us Latinas. We hid when we undressed, modestly facing a wall, or, in my case, dressing in a bathroom stall. We were the ones who still used bulky sanitary pads instead of tampons, thinking ourselves morally superior to our white classmates. *My mama said you can't use tampons till after you're married.* All Latina mamas said this, yet how come none of us thought to ask our mothers why they didn't use tampons *after* getting married?

Womanhood was full of mysteries. I was as ignorant about my own body as any female ancestor who hid behind a sheet with a hole in the center when husband or doctor called. Religion and our culture, our culture and religion, helped to create that blur, a vagueness about what went on "down there." So ashamed was I about my own "down there" that until I was an adult I had no idea I had another orifice called the vagina; I thought my period would arrive via the urethra or perhaps through the walls of my skin.

No wonder, then, it was too terrible to think about a doctor—a man!— looking at you down there when you could never bring yourself to look yourself. *¡Ay, nunca!* How could I acknowledge my sexuality, let alone enjoy sex, with so much guilt? In the guise of modesty my culture locked me in a double chastity belt of ignorance and *vergüenza*, shame.

I had never seen my mother nude. I had never taken a good look at myself either. Privacy for self-exploration belonged to the wealthy. In my home a private space was practically impossible; aside from the doors that opened to the street, the only room with a lock was the bathroom, and how could anyone who shared a bathroom with eight other people stay in there for more than a few minutes? Before college, no one in my family had a room of their own except me, a narrow closet just big enough for my twin bed and an oversized blond dresser we'd bought in the bargain basement of *el Sears*. The dresser was as long as a coffin and blocked the door from shutting completely. I had my own room, but I never had the luxury of shutting the door.

I didn't even see my own sex until a nurse at the Emma Goldman Clinic showed it to me—*Would you like to see your cervix? Your os is dilating. You must be ovulating. Here's a mirror; take a look.* When had anyone ever suggested I take a look or allowed me a speculum to take home and investigate myself at leisure!

I'd only been to one other birth control facility prior to the Emma Goldman Clinic, the university medical center in grad school. I was 21 in a strange town far from home for the first time. I was afraid and I was ashamed to seek out a gynecologist, but I was more afraid of becoming pregnant. Still, I agonized about going for weeks. Perhaps the anonymity and distance from my family allowed me finally to take control of my life. I remember wanting to be fearless like the white women around me, to be able to have sex when I wanted, but I was too afraid to explain to a would-be lover how I'd only had one other man in my life and we'd practiced withdrawal. Would he laugh at me? How could I look anyone in the face and explain why I couldn't go see a gynecologist?

One night, a classmate I liked too much took me home with him. I meant all along to say something about how I wasn't on anything, but I never quite found my voice, never the right moment to cry out—*Stop, this is dangerous to my brilliant career!* Too afraid to sound stupid, afraid to ask him to take responsibility too, I said nothing, and I let him take me like that with nothing protecting me from motherhood but luck. The days that followed were torture, but fortunately on Mother's Day my period arrived, and I celebrated my nonmaternity by making an appointment with the family planning center.

When I see pregnant teens, I can't help but think that could've been me. In high school I would've thrown myself into love the way some warriors throw themselves into fighting. I was ready to sacrifice everything in the name of love, to do anything, even risk my own life, but thankfully there were no takers. I was enrolled at an all-girls' school. I think if I had met a boy who would have me, I would've had sex in a minute, convinced this was love. I have always had enough imagination to fall in love all by myself, then and now.

I tell you this story because I am overwhelmed by the silence regarding Latinas and our bodies. If I, as a graduate student, was shy about talking to anyone about my body and sex, imagine how difficult it must be for a young girl in middle school or high school living in a home with no lock on the bedroom door, perhaps with no door, or maybe with no bedroom, no information other than misinformation from the girlfriends and the boyfriend. So much guilt, so much silence, and such a yearning to be loved; no wonder young women find themselves having sex while they are still children, having sex without sexual protection, too ashamed to confide their feelings and fears to anyone.

What a culture of denial. Don't get pregnant! But no one tells you how not to. This is why I was angry for so many years every time I saw *la Virgen de Guadalupe*, my culture's role model for brown women like me. She was damn dangerous, an ideal so lofty and unrealistic it was laughable. Did boys have to aspire to be Jesus? I never saw any evidence of it. They were fornicating like rabbits while the Church ignored them and pointed us women toward our destiny—marriage and motherhood. The other alternative was *puta*hood.

In my neighborhood I knew only real women, neither saints nor whores, naive and vulnerable *huerquitas* like me who wanted desperately to fall in love, with the heart and soul. And yes, with the *panocha* too.

As far as I could see, *la Lupe* was nothing but a Goody Two-shoes meant to doom me to a life of unhappiness. Thanks, but no thanks. Motherhood and/or marriage were anathema to my career. But being a bad girl, that was something I could use as a writer, a Molotov cocktail to toss at my papa and *el Papa*, who had their own plans for me.

Discovering sex was like discovering writing. It was powerful in a way I couldn't explain. Like writing, you had to go beyond the guilt and shame to get to anything good. Like writing, it could take you to deep and mysterious subterranean levels. With each new depth I found out things about myself I didn't know I knew. And, like writing, for a slip of a moment it could be spiritual, the cosmos pivoting on a pin, could empty and fill you all at once like a Ganges, a Piazzolla tango, a tulip bending in the wind. I was no one, I was nothing, and I was everything in the universe little and large—twig, cloud, sky. How had this incredible energy been denied me!

When I look at *la Virgen de Guadalupe* now, she is not the Lupe of my childhood, no longer the one in my grandparents' house in Tepeyac, nor is she the one of the Roman Catholic Church, the one I bolted the door against in my teens and twenties. Like every woman who matters to me, I have had to search for her in the rubble of history. And I have found her. She is Guadalupe the sex goddess, a goddess who makes me feel good about my sexual power, my sexual energy, who reminds me that I must, as Clarissa Pinkola Estés so aptly put it, "[speak] from the vulva . . . speak the most basic, honest truth," and write from my *panocha*.

In my research of Guadalupe's pre-Columbian antecedents, the she before the Church desexed her, I found Tonantzin, and inside Tonantzin a pantheon of other mother goddesses. I discovered Tlazolteotl, the goddess of fertility and sex, also referred to as Totzin, Our Beginnings, or Tzinteotl, goddess of the rump. *Putas*, nymphos, and other loose women were known as "women of the sex goddess." Tlazolteotl was the patron of sexual passion, and though she had the power to stir you to sin, she could also forgive you and cleanse you of your sexual transgressions via her priests who heard confession. In this aspect of confessor Tlazolteotl was known as Tlaelcuani, the filth eater. Maybe you've seen her; she's the one whose image is sold in the tourist markets even now, a statue of a woman squatting in childbirth, her face grimacing in pain. Tlazolteotl, then, is a duality of maternity *and* sexuality. In other words, she is a sexy mama.

To me, *la Virgen de Guadalupe* is also Coatlicue, the creative/destructive goddess. When I think of the Coatlicue statue in the National Museum of Anthropology in Mexico City, so terrible it was unearthed and then reburied because it was too frightening to look at, I think of a woman enraged, a woman as tempest, a woman *bien berrinchuda*, and I like that. *La Lupe* as *cabrona*. Not silent and passive, but silently gathering force.

Most days, I too feel like the creative/destructive goddess Coatlicue, especially the days I'm writing, capable of fabricating pretty tales with pretty words, as well as doing demolition work with a volley of *palabrotas* if I want to. I am the Coatlicue-Lupe whose square column of a body I see in so many

Indian women, in my mother, and in myself each time I check out my thick-waisted, flat-assed torso in the mirror.

Coatlicue, Tlazolteotl, Tonantzin, *la Virgen de Guadalupe*. They are each telescoped one into the other, into who I am. And this is where *la Lupe* intrigues me—not the Lupe of 1531 who appeared to Juan Diego, but the one of the 1990s who has shaped who we are as Chicanas/*mexicanas* today, the one inside each Chicana and *mexicana*. Perhaps it's the Tlazolteotl-Lupe in me whose *malcriada* spirit inspires me to leap into the swimming pool naked or dance on a table with a skirt on my head. Maybe it's my Coatlicue-Lupe attitude that makes it possible for my mother to tell me, "No wonder men can't stand you." Who knows? What I do know is this: I am obsessed with becoming a woman comfortable in her skin.

I can't attribute my religious conversion to a flash of lightning on the road to Laredo or anything like that. Instead, there have been several lessons learned subtly over a period of time. A grave depression and near suicide in my thirty-third year and its subsequent retrospection. Vietnamese Buddhist monk Thich Nhat Hanh's writing that has brought out the Buddha-Lupe in me. My weekly peace vigil for my friend Jasna in Sarajevo. The writings of Gloria Anzaldúa. A crucial trip back to Tepeyac in 1985 with Cherríe Moraga and Norma Alarcón. Drives across Texas, talking with other Chicanas. And research for stories that would force me back inside the Church from where I'd fled.

My *Virgen de Guadalupe* is not the mother of God. She is God. She is a face for a god without a face, an *indigena* for a god without ethnicity, a female deity for a god who is genderless, but I also understand that for her to approach me, for me to finally open the door and accept her, she had to be a woman like me.

Once watching a porn film, I saw a sight that terrified me. It was the film star's *panocha*—a tidy, elliptical opening, pink and shiny like a rabbit's ear. To make matters worse, it was shaved and looked especially childlike and unsexual. I think what startled me most was the realization that my own sex has no resemblance to this woman's. My sex, dark as an orchid, rubbery and blue-purple as *pulpo*, an octopus, does not look nice and tidy, but other-worldly. I do not have little rosette nipples. My nipples are big and brown like the Mexican coins of my childhood.

When I see *la Virgen de Guadalupe* I want to lift her dress as I did my dolls, and look to see if she comes with *chones* and does her *panocha* look like mine, and does she have dark nipples too? Yes, I am certain she does. She is not neuter like Barbie. She gave birth. She has a womb. *Blessed art thou and blessed is the fruit of thy womb....* Blessed art thou, Lupe, and, therefore, blessed am I.

Analyze

1. Why does Cisneros begin her essay with a description of how she "marveled" at the white women in the locker room? How does this set up what follows?

2. Cisneros states that she writes her story because she is "overwhelmed by the silence regarding Latinas and our bodies." What creates the need for this silence?

3. How does Cisneros's research into Guadalupe's pre-Columbian antecedents help her form an empowered Chicana identity?

Explore

1. "The personal is political" was a feminist slogan that became popular in the late 1960s and 1970s. The phrase was used to emphasize how what was happening in women's personal lives were also political issues that needed to be addressed. It was also meant to inspire women to be politically active in regard to these issues. How does Cisneros make the personal political? And how does the act of writing become political activism?

2. Cisneros asserts that *La Virgen de Guadalupe* is her culture's role model for women. What makes her "an ideal so lofty and unrealistic it was laughable"? And why does Cisneros then ask, "Did boys have to aspire to be Jesus"? What does this question (as well as her response), in contrast to her description of Guadalupe, reveal about her culture's differing expectations of men and women? Additionally, how does her essay suggest that culture shapes our attitudes about sex and sexuality?

3. Cisneros claims that the Church "desexed" Guadalupe. This is reiterated by authors such as Gloria Anzaldúa in her book *Borderlands/La Frontera: The New Mestiza*. What do these authors mean when they say that the Church desexed Guadalupe? Do some research on how Guadalupe emerged from the different indigenous deities to which Cisneros refers, as well as what she represents as a cultural icon. How, then, does Guadalupe impact Chicana notions of identity, gender, and sexuality?

Zachary Pullin
"Two Spirit: The Story of a Movement Unfolds"

Zachary Pullin is a Chippewa Cree tribal member and President of the Capital Hill Community Council in Seattle, Washington. He is also a freelance writer and a community activist; he was a part of the Soulforce Equality Ride, a two-month social justice tour, in 2012, and prior to his involvement with Soulforce, Pullin served with the Peace Corps in Belize as an organizational development volunteer. He writes about the intersection of his identity as a Chippewa Cree tribal member and his identity as a gay man. In "Two Spirit: The Story of a Movement Unfolds," which was published in the magazine *Native Peoples* in 2014, he explores not only this intersection, but also the Native American gender tradition. As you read this essay, think about how Pullin weaves the historical tradition of Native cultures into his essay to make a contemporary argument about a two-spirit identity.

Growing up, I never truly felt like dancing at powwows. I spent my early childhood on the Rocky Boy Reservation in Montana before moving to Spokane, Wash., with my family, and despite a warm and welcoming upbringing, I never entered the dance arena with confidence like the male grass, Plains traditional and fancy dancers at grand entry. I had grown up with the idea in my own mind that I was less of a man, and also, being both physically or characteristically different, I felt vulnerable in expressing myself in those circles. Even if the notion was all in my head, there was a deep sense that I couldn't present my whole self in that space.

I was different because I was two spirit, meaning a Native LGBTQ person.

It wasn't until I attended a two-spirit gathering—a cultural event that draws together two-spirit individuals for traditional dancing, storytelling and other customs—that I entered a dance arena and felt authentic about who I was in my place in the circle. While I don't wear regalia, like many of the others, I still join in when invited, not feeling I should defend or hide my identity as a gay or Native man.

I am part of a Native American gender tradition that has come to be defined in modern times as "two spirit." The term stems from the Ojibwe phrase *niizh manidoowag* and replaces the outdated, oversimplified term *berdache*, which appeared frequently in research and anthropological studies that aimed to describe the place of gay men in Native society in the 18th and early 19th centuries. *Berdache* is a derivative of a French term meaning "kept boy." So not only is the word offensive, it also falls short in defining the diverse experiences of Native people who weren't of only the male and female genders in their cultures.

The phrase "two spirit" began to gain traction across Native America after 1990, when 13 men, women and transgender people from various tribes met in Winnipeg, Canada, with the task of finding a term that could unite the LGBTQ Native community. Numerous terms in tribal languages identified third genders in their cultures that encompassed both masculine and feminine, and the struggle for those gathered in Winnipeg was finding a contemporary term that would be embraced across all tribal cultures.

The attendees at the gathering settled on "two spirit." They wanted a term that "reflected the combination of masculinity and femininity which was attributed to males in a feminine role and females in a masculine role," says author Sabine Lang in the book *Men as Women, Women as Men: Changing Gender in Native American Cultures.* Many two spirit, historically, were keepers of traditions, tellers of the stories of creation, and healers.

The efforts of those in Winnipeg proved necessary in the years that followed. Anti-transgender bias and persistent structural and interpersonal acts of racism have been especially devastating for American Indian and Alaska Native transgender people, according to a 2012 report by the National Gay & Lesbian Task Force. And there are tragic stories that support this finding, including that of Fred Martinez (Navajo), a 16-year-old transgender person who was murdered in a violent beating near Cortez, Colo., in 2001. Martinez's story is told in the 2011 documentary *Two Spirits*, which also looks at the history of gay identity in many Native cultures.

Martinez was *nadleeh*—in the Navajo language, "the changing one," a person whose gender identity exists beyond male or female.

Although not all tribes identify or name a concept for gender or sexual-orientation-variant members, many of them have, including the Zuni, with *lhaman*; the Lakota, with both *lila witkowin* and *winkte*; and the Plains Cree, my people, with *a'yahkwêw*. At least 165 tribal gender traditions existed in North America historically, when many of our Native cultures accepted and respected individuals encompassing a balance of both feminine and masculine qualities.

The two-spirit tradition centers primarily on gender, not sexual orientation, and the distinction is important. While sexual orientation describes the sexual relationship that a person of one gender has with another person, gender describes an individual's expected role within a community.

Many of the great visionaries, dreamers, shamans or medicine givers were two-spirit people. Among the Crow, Ohchiish, also known as Woman Jim, gained prominence in the 1870s by joining a battle against enemy tribes. Woman Jim was an accomplished craftsperson of the Crow tribe. As a *boté*, a term for a two-spirit person in Crow, Woman Jim made large tipis and other leather goods intricately decorated with quill- and beadwork. The translation of Ohchiish's name in English was Finds-Them-and-Kills-Them.

Among the Navajo, weavers are usually female, and *hataalii*—singers, chanters or medicine men—are usually male. Many times Hastiin Klah, in early life known as Charlie the Weaver, identified as a *nadleeh*. Klah filled both male and female roles, becoming a renowned spiritual chanter and developing a weaving style still used today.

One of the most well-known two spirit in history is We-wha, an honored Zuni Pueblo cultural ambassador who traveled to Washington, D.C., in 1886 and shared the story and values of her people, who live in what is now eastern New Mexico. In Zuni tradition, We-wha was referred to as *lhaman*, or mixed gender. Many *lhaman* expressed as female, took on female gender roles and served as mediators. Tall and broad shouldered, she was a skilled potter and weaver of the Zuni people.

On any given reservation today there can be different levels of acceptance and understanding, and not all Native communities regard two spirit equally. There are complicated debates about the rights of LGBTQ Native men and women on reservations, like the one taking place on the Navajo Nation, where LGBT rights advocates have received support from some and resistance from others in their attempt to undo the 2005 Dine Marriage Act, which defines marriage as being only between a man and a woman.

But there are also signs that Native people—gay and straight—are returning to a culturally connected awareness of who two-spirit people are and what they have contributed. In many cases, the clearest indications of acceptance have come from tribes themselves. At least seven Native governments in the United States have passed laws recognizing same-sex marriage since 2008, and most of the tribes did so in states where same-sex marriage was not yet legal, like the Suquamish near Seattle.

The Suquamish law came at the request of tribal member Heather Purser, who at age 28 asked for a vote on the issue in 2011—a year before the state of Washington recognized same-sex marriage. More than a year after initial conversations with some tribal leaders on the issue, she decided to take her proposal to the people. As she stood at the annual tribal meeting, hands trembling and with a slightly sweaty forehead, she asked her fellow Suquamish citizens in attendance to allow marriage rights for all people in the tribal law. Purser remembers that day vividly.

"We are braided together, indefinitely braided together. For the rest of our lives—for the rest of the history of our people," she recalls telling the crowd of 300.

Once her swift appeal was finished, the crowd voted unanimously in favor of same-sex marriage, making it the first jurisdiction in the state of Washington to do so. "It was less a vote and more an affirmation of me and an understanding of my struggle," Purser says.

Two Spirit

For Purser, coming to terms with her two-spirit identity was part of a larger journey of self-acceptance. Understanding two-spirit history helps her "understand—more fully—my own beautiful complexity" as a woman, Native American and LGBT person, she says.

For me, the term "two spirit" resists a Western definition of who we are and what we should be. Two spirit are integral to the struggle of undoing the impacts of historical trauma, because our roles in tribes historically were part of the traditions taken away from us with Westernization. We aren't attempting necessarily to convince the Native community that we exist—historically and presently—but that our history is just as much wrapped up in the story of Indian Country as is each other Native American's.

Two spirit—the movement, the societies and the term itself—marks a return to a tradition that historically recognized more than two genders. It's meant to honor Native American languages and traditions that were nearly forgotten in some cases.

"We're reclaiming our place in the circle," said Steven Barrios, of the Montana Two Spirit Society, at a Two-Spirit Gathering in Tulsa, Okla. "Until the two-spirit people are brought back into that circle, that circle is never going to be completely mended."

As two-spirit people, we are finally ready for our grand entry.

Analyze

1. Pullin pays special attention to the terms he uses throughout this piece, such as "two spirit," "*berdache*," and "*nadleeh*," carefully defining each term and, in many cases, noting its historic and/or cultural use. Why is it necessary for him to do so? He also notes the specific terms used by several different North American tribes for gender- or sexual orientation–variant members. How is the reference to multiple, tribe-specific terms important to our understanding of the term "two spirit"?

2. Why does Pullin note that the two-spirit tradition "centers primarily on gender, not sexual orientation"? And why does he assert that "the distinction is important"?

3. Pullin shares not only his own story, but also the stories of Fred Martinez (Navajo) and Heather Purser (Suquamish). Why does he include their stories, and how do they enhance his argument?

4. Pullin begins the essay by noting his reluctance to enter the dance arena at grand entry. He ends the essay by stating, "As two-spirit people, we are finally ready for our grand entry." What is his purpose in repeating the phrase "grand entry" at the end of the essay, and how does it give a sense of wholeness to the essay?

Explore

1. Anne Fausto-Sterling's article "The Five Sexes: Why Male and Female Are Not Enough" argues for a broader understanding of gender beyond male and female. How does Pullin's essay reinforce this while also making the additional claim that this understanding must be culturally specific?

2. Working with a classmate, create a list of keywords used by Pullin in this article. Then use these keywords to do some presearching on Google, Wikipedia, or a social media site. What additional resources

can you find to help you better understand what it is to be two spirit? List a few of these, evaluating each to determine whether the source is reliable.

3. Watch the short film "Two Spirits" (Frameline) on YouTube. How does Ruth Fertig's film about Joey Criddle add to the conversation about gay and Native identities? About reclaiming the position held by two-spirit individuals prior to colonization? And about the two-spirit movement?

Julia R. Johnson
"Cisgender Privilege, Intersectionality, and the Criminalization of CeCe McDonald: Why Intercultural Communication Needs Transgender Studies"

Julia R. Johnson is the associate dean of liberal studies at the University of Wisconsin–La Crosse. Her specialties include diversity and social justice. In her work, Johnson studies how individuals construct their identities, how they identify with particular social groups and mores, and how we can work to disrupt power inequalities.

Johnson's article "Cisgender Privilege, Intersectionality, and the Criminalization of CeCe McDonald: Why Intercultural Communication Needs Transgender Studies" was published by the *Journal of International and Intercultural Communication* in 2013. In this piece, she uses the story of CeCe McDonald, a transfeminine woman who was assaulted and arrested for defending herself outside a bar in 2011, to advocate for the importance of the role of transgender studies in her field, communication. As you read, think about how Johnson uses McDonald's story to make her argument. How does beginning with McDonald's story sway the reader to agree with Johnson's overall claim, and how does Johnson continue to use McDonald's story as evidence throughout her essay?

In June 2011, CeCe McDonald faced an interaction all too familiar to trans[*1]-identified people, particularly working class or poor transgender women of color. While walking to a nearby grocery store with friends, all of whom were African American and queer-identified (or allies), a group of cisgender (non-transgender), heterosexual, white people yelled racist, homophobic, and transphobic epithets at McDonald. The attackers yelled, "faggots," "niggers," "chicks with dicks." They frantically accused McDonald of being "'dressed as a woman' in order to 'rape' Dean Schmitz, one of the attackers" (Support CeCe McDonald! "Background"). After McDonald confronted the group and said that she "would not tolerate hate speech," the attack turned physical: Molly Shannon Flaherty, a white woman and Schmitz's ex-girlfriend, screamed, "'I'll take all three of you bitches on!'" (Mannix, 2012) and then crushed a glass on McDonald's face cutting a salivary gland. McDonald tried to walk away from the kerfuffle, but Schmitz followed her and "clenched his fists and approached her" (Mannix, 2012). In an effort to defend herself, McDonald reportedly pulled a pair of scissors out of her bag and turned to face Schmitz (*State of Minnesota*, 2012). Schmitz was stabbed and died at the scene.[2]

In spite of the fact that McDonald survived a vicious attack, she was the only person arrested. She was charged with second-degree murder and denied medical treatment for two months after receiving stitches. In May 2012, McDonald pled guilty to second-degree manslaughter and is now serving a 41-month sentence in a men's prison (Support CeCe McDonald! "Accepts plea agreement"). Flaherty was eventually charged with second and third-degree assault in May 2012 (Simons, 2012). Schmitz's swastika tattoo and history of violence were excluded from court proceedings.

The treatment of McDonald illustrates the layers of violence often imposed on persons who are transgender, particularly trans* persons of color who are (or are perceived to be) working class or poor. For intercultural communication (IC) scholars committed to the study of power, oppression, and privilege, the case of CeCe McDonald holds particular relevance: it illustrates the pervasiveness of cisgender privilege, the use of identity to justify violence, and the importance of intersectional analyses for challenging privilege and oppression. Cases like McDonald's are significant and all too common. IC scholars need to address transgenderism (identity) and transgender studies (TS) (an interdisciplinary field) in order to deepen analyses of gender, including intersectionality. The concepts of cisprivilege and cissexism, partnered with an expanded conception of intersectionality that includes transgender, offer the potential to expand intercultural scholarship on sexuality and gender. I begin this analysis by exploring the relevance of TS to IC. Second, I address how the concepts of trans- and cis- can enhance gender analyses. Finally, I examine the importance of transness for developing IC research in intersectionality. Throughout the essay, I utilize the criminalization of McDonald to contextualize my claims.

Trans- ing Intercultural Communication Research

Most gender research published in communication studies assumes a gender and sex binary, even in cases where the authors commit to examining gendered power and oppression (Dow & Wood, 2006). This perpetuates thinking about sex, gender, and sexuality in terms of woman/man, feminine/masculine, and gay/straight. Scholarship that subverts normative gendering, much of which examines questions of heteronormativity or queerness (Pérez & Goltz, 2010), tends to focus on the activities of persons whose morphological sex aligns with their gender identity. There exists a growing body of communication scholarship that examines transgenderism (Booth, 2011; Butler, 2003; Sloop, 2000; West, 2008), some of which has an explicitly intercultural focus (Chávez, 2010b; Johnson, 2013; Moreman & McIntosh, 2010), although transgender identities are often absent from queer scholarship (Yep, 2003) and IC research. TS can enhance IC research because of its focus on the material and representational practices of trans* subjects (Stryker, 2006). TS addresses IC topics including the cultural construction of gender identity categories (Hale, 2006), the performance of gender identity in everyday life (Namaste, 2000), and the importance of intersectionality (Juang, 2006). Furthermore, TS attends to the ways cultural dominance is exercised to surveil and/or constrain non-normative gendering as well as to the relational and personal dynamics through which institutional power manifests and is resisted—foci integral to critical intercultural scholarship (Nakayama & Halualani, 2010).

Trans-, Cis-, and Privilege

There are many identity markers used by persons who identify as trans*, including the term transgender itself. I use transgender as an umbrella term for persons who challenge gender normativity, which includes persons who identify as transfeminine, transmasculine, transsexual, Two-Spirit, cross-dresser, genderqueer, same-gender-loving, in the life, female-to-male (FTM), male-to-female (MTF), intersex and more. In general, transsexual references a person whose gender identity is not aligned with their assigned birth sex and who may use hormones and/or seek surgical procedures to align their body and identity. As with any label or category, transgender is contested and considered problematic in some contexts. For example, for some people of color, transgender signals whiteness and a corresponding western conception of gender binarisms (Driskill, 2004; Roen, 2001) and for some transpersons who uphold the binary through normative gender performances, transgender is considered an inaccurate depiction of their gender identity (Serano, 2007). For some, transgender is equated with transsexual while others adopt transgender as a political position that challenges the medical establishment's pathologizing of transness (Bettcher, 2007). In general, TS scholars challenge the dominant cultural assumption that gender is invariant and that a misalignment between the body and identity is deceptive or less "real" than someone whose body and selfhood are congruent.

Stryker, Currah, and Moore (2008) use the term "transing" to highlight transgenderism as a practice that disrupts gender discreteness (p. 13). They offer trans* with a hyphen (*trans-*) as a way to approach transgenderism as one part of "contingent structures of association with other attributes of bodily being" (p. 13), including nationhood, racialization, social class, ability status, etc. From this point forward, I use *trans*- (asterisk and hyphen) to signal gender nonconformity of all kinds and to continually foreground that gender is best understood in its interplay with other identity vectors.

One way that TS contributes to the study of culture is by challenging gender dominance, which is created when we label non-normative identities as "different" and refuse to address privilege. As Nakayama and Krizek (1995) argued, the dominant norm against which otherness is measured must be named in order to disrupt normativity (p. 292). In TS, the concepts of cisgender and cissex are designed to disrupt gendered normativity and were coined to "resist the way that 'woman' or 'man' can mean 'non-transgendered woman' or 'nontransgendered man' by default . . . The prefix *cis-* means 'on the same side as'" (Stryker, 2008, p. 22). If one's sex identity matches her/his morphology, then s/he is cissexual. If one's gender identity aligns with sex morphology, s/he is said to be cisgender. These definitions emphasize that sex and gender are most frequently identified in relationship to a stable and socially binding center when, in fact, the categories of sex and gender are constructed and performed. The labels cisgender and cissex also highlight that there are transpersons whose gender identity has never shifted, although their bodies have been altered physically and/or chemically to align with their selfhood.

The terms cisgender and cissexual are also important for examining how specific forms of privilege operate. Cisgender privilege is given to persons whose morphology aligns with socially-sanctioned gender categories. Following McIntosh's (1988) white privilege checklist, transgender activists and scholars have articulated the ways cispersons received unearned privileges for the ways their bodies and identities align. Some forms of cisgender privilege include: Having a government-issued identification that accurately represents one's identity; not being "asked . . . what my genitals look like, or whether or not my breasts are real, what medical procedures I have had" (Taking up too much space, para. 14); not being forced "to adopt a different gender presentation" (para. 18) or denied medical care; or being refused "access to, and fair treatment within, sex segregated facilities" such as bathrooms, homeless shelters, prisons, and domestic violence shelters (para. 17).

Gender dominance often manifests in cissexism and transphobia. According to Serano (2007), cissexism is "the belief that transsexuals' identified genders are inferior to, or less authentic than, those of cissexuals" (p. 12). Transphobia is all manner of hostility toward trans-persons, including ". . . hatred, loathing, rage, or moral indignation . . ." (Bettcher, 2007, p. 46) as well as "irrational fear, discrimination against, social rejection, hatred or persecution" (Scott-Dixon, 2006, p. 248). As is true of all discourses, cissexism and transphobia manifest in our gendered attitudes and actions, including our assumptions about what are considered "normal" (legitimate) embodiment, activity, and modes of being/belonging.

The case of CeCe McDonald illustrates common cultural assumptions about gender, cis-privilege, cissexism, and transphobia. The altercation prompting the arrest and conviction of McDonald was started by Schmitz and his friends as they yelled racist, homophobic, and transphobic epithets. Such pejoratives are a primary mechanism for marking difference and belonging. By using the words "nigger," "faggot," and "chicks with dicks," Schmitz and his friends established clearly gendered, racialized, and sexed boundaries between themselves and McDonald. Furthermore, the boundary Schmitz asserted was a binary in which he established his normality and privilege as white, male, and cisgender in relation to McDonald's "abnormality" of transfeminity and blackness.

When Schmitz stated that McDonald was "dressed in women's clothing to 'rape'" him, he invoked a common claim made by cisgender men against transfeminine women (Bettcher, 2007). These accusations construct trans*- identities as fake and validate cissexists' "gender as 'real' or 'natural'" (Serano, 2007, p. 13). This performance of cissexism undermines McDonald's gender identification, "reverses blame" to affirm cis- identity, and re-asserts heterosexuality and heteronormativity. After all, a "real" man can never wear a dress, surgically and/or hormonally alter a body, or be sexually attracted to other "men." Schmitz's rhetoric also indicates that a real man cannot be black, a point I address more fully below.

In addition to enduring Schmitz's vitriol, McDonald faced cissexism through the court system. McDonald was placed in a men's prison in spite of her identification and presentation as a woman. Culturally, we treat genitals as "the essential determinants of sex" (Bettcher, 2007, p. 48) and invalidate genital reassignment as "artificial or invalid" (p. 49). Assigning prisons by genital sex does not account for gender avowal and is detrimental for most trans*- persons because they are subject to significant violence in general populations or protective custody (Léger, 2012). Furthermore, McDonald's personal history was featured in the courtroom and her attacker's history was precluded from proceedings, which made McDonald hypervisible. During one hearing, McDonald was asked about whether her prior hospitalization for depression or use of "hormone patch treatment" impacted her decision-making or allocution (*State of Minnesota*, 2012). Dean Spade, a lawyer and advocate who was present during McDonald's court hearing explained that the judge patronized her by asking:

> "Do you freely take this plea deal, do you freely and voluntarily take it?" . . . What does freely and voluntary mean in this system? What options does CeCe have in this system where she's being caged for being a target of a racist and transphobic attack? (Léger, 2012, para. 14)

In contrast to the scrutiny McDonald experienced, Schmitz's criminal background was determined to be inadmissible, even though he had a history of physically assaulting others and had a swastika tattooed to his stomach. While there are any number of legal justifications for including or excluding information from court proceedings, it is meaningful that McDonald was subjected to strategies commonly used to discredit people of color, women, and/or people who are poor (i.e., attacks on mental health, questioning the capacity for reasoned thought, questioning the influence of female hormones), while Schmitz's prior reliance on violence and overt affiliation with racist ideology was deemed irrelevant.

Intersectionality

As feminist scholars of color have long argued, intersectional analysis is integral to understanding how identity is navigated and how oppression manifests structurally and interpersonally (Collins, 1990; Crenshaw, 1991). Scholars from various fields within communication studies have addressed the importance of intersectionality for enhancing our analysis of culture, identity, and difference (Chávez, 2010b; Chávez & Griffin, 2012; Houston, 1992, 2012; Johnson, 2001; Johnson, Bhatt, & Patton, 2007; Jones & Calafell, 2012; Lee, 2003; Moreman & McIntosh, 2010). This work has been instrumental in illustrating ways oppressions overlap and how privilege and oppression manifest simultaneously (Allen, 2010). Unfortunately, while IC scholars articulate the need for intersectional analyses, few studies address non-normative gendering or transgenderism. For example, in the recently released *The Handbook of Critical Intercultural Communication* intersectionality is only indexed on five pages and only a few essays examine identity intersections (see Alexander, 2010).

TS scholars also call for intersectional analyses in their work. TS relies on intersectional analysis to discern how gender is shaped by discourses such as racism (Juang, 2006; Roen, 2006). For instance, TS has illustrated how working class and poor trans*- people of color have always been a part of LGBT communities (Saffin, 2011), and how trans*- persons of color, particularly trans*- women, are disproportionately targeted for violence and state sanction (National Gay and Lesbian Task Force, 2011). In addition, the conflations of gender, sex, and sexual orientation impact how trans*- persons are targeted for violence (Bettcher, 2007) as well as how race, immigration status, and gender play figure into the treatment of transgender and/or queer persons in the immigration and prison systems (Chávez, 2010b; Nair, 2011). Page and Richardson (2010) remind us that nation-states mark difference in order to construct classes of people as social problems. In fact, the identity of the nation-state is often built on the creation of "minority" statuses that enable states to terrorize (racialized, gendered, classed) citizen "Others." For example, nation-states engage in "racialized discipline"—such as terrorizing non-dominant racial groups and promoting whiteness—to enforce "compulsory heterosexist racializations" against those who are gender non-conforming or who violate heternormativity (p. 59). The U.S. nation-state's historical positioning of race against gender and sexuality established the context for the contemporary "Marriage Mimesis" Snorton analyzes in this issue. Not only are queer and/or trans*- persons of color erased in the "animus between people of color and queer folks,"—blackness and other historically targeted racialized embodiments are constructed as necessary foils for white racial viability, including white lesbian and gay "progress."

McDonald in particular faced interpersonal and state terror based on the intersectional interplay of white supremacy, gender conformity, and heteronormativity. Growing up African American and trans*-, McDonald was regularly confronted with violence: "[W]ith the fact of me just being a minority in this society was bad, being African American and trans is an ultimate challenge. I can remember having loaded guns being put to my head and being beat until bloody" (Support CeCe McDonald!, 2011). Her early experiences were mirrored in June 2011. By yelling "nigger," Schmitz targeted her blackness and its relationship to her transness, which he worked to disparage by labeling her as a "chick with a dick." He erased her femininity and simultaneously disparaged maleness by calling her a "faggot," demonstrating how transfemininity is a threat to heteronormative masculinity and patriarchy. Schmitz's attack thus interimbricated race, sex, gender, and sexual orientation—his own and McDonald's. His rhetorical choices reinforced his intersectional identity supremacy as he enacted the legacy of violence against McDonald's sex–gender variance, blackness, and working classness.

The arrest, sentencing, and imprisonment of McDonald illustrates the history of intersectional and discriminatory treatment trans*- people of color experience within the prison system. Although transgender persons are imprisoned at lower rates than African American cisgender men (the population most targeted by the penal system), transpersons—particularly those who are underemployed and/or people of color—are incarcerated at higher rates than cisgender persons and, when incarcerated, are often placed in a prison incongruent with their gender identification. Transgender prisoners are often denied access to hormones in spite of federal policies protecting hormone use (National Center for Lesbian Rights, 2006) and are sexually assaulted at significantly higher rates than cisgender inmates (Wallace, 2007).[3] Understanding the attack on McDonald and her subsequent imprisonment requires attention to the multiple, intertwined identities that were iterated and scrutinized by the people and institutions that targeted her.

Conclusion

In this essay, I argued that IC scholarship is enhanced by attending to concepts from TS such as cisgenderism, cisprivilege, and cissexism, which extend and deepen analyses of gender and intersectionality. As the case of CeCe McDonald illustrates, racialization, social class, and gender expression are just some of the intersecting identities that impact how trans*- persons experience oppression and how cispersons experience privilege. Future studies should investigate these dynamics more fully as well as the ways privilege and oppression are experienced simultaneously.

Crucially, analyzing cultural constructions of transness provides IC scholars an entry point for learning how to be allies in the struggle for trans*- justice. As scholars of alliance and coalition have argued, challenging oppression requires that we be "implicated in the dehumanization of each other" (Chávez, 2010a, p. 147) and work to disrupt our privileges and confront each other's oppression (Johnson, 2013; Johnson et al., 2007). We must interrogate interpersonal interactions as well as structural dynamics, including the state-sanctioned actions imposed on the bodies and minds of trans*- persons. Critical and reflective engagement is a first step to this end. While it cannot replace collective action, IC scholarship and its applications are sites of politicization where we can move over, make room, and engage in resistive world making.

NOTES

1. I follow gender activists who often use trans* to signal gender nonconformity that includes persons who identify as women and men as well as persons who

may reject or disrupt the gender binary altogether. Also, McDonald self-identifies as African American and trans* (As Long As We Live in Fear). To respect McDonald's identity, I use her chosen name and not the name assigned to her at birth.

2. There have been conflicting reports about whether McDonald pulled out a pair of scissors or a knife, although lawyers and McDonald referred to scissors during allocution (*State of Minnesota*, 2012). As Farrow (2012) reports, no weapon was found.

3. As reported by the Transgender Law Center of San Francisco, the Department of Justice has developed national standards to help prevent sexual assault in prisons and jails.

REFERENCES

Alexander, B. (2010). Br(other) in the Classroom: Testimony, Reflection, and Cultural Negotiation. In T. K. Nakayama & R. T. Halualani (Eds.), *The Handbook of Critical Intercultural Communication* (pp. 364–381). Malden, MA: Wiley-Blackwell.

Allen, B. J. (2010). A Proposal for Concerned Collaboration between Critical Scholars of Intercultural and Organizational Communication. In T. K. Nakayama & R. T. Halualani (Eds.), *The Handbook of Critical Intercultural Communication* (pp. 585–592). Malden, MA: Wiley–Blackwell.

Bettcher, T. M. (2007). Evil Deceivers and Make-Believers: On Transphobic Violence and the Politics of Illusion. *Hypatia, 22*(3), 43–65.

Booth, E. T. (2011). Queering *Queer Eye:* The Stability of Gay Identity Confronts the Liminality of Trans Embodiment. *Western Journal of Communication, 75*(2), 185–204.

Butler, J. R. (2003). Transgender DeKalb: Observations of an Advocacy Campaign. In G. A. Yep, K. E. Lovaas, & J. P. Elia (Eds.), *Queer Theory and Communication: From Disciplining Queers to Queering the Discipline(s)* (pp. 277–296). Binghamton, NY: Harrington Park Press.

Chávez, K. R. (2010a). Border (In)securities: Normative and Differential Belonging in LGBTQ and Immigrant Rights Discourse. *Communication and Critical/ Cultural Studies, 7*(2), 136–155.

Chávez, K. R. (2010b). Spatializing Gender Performativity: Ecstasy and Possibilities for Livable Life in the Tragic Case of Victoria Arellano. *Women's Studies in Communication, 33*(1), 1–15.

Chávez, K. R., & Griffin, C. L. (eds.). (2012). *Standing in the Intersection: Feminist Voices, Feminist Practices in Communication Studies.* Albany: State University of New York Press.

Collins, P. H. (1990). *Black Feminist Thought: Knowledge, Consciousness, and the Politics of Empowerment.* New York: Routledge.

Crenshaw, K. (1991). Mapping the Margins: Intersectionality, Identity Politics, and Violence against Women of Color. *Stanford Law Review, 43*(6), 1241–1299.

Dow, B. J., & Wood, J. T. (2006). *The Sage Handbook of Gender and Communication.* Thousand Oaks, CA: Sage Publications.

Driskill, Q.-L. (2004). Stolen from Our Bodies: First Nations Two-Spirits/Queers and the Journey to a Sovereign Erotic. *SAIL: Studies in American Indian Literatures, 16*(2), 50–64.

Farrow, K. (2012, May 4). CeCe McDonald Deserves Our Support, "Innocent" or Not. *ColorLines: News for Action.* Retrieved from http://colorlines.com/archives/2012/05/cece_mcdonald_and_the_high_cost_of_black_and_trans_self-defense.html

Hale, J. (2006). Are Lesbians Women? In S. Stryker & S. Whittle (Eds.), *The Transgender Studies Reader* (pp. 281–299). New York: Routledge.

Houston, M. (1992). The Politics of Difference: Race, Class, and Women's Communication. In L. F. Rakow (Ed.), *Women Making Meaning: New Feminist Directions in Communication* (pp. 45–59). New York: Routledge.

Houston, M. (2012). Foreword: Difficult Dialogues: Intersectionality as Lived Experience. In K. R. Chávez & C. L. Griffin (Eds.), *Standing in the Intersection: Feminist Voices, Feminist Practices in Communication Studies* (pp. ix–xii). Albany: State University of New York Press.

Johnson, E. P. (2001). "Quare" Studies, or (Almost) Everything I Know about Queer Studies I Learned from My Grandmother. *Text and Performance Quarterly, 21*(1), 1–25.

Johnson, J. R. (2013). Qwe're Performances of Silence: Many Ways to Live "Out Loud." In S. Malhotra & A. C. Rowe (Eds.), *Silence, Feminism, Power: Reflections at the Edges of Sound* (pp. 50–64). Basingstoke, UK: Palgrave Macmillan.

Johnson, J. R., Bhatt, A. P., & Patton, T. O. (2007). Dismantling Essentialisms in Academic Organizations: Intersectional Articulation and Possibilities for Alliance Formation. In B. J. Allen, L. A. Flores, & M. P. Orbe (Eds.), *International and Intercultural Communication Annual XXX* (pp. 21–50). Washington, DC: National Communication Association.

Jones, R. G., & Calafell, B. M. (2012). Contesting Neoliberalism through Critical Pedagogy, Intersectional Reflexivity, and Personal Narrative: Queer Tales of Academia. *Journal of Homosexuality, 57*(7), 957–981.

Juang, R. (2006). Transgendering the Politics of Recognition. In S. Stryker & S. Whittle (Eds.), *The Transgender Studies Reader* (pp. 706–720). New York: Routledge.

Lee, W. (2003). *Kuaering* Queer Theory: My Autocritography and a Race-Conscious, Womanist, Transnational Turn. *Journal of Homosexuality, 45*(2–4), 147–170.

Léger, T. (2012, May 2). Dean Spade Speaks on CeCe McDonald Trial. *Prettyqueer.* Retrieved from http://www.prettyqueer.com/2012/05/02/dean-spade-speaks-on-cece-mcdonald-trial/

Mannix, A. (2012, May 9). CeCe McDonald Murder Trial: Behind the Scenes of the Transgender Woman's Case. Retrieved from http://www.citypages .com/2012-05-09/news/cece-mcdonald-murder-trial/

McIntosh, P. (1988). White Privilege: Unpacking the Invisible Knapsack. Retrieved from http://www.amptoons.com/blog/files/mcintosh.html

Moreman, S. T., & McIntosh, D. M. (2010). Brown Scriptings and Rescriptings: A Critical Performance Ethnography of Latina Drag Queens. *Communication and Critical/Cultural Studies, 7*(2), 115–135.

Nair, Y. (2011). How to Make Prisons Disappear: Queer Immigrants, the Shackles of Love, and the Invisibility of the Prison Industrial Complex. In E. A. Stanley & N. Smith (Eds.), *Captive Genders: Trans Embodiment and the Prison Industrial Complex* (pp. 123–139). Oakland, CA: AK Press.

Nakayama, T. K., & Halualani, R. T. (eds.). (2010). *The Handbook of Critical Intercultural Communication*. Malden, MA: Wiley–Blackwell.

Nakayama, T. K., & Krizek, R. L. (1995). Whiteness: A Strategic Rhetoric. *Quarterly Journal of Speech, 81,* 291–309.

Namaste, V. K. (2000). *Invisible Lives: The Erasure of Transsexual and Transgendered People*. Chicago: University of Chicago Press.

National Center for Lesbian Rights (2006). Rights of Transgender Prisoners. Retrieved from http://www.nclrights.org/site/DocServer/RightsofTransgenderPrisoners.pdf?docID=6381

National Gay and Lesbian Task Force and the National Center for Transgender Equality (2011, February 3). *Injustice at Every Turn: A Report of the National Transgender Discrimination Survey*. Retrieved from http://www.thetaskforce .org/reports_and_research/ntds

Page, E. H., & Richardson, M. U. (2010). On the Fear of Small Numbers: A Twenty-First-Century Prolegomenon of the U.S. Black Transgender Experience. In J. Battle & S. L. Barnes (Eds.), *Black Sexualities: Probing Powers, Passions, Practices, and Policies* (pp. 57–81). New Brunswick, NJ: Rutgers University Press.

Pérez, K, & Goltz, D. B. (2010). Treading across Lines in the Sand: Performing Bodies in Coalitional Subjectivity. *Text and Performance Quarterly, 30*(3), 247–268.

Roen, K. (2001). Transgender Theory and Embodiment: The Risk of Racial Marginalization. *Journal of Gender Studies, 10*(3), 253–263.

Roen, K. (2006). Transgender Theory and Embodiment: The Risk of Racial Marginalisation. In S. Stryker & S. Whittle (Eds.), *The Transgender Studies Reader* (pp. 656–665). New York: Routledge.

Saffin, L. A. (2011). Identities under Siege: Violence against Transpersons of Color. In E. A. Stanley & N. Smith (Eds.), *Captive Genders: Trans Embodiment and the Prison Industrial Complex* (pp. 141–162). Oakland, CA: AK Press.

Scott-Dixon, K. (2006). *Trans/forming Feminisms: Trans-feminist Voices Speak Out*. Toronto: Sumach Press.

Serano, J. (2007). *Whipping Girl: A Transsexual Woman on Sexism and the Scapegoating of Femininity*. Berkeley: Seal Press.

Simons, A. (2012, May 23). Woman Charged in Attack on Friend's Killer during Melee outside Mpls. Bar. *Minneapolis Star Tribune*. Retrieved from http://www.startribune.com/local/minneapolis/152785405.html?refer=y

Sloop, J. (2000). Disciplining the Transgendered: Brandon Teena, Public Representation, and Normativity. *Western Journal of Communication, 64*(2), 165–189.

State of Minnesota v. Chrisahun Reed McDonald. 27-CR-11–16485. (2012). Retrieved from http://supportcece.files.wordpress.com/2012/08/mcdonald-chrishaun-11-16485-5-2-12-plea.pdf

Stryker, S. (2006). (De)subjugated Knowledges: An Introduction to Transgender Studies. In S. Stryker & S. Whittle (Eds.), *The Transgender Studies Reader* (pp. 1–17). New York: Routledge.

Stryker, S. (2008). *Transgender History*. Berkeley, CA: Seal Press.

Stryker, S., Currah, P., & Moore, L. (2008). Introduction: Trans-, Trans, or Transgender? *Women's Studies Quarterly, 36*(3–4), 11–22.

Support CeCe McDonald! (2011, November 20). As Long as We Live in Fear, We Live in Ignorance. [Web log post]. Retrieved from http://supportcece.wordpress.com/2011/11/20/as-long-as-we-live-in-fear-we-live-in-ignorance/

Support CeCe McDonald! (n.d.). Background. Retrieved from http://supportcece.wordpress.com/about-2/background/.

Support CeCe McDonald! (n.d.). Chrishaun "CeCe" McDonald Accepts Plea Agreement to Reduced Manslaughter Charge. Retrieved from http://supportcece.wordpress.com/category/updates/

Taking up Too Much Space. (n.d.) Retrieved from http://takesupspace.wordpress.com/cis-privilege-checklist/

Wallace, L. (2007, October 31). Transgendered behind Bars. *In These Times*. Retrieved from http://www.inthesetimes.com/article/3372/transgendered_behind_bars/

West, I. (2008). Debbie Mayne's Trans/scripts: Performative Repertoires in Law and Everyday Life. *Communication and Critical/Cultural Studies, 5*(3), 245–263.

Yep, G. A. (2003). The Violence of Heteronormativity in Communication Studies: Notes on Injury, Healing, and Queer World-making. In G.A. Yep, K.E. Lovaas, & J.P. Elia (Eds.), *Queer Theory and Communication: From Disciplining Queers to Queering the Discipline(s)* (pp. 11–59). Binghamton, NY: Harrington Park Press.

Analyze

1. How does Johnson define "transgender" in this essay, and why does she argue that her definition is problematic? What term does Johnson ultimately settle on using for the purposes of this essay, and why?

2. How does Johnson define "cissexual" and "cisgender," and why does she argue that those definitions are significant? How does CeCe McDonald's case connect to definitions of cisgender? Of cissexual?

3. According to Johnson, how does the intersection of race, gender, and sexuality impact McDonald's life and, in particular, this case against her?

Explore

1. In this essay, Johnson argues that intercultural communication "is enhanced by attending to concepts such as cisgenderism, cisprivilege, and cissexism." Although Johnson is speaking specifically to her own field, to what extent could her argument be applied to your own field of study? Consider the way in which gender and sexuality are perceived in your own discipline. For instance, would a trans*- individual be able to openly secure a job in your field? Why or why not?

2. In Anne Fausto-Sterling's article "The Five Sexes: Why Male and Female Are Not Enough," she argues for a broader understanding of gender beyond male and female. Would Johnson agree with Fausto-Sterling's argument, and why or why not? How might McDonald's situation have been altered, given a different perception of gender?

3. According to Johnson, how was McDonald's identity presented as "fake" or "invalid" during court proceedings and after, when she was sentenced to time in prison? Consider the readings we have done thus far (especially Judith Lorber's essay): To what extent does society determine what is a "real" identity? Write an essay, drawing on what you've read so far, that presents an argument detailing society's role in constructing identity (gender and otherwise).

Tommi Avicolli Mecca
"He Defies You Still: The Memoirs of a Sissy"

Tommi Avicolli Mecca is an Italian American writer, performer, and activist who helped organize the first gay pride march in Philadelphia in 1972. He has been published in numerous anthologies and has written for

Philadelphia Magazine, *San Francisco Bay Guardian*, and the *Bay Times*. He has also had plays and performance pieces produced on stages in Philadelphia, New York, and San Francisco. Most recently, he edited the collection *Smash the Church, Smash the State: The Early Years of Gay Liberation* (2009), an anthology of writings about the post-Stonewall gay liberation movement. "He Defies You Still: The Memoirs of a Sissy," originally published by *Radical Teacher* in 1985, is his account of realizing he was gay while attending a Catholic high school, where he was bullied and branded a sissy because he didn't act "like a boy."

Scene One:

A homeroom in a Catholic high school in South Philadelphia. The boy sits quietly in the first aisle, third desk, reading a book. He does not look up, not even for a moment. He is hoping no one will remember he is sitting there. He wishes he were invisible. The teacher is not yet in the classroom so the other boys are talking and laughing loudly.

Suddenly, a voice from beside him: "Hey, you're a faggot, ain't you?"

The boy does not answer. He goes on reading his book, or rather pretending he is reading his book. It is impossible to actually read now.

"Hey, I'm talking to you!"

The boy still does not look up. He is so scared his heart is thumping madly. But he can't look up.

"Faggot, I'm talking to you!"

To look up is to meet the eyes of the tormentor.

Suddenly a sharp pencil point is thrust into the boy's arm. He jolts, shaking off the pencil, aware that there is blood seeping from the wound.

"What did you do that for?" he asks timidly.

"Cause I hate faggots," the other boy says, laughing. Some other boys begin to laugh, too. A symphony of laughter. The boy feels as if he's going to cry. But he must not cry. Must not cry. So he holds back the tears and tries to read the book again. He must read the book. Read the book.

When the teacher arrives a few minutes later, the class quiets down. The boy does not tell the teacher what has happened. He spits on the wound to clean it, dabbing it with a tissue until the bleeding stops. For weeks he fears some dreadful infection from the lead in the pencil point.

Scene Two:

The boy is walking home from school. A group of boys (two, maybe three, he is not certain) grab him from behind, drag him into an alley and beat him up. When he gets home, he races up to his room, refusing dinner ("I don't feel well," he tells his mother through the locked door) and spends the night alone in the dark wishing he would die. . . .

These are not fictitious accounts—I *was* that boy. Having been branded a sissy by neighborhood children because I preferred jump rope to baseball and dolls to playing soldiers, I was often taunted with "hey sissy" or "hey faggot" or "yoo hoo, honey" when I left the house.

To avoid harassment, I spent many summers alone in my room. I went out on rainy days when the street was empty.

I came to like being alone. I didn't need anyone, I told myself over and over. I was an island. Contact with others meant pain. Alone, I was protected. I began writing poems, then short stories. There was no reason to go outside anymore. I had a world of my own.

> *In the schoolyard today*
> *they'll single you out*
> *Their laughter will leave your ears ringing*
> *like the church bells*
> *that once awed you . . .*[1]

School was one of the more painful experiences of my youth. The neighborhood bullies could be avoided. The taunts of the children living in those endless row houses could be evaded by staying in my room. But school was something I had to face day after day for some two hundred mornings a year.

I had few friends in school. Some kids would talk to me, but few wanted to be known as my close friend. Afraid of labels. If I was a sissy, then they would be sissies, too. I was condemned to loneliness.

Fortunately, a new boy moved into our neighborhood and befriended me; he wasn't afraid of the labels. He protected me when the other guys threatened to beat me up. He walked me home from school; he broke through the terrible loneliness. We were in third or fourth grade at the time.

We spent a summer or two together. Then his parents sent him to camp and I was once again confined to my room.

Scene Three:

High school lunchroom. The boy sits at a table near the back of the room. Without warning, his lunch bag is grabbed and tossed to another table. Someone opens it and confiscates a package of Tastykakes; another boy takes the sandwich. The empty bag is tossed back to the boy who stares at it, dumbfounded. He should be used to this; it has happened before.

Someone says, "Faggot," laughing. There is always laughter. It does not annoy him anymore.

There is no teacher nearby. There is never a teacher around. And what would he say if there were? Could he report the crime? He would be jumped after school if he did. Besides, it would be his word against theirs. Teachers never noticed anything. They never heard the taunts. Never heard the word, "faggot." They were the great deaf mutes, pillars of indifference; a sissy's pain was not relevant to history and geography and god made me to love honor and obey him, amen.

The boy reaches into his pocket for some money, but there's only a few coins. Always just a few coins. He cleans windshields at his father's gas station on Saturdays and Sundays to earn money. But it's never much. Only enough now to buy a carton of milk and some cookies. Only enough to watch the other boys eat and laugh, hoping they'll choke on their food. . . .

Scene Four:

High school religion class. Someone has a copy of *Playboy*. Father N. is not in the room yet; he's late, as usual. Someone taps the boy roughly on the shoulder. He turns. A finger points to the centerfold model, pink fleshy body, thin and sleek. Almost painted. Not real. The other asks in a mocking voice, "Hey, does she turn you on? Look at those tits!"

The boy smiles, nodding meekly; turns away.

The other jabs him harder on the shoulder, "Hey, what'samatter, don't you like girls?"

Laughter. Thousands of mouths; unbearable din of laughter. In the arena: thumbs down. Don't spare the queer.

"Wanna suck my dick, huh? That turn you on, faggot!"

What did being a sissy really mean? It was a way of walking (from the hips rather than the shoulders); it was a way of talking (often with a lisp or in a high-pitched voice); it was a way of relating to others (gently, not wanting to fight, or hurt anybody's feelings). It was being intelligent ("an egghead" they called it sometimes); getting good grades. It meant not being interested in sports, not playing football in the street after school; not discussing teams and scores and playoffs. And it involved not showing a fervent interest in girls, not talking about scoring or tits or *Playboy* centerfolds. Not concealing pictures of naked women in your history book; or porno books in your locker.

On the other hand, anyone could be a "faggot." It was a catchall. If you did something that didn't conform to the acceptable behavior of the group, then you risked being called a faggot. It was the most commonly used putdown. It kept guys in line. They became angry when somebody called them a faggot. More fights started over calling someone a faggot than anything else. The word had power. It toppled the male ego, shattered his delicate facade, violated the image he projected. He was tough. Without feeling. Faggot cut through all this. It made him vulnerable. Feminine. And feminine was the worst thing he could possibly be. Girls were fine for fucking, but no boy in his right mind wanted to be like them. A boy was the opposite of a girl. He was not feminine. He was not feeling. He was not weak.

Just look at the gym teacher who growled like a dog; or the priest with the black belt who threw kids against the wall in rage when they didn't know their Latin. They were men, they got respect.

But not the physics teacher who preached pacificism during lectures on the nature of atoms. Everybody knew what he was—and why he believed in the antiwar movement.

Scene Five:

FATHER: I wanna see you walk, Mark.
MARK: What do you mean?
FATHER: Just walk, Mark.
MARK: (Starts to walk) I don't understand.

FATHER: That's it, just walk.
MARK: (Walks back and forth)
FATHER: Now come here.

   (*Mark approaches; father slaps him across the face, hard*)

MARK: What was that for?
FATHER: I want you to walk right now.
MARK: What do you mean?
FATHER: Stop fooling around, Mark, I want you to walk like a man.
MARK: Dad, I . . .
FATHER: (Interrupting) Don't say another word. Just get over there and
   walk right—walk like a man.[2]

My parents only knew that the neighborhood kids called me names.
They begged me to act more like the other boys. My brothers were ashamed
of me. They never said it, but I knew. Just as I knew that my parents were
embarrassed by my behavior.

At times, they tried to get me to act differently. Once my father lectured
me on how to walk right. I'm still not clear on what that means. Not from
the hips, I guess; don't "swish" like faggots do.

A nun in elementary school told my mother at open house that there
was "something wrong with me." I had draped my sweater over my shoulders like a girl, she said. I was a smart kid, no complaints about my grades,
but I should know better than to wear my sweater like a girl.

My mother stood there, mute. I wanted her to say something, to
chastise the nun, to defend me. But how could she? This was a nun
talking—representative of Jesus, protector of all that was good and decent.

An uncle once told me I should start "acting like a boy" instead of a girl.
Everybody seemed ashamed of me. And I guess I was ashamed of myself,
too. It was hard not to be.

Scene Six:

PRIEST: Do you like girls, Mark?
MARK: Uh-huh.
PRIEST: I mean REALLY like them?
MARK: Yeah—they're okay.
PRIEST: There's a role they play in your salvation. Do you understand it,
   Mark?

MARK: Yeah.

PRIEST. You've got to like girls. Even if you should decide to enter the seminary, it's important to keep in mind God's plan for a man and a woman. . . .[3]

Catholicism of course condemned homosexuality. Effeminacy was tolerated as long as the effeminate person did not admit to being gay. Thus, priests could be effeminate because they weren't gay.

As a sissy, I couldn't count on support from the church. A male's sole purpose in life was to father children—souls for the church to save. The only hope a homosexual had of attaining salvation was to remain totally celibate. Don't even think of touching another boy. To think of a sin was a sin. And to sin was to put a mark on the soul. Sin—led to hell. There was no way around it. If you sinned, you were doomed.

Realizing I was gay wasn't an easy task. Although I knew I was attracted to boys by the time I was about eleven, I didn't connect this attraction to homosexuality. I was not queer. Not I. I was merely appreciating a boy's good looks, his fine features, his proportions. It didn't seem to matter that I didn't appreciate a girl's looks in the same way. There was no twitching in my thighs when I gazed upon a beautiful girl. But I wasn't queer.

We sat through endless English classes, and history courses about the wars between men who were not allowed to love each other. No gay history was ever taught. You're just a faggot. Homosexuals had never contributed to the human race. God destroyed the queers in Sodom and Gomorrah.

I resisted that label—queer—for the longest time. Even when everything pointed to it, I refused to see it. I was certainly not queer. Not I.

Near the end of my junior year in high school, most of the teasing and taunting had let up. Now I was just ignored. Besides, I was getting a reputation for being a hippie, since I spoke up in social studies classes against the war, and wore my hair as long as I could without incurring the wrath of the administration. When your hair reached a certain length, you were told to get a hair cut. If you didn't, you were sent down to the vice principal's office where you were given a hair cut.

I had a friend toward the end of junior year; his name was Joe. He introduced me to Jay at the bowling alley in South Philadelphia. I knew immediately I was in love with Jay.

A relationship developed. It was all very daring; neither of us understood what was happening. I still rejected the label. I wasn't queer. He wasn't queer. But I knew I was in love with him. I told myself that all the time. Yet I wasn't a homosexual.

Franny was a queer. He lived a few blocks away. He used to dress in women's clothes and wait for the bus on the corner. Everybody laughed at Franny. Everybody knew he was queer.

Then, one night, Halloween, a chilly October night, Jay called:

Scene Seven:

... "What?"

"It's wrong."

"What's wrong."

Tossing in my sleep—sweating. It was the winter of '69. The heavy woolen cover became a thick shroud on top of me. The heat pricked me like so many needles.

"Why can't I see you tonight?"

"We can't see each other anymore...."

My heart was an acrobat. It leaped like a frog. Landed in a deep puddle. Help, it shouted. It was going down for the third time.

"Why?" I felt nauseous. I was going to vomit.

"We can't. I've got to go."

"Wait—!"

"What?"

There were tears running down my cheeks in streams that left a salty residue at the corners of my lips. The record player in the background shut off, closing me in. The walls of the room collapsed. I was entombed.

"Please, talk to me. I can't let you go like this. I want to know what's wrong. Please ..."

"I can't see you anymore. It's over. It was a mistake."

"It wasn't a mistake, Jay. I—I love you."

"Don't say that!" Voice quivering; don't force me to see things I don't want to see right now.

"But I do. And you love me. Admit it. Don't break it off now. Admit it. Admit that you love me."

"I've got to go."

"You can't go. Admit it!"

"Goodbye."

"Jay?"

Silence.[4]

We learned about Michelangelo, Oscar Wilde, Gertrude Stein—but never that they were queer. They were not queer. Walt Whitman, the "father of American poetry," was not queer. No one was queer. I was alone, totally unique. One of a kind. Except for Franny who wore dresses and makeup. Where did Franny go every night? Were there others like me somewhere? Another planet, perhaps?

In school, they never talked of queers. They did not exist. The only hint we got of this other species was in religion class. And even then it was clouded in mystery—never spelled out. It was a sin. Like masturbation. Like looking at *Playboy* and getting a hard-on. A sin.

Once a progressive priest in senior-year religion class actually mentioned homosexuals—he said the word, broke the silence—but he was talking about homosexuals as pathetic and sick. Fixated at some early stage; penis, anal, whatever. Only heterosexuals passed on to the nirvana of sexual development.

No other images from the halls of the Catholic high school except those the other boys knew: swishy faggot sucking cock in an alley somewhere, grabbing asses in the bathroom. Never mentioning how straight boys craved blow jobs, too.

It was all a secret. You were not supposed to talk about queers. Whisper maybe. Laugh about them, yes. But don't be open, honest; don't try to understand. Don't cite their accomplishments. No history faces you this morning. You're a faggot. No history—a faggot.

Epilogue:

The boy marching down Spruce Street. Hundreds of queers. Signs proclaiming gay pride. Speakers. Tables with literature from gay groups. A miracle, he is thinking. Tears are coming loose now. Someone hugs him.

> *You could not control*
> *the sissy in me*
> *nor could you exorcise him*
> *nor electrocute him*
> *You declared him illegal illegitimate*
> *insane and immature*
> *but he defies you still.*[5]

NOTES

1. From the poem "Faggot," by Tommi Avicolli, published in *GPU News*, September 1979.
2. From the play *Judgement of the Roaches*, by Tommi Avicolli, produced in Philadelphia at the Gay & Lesbian Coffee House, the Painted Bride Arts Center, and the University of Pennsylvania; aired over WXPN-FM in four parts; and presented at the Lesbian/Gay Conference in Norfolk, VA, July 1980.
3. Ibid.
4. From the novel *Deaf Mute's Final Dance*, by Tommi Avicolli.
5. From the poem "Sissy Poem," published in *Magic Doesn't Live Here Anymore*, Spruce Street Press, 1976.

Analyze

1. In Scene One, Mecca uses the third person, referring to "the boy," before switching to the first person in Scene Two. He makes this switch again later in this piece. What is his purpose in doing so?
2. What's the difference between a "sissy" and a "faggot," according to Mecca?
3. Why does Mecca present his memoir in scenes, as if from a play?

Explore

1. Compare the way Mecca is treated by his classmates with the way X, Lois Gould's protagonist (Chapter 1), is treated. What accounts for the differences between the two?
2. How often do you hear the words "faggot" and "sissy" used on a regular basis? In what context? Do these terms still hold the same meaning that Mecca suggests they do? Watch the poker scene (available on YouTube) from Episode Two, "Poker/Divorce," of *Louie*, comedian Louis C. K.'s hit show for FX. How does this candid conversation about the word "faggot" complicate our understanding of the word?
3. Mecca ends his memoir with an epilogue, describing his experience at a gay pride parade. Why is this a "miracle" to him? Do you know anyone who has recently attended a gay pride parade? If so, interview him/her. (See the appendix for tips on preparing and conducting an interview.) How did attending a pride parade affect your interviewee? Was his/her experience similar to or different from Mecca's experience? How so?

4. Certainly Mecca's story hints at the preponderance of bullying. Do some research on bullying as it is tied to sexual orientation and/or gender identification. Look for both anecdotes of those who have been bullied and more academic sources that offer analysis of bullying. What do you learn about why this demographic is often targeted? What are the negative impacts of bullying? What should be done about it? Write a researched essay that proposes a solution to the problem.

Vanessa Vitiello Urquhart
"Why I'm Still a Butch Lesbian"

Vanessa Vitiello Urquhart is a freelance writer who also draws the web comic *Tiny Butch Adventures*. "Why I'm Still a Butch Lesbian," written for *Slate* in 2014, explores the author's need to reject a nonbinary gender identity. Think about how self-identification can be powerful as your read her essay.

I first began wearing men's clothing a few years ago, because I thought that looking like a lesbian might help me get girls. Once I'd started, I realized almost immediately that I was feeling far more comfortable and confident and that I liked the way I looked in the mirror for the first time in my life. Other people who knew me said I looked more natural, more like my clothing fit my personality. It felt a bit like I'd been wearing an uncomfortable, ill-fitting costume all my life.

As I adjusted to this new information, it was hard not to notice that many of the people who shared my preference for the men's section and my subtly masculine mannerisms had gone a step further and stopped identifying as women entirely. At times, it almost seemed as if, by not throwing my lot in with these pronoun creators and binary-rejecters, I might be just a little bit behind the times—a little square, uncool, perhaps even cis-sexist. Facebook has more than 50 possible gender identifiers. So why have I, a female-bodied person who wears men's clothing, decided to stick with the increasingly old-fashioned "butch lesbian woman"?

In part, it's because the language of gender identity has always been a bit bewildering to me—I've felt hungry, happy, gassy, and anxious, but never male or female. Even so, it has been tempting to interpret my experience in ways that separated it from that of other women. This is especially true because cis-gendered women have a distinct tendency to define themselves in ways that don't include me. I hear women throw out things like, "As women, we all know how important it is to feel pretty," or "We, as women, are naturally more tender and nurturing," statements that never seem to include women like me. Not only do I dislike feeling pretty and prefer arguing to nurturing, I don't even particularly like eating chocolate. Popular culture, and women themselves, often imply that I lack many of the most essential qualities of womanhood.

So in the past I've been quite tempted by the idea that *perhaps I'm not a woman after all*. I mean, I'm masculine in all sorts of ways—I am ambitious, logical, aggressive, strong, and highly competitive. And I'm certainly not silly, frivolous, dainty, weak, or overly emotional . . . Oh dear. That's where I run into a major problem, isn't it? When I start listing traits of mine that I'd call masculine, they're always positive. They're points of pride. Whereas when I list traits I lack that I'd call feminine, they're negatives. It seems I can't consider my own masculinity or lack of femininity without relying on some of the worst and most pernicious sex-based stereotypes. This suggests to me that the enterprise itself is suspect.

In our culture, the impulse to distance oneself from negatives associated with women and femininity is endemic. When we insult men, we do it by comparing them to women. When we compare women to men, we're generally praising them. In fact, I've probably known more straight, cis-gendered women who've bragged about how they're "one of the guys" than I've known lesbians. Ironically, one of the things I share with many women is my eagerness to point out all the ways in which I'm not like other women.

As girls grow up, they are bombarded by rules and restrictions governing the ways that they can be. I know I was—otherwise I wouldn't have been a fully grown adult before I started wearing clothes that I found comfortable. These gendered rules confine girls' choices and constrain their self-expression. Perhaps one day the gender binary will be dismantled totally, and we'll all stop limiting our children by bringing them up as either males or females. But, in the meantime, gender continues to be one of the first things children learn to recognize about themselves and others, and for that reason I think it's important to keep the boundaries of what can and can't potentially be male or female propped open as wide as possible. It's wonderful that people who feel uncomfortable with the gender they were assigned at birth are gaining strength and visibility. But, it's just as important that young people, girls and boys and genderqueers alike, can have as many examples as possible of men and women who don't conform to gender stereotypes. I like to think I'm doing my part for that by living as an aggressive, competitive, logical, and strong butch woman.

Analyze

1. Urquhart says that after beginning to wear men's clothing, she realized that it previously felt like she'd been wearing an "uncomfortable, ill-fitting costume" her whole life up to that point. Why does she use the word "costume," and what does this imply?

2. Why was Urquhart "tempted by the idea that *perhaps I'm not a woman at all*"? What does this say about the pressure placed on men and women by our culture to perform gender in only one way?

3. When Urquhart describes the way she feels excluded by cis-gendered women, why does she add, "I don't even particularly like eating chocolate"?

Explore

1. Urqhart asserts, "When we insult men, we do it by comparing them to women. When we compare women to men, we're generally praising them." Have you experienced this in your own life? If so, how did this make you feel?

2. Why is the language of gender identity "bewildering" to Urquhart? Look at the list of possible gender identifiers that Facebook now offers. Does this reinforce Urquhart's decision to identify as a "butch lesbian woman"? And is this one of her options? Should it be? Why or why not?

3. Read some of Urquhart's web comics. What additional issues related to gender identity and performance do her *Tiny Butch Adventures* reveal?

Forging Connections

1. Both Zachary Pullin, in "Two Spirit," and Sandra Cisneros, in "Guadalupe the Sex Goddess," note that their cultural understandings

of gender and sexuality were impacted by Westernization. How do both authors draw on their cultures' histories prior to colonization as a source of empowerment? And what does their desire to do so reveal about the effects of colonization and Westernization on indigenous communities and identities?

2. Anne Fausto-Sterling argues that "if the state and legal system have an interest in maintaining a two-party sexual system, they are in defiance of nature." How do we see this at work in the trial of CeCe McDonald? How might Fausto-Sterling advocate for McDonald's case, and why?

Looking Further

1. Rich argues that the media seems to inundate us with "feminist" messages that encourage women to claim their identities as women, but that ultimately these messages use feminism to sell products, thus usurping the feminist message and the feminist identity. Look through a recent women's magazine and/or watch a program more specifically geared toward women (such as a soap opera) and study the advertising. To what extent do you see language that suggests that women are equal to men? Why do you think this is—how does it serve the purposes of the advertisement? Write an essay in which you construct an argument that examines the connection between the language the ad uses and the message it wants to convey to the reader.

2. Urquhart states, "In our culture, the impulse to distance oneself from negatives associated with women and femininity is endemic. When we insult men, we do it by comparing them to women." Boys are frequently told to "stop acting like a girl." What does it mean to do something "like a girl"? How is this damaging to boys? To girls? Watch the video "Like a Girl," created by filmmaker Lauren Greenfield for Always, the feminine hygiene brand. How does this video both reinforce and challenge what it means to do something like a girl?

3

Gender and Stereotypes

Popular television shows often become the window into the values of society. The characters embody identities that are easy for audiences to relate to, whether treated seriously or poked fun at. And the narratives of these shows often capture current issues and ideologies.

One reason that television characters are easy to relate to is that they are often written as *tropes*, or as characters whose qualities are recurrent in the media. For instance, on the show *Modern Family*, Phil Dunphy is the Bumbling Dad; Claire Dunphy is the Overworked, Exasperated Mom; Jay Pritchett is the Older Man with a Younger, Hotter Wife; Gloria Pritchett is the Sexy Trophy Wife; Mitchell Pritchett is the Overachieving Gay Man; and Cameron Tucker is the Flamboyant Gay Man. You could think of countless examples of other shows where these characters appear, albeit with a different name and played by a different actor. (For instance,

Mitchell and Cameron could easily be *Will and Grace*'s Will and Jack.) Because these identities are displayed so frequently, they can be assumed to be real identities as we conflate the real world with the world of television. For example, when we see a family, we might assume that the father is bumbling and the mother is overworked and exasperated even before we meet them. Thus, these qualities are not just *tropes* that exist on television; they become *stereotypes* that infiltrate our daily lives.

The readings in this chapter examine the extent to which stereotypes play a role in our identities—how much we define ourselves and others by what are assumed to be the qualities we should hold. We begin with Brian Frazer's quiz, "How Big Are Your Balls?," a humorous piece that asks readers a series of questions, based on stereotypes of manliness, to gauge their masculinity. Robert Jensen's essay "The High Cost of Manliness" questions the stereotypes of masculinity and argues for an end to common conceptions of both masculinity and femininity. In "If Men Could Menstruate," Gloria Steinem riffs on the privilege afforded stereotypical men by exploring how menstruation would be thought of differently were it a male bodily function. Alice Walker's "In Search of Our Mothers' Gardens" explores the extent to which stereotypes about African American women have oppressed their creativity and artistry. Jade Chong-Smith's essay "Hard Time: Lessons from a Maximum-Security Prison" is a reflective piece in which Chong-Smith questions her own stereotypes about inmates to craft a call to change the prison system. In "The Coming Out We All Ignored," Jonathan Zimmerman looks at stereotypes of female athletes to demonstrate why WNBA star Brittney Griner's coming out was not watched as closely or as celebrated as that of NBA player Jason Collins. And Sarah McMahon's essay "Rape Myth Beliefs and Bystander Attitudes among Incoming College Students" examines the connection between stereotypes about sexual assault and a bystander's willingness to intervene.

Brian Frazer
"How Big Are Your Balls?"

Brian Frazer is a former stand-up comedian who has written for magazines such as *ESPN* and *Vanity Fair*. This quiz, "How Big Are Your Balls?," originally published in *Esquire* magazine in 2007, is a tongue-in-cheek quiz that asks readers to define their masculinity. As you take the quiz, think about which answers earn the most points, and why, and which earn the least points, and why.

---

1. What tattoos do you have?
   a. My girlfriend's name on my ankle. (0)
   b. None. (-3)
   c. Chinese symbol for strength on my shoulder blade. (1)
   d. Whatever's on sale that day that'll look good on my face. (9)
2. When was the last time you were in a fistfight?
   a. Third grade, when I got beaten up by a bully for wearing my red velour shirt. (-6)
   b. Within the last two years. (2)
   c. I'm in a fight right now and am using this magazine to sodomize my opponent. (10)
3. What's the most expensive thing you've ever stolen?
   a. That's a trick question! Stealing is wrong. (-8)
   b. A Charleston Chew. (1)
   c. An Oasis CD in 1998. (3)
   d. The babysitter's virginity. (11)
4. Complete this sentence: "The craziest thing I've ever eaten is _____."
   a. A bowl of Franken Berry mixed with Count Chocula—without any milk. (-4)
   b. A worm at recess. (-1)
   c. A cactus. (5)
   d. A mouse I was gonna give my snake. (7)
5. Indicate the position you played in high school football.
   a. Clarinet. (-10)
   b. 227-pound field-goal kicker. (1)
   c. 153-pound middle linebacker. (9)
   d. Legally blind punt returner. (17)
6. What is the most confrontational remark you've ever made to your boss?
   a. "May I go to lunch now? It's almost midnight." (-13)
   b. "Are you sure about that, sir?" (1)
   c. "You'll take lunch when I tell you to take lunch!" (15)

7. You're supposed to pick your girlfriend up at the airport. You . . .
   a. Get there an hour early just in case her flight makes good time against the headwinds. (-9)
   b. Get there ten minutes late, 'cause it always takes a while at baggage claim. (-1)
   c. Watch the entire Ohio State game, kick a dent in my car at half-time, and lie and say I was in a car accident. (8)
   d. Pick her up as soon as her best friend finishes blowing me. (19)

8. When you watched *Jackass Number Two*, what thoughts went through your head?
   a. Didn't see it. (0)
   b. "Jesus and a half! These guys are nuts!" (-5)
   c. "I wonder how many calories are in cow manure?" (4)
   d. "That particular stunt actually works better if you attach the electrode directly to your scrotum." (10)

9. When at the dentist having a root canal, you choose . . .
   a. The happy gas that goes over your nose. (-3)
   b. Injection into your gums. (0)
   c. Nothing. (13)
   d. Waterboarding. (30)

10. You are dealt this hand in a game of poker. What's your move?
    a. I actually don't play poker, but when I go to Vegas, I do enjoy the nickel *I Dream of Jeannie* slot machine! (-7)

b. I'd fold before you could say, "Ten high." (0)
c. Raise $15,000. (20)

11. Have you ever ... (check all that apply)
    a. Drank an entire Big Gulp? (0)
    b. Gone to a taping of *The Tyra Banks Show*? (-3)
    c. Hot-wired a car? (16)
    d. Fought more than one person at the same time? (23)
    e. Ridden a motorcycle without a helmet? (5)
    f. Kissed a cat? (-7)
    g. Kissed a cat despite being allergic to cats? (-6)
    h. Wrestled with a bear? (34)
    i. Eaten ice cream really, really fast? (1)

12. If you were at a presidential press conference and able to ask a question, what would it be?
    a. Too nervous to speak in front of our commander in chief. Sorry. (-15)
    b. "Can more be done about global warming, Mr. President?" (2)
    c. "Does Mr. Cheney tie your ties and then you just loop them over your head?" (17)

13. What was your response the last time you were turned away by a bouncer?
    a. Asked him where the nearest bar that I could get into would be. (-6)
    b. Said, "That's cool," then gave him the finger and walked away. (6)
    c. Asked him if, after taxes, he pockets more than $180 a week. (10)

14. Read the following list of phrases and circle any you have used when negotiating a business deal. (One point each.)
    a. "I'm outta here."
    b. "Fuck you."
    c. "Say hello to my little friend."
    d. "I'll eat you for breakfast and shit you out by lunch."
    e. "Right kneecap or left? It's your choice."
    f. "There's only one bullet in this gun. You first."
    g. "If you ever want to see your daughter again . . ."

15. What would you do for a PlayStation 3?
    a. Nothing. Video games are bad for my eyes. (-7)
    b. Wait patiently in line, as long as it isn't too cold out. (-1)
    c. Mug a Wal-Mart employee, steal his uniform, and pretend I work there. (5)
    d. Fuck a panda. (12)

16. Which of the following people would you fight?

    (No minimum or maximum number required; add or subtract number of points in parentheses after each name.)

    a. Ron Artest. (27)

    b. Neil Patrick Harris. (-1)

    c. Brett Favre. (13)

    d. Michael J. Fox. (-5)

    e. Stephen Jackson. (14)

    f. Stephen Hawking. (-40)

    g. Barry Bonds. (20)

    h. Mike Tyson. (25)

    i. Tom Hanks. (0)

    j. Mike Ditka. (23)

    k. Russell Crowe. (19)

17. You accidentally obtain some inside stock information that is technically illegal. What do you do?

    a. Nothing! Are you crazy? (-5)

    b. Buy five shares and pray that Jesus forgives me. (5)

    c. Buy as many shares as I can afford after selling the information on my Web site. (10)

18. What's the most daring public place you've had sex?

    a. I once adjusted my privates in a freight elevator, and there may have been a surveillance camera. Yikes! (-11)

    b. On the monkey bars at an elementary-school playground. (8)

    c. On the hood of my ex-girlfriend's car, on a weekend, in her husband's driveway. (20)

19. You're a huge Jets fan in Oakland at a Jets–Raiders game. How are you dressed?

    a. In black and silver, to blend in. (-15)

    b. Khaki slacks and a sensible maroon V-neck sweater, or whatever I wore to church. (-9)

    c. Shirtless with my torso and face painted green and white. (10)

    d. Naked with my body painted green and white and holding a sign that says "You can't spell Raiders without AIDS." (24)

20. What's the ballsiest thing you've ever attempted while drunk?

    a. Sewing a button on a shirt. (-10)

    b. Making a grilled cheese on my George Foreman grill. (1)

    c. Breaking up with a girl. (2)

    d. The Indy 500. (15)

21. What did you take this quiz with?

    a. By memory. I'm in a doctor's office right now and don't want to deface his magazine. (-10)

    b. Pencil. (-5)

    c. Sharpie. (5)

    d. Can of spray paint. (10)

Scoring Guide

Less than 0

The only balls you have came with your Ping-Pong table.

0 to 200

Your balls have the manufacturer's recommended pressure per square inch. Still, they could be bigger.

More Than 200

Russell Crowe, Jack Murtha, and Johnny Knoxville recently got together and started your fan club.

> "The only balls you have came with your Ping-Pong table."

Analyze

1. How does the first question of the quiz—both the question and the answers—set up the tenor for the rest of the questions?

2. Consider Question 5, its choices, and the points awarded for each choice. How does the framing of the question set up the expectations for the choices that will be available? What do the choices and the points awarded suggest about what aspects of high school football we value most?

3. Consider Frazer's overall tone in this quiz. In what ways is it humorous, and why? Choose one of the questions and look at it more deeply. How does the question itself invite humor—what words and/or phrases strike you as funny, and why? How about the answers? Are the answers what you would have expected, given the question? Finally, consider the points awarded for each answer. How do the points awarded contribute to the comedic quality of the question?

4. Take a look at the "Scoring Guide." What does the Scoring Guide suggest about the way in which a man's "balls" are associated with his masculinity? And how does the Scoring Guide use wit to help convey this idea?

Explore

1. If you haven't already, take the quiz and reflect on why you believe you got the score that you did. What experiences/values/beliefs informed your answers to these questions?

2. Read Question 16 carefully. What do you know about the eleven men represented in the answer choices? Why do you think that Frazer attributed the points to each man in the way that he did? What does this say about how society defines a "real" man and how society defines "masculinity"? Write an essay in which you consider how these men represent different aspects of society's definition(s) of masculinity, and why.

3. Watch "The Flip Side Workout" (Yahoo). Both "The Flip Side Workout" and "How Big Are Your Balls?" use comedy to make specific claims about representations of masculinity and femininity. Write an essay in which you compare and contrast the ways in which both pieces use humor to convey those claims.

Robert Jensen
"The High Cost of Manliness"

Robert Jensen is a journalism professor at the University of Texas at Austin. His writing and teaching focus on interrogating power structures of race and gender. He is the author of books such as *Arguing for Our Lives: A User's Guide to Constructive Dialogue* (2013) and *Getting Off: Pornography and the End of Masculinity* (2007).

In this essay, "The High Cost of Manliness," published by the website AlterNet in 2006, Jensen argues for an end to the idea of masculinity as we know it. As you read this essay, think about the way in which Jensen argues that our current concept of masculinity is dangerous. How does Jensen perceive masculinity as problematic—for both men and women—and why?

It's hard to be a man; hard to live up to the demands that come with the dominant conception of masculinity, of the tough guy.

So, guys, I have an idea—maybe it's time we stop trying. Maybe this masculinity thing is a bad deal, not just for women but for us.

We need to get rid of the whole idea of masculinity. It's time to abandon the claim that there are certain psychological or social traits that inherently come with being biologically male. If we can get past that, we have a chance to create a better world for men and women.

That dominant conception of masculinity in U.S. culture is easily summarized: Men are assumed to be naturally competitive and aggressive, and being a real man is therefore marked by the struggle for control, conquest and domination. A man looks at the world, sees what he wants and takes it. Men who don't measure up are wimps, sissies, fags, girls. The worst insult one man can hurl at another—whether it's boys on the playground or CEOs in the boardroom—is the accusation that a man is like a woman. Although the culture acknowledges that men can in some situations have traits traditionally associated with women (caring, compassion, tenderness), in the end it is men's strength-expressed-as-toughness that defines us and must trump any female-like softness. Those aspects of masculinity must prevail for a man to be a "real man."

That's not to suggest, of course, that every man adopts that view of masculinity. But it is endorsed in key institutions and activities—most notably in business, the military and athletics—and is reinforced through the mass media. It is particularly expressed in the way men—straight and gay alike—talk about sexuality and act sexually. And our culture's male heroes reflect those characteristics: They most often are men who take charge rather than seek consensus, seize power rather than look for ways to share it and are willing to be violent to achieve their goals.

That view of masculinity is dangerous for women. It leads men to seek to control "their" women and define their own pleasure in that control, which leads to epidemic levels of rape and battery. But this view of masculinity is toxic for men as well.

If masculinity is defined as conquest, it means that men will always struggle with each other for dominance. In a system premised on hierarchy and power, there can be only one king of the hill. Every other man must in some way be subordinated to the king, and the king has to always be nervous about who is coming up that hill to get him. A friend who once worked on Wall Street—one of the preeminent sites of masculine competition—described coming to work as like walking into a knife fight when all the good spots along the wall were taken. Masculinity like this is life lived as endless competition and threat.

No one man created this system, and perhaps none of us, if given a choice, would choose it. But we live our lives in that system, and it deforms men, narrowing our emotional range and depth. It keeps us from the rich connections with others—not just with women and children, but other men—that make life meaningful but require vulnerability.

This doesn't mean that the negative consequences of this toxic masculinity are equally dangerous for men and women. As feminists have long pointed out, there's a big difference between women dealing with the possibility of being raped, beaten and killed by the men in their lives, and men not being able to cry. But we can see that the short-term material gains that men get are not adequate compensation for what we men give up in the long haul—which is to surrender part of our humanity to the project of dominance.

Of course there are obvious physical differences between men and women—average body size, hormones, reproductive organs. There may be other differences rooted in our biology that we don't yet understand. Yet it's also true that men and women are more similar than we are different, and that given the pernicious effects of centuries of patriarchy and its relentless devaluing of things female, we should be skeptical of the perceived differences.

What we know is simple: In any human population, there is wide individual variation. While there's no doubt that a large part of our behavior is rooted in our DNA, there's also no doubt that our genetic endowment is highly influenced by culture. Beyond that, it's difficult to say much with any certainty. It's true that only women can bear children and breastfeed. That fact likely has some bearing on aspects of men's and women's personalities. But we don't know much about what the effect is, and given the limits of our tools to understand human behavior, it's possible we may never know much.

At the moment, the culture seems obsessed with gender differences, in the context of a recurring intellectual fad (called "evolutionary psychology" this time around, and "sociobiology" in a previous incarnation) that wants to explain all complex behaviors as simple evolutionary adaptations—if a pattern of human behavior exists, it must be because it's adaptive in some ways. In the long run, that's true by definition. But in the short-term it's hardly a convincing argument to say, "Look at how men and women behave so differently; it must be because men and women are fundamentally different" when a political system has been creating differences between men and women.

From there, the argument that we need to scrap masculinity is fairly simple. To illustrate it, remember back to right after 9/11. A number of commentators argued that criticisms of masculinity should be rethought. Cannot we now see—recognizing that male firefighters raced into burning buildings, risking and sometimes sacrificing their lives to save others—that masculinity can encompass a kind of strength that is rooted in caring and sacrifice? Of course men often exhibit such strength, just as do women. So, the obvious question arises: What makes these distinctly masculine characteristics? Are they not simply human characteristics?

We identify masculine tendencies toward competition, domination and violence because we see patterns of differential behavior; men are more prone to such behavior in our culture. We can go on to observe and analyze the ways in which men are socialized to behave in those ways, toward the goal of changing those destructive behaviors. That analysis is different than saying that admirable human qualities present in both men and women are somehow primarily the domain of one gender. To assign them to a gender is misguided and demeaning to the gender that is then assumed not to possess them to the same degree. Once we start saying "strength and courage are masculine traits," it leads to the conclusion that women are not as strong or courageous.

Of course, if we are going to jettison masculinity, we have to scrap femininity along with it. We have to stop trying to define what men and women are going to be in the world based on extrapolations from physical sex differences. That doesn't mean we ignore those differences when they matter, but we have to stop assuming they matter everywhere.

I don't think the planet can long survive if the current conception of masculinity endures. We face political and ecological challenges that can't be met with this old model of what it means to be a man. At the more intimate level, the stakes are just as high. For those of us who are biologically male, we have a simple choice: We men can settle for being men, or we can strive to be human beings.

Analyze

1. How does Jensen establish the prevailing concept of masculinity for us and demonstrate how/why that concept is problematic for men?
2. Why is this concept of masculinity problematic for women as well?
3. What, ultimately, is Jensen's goal in this essay? What does he want us to do with concepts of masculinity and femininity, and why?

Explore

1. Compare the quiz "How Big Are Your Balls?" to "The High Cost of Manliness." How might Jensen respond to the construction of masculinity presented in this quiz, and why?
2. How might Jensen's definition of masculinity be a result of the way in which heterosexuality has been constructed over time? Write an essay in which you place Jensen's theory of masculinity in conversation with Judith Lorber's essay "'Night to His Day': The Social Construction of Gender" and consider the extent to which Jensen's definition of masculinity evolves from Lorber's discussion of gender.
3. Watch the video "Male Restroom Etiquette" on YouTube. In what ways does this video rely on the concept of masculinity that Jensen outlines in his essay? How does the video poke fun at this concept?

Gloria Steinem
"If Men Could Menstruate"

Famed feminist and activist **Gloria Steinem** is a writer, journalist, and lecturer on issues of equality. She has written for publications such as *Esquire* and the *New York Times Magazine*; founded, cofounded, and chaired a wide variety of organizations advocating for women's rights, such as the National Women's Political Caucus and the Women's Media Center; and received countless awards for her activist and literary work over her five-decade career.

"If Men Could Menstruate" was originally published by *Ms.* magazine (a magazine that Steinem helped found) in 1978. In this essay, Steinem reflects on how male privilege causes our culture to embrace certain ideals over others—more specifically, how women's bodies are seen as "less than" in comparison to men's. As you read this essay, think about Steinem's tone in this piece. As a piece published in *Ms.*, who was Steinem's original audience? How does the tone of the essay attempt to reach that audience?

A white minority of the world has spent centuries conning us into thinking that a white skin makes people superior—even though the only thing it really does is make them more subject to ultraviolet rays and to wrinkles. Male human beings have built whole cultures around the idea that penis-envy is "natural" to women—though having such an unprotected organ might be said to make men vulnerable, and the power to give birth makes womb-envy at least as logical.

In short, the characteristics of the powerful, whatever they may be, are thought to be better than the characteristics of the powerless—and logic has nothing to do with it.

What would happen, for instance, if suddenly, magically, men could menstruate and women could not?

The answer is clear—menstruation would become an enviable, worthy, masculine event:

Men would brag about how long and how much.

Boys would mark the onset of menses, that longed-for proof of manhood, with religious ritual and stag parties.

Congress would fund a National Institute of Dysmenorrhea to help stamp out monthly discomforts.

Sanitary supplies would be federally funded and free. (Of course, some men would still pay for the prestige of commercial brands such as John Wayne Tampons, Muhammad Ali's Rope-a-dope Pads, Joe Namath Jock Shields—"For Those Light Bachelor Days," and Robert "Baretta" Blake Maxi-Pads.)

Military men, right-wing politicians, and religious fundamentalists would cite menstruation ("men- struation") as proof that only men could serve in the Army ("you have to give blood to take blood"), occupy political office ("can women be aggressive without that steadfast cycle governed by the planet Mars?"), be priests and ministers ("how could a woman give her blood for our sins?") or rabbis ("without the monthly loss of impurities, women remain unclean").

Male radicals, left-wing politicians, mystics, however, would insist that women are equal, just different, and that any woman could enter their ranks if she were willing to self-inflict a major wound every month ("you *must* give blood for the revolution"), recognize the preeminence of menstrual issues, or subordinate her selfness to all men in their Cycle of Enlightenment.

Street guys would brag ("I'm a three pad man") or answer praise from a buddy ("Man, you lookin' good!") by giving fives and saying, "Yeah, man, I'm on the rag!"

TV shows would treat the subject at length. ("Happy Days": Richie and Potsie try to convince Fonzie that he is still "The Fonz," though he has missed two periods in a row.) So would newspapers. (SHARK SCARE THREATENS MENSTRUATING MEN. JUDGE CITES MONTHLY STRESS IN PARDONING RAPIST.) And movies. (Newman and Redford in "Blood Brothers"!)

Men would convince women that intercourse was more pleasurable at "that time of the month." Lesbians would be said to fear blood and therefore life itself—though probably only because they needed a good menstruating man.

Of course, male intellectuals would offer the most moral and logical arguments. How could a woman master any discipline that demanded a sense of time, space, mathematics, or measurement, for instance, without that in-built gift for measuring the cycles of the moon and planets—and thus for measuring anything at all? In the rarefied fields of philosophy and religion, could women compensate for missing the rhythm of the universe? Or for their lack of symbolic death-and-resurrection every month?

Liberal males in every field would try to be kind: the fact that "these people" have no gift for measuring life or connecting to the universe, the liberals would explain, should be punishment enough.

And how would women be trained to react? One can imagine traditional women agreeing to all arguments with a staunch and smiling masochism. ("The ERA would force housewives to wound themselves every month": Phyllis Schlafly. "Your husband's blood is as sacred as that of Jesus—and so sexy, too!": Marabel Morgan.) Reformers and Queen Bees would try to imitate men, and pretend to have a monthly cycle. All feminists would explain endlessly that men, too, needed to be liberated from the false idea of Martian aggressiveness, just as women needed to escape the bonds of menses-envy. Radical feminists would add that the oppression of the nonmenstrual was the pattern for all other oppressions ("Vampires were our first freedom fighters!"). Cultural feminists would develop a bloodless imagery in art and literature. Socialist feminists would insist that only under capitalism would men be able to monopolize menstrual blood. . . .

In fact, if men could menstruate, the power justifications could probably go on forever.

If we let them.

Analyze

1. Steinem begins her essay by noting that a "white minority of the world has spent centuries conning us into thinking that a white skin makes people superior." Why does she begin the essay with this observation? What's the connection between white privilege and patriarchy?

2. Why does Steinem choose menstruation as the focus of her essay? What is her goal in getting the reader to imagine a world in which men could menstruate? Additionally, what does she want the reader to understand about men's and women's positions in society?

3. The crux of Steinem's argument rests in the reader being able to see that, if men menstruated, menstruation would be perceived differently than it currently is because women do it. One way she works to convince the reader is using humor. In what paragraphs do you see Steinem using humor, and to what extent is the humor effective?

Explore

1. Do a little research on how menstruation is perceived either historically or in other countries. Could Steinem's argument be applied across cultures, and if so, how?

2. This essay was written in 1978. To what extent is Steinem's argument still relevant? In what ways might you find her argument dated? Why?

3. Consider Steinem's essay in conversation with Frazer's quiz and Jensen's piece. How does Steinem's text fit in the context of the discussion of masculinity begun by those two writers?

Alice Walker
"In Search of Our Mothers' Gardens"

Alice Walker is best known for writing *The Color Purple*, which made her the first African American woman to receive the Pulitzer Prize for fiction. "In Search of Our Mothers' Gardens" (1983) is the title essay in a collection of what she calls "womanist" prose. In it, Walker explores how African American women's artistic talents were suppressed while asserting that wisdom and artistry can emerge from the everyday—even the private sphere of home and garden. Her essay is rhetorically rich; it weaves together autobiography, poetry, literary criticism, and historical narrative. As you read, pay attention to the moves she makes and how these moves work to reveal the artistry she discusses.

> I described her own nature and temperament. Told how they needed a larger life for their expression. . . . I pointed out that in lieu of proper channels, her emotions had overflowed into paths that dissipated them. I talked, beautifully I thought, about an art that would be born, an art that would open the way for women the likes of her. I asked her to hope, and build up an inner life against the coming of that day. . . . I sang, with a strange quiver in my voice, a promise song.
>
> —Jean Toomer, "Avey," CANE

The poet speaking to a prostitute who falls asleep while he's talking— When the poet Jean Toomer walked through the South in the early twenties, he discovered a curious thing: black women whose spirituality was so intense, so deep, so *unconscious*, that they were themselves unaware of the richness they held. They stumbled blindly through their lives: creatures so abused and mutilated in body, so dimmed and confused by pain, that they considered themselves unworthy even of hope. In the selfless abstractions their bodies became to the men who used them, they became more than "sexual objects," more even than mere women: they became "Saints." Instead of being perceived as whole persons, their bodies became shrines: what was thought to be their minds became temples suitable for worship. These crazy Saints stared out at the world, wildly, like lunatics—or quietly, like suicides; and the "God" that was in their gaze was as mute as a great stone.

Who were these Saints? These crazy, loony, pitiful women?

Some of them, without a doubt, were our mothers and grandmothers.

In the still heat of the post-Reconstruction South, this is how they seemed to Jean Toomer: exquisite butterflies trapped in an evil honey, toiling away their lives in an era, a century, that did not acknowledge them, except as "the *mule* of the world." They dreamed dreams that no one knew—not even themselves, in any coherent fashion—and saw visions no one could understand. They wandered or sat about the countryside crooning lullabies to ghosts, and drawing the mother of Christ in charcoal on courthouse walls.

They forced their minds to desert their bodies and their striving spirits sought to rise, like frail whirlwinds from the hard red clay. And when those frail whirlwinds fell, in scattered particles, upon the ground, no one mourned. Instead, men lit candles to celebrate the emptiness that remained, as people do who enter a beautiful but vacant space to resurrect a God.

Our mothers and grandmothers, some of them: moving to music not yet written. And they waited.

They waited for a day when the unknown thing that was in them would be made known; but guessed, somehow in their darkness, that on the day of their revelation they would be long dead. Therefore to Toomer they walked, and even ran, in slow motion. For they were going nowhere immediate, and the future was not yet within their grasp. And men took our mothers and grandmothers, "but got no pleasure from it." So complex was their passion and their calm.

To Toomer, they lay vacant and fallow as autumn fields, with harvest time never in sight: and he saw them enter loveless marriages, without joy; and become prostitutes, without resistance; and become mothers of children, without fulfillment.

For these grandmothers and mothers of ours were not Saints, but Artists; driven to a numb and bleeding madness by the springs of creativity in them for which there was no release. They were Creators, who lived lives of spiritual waste, because they were so rich in spirituality—which is the basis of Art—that the strain of enduring their unused and unwanted talent drove them insane. Throwing away this spirituality was their pathetic attempt to lighten the soul to a weight their work-worn, sexually abused bodies could bear.

What did it mean for a black woman to be an artist in our grandmothers' time? In our great-grandmothers' day? It is a question with an answer cruel enough to stop the blood.

Did you have a genius of a great-great-grandmother who died under some ignorant and depraved white overseer's lash? Or was she required to bake biscuits for a lazy backwater tramp, when she cried out in her soul to paint watercolors of sunsets, or the rain falling on the green and peaceful pasturelands? Or was her body broken and forced to bear children (who were more often than not sold away from her)—eight, ten, fifteen, twenty children—when her one joy was the thought of modeling heroic figures of rebellion, in stone or clay?

How was the creativity of the black woman kept alive, year after year and century after century, when for most of the years black people have been in America, it was a punishable crime for a black person to read or write? And the freedom to paint, to sculpt, to expand the mind with action did not exist. Consider, if you can bear to imagine it, what might have been the result if singing, too, had been forbidden by law. Listen to the voices of Bessie Smith, Billie Holiday, Nina Simone, Roberta Flack, and Aretha Franklin, among others, and imagine those voices muzzled for life. Then you may begin to comprehend the lives of our "crazy," "Sainted" mothers and grandmothers. The agony of the lives of women who might have been Poets, Novelists, Essayists, and Short-Story Writers (over a period of centuries), who died with their real gifts stifled within them.

And, if this were the end of the story, we would have cause to cry out in my paraphrase of Okot p'Bitek's great poem:

> *O, my clanswomen*
> *Let us all cry together!*
> *Come,*
> *Let us mourn the death of our mother,*
> *The death of a Queen*
> *The ash that was produced*
> *By a great fire!*
> *O, this homestead is utterly dead*
> *Close the gates*
> *With* lacari *thorns,*
> *For our mother*
> *The creator of the Stool is lost!*
> *And all the young women*
> *Have perished in the wilderness!*

But this is not the end of the story, for all the young women—our mothers and grandmothers, *ourselves*—have not perished in the wilderness. And if we ask ourselves why, and search for and find the answer, we will know beyond all efforts to erase it from our minds, just exactly who, and of what, we black American women are.

One example, perhaps the most pathetic, most misunderstood one, can provide a backdrop for our mothers' work: Phillis Wheatley, a slave in the 1700s.

Virginia Woolf, in her book *A Room of One's Own*, wrote that in order for a woman to write fiction she must have two things, certainly: a room of her own (with key and lock) and enough money to support herself.

What then are we to make of Phillis Wheatley, a slave, who owned not even herself? This sickly, frail black girl who required a servant of her own at times—her health was so precarious—and who, had she been white, would have been easily considered the intellectual superior of all the women and most of the men in the society of her day.

Virginia Woolf wrote further, speaking of course not of our Phillis, that "any woman born with a great gift in the sixteenth century [insert "eighteenth century," insert "black woman," insert "born or made a slave"] would certainly have gone crazed, shot herself, or ended her days in some lonely cottage outside the village, half witch, half wizard [insert "Saint"], feared and mocked at. For it needs little skill and psychology to be sure that a highly gifted girl who had tried to use her gift for poetry would have been so thwarted and hindered by contrary instincts [add "chains, guns, the lash, the ownership of one's body by someone else, submission to an alien religion"], that she must have lost her health and sanity to a certainty."

The key words, as they relate to Phillis, are "contrary instincts." For when we read the poetry of Phillis Wheatley—as when we read the novels of Nella Larsen or the oddly false-sounding autobiography of that freest of all black women writers, Zora Hurston—evidence of "contrary instincts" is everywhere. Her loyalties were completely divided, as was, without question, her mind.

But how could this be otherwise? Captured at seven, a slave of wealthy, doting whites who instilled in her the "savagery" of the Africa they "rescued" her from . . . one wonders if she was even able to remember her homeland as she had known it, or as it really was.

Yet, because she did try to use her gift for poetry in a world that made her a slave, she was "so thwarted and hindered by . . . contrary instincts, that she . . . lost her health. . . ." In the last years of her brief life, burdened not only with the need to express her gift but also with a penniless, friendless "freedom" and several small children for whom she was forced to do strenuous work to feed, she lost her health, certainly. Suffering from malnutrition and neglect and who knows what mental agonies, Phillis Wheatley died.

So torn by "contrary instincts" was black, kidnapped, enslaved Phillis that her description of "the Goddess"—as she poetically called the Liberty she did not have—is ironically, cruelly humorous. And, in fact, has held Phillis up to ridicule for more than a century. It is usually read prior to hanging Phillis's memory as that of a fool. She wrote:

> *The Goddess comes, she moves divinely fair,*
> *Olive and laurel binds her golden hair.*
> *Wherever shines this native of the skies,*
> *Unnumber'd charms and recent graces rise.* [My italics]

It is obvious that Phillis, the slave, combed the "Goddess's" hair every morning; prior, perhaps, to bringing in the milk, or fixing her mistress's lunch. She took her imagery from the one thing she saw elevated above all others.

With the benefit of hindsight we ask, "How could she?"

But at last, Phillis, we understand. No more snickering when your stiff, struggling, ambivalent lines are forced on us. We know now that you were not an idiot or a traitor; only a sickly little black girl, snatched from your home and country and made a slave; a woman who still struggled to sing the song that was your gift, although in a land of barbarians who praised you for your bewildered tongue. It is not so much what you sang, as that you kept alive, in so many of our ancestors, *the notion of song.*

Black women are called, in the folklore that so aptly identifies one's status in society, "the *mule* of the world," because we have been handed the burdens that everyone else—*everyone* else—refused to carry. We have also been called "Matriarchs," "Superwomen," and "Mean and Evil Bitches." Not to mention "Castraters" and "Sapphire's Mama." When we have pleaded for understanding, our character has been distorted; when we have asked for simple caring, we have been handed empty inspirational appellations, then stuck in the farthest corner. When we have asked for love, we have been given children. In short, even our plainer gifts, our labors of fidelity and love, have been knocked down our throats. To be an artist and a black woman, even today, lowers our status in many respects, rather than raises it: and yet, artists we will be.

Therefore we must fearlessly pull out of ourselves and look at and identify with our lives the living creativity some of our great-grandmothers were not allowed to know. I stress *some* of them because it is well known that the majority of our great-grandmothers knew, even without "know-ing" it, the reality of their spirituality, even if they didn't recognize it beyond what happened in the singing at church—and they never had any intention of giving it up.

How they did it—those millions of black women who were not Phillis Wheatley, or Lucy Terry or Frances Harper or Zora Hurston or Nella Larsen or Bessie Smith; or Elizabeth Catlett, or Katherine Dunham, either—brings me to the title of this essay, "In Search of Our Mothers' Gardens," which is a personal account that is yet shared, in its theme and its meaning, by all of us. I found, while thinking about the far-reaching world of the creative black woman, that often the truest answer to a question that really matters can be found very close.

In the late 1920s my mother ran away from home to marry my father. Marriage, if not running away, was expected of seventeen-year-old girls. By the time she was twenty, she had two children and was pregnant with a third. Five children later, I was born. And this is how I came to know my mother: she seemed a large, soft, loving-eyed woman who was rarely impa-tient in our home. Her quick, violent temper was on view only a few times a year, when she battled with the white landlord who had the misfortune to suggest to her that her children did not need to go to school.

She made all the clothes we wore, even my brothers' overalls. She made all the towels and sheets we used. She spent the summers canning vegeta-bles and fruits. She spent the winter evenings making quilts enough to cover all our beds.

During the "working" day, she labored beside—not behind—my father in the fields. Her day began before sunup, and did not end until late at night. There was never a moment for her to sit down, undisturbed, to un-ravel her own private thoughts; never a time free from interruption—by work or the noisy inquiries of her many children. And yet, it is to my mother—and all our mothers who were not famous—that I went in search of the secret of what has fed that muzzled and often mutilated, but vibrant, creative spirit that the black woman has inherited, and that pops out in wild and unlikely places to this day.

But when, you will ask, did my overworked mother have time to know or care about feeding the creative spirit?

The answer is so simple that many of us have spent years discovering it. We have constantly looked high, when we should have looked high—and low.

For example: in the Smithsonian Institution in Washington, D.C., there hangs a quilt unlike any other in the world. In fanciful, inspired, and yet simple and identifiable figures, it portrays the story of the Crucifixion. It is considered rare, beyond price. Though it follows no known pattern of quilt-making, and though it is made of bits and pieces of worthless rags, it is obviously the work of a person of powerful imagination and deep spiritual feeling. Below this quilt I saw a note that says it was made by "an anonymous Black woman in Alabama, a hundred years ago."

If we could locate this "anonymous" black woman from Alabama, she would turn out to be one of our grandmothers—an artist who left her mark in the only materials she could afford, and in the only medium her position in society allowed her to use.

As Virginia Woolf wrote further, in *A Room of One's Own*:

> Yet genius of a sort must have existed among women as it must have existed among the working class. [Change this to "slaves" and "the wives and daughters of sharecroppers."] Now and again an Emily Brontë or a Robert Burns [change this to "a Zora Hurston or a Richard Wright"] blazes out and proves its presence. But certainly it never got itself on to paper. When, however, one reads of a witch being ducked, of a woman possessed by devils [or "Sainthood"], of a wise woman selling herbs [our root workers], or even a very remarkable man who had a mother, then I think we are on the track of a lost novelist, a suppressed poet, of some mute and inglorious Jane Austen. . . . Indeed, I would venture to guess that Anon, who wrote so many poems without signing them, was often a woman. . . .

And so our mothers and grandmothers have, more often than not anonymously, handed on the creative spark, the seed of the flower they themselves never hoped to see: or like a sealed letter they could not plainly read.

And so it is, certainly, with my own mother. Unlike "Ma" Rainey's songs, which retained their creator's name even while blasting forth from Bessie Smith's mouth, no song or poem will bear my mother's name. Yet so many of the stories that I write, that we all write, are my mother's stories. Only recently did I fully realize this: that through years of listening to my mother's stories of her life, I have absorbed not only the stories themselves, but something of the manner in which she spoke, something of the urgency that involves the knowledge that her stories—like her life—must be recorded.

It is probably for this reason that so much of what I have written is about characters whose counterparts in real life are so much older than I am.

But the telling of these stories, which came from my mother's lips as naturally as breathing, was not the only way my mother showed herself as an artist. For stories, too, were subject to being distracted, to dying without conclusion. Dinners must be started, and cotton must be gathered before the big rains. The artist that was and is my mother showed itself to me only after many years. This is what I finally noticed:

Like Mem, a character in *The Third Life of Grange Copeland*, my mother adorned with flowers whatever shabby house we were forced to live in. And not just your typical straggly country stand of zinnias, either. She planted ambitious gardens—and still does—with over fifty different varieties of plants that bloom profusely from early March until late November. Before she left home for the fields, she watered her flowers, chopped up the grass, and laid out new beds. When she returned from the fields she might divide clumps of bulbs, dig a cold pit, uproot and replant roses, or prune branches from her taller bushes or trees—until night came and it was too dark to see.

Whatever she planted grew as if by magic, and her fame as a grower of flowers spread over three counties. Because of her creativity with her flowers, even my memories of poverty are seen through a screen of blooms—sunflowers, petunias, roses, dahlias, forsythia, spirea, delphiniums, verbena . . . and on and on.

And I remember people coming to my mother's yard to be given cuttings from her flowers; I hear again the praise showered on her because whatever rocky soil she landed on, she turned into a garden. A garden so brilliant with colors, so original in its design, so magnificent with life and creativity, that to this day people drive by our house in Georgia—perfect strangers and imperfect strangers—and ask to stand or walk among my mother's art.

I notice that it is only when my mother is working in her flowers that she is radiant, almost to the point of being invisible—except as Creator: hand and eye. She is involved in work her soul must have. Ordering the universe in the image of her personal conception of Beauty.

Her face, as she prepares the Art that is her gift, is a legacy of respect she leaves to me, for all that illuminates and cherishes life. She has handed down respect for the possibilities—and the will to grasp them.

For her, so hindered and intruded upon in so many ways, being an artist has still been a daily part of her life. This ability to hold on, even in very simple ways, is work black women have done for a very long time.

This poem is not enough, but it is something, for the woman who literally covered the holes in our walls with sunflowers:

> *They were women then*
> *My mama's generation*
> *Husky of voice—Stout of*
> *Step*
> *With fists as well as*
> *Hands*
> *How they battered down*
> *Doors*
> *And ironed*
> *Starched white*
> *Shirts*
> *How they led*
> *Armies*
> *Headragged Generals*
> *Across mined*
> *Fields*
> *Booby-trapped*
> *Kitchens*
> *To discover books*
> *Desks*
> *A place for us*
> *How they knew what we*
> Must *know*
> *Without knowing a page*
> *Of it*
> *Themselves.*

Guided by my heritage of a love of beauty and a respect for strength—in search of my mother's garden, I found my own.

And perhaps in Africa over two hundred years ago, there was just such a mother; perhaps she painted vivid and daring decorations in oranges and yellows and greens on the walls of her hut; perhaps she sang—in a voice like Roberta Flack's—*sweetly* over the compounds of her village; perhaps she wove the most stunning mats or told the most ingenious stories of all the village storytellers. Perhaps she was herself a poet—though only her daughter's name is signed to the poems that we know.

Perhaps Phillis Wheatley's mother was also an artist.

Perhaps in more than Phillis Wheatley's biological life is her mother's signature made clear.

Analyze

1. Walker quotes Virginia Woolf directly, but inserts historical women of color into Woolf's text. What effect does this have? How does it contribute to her overall argument?

2. What are "contrary instincts"? How does Walker use Phillis Wheatley's story to illustrate this idea?

3. How does Walker manage to create a sense of hopefulness while still critically addressing oppression, trauma, and stifled creativity?

Explore

1. Walker challenges her readers: "Listen to the voices of Bessie Smith, Billie Holiday, Nina Simone, Roberta Flack, and Aretha Franklin, among others, and imagine those voices muzzled for life." Find and listen to recordings by a few of these artists. Does hearing these voices make Walker's argument less abstract and more real? How so?

2. Look more closely at the poem Walker includes at the end of her essay "for the woman who literally covered the holes in our walls with sunflowers." Write an explication of this poem using Walker's text as support for your interpretation.

3. Look up Walker's definition of "womanist." How is her essay an example of womanist prose?

Jade Chong-Smith
"Hard Time: Lessons from a Maximum-Security Prison"

Jade Chong-Smith is a student at Yale Law School. Before beginning her studies at Yale, she worked for the Canadian federal government and as a legal literacy consultant for the Commonwealth of Learning, an intergovernmental agency that helps developing countries improve access to quality education. In "Hard Time: Lessons from a Maximum-Security Prison," published by the *Huffington Post* in 2014, Chong-Smith uses personal narrative to examine issues of race, class, and gender within the prison industrial complex. As you read, consider whether her narrative approach helps or hinders her argument.

I first went to prison a year ago. I left the city I was familiar with, took a winding drive through faded towns, passed diners I imagined once saw better days, passed the final gas station.

I arrived at a maximum-security prison in a corner of New York state. It was an imposing fortress of concrete, loops of barbed wire, and layers of fencing, and corridors upon corridors divided by sliding metal doors, which locked in over 2,000 men, most of them serving sentences of 25 years to life.

In the entranceway, a long line of women slowly shuffled forward, each laden with grocery bags stuffed with potato chips and other processed snacks. Guards with wooden batons holstered at their hips, thumbs hooked into their belts, strolled about. The women were waiting for prison officials to inspect their food items and then transfer them to prisoners who missed the taste of what were now, to them, luxuries. Those behind bars here were likely the husbands, boyfriends, fathers, sons, or brothers of those patiently waiting in line.

It was impossible not to notice that every woman in line was a woman of color.

When I tell the guards I'm a law school student, they look confused. *What is she doing here?*

I'm with a small delegation of other Yale students, participating in a seminar twice a month that brings together law students and convicted felons to break down communication barriers between those inside and outside of prison.

This prison is not that different from other big prisons across America, built on the outskirts of small towns, typically with high rates of unemployment. Since the 1980s, the majority of prisons in America have been built in depressed, rural areas in an attempt to create jobs and spur growth. These areas are also predominantly white; as a consequence, guards who are primarily white watch over prisoners who are primarily minorities.

The guards told me much the same story: they sacrifice their lives to working in prison so that their children won't have to. "I drive exactly 48 miles to work and back every day to pay for my son to go to college, so he won't ever work here," one male guard said. "I know it's a 48-mile drive because I dread going to work, and I can't wait to get home."

I asked some of the guards what they thought of the prisoners. "Some of them just need to go home," said one. "But some of them are 'baby rapers'— they deserve to be here." Another declared: "We always have to watch our backs, because you never know when violence will break out, and you can never be too careful." Yet another hardened guard warned me: "Never tell anyone your full name, where you live, or any other identifying information about yourself. You don't want convicted felons to find you when they get out."

I was intimidated before I even entered the cellblocks.

My classmates and I had to go through the metal detector. The underwire in my bra set it off. I was directed towards a nearby broom closet, where I removed my bra from underneath my thick sweater. I placed it in a brown paper bag, and reemerged to hand it to a guard. The second time through, shoulders hunched, I passed. I was allowed back in the closet to put my bra back on.

Next, we went through a series of metal doors. Each opened before me only after the ones behind me clanged shut.

Yellow lines down the center divided the hallways like roadways, with stop signs at each intersection.

"NO TALKING," demanded the signs on the walls.

Even when only one or two guards were in sight, there was an overwhelming sense of control.

We reached the prison block for educational programs. I found myself in a room full of prisoners. All wore the standard one-color prison uniform. Scars and tattoos snaked around their necks and arms.

These men greeted me with warm smiles and friendly handshakes.

I was embarrassed to think that if I had been on the street and seen them, I probably would have been intimidated and crossed to the other side.

Conversation flowed and laughter came easily as they peppered us with questions.

What is it like to live on your own, and to do your own laundry? What is it like to go to a bar? What is it like to own a cell phone? What is Facebook like?

I learned most of these men had been incarcerated since they were as young as 17-years-old, and had been sentenced as adults. They hadn't done many of the mundane daily things that I did without a second thought, but they had also lived through much more than I had.

They spoke of growing up in public housing in Harlem, the Bronx, or Queens, where violence was the default way of resolving issues, and where they were at once over-policed and under-protected. Even before their teenage years, they took for granted that, in all likelihood, they would spend some time in jail. After all, most men in their community they knew had.

Despite the challenges the prisoners still faced, I found a sense of resilience. Curious and hard working, most of them had completed their high school equivalencies in prison, and they were studying, among other courses, business, paralegal skills, creative writing, and communication skills. One man had learned to read ancient Egyptian hieroglyphs. Another spoke of his plans to start a charity and counseling program for at-risk youth when he got out. A third man described the lawsuit he was filing in federal court to challenge what he perceived as the unconstitutional vagueness of the felony statute he had been charged under.

"Do you want to go home?" I asked the men.

Only about half raised their hands. They knew all too well the challenges they will likely face upon release because of their status as convicted felons: they may struggle to make ends meet without food stamps or temporary assistance benefits; they might be ineligible for public housing, and may face homelessness; they could be denied the right to vote; and they will have great difficulty finding a job. As a condition of their parole, they could be prohibited from associating with previously convicted felons, denying them the support of friendships they made and relied on while in prison.

As a society, we have repeatedly let all such individuals down.

First, we have perpetuated the social and economic inequality that disproportionately disadvantages those who are impoverished, or minorities, or both. In part due to the legacy of segregation and other racially discriminatory policies, African Americans and Hispanics are more likely to be living in poverty, and to be targeted by more aggressive policing tactics. A white person or anyone growing up in the middle-class is much less likely to fall under the supervision of the criminal justice system. According to the NAACP, in 2008, African Americans and Hispanics, who accounted for about 25 percent of the American population, comprised 58 percent of all prisoners in the U.S. If these two groups were incarcerated at the same rate as white Americans, the U.S. prison and jail populations would be cut in half. These patterns partly explain why the U.S. has more persons in prison than any other country in the world, ahead of China and Russia in absolute and per capita terms.

Second, we have substituted prisons for mental hospitals. Instead of treating people with mental illnesses, we lock them up and punish them. A 2014 report by the Treatment Advocacy Center found that America's prisons hold more than 10 times as many mentally ill people than its mental hospitals do. While in prison, individuals are unable to access the mental health services they need, and many aspects of incarceration only worsen their mental health problems.

Third, we impose obstacles and deny ex-felons the support they most need upon re-entering society, in rehabilitation programs and social services. By doing so, we actually make it more likely they will commit another crime, or harm themselves. According to the Bureau of Justice Statistics, about two-thirds of those released from prison will reoffend within three years of their release. Recently released prisoners are at a much higher risk of suicide or drug overdose compared to the general population.

These three failures deny young men of color, and their families, an equal shot at success available to other Americans.

This past summer, while working in the Harlem Community Law Office of New York City's Legal Aid Society, I witnessed some of these consequences firsthand. My job was to sort out problems with access to public benefits, including helping those whose applications for welfare had been unjustly denied or whose benefits had been erroneously terminated. All of my clients were women of color. Almost all were single mothers struggling to provide for their families. The men who had been in their lives were incarcerated. The only child support those men could pay was drawn from what they earned from prison labor, at 12 cents to $1.15 an hour. The women I represented this summer could have been the very same women I saw struggling to visit their family members in prison on weekends.

At my most recent bi-monthly session at the maximum-security prison, the group of prisoners spoke of their struggles to parent from within the prison walls. Some said they felt their children were making bad decisions, and they didn't know how to stop them from doing so. They concluded it was best to act as a listener rather than an instructor. I could tell that they were deeply dissatisfied that this was all they could do.

Republicans argue that punitive sentences are essential to a tough-on-crime approach that keeps our streets safe.

I see building stronger communities with adequate support mechanisms, not building stronger prisons, as the path to a safer society.

The average annual cost of incarcerating one person in a maximum-security facility is upwards of $33,000. Do we want to spend $33,000 a year to separate a man from his family, to leave his children fatherless, and to subject him to a thousand indignities that are focused more on punishment than on rehabilitation? In punishing this man, we rob his family of his presence and support. We rob him of the very services that would make it less likely he would re-offend upon release. We fracture communities and ultimately leave them more dangerous.

Surely we could better keep our streets safe by using some of the millions we spend on prisons on socioeconomic policies and programs that reduce inequality, promote education, and make available more mental health services, putting more of an emphasis on prevention and rehabilitation, rather than punishment.

Every two weeks, I go back to the maximum-security prison. With each visit, the men affirm to me that individuals are so much more than a set of legal problems; more than just victims of circumstances beyond their control; more than a single wrongful act, and more than innately good or bad.

I don't expect people to take my word about this. Instead, people should see for themselves.

See the disproportionate effect mandatory minimum sentences, harsh parole policies, and three-strike rules have had on already marginalized communities. See how dehumanizing the prison experience is, for guards and prisoners alike. Understand the world from another lived reality and seriously reflect on the actual on-the-ground consequences of the large-scale policy issues we consider so abstractly.

If every American could visit a prison, they might better see why we need to change this broken system.

Analyze

1. Why does Chong-Smith choose to create space around the statement, "It was impossible not to notice that every woman in line was a woman of color," leaving it separate from the text that precedes and follows it?

2. Chong-Smith could have easily omitted the section of her piece where she describes having to go into a closet to remove and then replace her underwire bra. It isn't needed for her to make her claim clear. Why does she choose to include this detail despite this fact?

3. What is her purpose in ending the essay with the claim, "If every American could visit a prison, they might better see why we need to change this broken system"?

Explore

1. Chong-Smith writes, "I found myself in a room full of prisoners. All wore the standard one-color prison uniform. Scars and tattoos snaked around their necks and arms. These men greeted me with warm smiles and friendly handshakes. I was embarrassed to think that if I had been on the street and seen them, I probably would have been intimidated and crossed to the other side." Why does she admit her embarrassment? Have you ever experienced something similar? Write a personal narrative that reveals how your expectations of a person or a community were changed because of this type of interaction.

2. Summarize the three failures Chong-Smith argues "deny young men of color, and their families, an equal shot at success available to other Americans." Do you agree with this part of her argument? Why or why not?

3. Do some research on the "school-to-prison pipeline." What is it? How does it add to the conversation begun here by Chong-Smith?

Jonathan Zimmerman
"The Coming Out We All Ignored"

Jonathan Zimmerman is a professor of history of education and the director of the history of education program in New York University's Steinhardt School of Culture, Education, and Human Development. Zimmerman's books include *Small Wonder: The Little Red Schoolhouse in History and Memory*

(2009) and *Innocents Abroad: American Teachers in the American Century* (2006). He is a frequent contributor to periodicals such as the *New York Times* and the *Washington Post*.

"The Coming Out We All Ignored," which was published by the *New York Daily News* in May 2013, is a critique of the media's coverage of Brittney Griner's coming out, which happened a few days after she was selected first overall in the WNBA draft on 15 April 2013. As you read this article, think about the stereotypes of female athletes that Zimmerman is evoking here. Why does he do this? What does he hope to get us to think about?

Hey, did you hear the big sports news? One of the best basketball players of our time just came out as gay. I'm not talking about Jason Collins, the journeyman NBA center who came out on Monday. This season, playing for two teams, he averaged just over 1 point a game.

I'm talking instead about Brittney Griner, the first NCAA player to score 2,000 points and block 500 shots. A three-time All-American, she was the No. 1 pick in the Women's National Basketball Association draft on April 15. A few days later, Griner told interviewers that she's gay.

And the world shrugged. "Can you imagine if it was a man who did the exact same thing?" asked one gay blogger. "Everyone's head would have exploded."

That's what happened after *Sports Illustrated* published an article by Collins acknowledging that he's homosexual. The airwaves and blogosphere lit up with praise for Collins, from sources as varied as Chelsea Clinton (who attended Stanford with him) and Kobe Bryant.

So why didn't Griner's coming out make headlines, too? Call it the Double Standard of Sports Sexuality: Male athletes can't be gay, but females are assumed to be. Far from shocking our sensibilities, Griner's announcement confirmed them.

And these beliefs go all the way back to the late 19th century, when schools began to sponsor male athletic teams. According to the era's doctrine of "Muscular Christianity," embraced most famously by Theodore Roosevelt, modern urban society was squelching men's "natural" energy and vigor. Sports would help men rediscover these rustic virtues and guard against the "feminization" of city life.

So any woman who played sports was also challenging a male preserve. Feminists such as Elizabeth Cady Stanton had long pressed for female exercise and athletics, which would help improve girls' health and counter claims of male "physical superiority," as Stanton wrote in 1850.

But a half-century later, amid new anxieties over American masculinity, athletic women were forced to demonstrate that they were not simply acting like men.

One female physical education teacher assured readers that girls' sports teams would not create "the loud masculinely dressed man-aping individual but the wholehearted rosy-cheeked health girl." Indeed, phys-ed programs often required that women entering the major have an "attractive" appearance.

The All-American Girls Professional Baseball League—memorialized in *A League of Their Own*—required players to follow what league managers called the "femininity principle": They had to wear skirts and makeup, keep their hair long and even attend an evening charm school. A player who got a bob haircut was fired.

And the most dominant female athlete of the early 20th century, Babe Didrikson, was ridiculed by newspapermen as "mannish" and "not quite female." So when Didrikson married a pro wrestler in 1938, America breathed a collective sigh of relief. "Along came a great big he-man and the Babe forgot all her man-hating chatter," one reporter gushed.

It wasn't until the 1980s that tennis greats Billie Jean King and Martina Navratilova could come out of the closet; more recently, basketball stars such as Sheryl Swoopes and Chamique Holdsclaw have done the same.

But all that also placed a new pressure on female athletes, who are now often assumed to be lesbians until proven otherwise. That might explain why the initial chorus of hosannas for Collins didn't include many prominent straight sportswomen. If they praised a gay athlete, wouldn't people think they were gay as well?

For male athletes, by comparison, it was a piece of cake. Bryant and other NBA stars rallied behind Collins, without anyone questioning their own sexuality.

The only people who took real flak were the handful of athletes who raised eyebrows about Collins. When Miami Dolphins wide receiver Mike Wallace tweeted, "All these beautiful women in the world and guys wanna mess with other guys," the reaction was so swift that Wallace quickly deleted the tweet and apologized.

We owe our biggest apology to all the gay athletes, male and female, who have been ridiculed and silenced over the years. And we should congratulate

Collins, who has boldly gone where no standing professional sportsman ventured before.

But in the process, we should also recognize this moment as a marker of gender inequality, not just of emerging gay rights. The taboo on male homosexuality remains far greater than the one on lesbianism. That makes it more difficult for male athletes to come out as gay, but it also extends the historic burden on sportswomen to prove that they're not. And it makes it harder for all of us to be what we should be, once and for all: ourselves.

Analyze

1. Why does Zimmerman begin his article by pointing out the difference between Collins's and Griner's quality of play? How does this help set up his argument that the media needed to pay more attention to Griner's coming out?

2. How does Zimmerman use the history of the treatment of women in sports to emphasize that there has been a long-standing assumption that women who play sports are not only mannish but also non-heterosexual?

3. Why does Zimmerman believe the media's silence on Griner's coming out both reflects a step forward in LGBT rights and demonstrates a continued gender inequality in sports?

Explore

1. Given Gloria Steinem's argument in "If Men Could Menstruate," how might she respond to Zimmerman's claims in this essay? Why?

2. Take a look at the article "Twitter Reaction to Jason Collins Coming Out," available on the NBA's website. Can you find a similar article documenting support for Griner? If so, what are Griner's supporters saying? If not, why don't you think this kind of article exists?

3. In this article, Zimmerman references several other famous female athletes who have come out as gay, including Billie Jean King, Martina Navratilova, Sheryl Swoopes, and Chamique Holdsclaw. How were these athletes treated when they came out? How do their stories compare to Griner's? Choose one of these women (or another female athlete who is LGBTQ+) and write an essay that discusses the way in which female athletes, especially gay female athletes, are perceived by society.

Sarah McMahon
"Rape Myth Beliefs and Bystander Attitudes among Incoming College Students"

Sarah McMahon is an assistant professor of social work at Rutgers University in New Jersey and the associate director of the Center on Violence against Women and Children. This article, which was published in the *Journal of American College Health* in 2010, examines the intersection between the acceptance of rape myths and bystander attitudes of college males and females. As you read, consider how McMahon's research contributes to the conversation about rape culture on college and university campuses.

It is widely demonstrated that rape is a major public health problem on college campuses, with research suggesting that 3% of college women are raped during a 9-month period and one fifth to one fourth of all women experience a completed or attempted rape during their 4- to 5-year college careers.[1] The devastating impact of rape on victims has been well documented, including negative outcomes on physical health, mental health, academic performance, and interpersonal relationships.[2-5] In response, many colleges now provide various services to respond to survivors, such as crisis intervention and counseling. Additionally, the federal government mandated that all higher education institutions receiving federal funds must provide rape prevention programs.[6]

One increasingly popular and promising approach for rape prevention is a focus on bystander intervention. The idea reflects the current shift in the field of rape prevention from a focus on victims and perpetrators to the role of community members, and suggests that individuals in a community can intervene when faced with situations involving sexual violence.[7,8] This is reinforced by a recent call from the Centers for Disease Control and Prevention[9] to shift efforts within the field of sexual violence to focus on primary prevention and the responsibility of the larger community. The call for this shift has impacted colleges and universities as well. For example, the American College Health Association recently issued a position statement calling for college health professionals to recognize the importance of the primary prevention of sexual violence, and to develop strategies to engage the campus community.[10]

The bystander approach holds particular promise for addressing rape on college campuses, which may be considered "at risk" environments.[11] On college campuses, most assaults are committed by someone known to the victim,[12] often involve alcohol intoxication[13,14] and occur in social settings with others present, such as residence halls or fraternities.[12] Burn[15] suggests that in these settings, bystanders are often present during the "preassault phase" where risk markers appear, and if equipped with the correct skills, can intervene to interrupt these situations. Hence, bystander intervention may be a potentially powerful prevention tool to ultimately reduce the occurrence of rape.[15,16] In addition to primary prevention, bystanders can also respond after an assault occurs, providing support and resources to victims.[7] Part of the appeal of this approach is that it offers all students an opportunity to take part in rape prevention, not just those identified as high-risk, which is consistent with the public health framework.[9]

However, for rape prevention programs to effectively prepare individuals to act as bystanders, we must further our understanding of what factors facilitate and prevent action, and thus what content to include in educational programming for students.[15,16] One of the factors that may influence whether bystanders intervene in situations involving sexual assault relates to their beliefs about rape and rape victims. Previous yet limited research suggests that an individual's willingness to intervene may be impacted by their perception of rape victims' "worthiness," responsibility for their own assault, and beliefs in other rape myths.[15] The present study further explores the relationship between acceptance of rape myths and willingness to engage in a range of bystander behaviors in a sample of university students.

Bystander Intervention and Rape Prevention

The idea of bystander intervention originated after the landmark case involving the murder of a woman named Kitty Genovese in New York in 1964. The assault occurred in public and there were numerous witnesses who did not intervene, and thus began the often-cited work of researchers Latane and Darley who studied how bystanders react to emergency situations and why they do not intervene.[17] The idea of bystander behavior is well established in the field of social psychology and is utilized internationally, largely to explore individuals' reactions to witnessing crimes and emergencies.[7,18,19]

In recent years, the role of bystander intervention has been extended by researchers as a possible technique for rape prevention, especially on college campuses. This strategy departs from previous program efforts that were focused on audience members as potential perpetrators or victims, and instead emphasizes the potential role of all community members in reducing rape.[7] According to the bystander approach, individuals play an important role in "interrupting situations that could lead to assault before it happens or during an incident, speaking out against social norms that support rape, and having skills to be an effective and supportive ally to survivors."[20(p464)]

The literature on sexual violence and bystander intervention is limited but promising.[21] Foubert has reported positive findings from *The Men's Program*, which focuses on approaching men as "potential helpers." Multiple evaluations of the program have demonstrated long-term changes in men's attitudes and behavior, including decreases in rape myth acceptance and likelihood of raping, increases in empathy towards rape victims, increased willingness to curtail sexist comments, and a greater likeliness to offer support to rape victims.[21-25] The Mentors in Violence Prevention (MVP) program is a nationally recognized education program for student-athletes and leaders to encourage leadership on issues of violence against women.[26] Internal evaluation of the MVP program indicates that among other findings, students feel more able to intervene, such as telling a friend to stop calling his girlfriend names.[27] "Bringing in the Bystander" was developed by Vicki Banyard and her colleagues and demonstrates the most empirically and theoretically supported bystander intervention (BI) model to date.[11] Their model has been developed rigorously over time and found to increase positive bystander attitudes and behaviors with both the general student population[20] and "high-risk" students such as athletes and members of sororities and fraternities,[28] and student leaders.[11]

Research on the factors that facilitate or hinder a bystander's decision to intervene in situations involving sexual assault is in its infancy. Greater acceptance of rape myths has been identified by Burn[15] and Banyard[16] as a potential barrier to the ability of bystanders to intervene in sexual assault situations. Although these studies identified acceptance of rape myths as barriers to bystander intervention, the specifics of the relationship have not been explored. Rape myths are a broad construct, including several related yet distinct types of myths, and the research has not yet explored how these are related to bystander intervention.

Rape Myths

Rape myths were originally defined by Burt[29(p217)] as "prejudicial, stereotyped, or false beliefs about rape, rape victims, and rapists" and later described by Lonsway and Fitzgerald[30(p134)] as "attitudes and beliefs that are generally false yet widely and persistently held and that serve to deny and justify male sexual aggression against women." Common rape myths cited over time include the belief that the way a woman dresses or acts indicates that "she asked for it," or that rape occurs because men cannot control their sexual impulses. Researchers have demonstrated that the acceptance of rape myths not only indicates problematic attitudes, but is also an explanatory predictor in the actual perpetration of sexual violence.[31,32]

Measurement of rape myths often views it as a unidimensional construct, but research indicates that there may be various, related constructs—with some that focus on beliefs about the act of rape itself, with others about the victim or perpetrator. For example, The Illinois Rape Myth Acceptance Scale (IRMA) is arguably the most reliable and psychometrically demonstrated rape myth scale to date.[33] The scale consists of a general rape myth construct as well as 7 subscale constructs, including *She asked for it*; *It wasn't really rape*; *He didn't mean to*; *She wanted it*; *She lied*; *Rape is a trivial event*; and *Rape is a deviant event*. The IRMA authors conducted a series of studies to demonstrate the scale's construct validity through the relationship of the IRMA to empirically and theoretically related rape acceptance variables.[33] In their study with 951 undergraduates, McMahon and Farmer[34] revised the IRMA to provide updated language and to focus specifically on victim blaming. They used 4 of the IRMA's subscales (*She asked for it, It wasn't really rape, He didn't mean to, She lied*) and found evidence of a fifth factor (*Alcohol*) that specifically excused the perpetrator for the rape because he was drunk.

The complexity of rape myths is especially apparent among college students, who likely received some exposure to rape prevention education in some shape or form by the time they graduate high school and therefore may have greater awareness that certain traditional rape myths are not socially acceptable.[35,36] For example, Hinck and Thomas[37] found that college students with previous rape education had less adherence to rape myth beliefs. However, these myths may exist in various, more subtle and covert forms, especially regarding expressions about victim-blaming.[34] Although those rape myths that blatantly blame girls and women for rape have become less acceptable, many of the underlying beliefs that the girls and women did something to contribute to the assault and that it is not completely the perpetrator's fault still exist but in more covert expressions. For example, in a study conducted with college student-athletes, McMahon[38] found that respondents would not directly blame the victim for her assault, but expressed the belief that women put themselves in bad situations by dressing a certain way, drinking alcohol, or demonstrating other behaviors such as flirting. Additionally, some respondents indicated a belief that rape could happen accidentally or unintentionally, and that there are certain situations where men should not be held entirely accountable for sexual assault. Similarly, in a recent study, Ferro et al[39] found that college students knew that forced sex was rape and that the victim should not be blamed, but they were less clear about how accountable the perpetrator should be.

If individuals accept rape myths, especially those that blame the victim or excuse the perpetrator, the question remains as to whether they would be less likely to intervene as bystanders. If so, information is lacking about whether certain types of rape myths (ie, using alcohol to excuse the perpetrator or believing that victims asked for it) are more strongly prohibitive of positive bystander attitudes. Other than the work of Banyard and Burn, however, the relationship between rape myth acceptance and bystander attitudes and behavior has yet to be substantiated or explored. This has important implications for bystander rape prevention programs. With limited time to present programming to students, administrators must be parsimonious about what educational information to include. Some program administrators may wonder if they need to choose to focus either on rape myths or bystander intervention, or both. The purpose of this study is to further our understanding of the relationship between rape myths and students' willingness to intervene as bystanders. The research questions used to guide this study include the following: (1) In a sample of university students, what types of rape myths were most accepted? (2) Was acceptance of rape myths related to a willingness to intervene as a bystander? (3) Were certain types of rape myths more related to bystander attitudes?

Methods

Sample

This exploratory study was conducted with a convenience sample of approximately 2,500 undergraduate students attending new student orientation at a large, northeastern public university. All students who participated in the survey were first-year students residing on campus. A total of 2,446 students returned surveys for a response rate of 98%. Of those surveys, a total of 108 surveys were discarded during data cleaning, for a total of 2,338, representing 93.5% response rate.

Within the sample, 52% of respondents were female, with the remaining male (48%). Additionally, the majority were White (53%) followed by Asian/South Asian (24%); 23% planned on pledging to a sorority or fraternity, and 24% identified themselves as on an athletic team. Finally, 36% of respondents had attended a rape prevention program before; 29% reported that they knew someone who had been raped.

Procedure

All incoming students at the university explored in this study were required to attend a rape prevention program at orientation. Before the program began, the researchers explained and distributed paper surveys, informed consent forms, and pencils, which were collected after completion which lasted approximately 15 minutes. This study was approved by the Institutional Review Board.

Measures

Rape Myth Acceptance

To measure rape myth acceptance, the revised version of the IRMA was selected because the scale includes updated language for college students as well as having a specific focus on accountability for rape and victim blaming.[34] The scale includes a total of 19 items scored on a 5-point Likert scale (1 = strongly disagree with rape myths to 5 = strongly agree). The alpha coefficient in a previous study with 951 undergraduates was .87[34] and .86 in the present study. The scale includes 5 subscales.

The first subscale, *She asked for it*, reflects the belief that the victim's behaviors invited sexual assault. A sample statement is, "When girls go to parties wearing slutty clothes, they're asking for trouble." Five items are included on this subscale ($\alpha = .72$). The second subscale, *It wasn't really rape*, consists of 3 items ($\alpha = .74$) that deny that an assault occurred due to either blaming the victim or excusing the perpetrator; for example, "If the rapist doesn't have a weapon, you can't really call it a rape." *She lied*, the third subscale, consists of items that indicate the belief that the victim fabricated the rape, such as, "Girls who say they were raped often led the guy on and then had regrets." Five items are included ($\alpha = .83$). The fourth subscale, *He didn't mean to*, reflects the belief that the perpetrator did not intend to rape, with items such as, "When guys rape, it is because of their strong desire for sex." Four items are included ($\alpha = .69$). *He didn't mean to—Alcohol*, the fifth and final subscale, is a related construct to *He didn't mean to*, with a focus on intoxication of the perpetrator, such as "If both people are drunk, it can't be rape." This subscale shares one item that cross-loads with *He didn't mean to*, "If a guy is drunk, he might rape someone unintentionally." This scale includes three items ($\alpha = .60$).

Bystander Attitudes

To measure bystander attitudes, the Bystander Attitude Scale, Revised (BAS-R) was administered, which is a modified version of Banyard's Bystander Scale.[40,41] The scale contains 16 statements about behaviors in which students can engage to intervene before, during, or after a sexual assault. The scale includes statements about intervening in overt acts of violence such as "Report a friend that committed a rape" as well as more covert acts, such as "Say something to my friend who is taking a drunk person back to his/her room at a party." Additionally, it contains statements about intervening as a bystander to impact a culture that supports sexual violence, such as "Challenge a friend who uses 'ho,' 'bitch,' or 'slut' to describe girls." For each of the 16 statements, participants indicate how likely they are to engage in the behavior on a Likert scale from 1 to 5, "Not likely" to "Extremely likely." The BAS-R was selected because its language was updated for college students to reflect relevant discourse and settings.[41]

Demographic Items

A variety of demographic items were collected to determine whether attitudes and behaviors about acting as an engaged bystander were consistent between groups, including gender, status as a college athlete, intention to pledge a fraternity or sorority, knowing someone sexually assaulted, and receiving previous rape education. Additionally, in order to increase reliability, a question was added in the middle of the rape myth questionnaire that stated, "If you are still reading this survey, please circle 2."

Data Analyses

All data were carefully cleaned and triple-spot checked for accuracy. Cases that failed the reliability check item were removed, leaving a total of 2,388 cases. Missing data were reviewed using SPSS Missing Value Analysis. Due to low levels of missing data, maximum likelihood estimates were obtained using Expectation Maximization (EM) algorithm and imputed for all missing data.[42] A mean score was created for the Rape Myth Scale and each of the 5 subscales, as well as the BAS-R. All demographic items were dummy coded. Descriptive statistics were run as well as correlations among the variables. t tests were conducted to review whether significant differences existed among groups for rape myth acceptance and bystander attitudes. To determine the impact of rape myth beliefs on bystander attitudes and behaviors, a series of linear regression analyses were conducted.

Results

The overall mean for the rape myth scale was 2.51 ($SD = .56$) and the subscales were as follows, from highest to lowest: *He didn't mean to* ($M = 2.81$, $SD = .82$), *She lied* ($M = 2.79$, $SD = .73$), *She asked for it* ($M = 2.76$, $SD = .77$), *Alcohol* ($M = 2.13$, $SD = .76$), and *It wasn't really rape* ($M = 1.68$, $SD = .73$). The mean score for each rape myth item ranged from 1.34 to 3.39, indicating that the results were skewed towards a lower acceptance of rape myths (Table 2).[2] For bystander attitudes, the mean score was 3.64 ($SD = .58$). The mean score for each item ranged from 2.96 to 4.45, suggesting an overall willingness to intervene in most situations (Table 3).

All of the demographic items revealed significant results in the t tests for rape myths, although ethnicity was not included due to the small representation of most groups, which prevented meaningful analysis. Those students who indicated a significantly greater acceptance of rape myths than their counterparts included males, those pledging a fraternity/sorority,

Table 2. **Mean Scores of Rape Myths Items**

Item	Mean	SD
If a girl is raped while she is drunk, she is at least somewhat responsible for what happened. (SA)	2.53	1.22
When girls go to parties wearing slutty clothes, they are asking for trouble. (SA)	2.90	1.12
If a girl goes to a room alone with a guy at a party, it is her own fault if she is raped. (SA)	2.19	1.06
If a girl acts like a slut, eventually she is going to get into trouble. (SA)	3.39	1.07
When guys rape, it is usually because of their strong desire for sex. (MT)	2.94	1.20
Guys don't usually intend to force sex on a girl, but sometimes they get too sexually carried away. (MT)	2.95	1.05
Rape happens when a guy's sex drive gets out of control. (MT)	2.69	1.14
If a guy is drunk, he might rape someone unintentionally. (MT, SA)*	2.65	1.12
If both people are drunk, it can't be rape. (A)	2.02	1.04
It shouldn't be considered rape if a guy is drunk and didn't realize what he was doing. (A)	1.70	0.84
If a girl doesn't physically resist sex—even if protesting verbally— it really can't be considered rape. (NR)	1.92	1.02
If a girl doesn't physically fight back, you can't really say it was rape. (NR)	1.74	0.93
A lot of times, girls who say they were raped agreed to have sex and then regret it. (LI)	2.94	0.93
Rape accusations are often used as a way of getting back at guys. (LI)	2.89	0.95
Girls who say they were raped often led the guy on and then had regrets. (LI)	2.84	0.90
A lot of times, girls who claim they were raped just have emotional problems. (LI)	2.38	0.96
If the accused "rapist" doesn't have a weapon, you really can't call it a rape. (NR)	1.34	0.68
Girls who are caught cheating on their boyfriends sometimes claim that it was rape. (LI)	2.89	0.93
If a girl doesn't say "no," she can't claim rape. (NR)	2.78	1.22

Note. Rating of these items were made on a 5-point scale (1 = strongly disagree, 5 = strongly agree).

The abbreviations represent the subscales of the Rape Myths: SA = She asked for it; NR = It wasn't really rape; MT = He didn't mean to; A = Alcohol; LI = She lied.

*Item cross-loaded.

Table 3. **Mean Scores of Bystander Attitude Items**

Item	Mean	SD
Ask for verbal consent when I am intimate with my partner, even if we are in a long-term relationship.	3.67	1.23
Stop sexual activity when asked to, even if I am already sexually aroused.	4.35	0.90
Check in with my friend who looks drunk when s/he goes to a room with someone else at a party.	4.05	1.10
Say something to my friend who is taking a drunk person back to his/her room at a party.	3.88	1.07
Challenge a friend who made a sexist joke.	2.96	1.30
Express my concern if a family member makes a sexist joke.	3.04	1.34
Use the word "ho," "bitch," or "slut" to describe girls.	3.04	1.37
Challenge a friend who uses "ho," "bitch," or "slut" to describe girls.	2.68	1.25
Confront a friend who plans to give someone alcohol to get sex.	3.95	1.08
Refuse to participate in activities where girls' appearances are ranked/rated.	3.09	1.23
Listen to music that includes "ho," bitch," or "slut."	3.70	1.25
Confront a friend who is hooking up with someone who was passed out.	4.09	1.05
Confront a friend if I hear rumors that s/he forced sex on someone.	3.86	1.01
Report a friend that committed a rape.	3.71	1.05
Stop having sex with a partner if s/he says to stop, even if it started consensually.	4.45	0.84
Decide not to have sex with a partner if s/he is drunk.	3.93	1.08

Note. Rating of these items were made on a 5-point scale (1 = not likely, 5 = extremely likely).

athletes, those without previous rape education, and those who did not know someone sexually assaulted. For bystander attitudes, only 3 of the demographic variables were significant including males, those who did not receive previous rape education, and those who did not know anyone sexually assaulted.

Further, within at-risk groups (ie, athletes and those pledging a fraternity/sorority), there was a significant difference by gender for both rape myth acceptance and bystander attitudes. Male athletes ($M = 2.70, SD = .53$) reported significantly higher rape myth acceptance than female athletes ($M = 2.38, SD = .55$), $t(593) = -7.074, p < .001$. Male athletes also reported significantly less positive bystander attitudes ($M = 3.47, SD = .53$) than female athletes ($M = 3.89, SD = .54$), $t(584) = 9.399, p < .001$. Similarly, males intending to pledge a fraternity reported significantly higher rape myth acceptance ($M = 2.74, SD = .53$) than females pledging sororities ($M = 2.43, SD = .52$), $t(561) = -7.063, p < .001$. Additionally, males pledging fraternities reported significantly less positive bystander attitudes ($M = 3.40, SD = .51$) than females pledging sororities ($M = 3.89, SD = .53$), $t(550) = 10.899, p < .001$.

Correlations among the Rape Myth subscales revealed small to moderate relationships, ranging from .30 to .54, $p < .001$. The correlation between the overall Rape Myth scores and the Bystander Attitude scores was small but significant, $r = .28, p < .001$.

For all regression analyses, the demographic variables gender, athlete status, fraternity/sorority status, knowing someone sexually assaulted, and having previous rape education were entered as predictor variables. For the first of the series, the mean rape myth scale score was entered along with the demographic variables as independent variables, with the Bystander Attitude scale as the dependent variable. Overall, the regression analysis indicated that the model significantly predicted bystander attitudes. The 19% of the variance (adjusted $R^2 = .19$) in bystander attitudes was explained by the model, $F(6, 2071) = 81.67, p < .001$. The results indicate that gender (female), knowing someone sexually assaulted, and athlete status (nonathletes) were all significant predictors, along with overall rape myth acceptance. For each additional score increase in rape myth acceptance, a .20 point decrease in bystander attitudes ($p < .001$) was predicted, controlling other variables in the model. Gender also predicted the bystander attitudes, its score decreased by .32 points for males, compared to females ($p < .001$).

To determine whether certain types of rape myths were related to bystander attitudes, a second series of regression analyses were conducted. Due to the moderate correlations among the subscales and the possibility of multicolinearity, a series of separate linear regressions were conducted for each subscale. Along with each of the 5 subscales, the demographic variables were entered as independent variables to determine the impact on Bystander Attitudes. In each of these analyses, the subscales were significant, along with gender. The strongest model was produced with the subscale *It wasn't really rape* as the predictor, explaining 20% of variability in bystander attitudes, adjusted $R^2 = .20$, $F(6, 2071) = 86.95$, $p < .001$, The other subscales also produced significant results, with *She asked for it* (adjusted $R^2 = .17$, $F[6, 2071] = 72.40$, $p < .001$); *She lied* (adjusted $R^2 = .17$, $F[6, 2069] = 72.240$, $p < .001$); *He didn't mean to* (adjusted $R^2 = .16$, $F[6, 2071] = 66.82$, $p < .001$); and *Alcohol* (adjusted $R^2 = .17$, $F[6, 2071] = 72.25$, $p < .001$).

COMMENT

The purpose of this exploratory study was to determine college students' level of rape myths and bystander attitudes and to determine if they are related as well as impacted by various demographic factors. The results indicate that college students in this sample moderately supported rape myths, with certain myths receiving more endorsement than others. The rape myth subcales *He didn't mean to* and *She lied* had the highest mean scores, although they were still skewed towards lower rape myth acceptance. The response items on these scales suggest that despite a new generation of college students who likely received some education on sexual violence and who have an awareness of political correctness, victim-blaming beliefs still persist as well as excusing the perpetrator. Those items with the highest means demonstrate the presence of victim blaming myths in this sample; for example, over 53% of students strongly agreed or agreed that "If a girl acts like a slut, she is eventually going to get into trouble." As administrators on college campuses debate what content should be included in rape prevention programming, the results of this study suggest that further work is needed to address victim blaming and excusing perpetrator behavior as innocent or accidental.

Students in this sample also reported a moderate overall willingness to intervene as a bystander in situations involving sexual violence. Those bystander items to which students responded most positively were related to their own sexual behavior. Although this may suggest that students are aware of the importance of obtaining consent in intimate situations, it may also suggest the influence of social desirability commonly associated with self-reported behavior. The other bystander items receiving more positive responses were related to more overt forms of sexual violence, such as confronting a friend who was taking advantage of someone passed out. Students reported less likeliness to challenge others around issues of sexist language and jokes. This replicates previous findings by McMahon et al[41] and suggests that students are more willing to intervene in those situations with more blatant demonstrations of sexual violence and perhaps do not see the relevance of behaviors on the other end of the continuum such as sexist language.

The results of this study suggest that beliefs in rape myths are negatively related to students' intentions to intervene as bystanders. The moderate relationship suggests that those students who endorse more rape myths are less likely to intervene as bystanders. This is an important finding because it supports the need for education about rape myths to accompany bystander intervention. As college administrators consider the incorporation of bystander intervention into their prevention education programs, the preliminary results from this study underscore the need to include content on rape myths as well.

Although the *It's not really rape* subscale had the lowest mean score, it also produced the strongest model for predicting bystander attitudes. This is important because it suggests that although there may be fewer students who support these particular myths, those that do endorse these beliefs are less likely to intervene as bystanders. Because bystander intervention is based on the premise of engaging communities, it is essential to pinpoint which members of the community are least likely to intervene and address their needs. Although further research is needed, the findings suggest that those students who do not believe that perpetrators have committed sexual assault are especially less likely to engage as bystanders. Education is clearly warranted to provide accurate information about what constitutes rape as well as addressing issues of perpetrator accountability.

In this study, gender was a salient factor for both rape myths and bystander behaviors, with males more accepting of rape myths and less positive about bystander intervention. This is consistent with previous research.[16,41] Additionally, gender was the strongest variable in predicting bystander attitudes in the regression model, including with the overall rape myth score as well as the various subscales. The fact that gender continues to emerge as significant in studies related to attitudes about sexual violence must be recognized by those designing rape prevention and education programs. The findings strongly support the case for separate programming for men and women, with an opportunity to address the role of gender in rape myth acceptance and willingness to intervene as a bystander.

The results of this study indicate that student athletes and those intending to pledge a fraternity or sorority hold significantly greater rape myth acceptance, although no difference related to bystander attitudes. Greater rape myth acceptance by these groups is consistent with previous research and emphasizes the need to develop community-specific prevention programs that address aspects of these cultures that may be unique.[38] The finding about bystander attitudes contradicts the previous yet limited research showing that athletes and those intending to pledge the Greek system held less positive bystander attitudes.[41] Analysis revealed that within these "high-risk" groups, gender was again salient, with male athletes and men intending to pledge fraternities with higher rape myth acceptance and less positive bystander attitudes than their female counterparts. This preliminary finding suggests that in addition to community-specific programming for these groups, the role of gender within the context of these communities must be addressed. Further research should investigate the intersection of gender and athlete/fraternity status and its relationship to bystander behavior. It is also important to note that those students who reported knowing someone who had been sexually assaulted and those who had previous rape education also held less rape myths and more positive bystander attitudes. This is consistent with previous literature and these mediating variables should be considered in future studies. Future research could also further examine the impact of previous rape education to determine if the content, length, or timing results impact rape myth acceptance and bystander attitudes.

Limitations

This study has a number of limitations that should be considered when interpreting the results. Measurement related to sexual violence may be influenced by social desirability bias due to its sensitive nature. Students' self-reports about their willingness to assist a victim of sexual violence are certainly subject to the pressure of social desirability. Future studies may wish to include measures to counteract social desirability bias.

Additionally, this study did not address some of the situational factors that may influence bystander attitudes. For example, future research can distinguish whether the willingness to intervene is influenced by how well the bystander knows the victim/perpetrator (ie, stranger versus friend). A related concern is that our sample was low in its representation of ethnic diversity, which prevented meaningful analysis by this demographic but which needs further exploration. In particular, questions remain about whether the race/ethnicity of the victim/perpetrator may influence the bystander's intentions to intervene.

This study was also limited to studying the relationship between rape myths and bystander attitudes and did not examine the impact on actual bystander behaviors. Future work should establish the predictive validity of the measure utilized in the study. A next step in research can be further examining the relationships among bystander attitudes, behaviors, rape myths, and other mediating variables.

Lastly, although the sample was large, it represented only one campus in the Northeast. The sample was rather homogenous for age (all first-year students) and race. Replication of studies on bystander attitudes and rape myths are needed on other campuses with varying demographic profiles.

Conclusions

Bystander intervention presents an appealing and promising approach to rape prevention efforts on college campuses. However, research on the bystander approach applied to sexual violence prevention is in its infancy and many questions remain. This exploratory study provided insight as to the prevalence of rape myths and bystander attitudes among a sample of incoming college students. The results indicate that gender was the most salient predictor of both rape myths and bystander attitudes, which deserves serious consideration when developing and implementing rape prevention programs. Additionally, the results indicate a negative relationship between rape myth acceptance and willingness to intervene as a bystander, which suggests that rape prevention programs must include content on both. In particular, students who scored higher on the *It's not really rape* myth subscale indicated less willingness to intervene, which warrants further investigation and the development of strategies to engage and educate this group of students.

ACKNOWLEDGMENTS

I would like to acknowledge the contributions to this study from the Department of Sexual Assault Services & Crime Victim Assistance at

Rutgers University, including the efforts of Director Ruth Anne Koenick, as well as support from the Center on Violence Against Women and Children at the Rutgers University School of Social Work, especially Judy Postmus and MiSung Kim.

NOTES

1. For comments and further information, address correspondence to Sarah McMahon, PhD, Assistant Professor, Center on Violence Against Women & Children, Rutgers University School of Social Work, 536 George Street, New Brunswick, NJ 08901, USA (e-mail: smcmahon@ssw.rutgers.edu).
2. Some tables have been removed due to space and length considerations.

REFERENCES

1. Karjane H, Fisher B, Cullen F. *Sexual Assault on Campus: What Colleges and Universities Are Doing About It.* Washington, DC: US Department of Justice, Office of Justice Programs, National Institute for Justice; 2005. Research Report 2005:NCJ 205521.
2. Bachar K, Koss M. From Prevalence to Prevention. In: Renzetti C, Edleson J, Bergen R, eds. *Sourcebook on Violence against Women.* Thousand Oaks, CA: Sage Publications; 2001:117–142.
3. Campbell, R. The Psychological Impact of Rape Victims' Experiences with the Legal, Medical, and Mental Health Systems. *Am Psychol.* 2008;63:702–717.
4. Koss M, Koss P, Woodruff J. Deleterious Effects of Criminal Victimization on Women's Health and Medical Utilization. *Arch Intern Med.* 1991;151:342–347.
5. Waigandt A, Wallace D, Phelps L, Miller D. The Impact of Sexual Assault on Physical Health Status. *J Trauma Stress.* 1990;3:93–101.
6. Neville H, Heppner M. Prevention and Treatment of Violence against Women: An Examination of Sexual Assault. In: Juntunen C, Atkinson D, eds. *Counseling across the Lifespan: Prevention and Treatment.* Thousand Oaks, CA: Sage Publications; 2002:261–277.
7. Banyard V, Plante E, Moynihan M. Bystander Education: Bringing a Broader Community Perspective to Sexual Violence Prevention. *J Community Psychol.* 2004;32:61–79.
8. Potter S, Moynihan M, Stapleton J, Banyard V. Empowering Bystanders to Prevent Campus Violence against Women: A Preliminary Evaluation of a Poster Campaign. *Violence against Women.* 2009;15:106–121.
9. Centers for Disease Control and Prevention (CDC). *Sexual Violence Prevention: Beginning the Dialogue.* Atlanta, GA: Centers for Disease Control and

Prevention; 2004. Available at: http://www.cdc.gov/Ncipc/dvp/SVPrevention.pdf. Accessed February 6, 2008.

10. American College Health Association. Position Statement on Preventing Sexual Violence on College and University Campuses. April, 2007. Available at: http://www.acha.org/info_resources/ACHA_SexualViolence_Statement07. pdf. Accessed February 6, 2008.

11. Banyard V, Moynihan M, Crossman M. Reducing Sexual Violence on Campus: The Role of Student Leaders as Empowered Bystanders. *J Coll Student Dev.* 2009;50:446–457.

12. Fisher B, Cullen F, Turner M. *The Sexual Victimization of College Women.* Washington, DC: US Department of Justice; 2001. Publication no. NCJ182369.

13. Abbey A, Ross L, McDuffie D, McAuslan P. Alcohol and Dating Risk Factors for Sexual Assault among College Women. *Psychol Women Q.* 1996;20: 147–169.

14. Messman-Moore T, Coates A, Gaffey K, Johnson C. Sexuality, Substance Abuse, and Susceptibility to Victimization: Risk for Rape and Sexual Coercion in a Prospective Study of College Women. *J Interpers Violence.* 2008;23: 1730–1746.

15. Burn S. A Situational Model of Sexual Assault Prevention through Bystander Intervention. *Sex Roles.* 2009;60:779–792.

16. Banyard V. Measurement and Correlates of Pro-social Bystander Behavior: The Case of Interpersonal Violence. *Violence Victims.* 2008;23:85–99.

17. Latane B, Darley J. *The Unresponsive Bystander: Why Doesn't He Help?* New York, NY: Appleton–Century–Crofts; 1970.

18. Fischer P, Greitmeyer T, Pollozek F, Frey D. The Unresponsive Bystander: Are Bystanders More Responsive in Dangerous Emergencies? *Eur J Soc Psychol.* 2006;36:267–278.

19. Levine M. Rethinking Bystander Nonintervention: Social Categorization and the Evidence of Witnesses at the James Bulger Murder Trial. *Human Relat.* 1999;52:1133–1155.

20. Banyard VL, Moynihan MM, Plante EG. Sexual Violence Prevention through Bystander Education: An Experimental Evaluation. *J Community Psychol.* 2007;35:463–481.

21. Foubert J. The Longitudinal Effects of a Rape-Prevention Program on Fraternity Men's Attitudes, Behavioral Intent, and Behavior. *J Am Coll Health.* 2000;48:158–163.

22. Foubert J, Cowell E. Perceptions of a Rape Prevention Program by Fraternity Men and Male Student Athletes: Powerful Effects and Implications for Changing Behavior. *NASPA J.* 2004;42:1–20.

23. Foubert J, LaVoy S. A Qualitative Assessment of "The Men's Program": The Impact of a Rape Prevention Program on Fraternity Men. *NASPA J.* 2000;38:18–30.

24. Foubert J, Perry B. Creating Lasting Attitude and Behavior Change in Fraternity Members and Male Student Athletes: The Qualitative Impact of an Empathy-based Rape Prevention Program. *Violence against Women.* 2007;13:70–86.

25. Foubert J, Newberry, JT, Tatum, JL. Behavior Differences Seven Months Later: Effects of a Rape Prevention Program. *NASPA J.* 2007;44:727–749.

26. Center for Sport in Society. Mentors in Violence Prevention Homepage. Available at: http://www.sportinsociety.org/vpd/mvp.php. Accessed November 9, 2007.

27. Ward, KJ. *1999–2000 Evaluation Report.* Boston, MA: Center for the Study of Sport in Society. Available at: http://www.sportinsociety.org/vpd/mvp .php. Accessed November 9, 2007.

28. Moynihan M, Banyard V. Community Responsibility for Preventing Sexual Violence: A Pilot Study with Campus Greeks and Intercollegiate Athletes. *J Prev Interv Commun.* 2008;36:23–38.

29. Burt M. Cultural Myths and Supports for Rape. *J Pers Soc Psychol.* 1980;38:217–230.

30. Lonsway K, Fitzgerald L. Rape Myths. *Psychol Women Q.* 1994;18:133–164.

31. Bohner G, Jarvis C, Eyssel F, Siebler F. The Causal Impact of Rape Myth Acceptance on Men's Rape Proclivity: Comparing Sexually Coercive and Noncoercive Men. *Eur J Soc Psychol.* 2005;35:819–828.

32. O'Donohue W, Yeater E, Fanetti M. Rape Prevention with College Males: The Roles of Rape Myth Acceptance, Victim Empathy, and Outcome Expectancies. *J Interpers Violence.* 2003;18:513–531.

33. Payne D, Lonsway K, Fitzgerald L. Rape Myth Acceptance: Exploration of Its Structure and Its Measurement Using the Illinois Rape Myth Acceptance Scale. *J Res Pers.* 1999;33:27–68.

34. McMahon S, Farmer G. An Updated Measure for Assessing Subtle Rape Myths. *Social Work Research.* In press.

35. Frazier P, Valtinson G, Candell S. Evaluation of Coeducational Interactive Rape Prevention Program. *J Couns Dev.* 1994;73:153–158.

36. Humphrey C. *Acquaintance Rape: Exploring the Relationship between Cognitions and Behavioral-Intentions through the Development of Contemporary Measures of Attitude* [dissertation]. Columbia: University of Missouri–Columbia; 2001.

37. Hinck S, Thomas R. Rape Myth Acceptance in College Students: How Far Have We Come? *Sex Roles.* 1999;40:815–832.

38. McMahon S. *Student-Athletes, Rape Supportive Culture, and Social Change* [dissertation]. New Brunswick, NJ: Rutgers University; 2005.

39. Ferro C, Cermele J, Saltzman A. Current Perceptions of Marital Rape: Some Good and Not-So-Good News. *J Interpers Violence.* 2008;23:764–779.

40. Banyard V, Plante E, Moynihan M. *Rape Prevention through Bystander Education: Final Report.* Washington, DC: US Department of Justice; 2005. Document No. 208701. Available at: www.ncjrs.org/pdffilesl/nij/grants/208701.pdf. Accessed November 9, 2007.

41. McMahon S, Postmus J, Koenick R. Engaging Bystanders: A Primary Prevention Approach to Sexual Violence on Campus. *J Coll Student Dev.* In press.

42. Enders C. The Performance of the Full Information Maximum Likelihood Estimator in Multiple Regression Models with Missing Data. *Educ Psychol Meas.* 2001;61:713–740.

Analyze

1. What is a "rape myth"? What different examples of these myths does McMahon provide?
2. Why are college campuses considered "at-risk" environments for rape? And why are student athletes and members of sororities and fraternities "high-risk" students?
3. Why have scales such as the IRMA had to provide updated language?

Explore

1. What kind of rape prevention education does your campus provide? Does it include bystander information? Do some research on what kinds of resources your college provides to students about rape prevention and, using McMahon's study, evaluate their effectiveness.
2. Examine the rape myth items listed in Table 2. Do any of these surprise you? Why or why not? Are there any that you would add to this list? Take a survey of students on your campus to determine rape myth acceptance and bystander attitudes using the scale items listed in Tables 2 and 3, adding any additional items you feel are necessary. Do your results support McMahon's findings? Why or why not? Write an essay in which you explain your findings using your own research as evidence.
3. Look at Daryl Cagle's cartoon, "Rape on Campus," Figure 7 in the color art insert. Look closely at the details in the image—the young woman's broken purse handle, her misplaced bra strap, and so on. Based on your interpretation of these details and using these as evidence, write a

paragraph or two that identifies the point Cagle is making about rape on campus. Does it support McMahon's findings or point to other issues about rape on campus that should be addressed? How so?

Forging Connections

1. Based on the readings in the first three sections of this book, what conclusions can you draw about the way society defines masculinity? What is a "real man," and what are both the positives and problems with this definition? Finally, where do you fit into the conversation on this issue—what do you think about how society defines a man, and why? In crafting your answer to this question, draw from at least three sources you've read thus far.

2. Claims about gender identity impact LGBTQ+ individuals, especially when those claims are made by others about another individual. Compare the way in which Mecca is perceived in "He Defies You Still: The Memoirs of a Sissy" with the assumptions made about Brittney Griner in Zimmerman's "The Coming Out We All Ignored." How do gender expectations play a role in how both Mecca and Griner are treated? How does Urquhart both face those same criticisms and seek to challenge them? Why is it important that gendered expectations be acknowledged and challenged, especially in the LGBTQ+ community?

Looking Further

1. At the beginning of this chapter, we proposed that the characters of *Modern Family* embody stereotypes present in the media. Can you come up with examples that support this hypothesis? If so, how do they support it? If this hypothesis is true, why is that significant? What does this suggest about how gender is presented in the media, and why? Draw from the texts by Rich, Cisneros, Mecca, Frazer, Jensen, Walker, or others in crafting your response.

2. Many women-of-color feminists, including authors/activists such as Sandra Cisneros and Alice Walker, have taken issue with white feminism, or what Gayatri Spivak calls "hegemonic feminism," because it is solely organized around the gender binary of male/female and didn't address race, class, culture, or sexuality in addition to this

binary. What emerged in response to hegemonic feminism was U.S. third-world feminism. According to Chela Sandoval, U.S. third-world feminism "represents the political alliance made during the 1960s and 1970s between a generation of U.S. feminists of color who were separated by culture, race, class, or gender identifications but united through similar responses to the experience of race oppression." Do some research on U.S. third-world feminism. Based on your research, how would you expand on Sandoval's description of what it is? Additionally, Sandoval hints at the concept of intersectional feminism, or "intersectionality" (the term was coined by Kimberlé Crenshaw in 1989). Do some additional research on this concept and write an essay that compares and contrasts U.S. third-world feminism with intersectional feminism.

4

Gender and the Body

"The body we are born into is one of the single most powerful determinants of who we will be. We may struggle against that shape of our body, or embody it with unexpected potential. The body is the vessel that carries us into our encounters with the world. Through it, we observe our world and it begins to perceive us, in a lifelong war-dance of inner and outer perspectives."

—Riva Lehrer

When we are born, no matter whether we are born male, female, or intersex; whether we are born white, black, Hispanic, Native American, or Asian; whether we are born Italian, Russian, or Brazilian; we are all born into a body. That body might have ten fingers and ten toes; it might have ten fingers and eleven toes.

That body might have fully formed lungs; those lungs may still need time to develop. That body might be able to hear; that body might not be able to hear. That body might have been born female, although we might one day identify as male and want to change that body to reflect our identity. Regardless of how that body is shaped, regardless of how we change it, it is still our body. It is the one we're stuck with our entire lives. And, as Riva Lehrer points out, it is the lens through which we see the world, and the lens through which the world sees us. It is one of the most powerful markers that defines us for others.

Take Chris from Chapter 1, for instance. We saw Chris as someone with dark hair and eyes, who is of medium build. Regardless of whether we perceive Chris as male or female, we also have a strong predilection to assign certain attributes to Chris as such. For instance, how do we see Chris if we view Chris as a male who is medium build, with blond hair and blue eyes? What does that mean to Chris's masculinity? Similarly, if we see Chris as a female, how does our perception of her body impact our understanding of her femininity? We might also view this situation from Chris's perspective. What might it mean to Chris that he is of medium build? Would he be satisfied with his body based on societal ideals? Or might he spend extra time working out and drinking protein shakes? If Chris is female, would she be satisfied with her body based on societal ideals? Or would she constantly be dieting and exercising, all in an attempt to reach that perfect (probably unattainable) weight?

The readings in this chapter will ask you to think about the way in which the body becomes a vessel through which the beliefs and values of a society are enacted, just as we described in the previous example with Chris. The way that Chris might feel the need to change his/her body to match the beliefs of society shows how his/her body is no longer just his/hers, but rather a body that belongs to a particular societal ideal. In each of these readings, the authors explore the implications of the "ideal body" on men and women and on hetero- and LGBTQ+ individuals. Susan Bordo's essay "The Body and the Reproduction of Femininity" takes a look at how women's bodies have historically become sites of social control and the ways that women have attempted to reclaim their bodies. In "Call Cornell Co-Ed the

Perfect Girl," we learn about Elsie Scheel, who, based on her appearance, was deemed the "Brooklyn Venus" in 1912. Then, in "Brooklyn Venus Much Too Large Is Verdict of Physical Horticulturists," we see how, even in 1912, women's bodies were critiqued and shamed. Brooke Kantor, Helen Clark, and Lydia Federico offer a different perspective on the body in "An Exercise in Body Image," as they argue that playing a sport like rugby, which gives multiple types of people a role in the game, allows for—and even celebrates—diversity in body types. In "It's a Big Fat Revolution," Nomy Lamm highlights what she calls "the revolution" and challenges the patriarchy's oppression of female bodies. In Kate Fridkis's "Why I'm Hot for Peter Dinklage," Fridkis argues that we shouldn't let the media's perception of the "ideal man" limit to whom we are attracted. And Sherman Alexie's essay "Jason Collins Is the Envy of Straight Men Everywhere" looks at perceptions of the male body and masculinity in popular culture and in sport to point out that heterosexual "real man" behaviors (remember our discussion in Chapter 3 on masculinity) and homosexual male behaviors are more similar than one might think.

Susan Bordo
"The Body and the Reproduction of Femininity"

Susan Bordo is a professor of women's and gender studies and the Otis A. Singletary chair in the humanities at the University of Kentucky. Her work in the field of feminist scholarship is considered highly accessible, and many of her writings are frequently anthologized. She has published numerous books in her discipline, including *The Male Body: A New Look at Men in Public and Private* (1999) and, most recently, *The Creation of Anne Boleyn: A New Look at England's Most Notorious Queen* (2013).

"The Body and the Reproduction of Femininity," from Bordo's book *Unbearable Weight: Feminism, Western Culture, and the Body* (1993), examines the way in which the female body has been ascribed ideals and regulated by societal norms. As you read this essay, think about the alternate points of view that Bordo offers on aspects of illnesses typically assigned to women (such as hysteria). Do you agree with her interpretations of these illnesses? Why or why not?

Reconstructing Feminist Discourse on the Body

The body—what we eat, how we dress, the daily rituals through which we attend to the body—is a medium of culture. The body, as anthropologist Mary Douglas has argued, is a powerful symbolic form, a surface on which the central rules, hierarchies, and even metaphysical commitments of a culture are inscribed and thus reinforced through the concrete language of the body.[1] The body may also operate as a metaphor for culture. From quarters as diverse as Plato and Hobbes to French feminist Luce Irigaray, an imagination of body morphology has provided a blueprint for diagnosis and/or vision of social and political life.

The body is not only a *text* of culture. It is also, as anthropologist Pierre Bourdieu and philosopher Michel Foucault (among others) have argued, a *practical*, direct locus of social control. Banally, through table manners and toilet habits, through seemingly trivial routines, rules, and practices, culture is "*made* body," as Bourdieu puts it—converted into automatic, habitual activity. As such it is put "beyond the grasp of consciousness . . . [untouchable] by voluntary, deliberate transformations."[2] Our conscious politics, social commitments, strivings for change may be undermined and betrayed by the life of our bodies—not the craving, instinctual body imagined by Plato, Augustine, and Freud, but what Foucault calls the "docile body," regulated by the norms of cultural life.[3]

Throughout his later "genealogical" works (*Discipline and Punish*, *The History of Sexuality*), Foucault constantly reminds us of the primacy of practice over belief. Not chiefly through ideology, but through the organization and regulation of the time, space, and movements of our daily lives, our bodies are trained, shaped, and impressed with the stamp of prevailing historical forms of selfhood, desire, masculinity, femininity. Such an emphasis casts a dark and disquieting shadow across the contemporary scene. For women, as study after study shows, are spending more time on the management and discipline of our bodies than we have in a long, long time. In a decade marked by a reopening of the public arena to women, the intensification of such regimens appears diversionary and subverting. Through the pursuit of an ever-changing, homogenizing, elusive ideal of femininity—a pursuit without a terminus, requiring that women constantly attend to minute and often whimsical changes in fashion—female bodies become docile bodies—bodies whose forces and energies are habituated to external regulation, subjection, transformation, "improvement." Through the exacting and normalizing disciplines of diet, makeup, and dress—central organizing principles of time and space in the day of many women—we are rendered less socially oriented and more centripetally focused on self-modification. Through these disciplines, we continue to memorize on our bodies the feel and conviction of lack, of insufficiency, of never being good enough. At the farthest extremes, the practices of femininity may lead us to utter demoralization, debilitation, and death.

Viewed historically, the discipline and normalization of the female body—perhaps the only gender oppression that exercises itself, although to different degrees and in different forms, across age, race, class, and sexual orientation—has to be acknowledged as an amazingly durable and flexible strategy of social control. In our own era, it is difficult to avoid the recognition that the contemporary preoccupation with appearance, which still affects women far more powerfully than men, even in our narcissistic and visually oriented culture, may function as a backlash phenomenon, reasserting existing gender configurations against any attempts to shift or transform power relations.[4] Surely we are in the throes of this backlash today. In newspapers and magazines we daily encounter stories that promote traditional gender relations and prey on anxieties about change: stories about latch-key children, abuse in day-care centers, the "new woman's" troubles with men, her lack of marriageability, and so on. A dominant visual theme in teenage magazines involves women hiding in the shadows of men, seeking solace in their arms, willingly contracting the space they occupy. The last, of course, also describes our contemporary aesthetic ideal for women, an ideal whose obsessive pursuit has become the central torment of many women's lives. In such an era we desperately need an effective political discourse about the female body, a discourse adequate to an analysis of the insidious, and often paradoxical, pathways of modern social control.

Developing such a discourse requires reconstructing the feminist paradigm of the late 1960s and early 1970s, with its political categories of oppressors and oppressed, villains and victims. Here I believe that a feminist appropriation of some of Foucault's later concepts can prove useful. Following Foucault, we must first abandon the idea of power as something possessed by one group and leveled against another; we must instead think of the network of practices, institutions, and technologies that sustain positions of dominance and subordination in a particular domain.

Second, we need an analytics adequate to describe a power whose central mechanisms are not repressive, but *constitutive*: "a power bent on generating forces, making them grow, and ordering them, rather than one dedicated to impeding them, making them submit, or destroying them." Particularly in the realm of femininity, where so much depends on the seemingly willing acceptance of various norms and practices, we need an analysis of power "from below," as Foucault puts it; for example, of the mechanisms that shape and proliferate—rather than repress—desire, generate and focus our energies, construct our conceptions of normalcy and deviance.[5]

And, third, we need a discourse that will enable us to account for the subversion of potential rebellion, a discourse that, while insisting on the necessity of objective analysis of power relations, social hierarchy, political backlash, and so forth, will nonetheless allow us to confront the mechanisms by which the subject at times becomes enmeshed in collusion with forces that sustain her own oppression.

This essay will not attempt to produce a general theory along these lines. Rather, my focus will be the analysis of one particular arena where the interplay of these dynamics is striking and perhaps exemplary. It is a limited and unusual arena, that of a group of gender-related and historically localized disorders: hysteria, agoraphobia, and anorexia nervosa.[6] I recognize that these disorders have also historically been class- and race-biased, largely (although not exclusively) occurring among white middle- and upper-middle-class women. Nonetheless, anorexia, hysteria, and agoraphobia may provide a paradigm of one way in which potential resistance is not merely undercut but *utilized* in the maintenance and reproduction of existing power relations.[7]

The central mechanism I will describe involves a transformation (or, if you wish, duality) of meaning, through which conditions that are objectively (and, on one level, experientially) constraining, enslaving, and even murderous, come to be experienced as liberating, transforming, and life-giving. I offer this analysis, although limited to a specific domain, as an example of how various contemporary critical discourses may be joined to yield an understanding of the subtle and often unwitting role played by our bodies in the symbolization and reproduction of gender.

The Body as a Text of Femininity

The continuum between female disorder and "normal" feminine practice is sharply revealed through a close reading of those disorders to
which women have been particularly vulnerable. These, of course, have
varied historically: neurasthenia and hysteria in the second half of the nineteenth century; agoraphobia and, most dramatically, anorexia nervosa and
bulimia in the second half of the twentieth century. This is not to say that
anorectics did not exist in the nineteenth century—many cases were described, usually in the context of diagnoses of hysteria[8]—or that women no
longer suffer from classical hysterical symptoms in the twentieth century.
But the taking up of eating disorders on a mass scale is as unique to the
culture of the 1980s as the epidemic of hysteria was to the Victorian era.[9]

The symptomatology of these disorders reveals itself as textuality. Loss
of mobility, loss of voice, inability to leave the home, feeding others while
starving oneself, taking up space, and whittling down the space one's
body takes up—all have symbolic meaning, all have *political* meaning
under the varying rules governing the historical construction of gender.
Working within this framework, we see that whether we look at hysteria,
agoraphobia, or anorexia, we find the body of the sufferer deeply inscribed
with an ideological construction of femininity emblematic of the period
in question. The construction, of course, is always homogenizing and normalizing, erasing racial, class, and other differences and insisting that all
women aspire to a coercive, standardized ideal. Strikingly, in these disorders the construction of femininity is written in disturbingly concrete,
hyperbolic terms: exaggerated, extremely literal, at times virtually carica-
tured presentations of the ruling feminine mystique. The bodies of disordered women in this way offer themselves as an aggressively graphic text
for the interpreter—a text that insists, actually demands, that it be read as
a cultural statement, a statement about gender.

Both nineteenth-century male physicians and twentieth-century feminist critics have seen, in the symptoms of neurasthenia and hysteria (syn-
dromes that became increasingly less differentiated as the century wore on),
an exaggeration of stereotypically feminine traits. The nineteenth-century
"lady" was idealized in terms of delicacy and dreaminess, sexual passivity,
and a charmingly labile and capricious emotionality.[10] Such notions were
formalized and scientized in the work of male theorists from Acton and
Krafft-Ebing to Freud, who described "normal," mature femininity in such

terms.[11] In this context, the dissociations, the drifting and fogging of perception, the nervous tremors and faints, the anesthesias, and the extreme mutability of symptomatology associated with nineteenth-century female disorders can be seen to be concretizations of the feminine mystique of the period, produced according to rules that governed the prevailing construction of femininity. Doctors described what came to be known as the hysterical personality as "impressionable, suggestible, and narcissistic; highly labile, their moods changing suddenly, dramatically, and seemingly for inconsequential reasons . . . egocentric in the extreme . . . essentially asexual and not uncommonly frigid"[12]—all characteristics normative of femininity in this era. As Elaine Showalter points out, the term *hysterical* itself became almost interchangeable with the term *feminine* in the literature of the period.[13]

The hysteric's embodiment of the feminine mystique of her era, however, seems subtle and ineffable compared to the ingenious literalism of agoraphobia and anorexia. In the context of our culture this literalism makes sense. With the advent of movies and television, the rules for femininity have come to be culturally transmitted more and more through standardized visual images. As a result, femininity itself has come to be largely a matter of constructing, in the manner described by Erving Goffman, the appropriate surface presentation of the self.[14] We are no longer given verbal descriptions or exemplars of what a lady is or of what femininity consists. Rather, we learn the rules directly through bodily discourse: through images that tell us what clothes, body shape, facial expression, movements, and behavior are required.

In agoraphobia and, even more dramatically, in anorexia, the disorder presents itself as a virtual, though tragic, parody of twentieth-century constructions of femininity. The 1950s and early 1960s, when agoraphobia first began to escalate among women, was a period of reassertion of domesticity and dependency as the feminine ideal. *Career woman* became a dirty word, much more so than it had been during the war, when the economy depended on women's willingness to do "men's work." The reigning ideology of femininity, so well described by Betty Friedan and perfectly captured in the movies and television shows of the era, was childlike, nonassertive, helpless without a man, "content in a world of bedroom and kitchen, sex, babies and home."[15] The housebound agoraphobic lives this construction of femininity literally. "You want me in this home? You'll have me in this home—with a vengeance!" The point, upon which many therapists have commented, does not need belaboring. Agoraphobia, as I. G. Fodor has put it, seems "the logical—albeit extreme—extension of the cultural sex-role stereotype for women" in this era.[16]

The emaciated body of the anorectic, of course, immediately presents itself as a caricature of the contemporary ideal of hyperslenderness for women, an ideal that, despite the game resistance of racial and ethnic difference, has become the norm for women today. But slenderness is only the tip of the iceberg, for slenderness itself requires interpretation. "C'est le sens qui fait vendre," said Barthes, speaking of clothing styles—it is meaning that makes the sale.[17] So, too, it is meaning that makes the body admirable. To the degree that anorexia may be said to be "about" slenderness, it is about slenderness as a citadel of contemporary and historical meaning, not as an empty fashion ideal. As such, the interpretation of slenderness yields multiple readings, some related to gender, some not. For the purposes of this essay I will offer an abbreviated, gender-focused reading. But I must stress that this reading illuminates only partially, and that many other currents not discussed here—economic, psychosocial, and historical, as well as ethnic and class dimensions—figure prominently.[18]

We begin with the painfully literal inscription, on the anorectic's body, of the rules governing the construction of contemporary femininity. That construction is a double bind that legislates contradictory ideals and directives. On the one hand, our culture still widely advertises domestic conceptions of femininity, the ideological moorings for a rigorously dualistic sexual division of labor that casts woman as chief emotional and physical nurturer. The rules for this construction of femininity (and I speak here in a language both symbolic and literal) require that women learn to feed others, not the self, and to construe any desires for self-nurturance and self-feeding as greedy and excessive.[19] Thus, women must develop a totally other-oriented emotional economy. In this economy, the control of female appetite for food is merely the most concrete expression of the general rule governing the construction of femininity: that female hunger—for public power, for independence, for sexual gratification—be contained, and the public space that women be allowed to take up be circumscribed, limited.*
... Slenderness, set off against the resurgent muscularity and bulk of the current male body-ideal, carries connotations of fragility and lack of power

---

*Figures have been removed for space and length considerations.

in the face of a decisive male occupation of social space. On the body of the anorexic woman such rules are grimly and deeply etched.

On the other hand, even as young women today continue to be taught traditionally "feminine" virtues, to the degree that the professional arena is open to them they must also learn to embody the "masculine" language and values of that arena—self-control, determination, cool, emotional discipline, mastery, and so on. Female bodies now speak symbolically of this necessity in their slender spare shape and the currently fashionable men's-wear look. . . . Our bodies, too, as we trudge to the gym every day and fiercely resist both our hungers and our desire to soothe ourselves, are becoming more and more practiced at the "male" virtues of control and self-mastery. . . . The anorectic pursues these virtues with single-minded, unswerving dedication. "Energy, discipline, my own power will keep me going," says ex-anorectic Aimee Liu, recreating her anorexic days. "I need nothing and no one else. . . . I will be master of my own body, if nothing else, I vow."[20]

The ideal of slenderness, then, and the diet and exercise regimens that have become inseparable from it offer the illusion of meeting, through the body, the contradictory demands of the contemporary ideology of femininity. Popular images reflect this dual demand. In a single issue of *Complete Woman* magazine, two articles appear, one on "Feminine Intuition," the other asking, "Are You the New Macho Woman?" In *Vision Quest*, the young male hero falls in love with the heroine, as he says, because "she has all the best things I like in girls and all the best things I like in guys," that is, she's tough and cool, but warm and alluring. In the enormously popular *Aliens*, the heroine's personality has been deliberately constructed, with near–comic book explicitness, to embody traditional nurturant femininity alongside breathtaking macho prowess and control; Sigourney Weaver, the actress who portrays her, has called the character "Rambolina."

In the pursuit of slenderness and the denial of appetite the traditional construction of femininity intersects with the new requirement for women to embody the "masculine" values of the public arena. The anorectic, as I have argued, embodies this intersection, this double bind, in a particularly painful and graphic way.[21] I mean *double bind* quite literally here. "Masculinity" and "femininity," at least since the nineteenth century and arguably before, have been constructed through a process of mutual exclusion. One cannot simply add the historically feminine virtues to the historically masculine ones to yield a New Woman, a New Man, a new ethics, or a new culture. Even on the screen or on television, embodied in created characters like the *Aliens* heroine, the result is a parody. Unfortunately, in this image-bedazzled culture, we find it increasingly difficult to discriminate between parodies and possibilities for the self. Explored as a possibility for the self, the "androgynous" ideal ultimately exposes its internal contradiction and becomes a war that tears the subject in two—a war explicitly thematized, by many anorectics, as a battle between male and female sides of the self.[22]

Protest and Retreat in the Same Gesture

In hysteria, agoraphobia, and anorexia, then, the woman's body may be viewed as a surface on which conventional constructions of femininity are exposed starkly to view, through their inscription in extreme or hyperliteral form. They are written, of course, in languages of horrible suffering. It is as though these bodies are speaking to us of the pathology and violence that lurks just around the corner, waiting at the horizon of "normal" femininity. It is no wonder that a steady motif in the feminist literature on female disorder is that of pathology as embodied *protest*—unconscious, inchoate, and counterproductive protest without an effective language, voice, or politics, but protest nonetheless.

American and French feminists alike have heard the hysteric speaking a language of protest, even or perhaps especially when she was mute. Dianne Hunter interprets Anna O.'s aphasia, which manifested itself in an inability to speak her native German, as a rebellion against the linguistic and cultural rules of the father and a return to the "mother-tongue": the semiotic babble of infancy, the language of the body. For Hunter, and for a number of other feminists working with Lacanian categories, the return to the semiotic level is both regressive and, as Hunter puts it, an "expressive" communication "addressed to patriarchal thought," "a self-repudiating form of feminine discourse in which the body signifies what social conditions make it impossible to state linguistically."[23] "The hysterics are accusing; they are pointing," writes Catherine Clément in *The Newly Born Woman*; they make a "mockery of culture."[24] In the same volume, Hélène Cixous speaks of "those wonderful hysterics, who subjected Freud to so many voluptuous moments too shameful to mention, bombarding his mosaic statute/law of Moses with their carnal, passionate body-words, haunting him with their inaudible thundering denunciations." For Cixous,

Dora, who so frustrated Freud, is "the core example of the protesting force in women."[25]

The literature of protest includes functional as well as symbolic approaches. Robert Seidenberg and Karen DeCrow, for example, describe agoraphobia as a "strike" against "the renunciations usually demanded of women" and the expectations of housewifely functions such as shopping, driving the children to school, accompanying their husband to social events.[26] Carroll Smith-Rosenberg presents a similar analysis of hysteria, arguing that by preventing the woman from functioning in the wifely role of caretaker of others, of "ministering angel" to husband and children, hysteria "became one way in which conventional women could express—in most cases unconsciously—dissatisfaction with one or several aspects of their lives."[27] A number of feminist writers, among whom Susie Orbach is the most articulate and forceful, have interpreted anorexia as a species of unconscious feminist protest. The anorectic is engaged in a "hunger strike," as Orbach calls it, stressing that this is a political discourse, in which the action of food refusal and dramatic transformation of body size "expresses with [the] body what [the anorectic] is unable to tell us with words"—her indictment of a culture that disdains and suppresses female hunger, makes women ashamed of their appetites and needs, and demands that women constantly work on the transformation of their body.[28]

The anorectic, of course, is unaware that she is making a political statement. She may, indeed, be hostile to feminism and any other critical perspectives that she views as disputing her own autonomy and control or questioning the cultural ideals around which her life is organized. Through embodied rather than deliberate demonstration she exposes and indicts those ideals, precisely by pursuing them to the point at which their destructive potential is revealed for all to see.

The same gesture that expresses protest, moreover, can also signal retreat; this, indeed, may be part of the symptom's attraction. Kim Chernin, for example, argues that the debilitating anorexic fixation, by halting or mitigating personal development, assuages this generation's guilt and separation anxiety over the prospect of surpassing our mothers, of living less circumscribed, freer lives.[29] Agoraphobia, too, which often develops shortly after marriage, clearly functions in many cases as a way to cement dependency and attachment in the face of unacceptable stirrings of dissatisfaction and restlessness.

Although we may talk meaningfully of protest, then, I want to emphasize the counterproductive, tragically self-defeating (indeed, self-deconstructing) nature of that protest. Functionally, the symptoms of these disorders isolate, weaken, and undermine the sufferers; at the same time they turn the life of the body into an all-absorbing fetish, beside which all other objects of attention pale into unreality. On the symbolic level, too, the protest collapses into its opposite and proclaims the utter capitulation of the subject to the contracted female world. The muteness of hysterics and their return to the level of pure, primary bodily expressivity have been interpreted, as we have seen, as rejecting the symbolic order of the patriarchy and recovering a lost world of semiotic, maternal value. But *at the same time*, of course, muteness is the condition of the silent, uncomplaining woman—an ideal of patriarchal culture. Protesting the stifling of the female voice through one's own voicelessness—that is, employing the language of femininity to protest the conditions of the female world—will always involve ambiguities of this sort. Perhaps this is why symptoms crystallized from the language of femininity are so perfectly suited to express the dilemmas of middle-class and upper-middle-class women living in periods poised on the edge of gender change, women who have the social and material resources to carry the traditional construction of femininity to symbolic excess but who also confront the anxieties of new possibilities. The late nineteenth century, the post–World War II period, and the late twentieth century are all periods in which gender becomes an issue to be discussed and in which discourse proliferates about "the Woman Question," "the New Woman," "What Women Want," "What Femininity Is."

Collusion, Resistance, and the Body

The pathologies of female protest function, paradoxically, as if in collusion with the cultural conditions that produce them, reproducing rather than transforming precisely that which is being protested. In this connection, the fact that hysteria and anorexia have peaked during historical periods of cultural backlash against attempts at reorganization and redefinition of male and female roles is significant. Female pathology reveals itself here as an extremely interesting social formation through which one source of potential for resistance and rebellion is pressed into the service of maintaining the established order.

In our attempt to explain this formation, objective accounts of power relations fail us. For whatever the objective social conditions are that create a pathology, the symptoms themselves must still be produced (however unconsciously or inadvertently) by the subject. That is, the individual must invest the body with meanings of various sorts. Only by examining this productive process on the part of the subject can we, as Mark Poster has put it, "illuminate the mechanisms of domination in the processes through which meaning is produced in everyday life"; that is, only then can we see how the desires and dreams of the subject become implicated in the matrix of power relations.[30]

Here, examining the context in which the anorexic syndrome is produced may be illuminating. Anorexia will erupt, typically, in the course of what begins as a fairly moderate diet regime, undertaken because someone, often the father, has made a casual critical remark. Anorexia *begins in*, emerges out of, what is, in our time, conventional feminine practice. In the course of that practice, for any number of individual reasons, the practice is pushed a little beyond the parameters of moderate dieting. The young woman discovers what it feels like to crave and want and need and yet, through the exercise of her own will, to triumph over that need. In the process, a new realm of meanings is discovered, a range of values and possibilities that Western culture has traditionally coded as "male" and rarely made available to women: an ethic and aesthetic of self-mastery and self-transcendence, expertise, and power over others through the example of superior will and control. The experience is intoxicating, habit-forming.

At school the anorectic discovers that her steadily shrinking body is admired, not so much as an aesthetic or sexual object, but for the strength of will and self-control it projects. At home she discovers, in the inevitable battles her parents fight to get her to eat, that her actions have enormous power over the lives of those around her. As her body begins to lose its traditional feminine curves, its breasts and hips and rounded stomach, begins to feel and look more like a spare, lanky male body, she begins to feel untouchable, out of reach of hurt, "invulnerable, clean and hard as the bones etched into my silhouette," as one student described it in her journal. She despises, in particular, all those parts of her body that continue to mark her as female. "If only I could eliminate [my breasts]," says Liu, "cut them off if need be."[31] For her, as for many anorectics, the breasts represent a bovine, unconscious, vulnerable side of the self. Liu's body symbolism is thoroughly continuous with dominant cultural associations. Brett Silverstein's studies on the "Possible Causes of the Thin Standard of Bodily Attractiveness for Women"[32] testify empirically to what is obvious from every comedy routine involving a dramatically shapely woman: namely, our cultural association of curvaceousness with incompetence. The anorectic is also quite aware, of course, of the social and sexual vulnerability involved in having a female body; many, in fact, were sexually abused as children.

Through her anorexia, by contrast, she has unexpectedly discovered an entry into the privileged male world, a way to become what is valued in our culture, a way to become safe, to rise above it all—for her, they are the same thing. She has discovered this, paradoxically, by pursuing conventional feminine behavior—in this case, the discipline of perfecting the body as an object—to excess. At this point of excess, the conventionally feminine deconstructs, we might say, into its opposite and opens onto those values our culture has coded as male. No wonder the anorexia is experienced as liberating and that she will fight family, friends, and therapists in an effort to hold onto it—fight them to the death, if need be. The anorectic's experience of power is, of course, deeply and dangerously illusory. To reshape one's body into a male body is *not* to put on male power and privilege. To *feel* autonomous and free while harnessing body and soul to an obsessive body-practice is to serve, not transform, a social order that limits female possibilities. And, of course, for the female to become male is only for her to locate herself on the other side of a disfiguring opposition. The new "power look" of female body-building, which encourages women to develop the same hulklike, triangular shape that has been the norm for male body-builders, is no less determined by a hierarchical, dualistic construction of gender than was the conventionally "feminine" norm that tyrannized female body-builders such as Bev Francis for years.

Although the specific cultural practices and meanings are different, similar mechanisms, I suspect, are at work in hysteria and agoraphobia. In these cases too, the language of femininity, when pushed to excess—when shouted and asserted, when disruptive and demanding—deconstructs into its opposite and makes available to the woman an illusory experience of power previously forbidden to her by virtue of her gender. In the case of nineteenth-century femininity, the forbidden experience may have been the bursting of fetters—particularly moral and emotional fetters. John Conolly, the asylum reformer, recommended institutionalization for women who "want that restraint over the passions without which the female character is lost."[33] Hysterics often infuriated male doctors by their lack of precisely this quality. S. Weir Mitchell described these patients as "the despair of physicians," whose "despotic selfishness wrecks the constitution of nurses and devoted relatives, and in unconscious or half-conscious self-indulgence destroys the comfort of everyone around them."[34] It must have given the Victorian patient some illicit pleasure to be viewed as capable of such disruption of the staid nineteenth-century household. A similar form of power, I believe, is part of the experience of agoraphobia.

This does not mean that the primary reality of these disorders is not one of pain and entrapment. Anorexia, too, clearly contains a dimension of physical addiction to the biochemical effects of starvation. But whatever the physiology involved, the ways in which the subject understands and thematizes her experience cannot be reduced to a mechanical process. The anorectic's ability to live with minimal food intake allows her to feel powerful and worthy of admiration in a "world," as Susie Orbach describes it, "from which at the most profound level [she] feels excluded" and unvalued.[35] The literature on both anorexia and hysteria is strewn with battles of will between the sufferer and those trying to "cure" her; the latter, as Orbach points out, very rarely understand that the psychic values she is fighting for are often more important to the woman than life itself.

Textuality, Praxis, and the Body

The "solutions" offered by anorexia, hysteria, and agoraphobia, I have suggested, develop out of the practice of femininity itself, the pursuit of which is still presented as the chief route to acceptance and success for women in our culture. Too aggressively pursued, that practice leads to its own undoing, in one sense. For if femininity is, as Susan Brownmiller has said, at its core a "tradition of imposed limitations,"[36] then an unwillingness to limit oneself, even in the pursuit of femininity, breaks the rules. But, of course, in another sense the rules remain fully in place. The sufferer becomes wedded to an obsessive practice, unable to make any effective change in her life. She remains, as Toril Moi has put it, "gagged and chained to [the] feminine role," a reproducer of the docile body of femininity.[37]

This tension between the psychological meaning of a disorder, which may enact fantasies of rebellion and embody a language of protest, and the practical life of the disordered body, which may utterly defeat rebellion and subvert protest, may be obscured by too exclusive a focus on the symbolic dimension and insufficient attention to praxis. As we have seen in the case of some Lacanian feminist readings of hysteria, the result of this can be a one-sided interpretation that romanticizes the hysteric's symbolic subversion of the phallocentric order while confined to her bed. This is not to say that confinement in bed has a transparent, univocal meaning—in powerlessness, debilitation, dependency, and so forth. The "practical" body is no brute biological or material entity. It, too, is a culturally mediated form; its activities are subject to interpretation and description. The shift to the practical dimension is not a turn to biology or nature, but to another "register," as Foucault puts it, of the cultural body, the register of the "useful body" rather than the "intelligible body."[38] The distinction can prove useful, I believe, to feminist discourse.

The intelligible body includes our scientific, philosophic, and aesthetic representations of the body—our cultural *conceptions* of the body, norms of beauty, models of health, and so forth. But the same representations may also be seen as forming a set of *practical* rules and regulations through which the living body is "trained, shaped, obeys, responds," becoming, in short, a socially adapted and "useful body."[39] Consider this particularly clear and appropriate example: the nineteenth-century hourglass figure, emphasizing breasts and hips against a wasp waist, was an intelligible *symbolic* form, representing a domestic, sexualized ideal of femininity. The sharp cultural contrast between the female and the male form, made possible by the use of corsets and bustles, reflected, in symbolic terms, the dualistic division of social and economic life into clearly defined male and female spheres. At the same time, to achieve the specified look, a particular feminine *praxis* was required—straitlacing, minimal eating, reduced mobility—rendering the female body unfit to perform activities outside its designated sphere. This, in Foucauldian terms, would be the "useful body" corresponding to the aesthetic norm.

The intelligible body and the useful body are two arenas of the same discourse; they often mirror and support each other, as in the above illustration. Another example can be found in the seventeenth-century philosophic conception of the body as a machine, mirroring an increasingly more automated productive machinery of labor. But the two bodies may also contradict and mock each other. A range of contemporary representations and images, as noted earlier, have coded the transcendence of female appetite and its public display in the slenderness ideal in terms of power, will, mastery, the possibilities of success in the professional arena. These associations are carried visually by the slender superwomen of prime-time television and popular movies and promoted explicitly in advertisements and articles appearing routinely in women's fashion magazines, diet books, and weight-training publications. Yet the thousands of slender girls and women who strive to embody these images and who in that service suffer from eating disorders, exercise compulsions, and continual self-scrutiny and self-castigation are anything *but* the "masters" of their lives.

Exposure and productive cultural analysis of such contradictory and mystifying relations between image and practice are possible only if the analysis includes attention to and interpretation of the "useful" or, as I prefer to call it, the practical body. Such attention, although often in inchoate and theoretically unsophisticated form, was central to the beginnings of the contemporary feminist movement. In the late 1960s and early 1970s the objectification of the female body was a serious political issue. All the cultural paraphernalia of femininity, of learning to please visually and sexually through the practices of the body—media imagery, beauty pageants, high heels, girdles, makeup, simulated orgasm—were seen as crucial in maintaining gender domination.

Disquietingly, for the feminists of the present decade, such focus on the politics of feminine praxis, although still maintained in the work of individual feminists, is no longer a centerpiece of feminist cultural critique.[40] On the popular front, we find *Ms.* magazine presenting issues on fitness and "style," the rhetoric reconstructed for the 1980s to pitch "self-expression" and "power." Although feminist theory surely has the tools, it has not provided a critical discourse to dismantle and demystify this rhetoric. The work of French feminists has provided a powerful framework for understanding the inscription of phallocentric, dualistic culture on gendered bodies, but it has offered very little in the way of concrete analyses of the female body as a locus of practical cultural control. Among feminist theorists in this country, the study of cultural representations of the female body has flourished, and it has often been brilliantly illuminating and instrumental to a feminist rereading of culture.[41] But the study of cultural representations alone, divorced from consideration of their relation to the practical lives of bodies, can obscure and mislead.

Here, Helena Mitchie's significantly titled *The Flesh Made Word* offers a striking example. Examining nineteenth-century representations of women, appetite, and eating, Mitchie draws fascinating and astute metaphorical connections between female eating and female sexuality. Female hunger, she argues, and I agree, "figures unspeakable desires for sexuality and power."[42] The Victorian novel's "representational taboo" against depicting women eating (an activity, apparently, that only "happens offstage," as Mitchie puts it) thus functions as a "code" for the suppression of female sexuality, as does the general cultural requirement, exhibited in etiquette and sex manuals of the day, that the well-bred woman eat little and delicately. The same coding is drawn on, Mitchie argues, in contemporary feminist "inversions" of Victorian values, inversions that celebrate female sexuality and power through images exulting in female eating and female hunger, depicting it explicitly, lushly, and joyfully.

Despite the fact that Mitchie's analysis centers on issues concerning women's hunger, food, and eating practices, she makes no mention of the grave eating disorders that surfaced in the late nineteenth century and that are ravaging the lives of young women today. The practical arena of women dieting, fasting, straitlacing, and so forth is, to a certain extent, implicit in her examination of Victorian gender ideology. But when Mitchie turns, at the end of her study, to consider contemporary feminist literature celebrating female eating and female hunger, the absence of even a passing glance at how women are *actually* managing their hungers today leaves her analysis adrift, lacking any concrete social moorings. Mitchie's sole focus is on the inevitable failure of feminist literature to escape "phallic representational codes."[43] But the feminist celebration of the female body did not merely deconstruct on the written page or canvas. Largely located in the feminist counterculture of the 1970s, it has been culturally displaced by a very different contemporary reality. Its celebration of female flesh now presents itself in jarring dissonance with the fact that women, feminists included, are starving themselves to death in our culture.

This is not to deny the benefits of diet, exercise, and other forms of body management. Rather, I view our bodies as a site of struggle, where we must *work* to keep our daily practices in the service of resistance to gender domination, not in the service of docility and gender normalization. This work requires, I believe, a determinedly skeptical attitude toward the routes of seeming liberation and pleasure offered by our culture. It also demands an awareness of the often contradictory relations between image and practice, between rhetoric and reality. Popular representations, as we have seen, may forcefully employ the rhetoric and symbolism of empowerment, personal freedom, "having it all." Yet female bodies, pursuing these ideals, may find themselves as distracted, depressed, and physically ill as female bodies in the nineteenth century were made when pursuing a feminine ideal of dependency, domesticity, and delicacy. The recognition and analysis of such contradictions, and of all the other collusions, subversions, and enticements through which culture enjoins the aid of our bodies in the reproduction of gender, require that we restore a concern for female praxis to its formerly central place in feminist politics.

NOTES

1. Mary Douglas, *Natural Symbols* (New York: Pantheon, 1982) and *Purity and Danger* (London: Routledge and Kegan Paul, 1966).

2. Pierre Bourdieu, *Outline of a Theory of Practice* (Cambridge: Cambridge University Press, 1977), p. 94 (emphasis in original).

3. On docility, see Michel Foucault, *Discipline and Punish* (New York: Vintage, 1979), pp. 135–69. For a Foucauldian analysis of feminine practice, see Sandra Bartky, "Foucault, Femininity, and the Modernization of Patriarchal Power," in her *Femininity and Domination* (New York: Routledge, 1990); see also Susan Brownmiller, *Femininity* (New York: Ballantine, 1984).

4. During the late 1970s and 1980s, male concern over appearance undeniably increased. Study after study confirms, however, that there is still a large gender gap in this area. Research conducted at the University of Pennsylvania in 1985 found men to be generally satisfied with their appearance, often, in fact, "distorting their perceptions [of themselves] in a positive, self-aggrandizing way ("Dislike of Own Bodies Found Common among Women," *New York Times*, March 19, 1985, p. C1). Women, however, were found to exhibit extreme negative assessments and distortions of body perception. Other studies have suggested that women are judged more harshly than men when they deviate from dominant social standards of attractiveness. Thomas Cash et al., in "The Great American Shape-Up," *Psychology Today*, (April 1986), p. 34, report that although the situation for men has changed, the situation for women has more than proportionally worsened. Citing results from 30,000 responses to a 1985 survey of perceptions of body image and comparing similar responses to a 1972 questionnaire, they report that the 1985 respondents were considerably more dissatisfied with their bodies than the 1972 respondents, and they note a marked intensification of concern among men. Among the 1985 group, the group most dissatisfied of all with their appearance, however, were teenage women. Women today constitute by far the largest number of consumers of diet products, attenders of spas and diet centers, and subjects of intestinal by-pass and other fat-reduction operations.

5. Michel Foucault, *The History of Sexuality*, Vol. 1, *An Introduction* (New York: Vintage, 1980), pp. 136, 94.

6. On the gendered and historical nature of these disorders: the number of female to male hysterics has been estimated at anywhere from 2:1 to 4:1, and as many as 80 percent of all agoraphobics are female (Annette Brodsky and Rachel Hare-Mustin, *Women and Psychotherapy* [New York: Guilford Press, 1980], pp. 116, 122). Although more cases of male eating disorders have been reported in the late eighties and early nineties, it is estimated that close to 90 percent of all anorectics are female (Paul Garfinkel and David Garner, *Anorexia Nervosa: A Multidimensional Perspective* [New York: Brunner/Mazel, 1982], pp. 112–13). For a sophisticated account of female psychopathology, with particular attention to nineteenth-century disorders but, unfortunately, little mention of agoraphobia or eating disorders, see Elaine Showalter, *The Female Malady: Women, Madness and English Culture, 1830–1980* (New York: Pantheon, 1985). For a discussion of social and gender issues in agoraphobia, see Robert Seidenberg and Karen DeCrow, *Women Who Marry Houses: Panic and Protest in Agoraphobia* (New York: McGraw–Hill, 1983). On the history of anorexia nervosa, see Joan Jacobs Brumberg, *Fasting Girls: The Emergence of Anorexia Nervosa as a Modern Disease* (Cambridge: Harvard University Press, 1988).

7. In constructing such a paradigm I do not pretend to do justice to any of these disorders in its individual complexity. My aim is to chart some points of intersection, to describe some similar patterns, as they emerge through a particular reading of the phenomenon—a political reading, if you will.

8. Showalter, *The Female Malady*, pp. 128–29.

9. On the epidemic of hysteria and neurasthenia, see Showalter, *The Female Malady*; Carroll Smith-Rosenberg, "The Hysterical Woman: Sex Roles and Role Conflict in Nineteenth-Century America," in her *Disorderly Conduct: Visions of Gender in Victorian America* (Oxford: Oxford University Press, 1985).

10. Martha Vicinus, "Introduction: The Perfect Victorian Lady," in Martha Vicinus, ed., *Suffer and Be Still: Women in the Victorian Age* (Bloomington: Indiana University Press, 1972), pp. x–xi.

11. See Carol Nadelson and Malkah Notman, *The Female Patient* (New York: Plenum, 1982), p. 5; E. M. Sigsworth and T. J. Wyke, "A Study of Victorian Prostitution and Venereal Disease," in Vicinus, *Suffer and Be Still*, p. 82. For more general discussions, see Peter Gay, *The Bourgeois Experience: Victoria to Freud*, Vol. 1, *Education of the Senses* (New York: Oxford University Press, 1984), esp. pp. 109–68; Showalter, *The Female Malady*, esp. pp. 121–44. The delicate lady, an ideal that had very strong class connotations (as does slenderness today), is not the only conception of femininity to be found in Victorian cultures. But it was arguably the single most powerful ideological representation of femininity in that era, affecting women of all classes, including those without the material means to realize the ideal fully. See Helena Mitchie, *The Flesh Made Word* (New York: Oxford University Press, 1987), for discussions of the control of female appetite and Victorian constructions of femininity.

12. Smith-Rosenberg, *Disorderly Conduct*, p. 203.

13. Showalter, *The Female Malady*, p. 129.

14. Erving Goffman, *The Presentation of Self in Everyday Life* (Garden City, N.Y.: Anchor Doubleday, 1959).

15. Betty Friedan, *The Feminine Mystique* (New York: Dell, 1962), p. 36. The theme song of one such show ran, in part, "I married Joan . . . What a girl . . . what a whirl . . . what a life! I married Joan . . . What a mind . . . love is blind . . . what a wife!"

16. See I. G. Fodor, "The Phobic Syndrome in Women," in V. Franks and V. Burtle, eds., *Women in Therapy* (New York: Brunner/Mazel, 1974), p. 119; see also Kathleen Brehoney, "Women and Agoraphobia," in Violet Franks and Esther Rothblum, eds., *The Stereotyping of Women* (New York: Springer, 1983).

17. In Jonathan Culler, *Roland Barthes* (New York: Oxford University Press, 1983), p. 74.

18. For other interpretive perspectives on the slenderness ideal, see "Reading the Slender Body" in *Unbearable Weight* (1993); Kim Chernin, *The Obsessions: Reflections on the Tyranny of Slenderness* (New York: Harper and Row, 1981); Susie Orbach, *Hunger Strike: The Anorectic's Struggle as a Metaphor for Our Age* (New York: W. W. Norton, 1985).

19. See "Hunger as Ideology" [in *Unbearable Weight*] for a discussion of how this construction of femininity is reproduced in contemporary commercials and advertisements concerning food, eating, and cooking.

20. Aimee Liu, *Solitaire* (New York: Harper and Row, 1979), p. 123.

21. Striking, in connection with this, is Catherine Steiner-Adair's 1984 study of high-school women, which reveals a dramatic association between problems with food and body image and emulation of the cool, professionally "together" and gorgeous superwoman. On the basis of a series of interviews, the high schoolers were classified into two groups: one expressed skepticism over the superwoman ideal, the other thoroughly aspired to it. Later administrations of diagnostic tests revealed that 94 percent of the pro-superwoman group fell into the eating-disordered range of the scale. Of the other group, 100 percent fell into the noneating-disordered range. Media notwithstanding, young women today appear to sense, either consciously or through their bodies, the impossibility of simultaneously meeting the demands of two spheres whose values have been historically defined in utter opposition to each other.

22. See "Anorexia Nervosa" [in *Unbearable Weight*].

23. Dianne Hunter, "Hysteria, Psychoanalysis and Feminism," in Shirley Garner, Claire Kahane, and Madelon Sprenger, eds., *The (M)Other Tongue* (Ithaca: Cornell University Press, 1985), p. 114.

24. Catherine Clément and Hélène Cixous, *The Newly Born Woman*, trans. Betsy Wing (Minneapolis: University of Minnesota Press, 1986), p. 42.

25. Clément and Cixous, *The Newly Born Woman*, p. 95.

26. Seidenberg and DeCrow, *Women Who Marry Houses*, p. 31.

27. Smith-Rosenberg, *Disorderly Conduct*, p. 208.

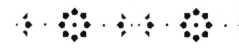

The following images offer a compliment to the articles we've included in this text. Throughout the book, there are questions inviting you to think about these images alongside the articles. However, we also imagine that you might find different ways that these images speak to the essays.

Figure 1: ThinkProgress, "Maternity Paid Leave Graphic:" This 2012 graphic highlights the difference in paid maternity leave allocated by various countries around the world. How do we know the United States is the focus of this chart? Why is the United States colored in black while the other countries are colored in a rainbow of colors ranging from red to blue? What does the image suggest about the difference between paid maternity leave in the United States and other countries?

Figures 2 and 3: Bluebella, "Ideal Men's Bodies and Ideal Women's Bodies:" In 2014, the lingerie and sex toy retailer Bluebella polled five hundred men and five hundred women on what makes a physically perfect man or woman. The result is four images—the ideal man and the ideal woman, from men's and women's perspectives. What do these images suggest women and men value about their own physical appearance versus the physical appearance of the other gender?

Figure 4: Memac Ogilvy and Mather Dubai, UN Women Ads against Sexism: The images presented here use genuine Google searches from March 2013 to reveal the widespread prevalence of sexism and discrimination against women from a global perspective. Why do Ogilvy and Dubai place the search results over the women's mouths? How do the ads work to expose negative stereotypes of women as well as the denial of women's rights?

Figure 5: MotorCorsa/Ducati, "Hot Mess" Desktop Wallpaper: In response to a series of desktop wallpapers published by MotorCorsa in 2014 that featured a scantily clad model on Ducati motorcycles, the company produced counterimages featuring men in the model's position. How does seeing a man used in the same way as a female model change the meaning of this ad?

Figure 6: Shelby Lin and Lydia Burns, photo of Rugby Players: This image accompanied the Chapter 4 essay "An Exercise in Body Image" (2014) in its original publication in *Harvard Political Review*. How does the photograph speak to the concept of ideal female beauty? How does it add to the conversation about exercise and beauty started by the authors of that essay?

Figure 7: John Darkow, "Rape on Campus:" This cartoon was featured on *The Cagle Post*, a website dedicated to political cartoons and commentary. What commentary is this cartoon offering about rape on college campuses? How do both the image and the text help contribute to that commentary?

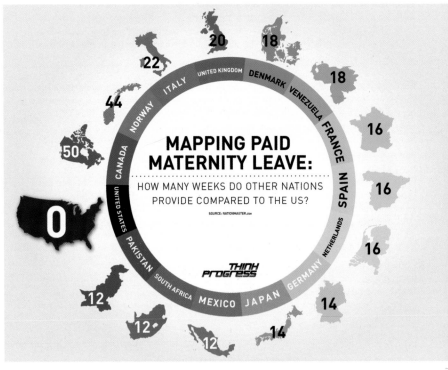

Figure 1 ThinkProgress, "Maternity Paid Leave Graphic."

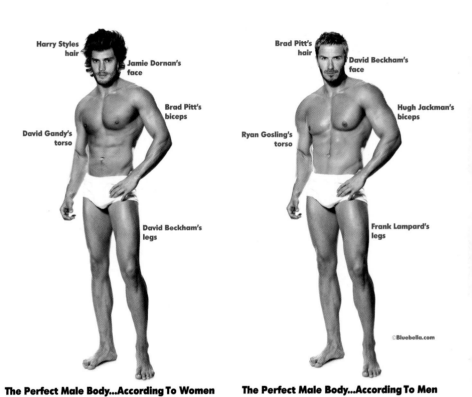

The Perfect Male Body...According To Women **The Perfect Male Body...According To Men**

Figure 2   Bluebella, "Ideal Men's Bodies."

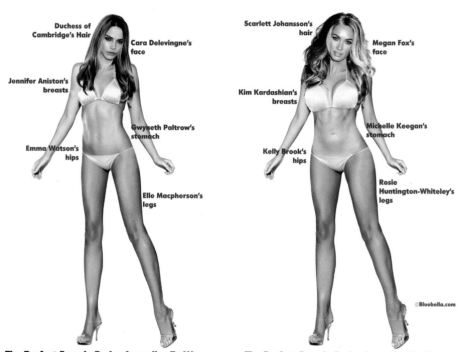

Duchess of
Cambridge's Hair

Cara Delevingne's
face

Jennifer Aniston's
breasts

Gwyneth Paltrow's
stomach

Emma Watson's
hips

Elle Macpherson's
legs

The Perfect Female Body...According To Women

Scarlett Johansson's
hair

Megan Fox's
face

Kim Kardashian's
breasts

Michelle Keegan's
stomach

Kelly Brook's
hips

Rosie
Huntington-Whiteley's
legs

©Bluebella.com

The Perfect Female Body...According To Men

Figure 3 Bluebella, "Ideal Women's Bodies."

Figure 4 Memac Ogilvy and Mather Dubai, UN Women Ads against Sexism.

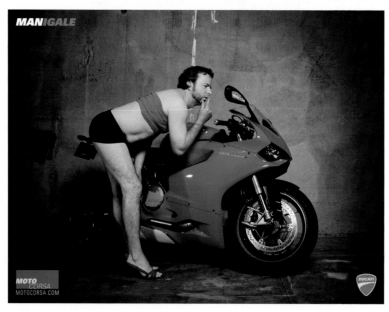

Figure 5 MotorCorsa/Ducati, "Hot Mess" Desktop Wallpaper.

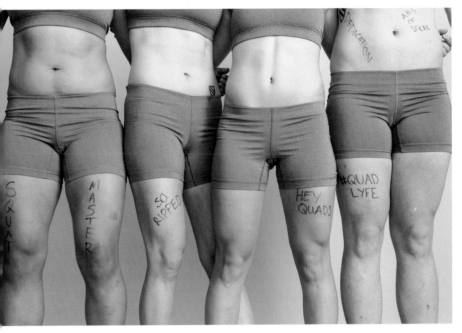

Figure 6   Shelby Lin and Lydia Burns, photo of Rugby Players.

Figure 7 John Darkow, "Rape on Campus."

28. Orbach, *Hunger Strike*, p. 102. When we look into the many autobiographies and case studies of hysterics, anorectics, and agoraphobics, we find that these are indeed the sorts of women one might expect to be frustrated by the constraints of a specified female role. Sigmund Freud and Joseph Breuer, in *Studies on Hysteria* (New York: Avon, 1966), and Freud, in the later *Dora: An Analysis of a Case of Hysteria* (New York: Macmillan, 1963), constantly remark on the ambitiousness, independence, intellectual ability, and creative strivings of their patients. We know, moreover, that many women who later became leading social activists and feminists of the nineteenth century were among those who fell ill with hysteria and neurasthenia. It has become a virtual cliché that the typical anorectic is a perfectionist, driven to excel in all areas of her life. Though less prominently, a similar theme runs throughout the literature on agoraphobia.

    One must keep in mind that in drawing on case studies, one is relying on the perceptions of other acculturated individuals. One suspects, for example, that the popular portrait of the anorectic as a relentless over-achiever may be colored by the lingering or perhaps resurgent Victorianism of our culture's attitudes toward ambitious women. One does not escape this hermeneutic problem by turning to autobiography. But in autobiography one is at least dealing with social constructions and attitudes that animate the subject's own psychic reality. In this regard the autobiographical literature on anorexia, drawn on in a variety of places [in *Unbearable Weight*], is strikingly full of anxiety about the domestic world and other themes that suggest deep rebellion against traditional notions of femininity.

29. Kim Chernin, *The Hungry Self: Women, Eating, and Identity* (New York: Harper and Row, 1985), esp. pp. 41–93.

30. Mark Poster, *Foucault, Marxism, and History* (Cambridge: Polity Press, 1984), p. 28.

31. Liu, *Solitaire*, p. 99.

32. Brett Silverstein, "Possible Causes of the Thin Standard of Bodily Attractiveness for Women," *International Journal of Eating Disorders* 5 (1986): 907–16.

33. Showalter, *The Female Malady*, p. 48.

34. Smith-Rosenberg, *Disorderly Conduct*, p. 207.

35. Orbach, *Hunger Strike*, p. 103.

36. Brownmiller, *Femininity*, p. 14.

37. Toril Moi, "Representations of Patriarchy: Sex and Epistemology in Freud's *Dora*," in Charles Bernheimer and Claire Kahane, eds., *In Dora's Case: Freud—Hysteria—Feminism* (New York: Columbia University Press, 1985), p. 192.

38. Foucault, *Discipline and Punish*, p. 136.

39. Foucault, *Discipline and Punish*, p. 136.

40. A focus on the politics of sexualization and objectification remains central to the anti-pornography movement (e.g., in the work of Andrea Dworkin,

Catherine McKinnon). Feminists exploring the politics of appearance include Sandra Bartky, Susan Brownmiller, Wendy Chapkis, Kim Chernin, and Susie Orbach. And a developing feminist interest in the work of Michel Foucault has begun to produce a poststructuralist feminism oriented towards practice; see, for example, Irene Diamond and Lee Quinby, *Feminism and Foucault: Reflections on Resistance* (Boston: Northeastern University Press, 1988).

41. See, for example, Susan Suleiman, ed., *The Female Body in Western Culture* (Cambridge: Harvard University Press, 1986).

42. Mitchie, *The Flesh Made Word*, p. 13.

43. Mitchie, *The Flesh Made Word*, p. 149.

Analyze

1. How is the body a "locus [central point] of social control"? In what ways can you see the body as a means to social control?

2. According to Bordo, previous notions of the feminine include hysteria and agoraphobia (fear of leaving the home). What are some contemporary notions of femininity? How do these relate to food (both women consuming food and women providing sustenance to others) and to masculinity?

3. Does Bordo see the "plight" of women (as obsessed with food, diet, and exercise) as hopeless? If so, why? Does she see any hope for women to move beyond this struggle and achieve some kind of stability with their bodies?

Explore

1. The motorcycle company Ducati commissioned a series of photos for desktop wallpaper featuring a motorcycle model in seductive poses. In response to complaints by "ladies who are sick and tired of bikes with bikini babes," Ducati then commissioned a series of photographs that feature men in place of the model. View the before and after image that we've included in the color art insert (Figure 5). How do contemporary notions of femininity play out in this ad? What ideas of femininity are these ads selling? How does the revision of the image to feature the man highlight those ideas and poke fun at them?

2. Jennifer Siebel Newsom's documentary *Miss Representation* (available in full on YouTube) also examines the way in which the female body

has been ascribed values by society. Watch the documentary and consider Bordo's argument in context with Newsom's. Would Bordo agree with the societal representation of the female body that Newsom offers? Why or why not?

3. One of Bordo's main focus points in this essay is to examine the anorectic body. Think about the ideal female body (Figure 3) presented in the color art insert in this book. Based on these images, along with your own sense of the perception of the female body (as crafted through the readings you've encountered in this book and your own experience), to what extent is this image of the "perfect female figure" as one that is slim fully ingrained in women? How might Bordo react to that ideal female body image, and why?

The New York Times
"Call Cornell Co-Ed the 'Perfect Girl'"

This article first appeared in *The New York Times* on 21 December 1912. According to the article, Dr. Esther Parker, a "medical examiner" at the university, studied the four hundred female students and determined twenty-four-year-old Elsie Scheel to be the "Perfect Girl." However, the idea of calling one woman the perfect girl caused controversy, even then. As you read this article, think about what in Dr. Parker's conclusions and what in Scheel's statements could be seen as problematic, given the time period (or even today), and why.

She Is Miss Elsie Scheel of Brooklyn, and Without a Single Physical Defect.

BEEFSTEAK HER MAINSTAY

Is Very Strong, Weighs 171 Pounds, and is 5 Feet 7 Inches Tall—Means to Grow Vegetables.

ITHACA, N.Y., Dec. 20.—The most nearly perfect physical specimen of womanhood at Cornell is Miss Elsie Scheel, a student in the College of Horticulture at Cornell University, who entered from Brooklyn, where she studied in the Packer Collegiate Institute. According to Dr. Esther Parker, Medical Examiner of the 400 "co-eds" in the university, Miss Scheel is not only a young woman of great strength, but in her physical makeup there is not a single defect.

Miss Scheel, who is a light-haired, blue-eyed girl whose very presence bespeaks perfect health, is 24 years old, weighs 171 pounds, and is 5 feet 7 inches tall. Her normal chest measurement is 34.6 inches, waist 30.3 inches, hips 40.4 inches. She is very fond of outdoor sports and walking; her hobby is motoring; her favorite sport basket ball; she is an ardent suffragette. She is much interested in horticulture, but if she were a man she would study mechanical engineering, as she likes to work about an automobile.

She eats but three meals in two days and almost always goes without breakfast. She does not believe in eating mechanically. Her favorite food is beefsteak; she doesn't care about delicacies, and has no liking for candy. She has never taken a drink of tea or coffee in her life, and keeps regular hours. She says she has never been ill and doesn't know what fear is. Girls would be happier if they got over the fear of things, she says. The girls at Sage College, she thinks, work too hard at their studies and too late at night.

When she finishes her course Miss Scheel is going to grow vegetables on her father's farm on Long Island.

Analyze

1. What are the reasons that Dr. Esther Parker gives for naming Scheel "the perfect girl"? Why do these reasons make Scheel an ideal woman?
2. What are some of Scheel's hobbies, and what are her long-term plans after graduation?
3. What is Scheel's philosophy on life, and how does that translate into advice that she gives to other girls?

Explore

1. Susan Bordo's book *Unbearable Weight*, from which the essay "The Body and the Reproduction of Femininity" was taken, was written about twenty years ago. Elsie Scheel was designated the "perfect woman" one

hundred years ago. Both texts allude to the power that women can—and should—have over their own bodies. To what extent do you believe that femininity is still tied to control over one's body and to power? Why?

2. Consider the ideal image of women, as perceived by both women and men, in the art insert at the middle of this textbook (Figure 3). To what extent is this idea of differing opinions on the ideal female body ongoing today?

3. Watch the Buzzfeed video "Women's Ideal Body Types throughout History" (available on YouTube). How does Elsie Scheel fit into the history of women's ideal bodies?

The New York Herald
"Brooklyn Venus Much Too Large Is Verdict of Physical Horticulturists"

This article is a response to the *New York Times*'s piece on Elsie Scheel previously featured in this book. Published by **The New York Herald** on 22 December 1912, this article declares that Elsie Scheel cannot be considered an "ideal woman" because her measurements do not match expectations of standard female beauty. In what ways is this article an early version of "body-shaming," and how?

Experts Declare That Avoirdupois Puts Miss Scheel Out of the Perfect Form Class.

WHY, SHE WEIGHS 171 LBS

If Figures Given Are Correct New York Specialists Say Dr. Parker, of Cornell, Has Made an Error.

Miss Elsie Scheel, the Brooklyn girl who, according to Dr. Esther Parker, of Cornell University, is the most perfectly formed "co-ed" ever entered at Cornell, may or may not rival the Venus de Milo for physical perfection, but several well known authorities on physical training and development last night said that the weight and measurements given by Dr. Parker cannot be reconciled with the accepted ideal of female beauty.

Miss Scheel, who is twenty-five years old, weighs 171 pounds and is 5 feet 7 inches tall. Her natural chest measurement is 34.6 inches, waist, 30.3 inches, and hips 40.4 inches.

Many of the authorities, questioned as to the proportion as indicated by the measurements, said that aside from being rather too tall for perfect womanly development Miss Scheel is at least twenty pounds over weight in relation to her height.

Dr. John Wilson Gibbs, of the Belleclaire Hotel, sent to the *Herald* a clipping of the announcement that Miss Scheel has been pronounced the most perfectly formed girl at Cornell and with it a brief note declaring the announcement absurd.

Seen in his apartment, Dr. Gibbs said that though Miss Scheel might possibly be attractive and might be an example of healthy development, she must, if her measurements are correctly stated, be far from perfection physically.

"No woman of Miss Scheel's height can possibly weigh 171 pounds and be in proportion," said Dr. Gibbs. "No matter how hardened by exercise she might be, it is inconceivable that with nearly twenty-two pounds over the proper weight the young woman could even approach the perfect female figure. The statement is merely the enthusiastic effusion of an enthusiastic friend, I fear."

Miss Kathryn Kahill, who conducts a gymnasium for the purpose of perfecting figures, said that she thought every one of the measurements of Miss Scheel indicated that she was much too large to be considered an ideal womanly figure.

William J. Brown, whose gymnasiums here and at Garrison-on-the-Hudson are well known, was of the opinion that Miss Scheel must be in splendid physical condition to carry 171 pounds and still be symmetrical. "The measurements given for Miss Scheel are remarkable in many ways," said Mr. Brown; "her chest measurement is small for the weight she is credited with; she is too tall to be considered an ideal type and her weight itself is out of all proportion. In the face of the figures given I cannot understand how the young woman could give the impression of perfection as to form. Only perfect physical condition can prevent her appearing absolutely clumsy."

Analyze

1. Based on the *New York Herald* article, why was Scheel's designation as the "Brooklyn Venus" incorrect?
2. Who are the people that deem her designation incorrect? What are their qualifications and their experience interacting with Scheel?
3. The "experts" critique not only Scheel's physicality, but also her appearance. What do they say about her appearance, and why? How does that critique further contribute to the concept of "body-shaming"?

Explore

1. In what ways does Bordo's discussion of the way that women's bodies are looked at in "The Body and the Reproduction of Femininity" relate to the *New York Herald*'s critique of Scheel? How might Bordo respond to the critique of Scheel's body? What in her argument leads you to believe this?
2. During this time period, there were two competing images of ideal female beauty: the "New Woman" and the "Gibson Girl." Do some research on both images. Which would you say that Scheel better represents? And how might that connect to the critique of her body?
3. How do you see the critique of Scheel play out in contemporary society? What examples suggest this kind of critique happens today? What examples suggest that society is beginning to move past critiques such as these? Write an essay that begins with the critique of Scheel and journeys into a discussion of contemporary critiques of women's bodies. How much has changed in the past one hundred years and how much has not? Why?

Brooke Kantor, Helen Clark, and Lydia Federico
"An Exercise in Body Image"

Harvard students and rugby players **Brooke Kantor** (Class of 2015), **Helen Clark** (Class of 2015), and **Lydia Federico** (Class of 2016) wrote this article for the *Harvard Political Review* in 2014. In this piece, using rugby as the focus of their discussion, they advocate for a different perspective on both diet and exercise and the female body. How does knowing that these authors are college students and rugby players add to their credibility in this piece?

Imagine a world in which every college-aged woman comes home from class in the afternoon, looks in the mirror, and thinks to herself "My body looks so strong and beautiful." The reader will likely recognize how far away this world is from where we are today. 86% of female students surveyed reported the existence of an eating disorder by age 20, and eating disorders claim more lives than any other mental illness in the United States. The main culprit may be what author and speaker Courtney Martin calls the "frightening normalcy of hating your body." Our society lacks a significant space for body positivity. Fortunately, one area that has the potential to provide this space for young females is women's athletics—in particular, the sport of rugby.

Loving Your Body Is a Statement

Loving one's body is an inherently political act. Maintaining pride in having a body that is "too big," "too small," or "not ideal" is a political statement against the many voices that tell us our bodies are problematic. Mainstream culture normalizes the flawless bodies that dominate every kind of mass media, sending girls the message that only slender, tall bodies are beautiful. At home, girls are taught to cross their legs in public and take up as little physical space as possible. They are taught that being beautiful is much more valuable than being smart and strong (try weighing Kim Kardashian's net worth against that of Condoleezza Rice). Magazines preach the gospel of constant diet and exercise to achieve "bikini bodies" that are meant to lounge poolside and be gazed upon. It is a true testament to the misogyny of our culture that women are encouraged to whittle away their bodies and maintain postures that make them as unobtrusive as possible.

Ultimately, it becomes a woman's responsibility to ensure that she arrives at this standard of beauty. Stand in the checkout line of any grocery store and you will see a plethora of magazines advertising the message that women are supposed to be in a constant state of self-improvement through beauty products, diets, and exercise. Exercise in particular has now taken its place as a piece of the "sexualization" of women phenomenon. Women are bombarded with the idea that the purpose of exercise is to attain a fit body, rather than to improve athletically. Workout videos and programs utilize slogans along the lines of, "receive the flat abs you always wanted," lending essentially zero value to the practicality of strengthening one's core muscles.

The Sport of Rugby

Rugby is undoubtedly one of the most physically demanding sports in the world. Lasting 80 minutes long with no substitutions, the amount of physical contact an individual on the field might receive makes American football look like a walk in the park. When most Americans think of rugby, they likely conjure up images of the movie *Invictus*, of people tackling each other with no protective gear of any kind. What is lesser known about rugby is that it is the only sport that has the exact same rules for men as it does for women. The number of players on the field is the same; unlike basketball, the ball size is the same; and unlike lacrosse, the level of contact is the same.

Rugby is a source of empowerment. Women players are taught to use the strength of their bodies in ways they had never even conceived. Where society appreciates the meek timidity that is supposed to accompany female beauty, rugby encourages women to be a dominating presence—fearless in pursuit of her goals. Contrary to the message that girls grow up receiving, rugby has no ideal body type. The ten separate rugby positions provide every kind of physique the opportunity to play a role on the field—tall, short, broad-shouldered, curvy, thick-legged, tiny. Each girl uses her unique strengths to make a significant contribution to the team. Every body type is celebrated and appreciated. There is no such thing as an ideal rugby body.

It is probable that more than a few girls on our rugby team have struggled with negative body image at some point in their lives. But if you ever had the chance to spend time with our team, you would never know it. We rejoice as a group when a girl proudly declares that she's gained a few pounds as the result of our weight training. We admire each other's widening thighs and thickening arms throughout the season. Words cannot adequately describe the liberating feeling that being a part of a team with such body positivity provides. Imagine the relief of taking a breath of fresh air after being drowned for so long in the pressure that society places on women to fit some unrealistic mold. Rugby, and our team in particular, only pressures players to utilize and to be proud of the parts of their bodies that make them unique.

The photo essay that accompanies this article is a testament to the power that a sport like rugby has. It demonstrates that there is the potential out there for women to be proud of their bodies, no matter what. It seeks to infiltrate the media landscape dominated by body negativity by inviting lookers to join us in our celebration of the distinctive beauty of each of our bodies. What you see are girls literally writing the things they love most about a fellow player's body or personality on that player's body with sharpie. Although it is extremely difficult to maintain a constant state of positive self-image in our culture, every time a woman celebrates the beauty of her own body or of another woman she is making a political statement. She is saying that she refuses to accept the messages spread by mainstream culture, and she is refusing to accept that her body is only valuable as a visual object.

Analyze

1. The authors are critical of a culture that promotes exercise to improve one's appearance. Why? What would they rather see society promote exercise as, and why?
2. Why do the authors believe that rugby can be a sport that encourages female empowerment and self-love?
3. Originally accompanying this essay was a photo essay by Shelby Lin and Lydia Burns featuring the Harvard rugby players. We've included one of the photos for you in the color art insert (Figure 6). After reading this essay, view the accompanying photograph (or the entire photo

essay, online). What do the authors believe is the true value of a female body? How do we know?

4. How does knowing that the authors are rugby players themselves influence our reading of this text? Why?

Explore

1. Compare the photograph of female rugby players in Figure 6 in the color art insert to the perception of female rugby players presented in the essay by Kantor, Clark, and Federico. How does the photo support the ideas in the essay?

2. In this essay, the authors argue that, to a large degree, diet and exercise have been sexualized. Talk to some women you know who eat healthily and follow an exercise routine. To what extent do they agree with the authors of this article? To what extent do they disagree?

3. Consider the authors' argument in this essay alongside the advice given to women by Elsie Scheel in "Call Cornell Co-Ed the 'Perfect Girl.'" What similarities do you notice? What might Scheel say about a sport for which women and men have the same rules? How do you know?

Nomy Lamm
"It's a Big Fat Revolution"

Nomy Lamm is a "bad ass, fat ass, Jew, dyke amputee" who was named *Ms.* magazine's 1997 "Woman of the Year." She is a writer, musician, political activist, and performer whose work challenges cultural constructions of beauty, femininity, ability, and sexual desirability. In "It's a Big Fat Revolution," originally featured in the book *Listen Up: Voices from the Next Feminist Generation* in 1995, Lamm uses writing to rebel against the patriarchy, the media, and the diet industry, as well as her friends, her family, and, importantly, herself. As you read, consider how Lamm seeks to incite revolution in her readers not only with *what* she says, but also with *how* she says it.

I am going to write an essay describing my experiences with fat oppression and the ways in which feminism and punk have affected my work. It will be clear, concise and well thought-out, and will be laid out in the basic thesis paper, college essay format. I will deal with these issues in a mature and intellectual manner. I will cash in on as many fifty-cent words as possible.

I lied. (You probably already picked up on that, huh?) I can't do that. This is my life, and my words are the most effective tool I have for challenging Whiteboyworld (that's my punk-rock cutesy but oh-so-revolutionary way of saying "patriarchy"). If there's one thing that feminism has taught me, it's that the revolution is gonna be on my terms. The revolution will be incited through my voice, my words, not the words of the universe of male intellect that already exists. And I know that a hell of a lot of what I say is totally contradictory. My contradictions can coexist, cuz they exist inside of me, and I'm not gonna simplify them so that they fit into the linear, analytical pattern that I know they're supposed to. I think it's important to recognize that all this stuff does contribute to the revolution, for real. The fact that I write like this cuz it's the way I want to write makes this world just that much safer for me.

I wanna explain what I mean when I say "the revolution," but I'm not sure whether I'll be able to. Cuz at the same time that I'm being totally serious, I also see my use of the term as a mockery of itself. Part of the reason for this is that I'm fully aware that I still fit into dominant culture in many ways. The revolution could very well be enacted against me, instead of for me. I don't want to make myself sound like I think I'm the most oppressed, most punk-rock, most revolutionary person in the world. But at the same time I do think that revolution is a word I should use as often as I can, because it's a concept that we need to be aware of. And I don't just mean it in an abstract, intellectualized way, either. I really do think that the revolution has begun. Maybe that's not apparent to mainstream culture yet, but I see that as a good sign. As soon as mainstream culture picks up on it, they'll try to co-opt it.

For now the revolution takes place when I stay up all night talking with my best friends about feminism and marginalization and privilege and oppression and power and sex and money and real-life rebellion. For now the revolution takes place when I watch a girl stand up in front of a crowd of people and talk about her sexual abuse. For now the revolution takes place when I get a letter from a girl I've never met who says that the zine I wrote changed her life. For now the revolution takes place when the homeless people in my town camp out for a week in the middle of downtown. For now the revolution takes place when I am confronted by a friend about something racist that I have said. For now the revolution takes place in my head when I know how fucking brilliant my girlfriends and I are.

And I'm living the revolution through my memories and through my pain and through my triumphs. When I think about all the marks I have against me in this society, I am amazed that I haven't turned into some worthless lump of shit. Fatkike-cripplecuntqueer. In a nutshell. But then I have to take into account the fact that I'm an articulate, white, middle-class college kid, and that provides me with a hell of a lot of privilege and opportunity for dealing with my oppression that may not be available to other oppressed people. And since my personality/being isn't divided up into a privileged part and an oppressed part, I have to deal with the ways that these things interact, counterbalance and sometimes even overshadow each other. For example, I was born with one leg. I guess it's a big deal, but it's never worked into my body image in the same way that being fat has. And what does it mean to be a white woman as opposed to a woman of color? A middle-class fat girl as opposed to a poor fat girl? What does it mean to be fat, physically disabled and bisexual? (Or fat, disabled and *sexual at all*?)

See, of course, I'm still a real person, and I don't always feel up to playing the role of the revolutionary. Sometimes it's hard enough for me to just get out of bed in the morning. Sometimes it's hard enough to just talk to people at all, without having to deal with the political nuances of everything that comes out of their mouths. Despite the fact that I do tons of work that deals with fat oppression, and that I've been working so so hard on my own body image, there are times when I really hate my body and don't want to deal with being strong all the time. Because I am strong and have thought all of this through in so many different ways, and I do have naturally high self-esteem, I've come to a place where I can honestly say that I love my body and I'm happy with being fat. But occasionally, when I look in the mirror and I see this body that is so different from my friends', so different from what I'm told it should be, I just want to hide away and not deal with it anymore. At these times it doesn't seem fair to me that I have to always be fighting to be happy. Would it be easier for me to just give in and go on another diet so that I can stop this perpetual struggle? Then I could still support the fat grrrl revolution without having it affect me personally in every way. And I know I know I know that's not the answer and I could never do that to myself, but I can't say that the thought never crosses my mind.

And it doesn't help much when my friends and family, who all know how I feel about this, continue to make anti-fat statements and bitch about how fat they feel and mention new diets they've heard about and are just dying to try. "I'm shaped like a watermelon." "Wow, I'm so happy, I now wear a size seven instead of a size nine." "I like this mirror because it makes me look thinner."

I can't understand how they could still think these things when I'm constantly talking about these issues, and I can't believe that they would think that these are okay things to talk about in front of me. And it's not like I want them to censor their conversation around me. . . . I just want them to not think it. I know that most of this is just a reflection of how they feel about themselves and isn't intended as an attack on me or an invalidation of my work, but it makes it that much harder for me. It puts all those thoughts inside me. Today I was standing outside of work and I caught a glimpse of myself in the window and thought, "Hey, I don't look that fat!" And I immediately realized how fucked up that was, but that didn't stop me from feeling more attractive because of it.

I want this out of me. This is not a part of me, and theoretically I can separate it all out and throw away the shit, but it's never really gone. When will this finally be over? When can I move on to other issues? It will never be over, and that's really fucking hard to accept.

I am living out this system of oppression through my memories, and even when I'm not thinking about them they are there, affecting everything I do. Five years old, my first diet. Seven years old, being declared officially "overweight" because I weigh ten pounds over what a "normal" seven-year-old should weigh. Ten years old, learning to starve myself and be happy feeling constantly dizzy. Thirteen years old, crossing the border from being bigger than my friends to actually being "fat." Fifteen years old, hearing the boys in the next room talk about how fat (and hence unattractive) I am. Whenever I perform, I remember the time when my dad said he didn't like the dance I choreographed because I looked fat while I was doing it. Every time I dye my hair I remember when my mom wouldn't let me dye my hair in seventh grade because seeing fat people with dyed hair made her think they were just trying to cover up the fact that they're fat, trying to look attractive despite it (when of course it's obvious what they should really do if they want to look attractive, right?). And these are big memorable occurrences that I can put my finger on and say, "This hurt me." But what about the lifetime of media I've been exposed to that tells me that only thin people are lovable, healthy, beautiful, talented, fun? I know that those messages are all packed in there with the rest of my memories, but I just can't label them and their effects on my psyche. They are elusive and don't necessarily feel painful at the time. They are well disguised and often even appear alluring and romantic. (I will never fall in love because I cannot be picked up and swung around in circles. . . .)

All my life the media and everyone around me have told me that fat is ugly. Which of course is just a cultural standard that has many, many medical lies to fall back upon. Studies have shown that fat people are unhealthy and have short life expectancies. Studies have also shown that starving people have these same peculiarities. These health risks to fat people have been proven to be a result of continuous starvation—dieting—and not of fat itself. I am not fat due to lack of willpower. I've been a vegetarian since I was ten years old. Controlling what I eat is easy for me. Starving myself is not (though for most of my life I wished it was). My body is supposed to be like this, and I've been on plenty of diets where I've kept off some weight for a period of several months and then gained it all back. Two years ago I finally ended the cycle. I am not dieting anymore because I know that this is how my body is supposed to be, and this is how I want it to be. Being fat does not make me less healthy or less active. Being fat does not make me less attractive.

On TV I see a thin woman dancing with a fabulously handsome man, and over that I hear, "I was never happy until I went on [fill in the blank] diet program, but now I'm getting attention from men, and I feel so good! I don't have to worry about what people are saying about me behind my back, because I know I look good. You owe it to yourself to give yourself the life you deserve. Call [fill in the blank] diet program today, and start taking off the pounds right away!" TV shows me a close-up of a teary-eyed fat girl who says, "I've tried everything, but nothing works. I lose twenty pounds, and I gain back twenty-five. I feel so ashamed. What can I do?" The first time I saw that commercial I started crying and memorized the number on the screen. I know that feeling of shame. I know that feeling of having nowhere left to turn, of feeling like I'm useless because I can't lose all that "unwanted fat." But I know that the unhappiness is not a result of my fat. It's a result of a society that tells me I'm bad.

Where's the revolution? My body is fucking beautiful, and every time I look in the mirror and acknowledge that, I am contributing to the revolution.

I feel like at this point I'm expected to try to prove to you that fat can be beautiful by going into descriptions of "rippling thighs and full smooth buttocks." I won't. It's not up to me to convince you that fat can be attractive. I refuse to be the self-appointed full-figured porno queen. Figure it out on your own.

It's not good enough for you to tell me that you "don't judge by appearances"—so fat doesn't bother you. Ignoring our bodies and "judging only by what's on the inside" is not the answer. This seems to be along the same line of thinking as that brilliant school of thought called "humanism": "We are all just people, so let's ignore trivialities such as race, class, gender, sexual preference, body type and so on." Bullshit! The more we ignore these aspects of ourselves, the more shameful they become and the more we are expected to be what is generally implied when these qualifiers are not given—white, straight, thin, rich, male. It's unrealistic to try to overlook these exterior (and hence meaningless, right?) differences, because we're still being brainwashed with the same shit as everyone else. This way we're just not talking about it. And I don't want to be told, "Yes you're fat, but you're beautiful on the inside." That's just another way of telling me that I'm ugly, that there's no way that I'm beautiful on the outside. Fat does not equal ugly, don't give me that. My body is me. I want you to see my body, acknowledge my body. True revolution comes not when we learn to ignore our fat and pretend we're no different, but when we learn to use it to our advantage, when we learn to deconstruct all the myths that propagate fat-hate.

My thin friends are constantly being validated by mainstream feminism, while I am ignored. The most widespread mentality regarding body image at this point is something along these lines: Women look in the mirror and think, "I'm fat," but really they're not. Really they're thin.

Really they're thin. But really I'm fat. According to mainstream feminist theory, I don't even exist. I know that women do often look in the mirror and think that they are fatter than they are. And yes, this is a problem. But the analysis can't stop there. There are women who *are* fat, and that needs to be dealt with. Rather than just reassuring people, "No, you're not fat, you're just curvy," maybe we should be demystifying fat and dealing with fat politics as a whole. And I don't mean maybe, I mean it's a necessity. Once we realize that fat is not "inherently bad" (and I can't even believe I'm writing that—"inherently bad"—it sounds so ridiculous), then we can work out the problem as a whole instead of dealing only with this very minute part of it. All forms of oppression work together, and so they have to be fought together.

I think that a lot of the mainstream feminist authors who claim to be dealing with this issue are doing it in a very wrong way. Susie Orbach, for example, with *Fat Is a Feminist Issue*. She tells us: Don't diet, don't try to lose weight, don't feed the diet industry. But she then goes on to say: But if you eat right and exercise, you will lose weight! And I feel like, great, nice, it's so very wonderful that that worked for her, but she's totally missing the point. She is trying to help women, but really she is hurting us. She is hurting us because she's saying that there's still only one body that's okay for us (and she's the one to help us get it!). It's almost like that *Stop the Insanity* woman, Susan Powter. One of my friends read her book and said that the first half of it is all about fat oppression and talks about how hard it is to be fat in our society, but then it says: So use my great new diet plan! This kind of thing totally plays on our emotions so that we think, Wow, this person really understands me. They know where I'm coming from, so they must know what's best for me.

And there are so many "liberal" reasons for perpetuating fat-hate. Yes, we're finally figuring out that dieting never works. How, then, shall we explain this horrible monstrosity? And how can we get rid of it? The new "liberal" view on fat is that it is caused by deep psychological disturbances. Her childhood was bad, she was sexually abused, so she eats and gets fat in order to hide herself away. She uses her fat as a security blanket. Or maybe when she was young her parents caused her to associate food with comfort and love, so she eats to console herself. Or maybe, like with me, her parents were always on diets and always nagging her about what she was eating, so food became something shameful that must be hoarded and kept secret. And for a long, long time I really believed that if my parents hadn't instilled in me all these fucked-up attitudes about food, I wouldn't be fat. But then I realized that my brother and sister both grew up in exactly the same environment, and they are both thin. Obviously this is not the reason that I am fat. Therapy won't help, because there's nothing to cure. When will we stop grasping for reasons to hate fat people and start realizing that fat is a totally normal and natural thing that cannot and should not be gotten rid of?

Despite what I said earlier about my friends saying things that are really hurtful to me, I realize that they are actually pretty exceptional. I don't want to make them seem like uncaring, ignorant people. I'm constantly talking about these issues, and I feel like I'm usually able to confront my friends when they're being insensitive, and they'll understand or at least try to. Sometimes when I leave my insular circle of friends I'm shocked at what the "real world" is like. Hearing boys on the bus refer to their girlfriends as their "bitches," seeing fat women being targeted for harassment on the street, watching TV and seeing how every fat person is depicted as a food-obsessed slob, seeing women treated as property by men who see masculinity as a right to power. . . . I leave these situations feeling like the punk scene, within which most of my interactions take place, is so sheltered. I cannot imagine living in a community where I had nowhere to go for support. I cannot imagine living in the "real world."

But then I have to remember that it's still there in my community— these same fucked-up attitudes are perpetuated within the punk scene as well; they just take on more subtle forms. I feel like these issues are finally starting to be recognized and dealt with, but fat hating is still pretty standard. Of course everyone agrees that we shouldn't diet and that eating disorders are a result of our oppressive society, but it's not usually taken much further than that. It seems like people have this idea that punk is disconnected from the media. That because we are this cool underground subculture, we are immune to systems of oppression. But the punkest, coolest kids are still the skinny kids. And the same cool kids who are so into defying mainstream capitalist "Amerika" are the ones who say that fat is a symbol of capitalist wealth and greed. Yeah, that's a really new and different way of thinking: Blame the victim. Perpetuate institutionalized oppression. Fat people are not the ones who are oppressing these poor, skinny emo boys.

This essay is supposed to be about fat oppression. I feel like that's all I ever talk about. Sometimes I feel my whole identity is wrapped up in my fat. When I am fully conscious of my fat, it can't be used against me. Outside my secluded group of friends, in hostile situations, I am constantly aware that at any moment I could be harassed. Any slight altercation with another person could lead to a barrage of insults thrown at my body. I am always ready for it. I've found it doesn't happen nearly as often as I expect it, but still I always remain aware of the possibility. I am "the Fat Girl." I am "the Girl Who Talks About Fat Oppression." Within the punk scene, that's my security blanket. People know about me and know about my work, so I assume that they're not gonna be laughing behind my back about my fat. And if they are, then I know I have support from other people around me.

The punk scene gives me tons of support that I know I wouldn't get elsewhere. Within the punk scene, I am able to put out zines, play music, do spoken-word performances that are intensely personal to me. I feel really strongly about keeping nothing secret. I can go back to the old cliché about the personal being political, and no matter how trite it may sound, it's true. I went for so long never talking about being fat, never talking about how that affects my self-esteem, never talking about the ways that I'm oppressed by this society. Now I'm talking. Now I'm talking, I'm talking all the time, and people listen to me. I have support.

And at the same time I know that I have to be wary of the support that I receive. Because I think to some people this is just seen as the cool thing, that by supporting me they're somehow receiving a certain amount of validation from the punk scene. Even though I am totally open and don't keep secrets, I have to protect myself.

This is the revolution. I don't understand the revolution. I can't lay it all out in black and white and tell you what is revolutionary and what is not. The punk scene is a revolution, but not in and of itself. Feminism is a revolution; it is solidarity as well as critique and confrontation. This is the fat grrrl revolution. It's mine, but it doesn't belong to me. Fuckin' yeah.

Analyze

1. Lamm begins her essay by describing how she will write it: "It will be clear, concise, and well thought-out, and will be laid out in the basic thesis paper, college essay format." Then she immediately eschews this approach. Why does she choose this rhetorical strategy?

2. How would you describe the tone of this piece? Is it effective? If so, why?

3. What does Lamm mean when she says "This is the fat grrrl revolution. It's mine, but it doesn't belong to me"? To whom does it belong?

Explore

1. Lamm claims that the "most widespread mentality regarding body image at this point is something along these lines: Women look in the mirror and think, 'I'm fat,' but really they're not. Really they're thin." Do you agree with this statement?

2. In 2012, the state of Georgia introduced the Strong 4 Life campaign, a series of ads aimed at combating childhood obesity. (Images from this campaign are easily found online.) "Warning," reads one message under a photo of a chubby boy. "Big bones didn't make me this way. Big meals did." Another, this time paired with a picture of a young girl, reads, "Warning: It's hard to be a little girl. If you're not." Do you think fat shaming is an effective way to promote weight loss? Why or why not?

3. Lamm notes the anti-fat statements she hears from friends and families: "I'm shaped like a watermelon." "Wow, I'm so happy, I now wear a size seven instead of a size nine." "I like this mirror because it makes me look thinner." These statements could also be considered microaggressions. According to Dr. Derald Sue, a professor of psychology at Columbia University, "microaggression" is defined as an "everyday slight, putdown, indignity, or invalidation unintentionally directed toward a marginalized group." Melissa McEwan created the hashtag #FatMicroaggressions to start a conversation about the hurtful comments directed at overweight people on a daily basis. View the #FatMicroaggressions feed on Twitter. What does this reveal about fat oppression and/or fat acceptance?

Kate Fridkis
"Why I'm Hot for Peter Dinklage"

Kate Fridkis is a Brooklyn-based writer whose work has appeared on/in *Salon, Slate, Cosmopolitan, The New York Times, xoJane,* and more. Her blog, *Eat the Damn Cake,* ran for four years and was featured on sites such as *Jezebel* and *The Huffington Post.* This article, "Why I'm Hot for Peter Dinklage," was written for the website *The Frisky's* "Girl Talk" column in 2012. As you read this essay, consider how Fridkis comes to an understanding of why she "is hot for Peter Dinklage." What ideas does she consider in this piece, and why? What is her thought process, and how does it help her arrive at a conclusion?

It's not that I have a thing, as it were, for little people. And, God, is that really the politically correct term? Are we serious about this? It's not that I have some sort of fetish or something. But Peter Dinklage is hot. And I said it long before he was on *Game of Thrones*.

I said it when I saw *The Station Agent*, back in the day, before college, even, when I went to see the flick with my lame boyfriend, and Peter Dinklage was so much hotter than him. And had so much more *gravitas*. And so much more *charisma*. And such a look of gentle weariness in his noble, manly eyes.

So when he showed up again, in *Game of Thrones*, I was willing to watch, despite all the casual rape and beheading and ripping out of throats and other body parts that no one should ever rip out.

He's still hot. He's commanding and funny and subtle. He's clearly a great actor. But when I say hot, I mean *hot*. Physically. He's a seriously good looking guy. And I get the sense that I am probably not supposed to think that, because women are talking about how Peeta is shorter than Katniss in *The Hunger Games*, and that's so weird and unappealing. And he's like, a half of an inch shorter than her.

I have friends who won't date a guy unless he's over 6'2". And friends who go on a first date with a guy and then won't go on another because he's an inch shorter than them. Or only an inch taller than them. Even though he is awesome, otherwise.

I am not saying that these friends are bad people. Attraction is attraction. You can't help it. And if you're not into the way someone looks, it's probably better to find someone else than to fake it. Not probably. *Definitely.*

I once dated a really tall guy. I remember his neck very clearly. Not his face, as much. I have definitely dismissed guys for silly, superficial, yet important-feeling reasons. In general, I stand up for the guys my friends dismiss based on height requirements, or other requirements that seem a little harsh. But that doesn't mean I understand why I think Peter Dinklage is hot. So here I am, wondering if maybe this is some sort of statement. Maybe this says something important about me. Maybe there's some profound secret of my psyche that is being revealed here.

I mean, Peter Dinklage looks different from the way that hot men are supposed to look. So I am different for thinking he's hot. He stands out in a way that might make people uncomfortable. In a way that goes against some pretty strict rules about masculinity. And maybe that's part of why he's hot to me. Because I know exactly what kind of guy I'm supposed to be into, and sometimes I can't tell them apart because it's a matter of how much gel is in this one's hair as opposed to how tan this other one is. They look like boys who have never had to deal with anything. Not even, like, the death of a family dog. They are untouched, pristine. They are flawless.

Peter Dinklage is not flawless.

And maybe I'm a little tired of attractiveness having to always be about flawlessness. About the most normal of the normal. Like when they do those studies where they ask guys to pick the most attractive face out of a stack of photos and they always pick the one that is the computer generated average of all the other faces. The most symmetrical and bland. Sometimes I wish someone would pick the girl with the bump on her nose and the flashing, but slightly uneven eyes. Sometimes I wish they would pick a girl who looks a little more like me. Or at least someone unusual.

Maybe I am open-minded.

I was thinking about all this for a while, as I watched Tyrion (Peter's character in *Game of Thrones*) crack a quick-witted and wry joke as he walked down a muddy road in a worn leather breastplate of the medieval variety. I thought about it, and then I decide that it was total crap.

I'm not deep and fascinating and open-minded for thinking Peter Dinklage is hot. I have not been liberated from the binds of superficiality and judgmentalness. I haven't made a profound statement or philosophically distinguished myself from the masses or managed to believe that, truly, everyone is beautiful at exactly the same level, if only we look at them the right way. No. Objectively, unthinkingly, automatically, I think Peter Dinklage is hot. And then I make up the rest of it to try to explain.

Would it be so weird if Peter Dinklage was just hot? Just because he *is*?

I think I'm just going to let him go ahead and be hot. And not analyze it anymore. And keep watching this damn show, where someone's throat is always about to be ripped out, and get turned on every time Peter Dinklage wears a leather breastplate.

Analyze

1. Why does Fridkis find Peter Dinklage hot? Why does she believe that she is not supposed to?
2. According to Fridkis, how does Dinklage defy the norms of masculinity?

3. What, ultimately, does Fridkis conclude about society's standard of beauty—for men *and* for women? Why?

Explore

1. Look up images of Peter Dinklage online, especially images of him as Tyrion Lannister on *Game of Thrones*. If you are unfamiliar with the book series or the show *Game of Thrones*, do a little research into Dinklage's character. How does the image of Dinklage as Lannister—and images that you see of Dinklage online—address the ideals of masculinity outlined by Frazer in "How Big Are Your Balls?"?

2. Consider Fridkis's argument in this essay alongside the images of the ideal male bodies in Figure 2 of the art insert. In what ways does her attraction to Peter Dinklage conform to (or deviate from) the ideal male body (for both women and men)?

3. How does Fridkis's insistence at the end of the essay that it should be enough to find Dinklage hot extend Jensen's argument in "The High Cost of Manliness" that we need to end society's current notions of masculinity and femininity? To what extent do you agree? Using Jensen and Fridkis (and any additional readings you find relevant), write an essay that addresses the extent to which masculinity needs to change, how, and why.

Sherman Alexie
"Jason Collins Is the Envy of Straight Men Everywhere"

Sherman Alexie is an award-winning writer and filmmaker who has published in a wide variety of genres, including poetry, short stories, and children's literature. The following essay was originally published on the Seattle-based website *The Stranger* in 2013. In this essay, think about how Alexie draws on his ethos as a heterosexual male "jock" (he was a star basketball player in high school) to challenge the notion that there are clear delineations between hetero- and non-heterosexual masculinity. How does Alexie's tone in this piece help construct his argument?

"If Collins does play in the NBA next year, I'm sure certain team-mates might feel threatened by his presence in the locker room. I'll be the straight boy who'd love to have a fraction of his physical near-perfection."

—Mark Kaufman

One of the best 1,000 basketball players in the world.

As a straight-boy jock, I have been showering with large groups of naked men for decades. And these showers have not taken place in bath-rooms where we straight men yell at one another from modest private stalls. No, we athletes clean ourselves in large, communal Roman gladiator bath-houses. My high-school locker room's showerheads were placed so that we boys soaped up while facing one another. And we did this soaping while standing two feet apart.

In other words, I, Sherman, a heterosexual lifelong basketball player, have seen a lot more cock and man-ass than many gay men.

As I age, my cock is essentially the same one I owned in 1983. But my balls and ass are loosening and threatening to avalanche down my body. I think I'm an attractive man wearing clothes, but when I'm naked . . . well, let's just say that I'm grateful I have a pleasant face. And, grading on a curve, I'm actually a relatively fit middle-aged man. All around me in the health clubs, I encounter mountainous guts that make my chubby belly look like a foothill. I see butt cheeks that look like two Sasquatches playing tennis. I recoil from feet so gnarled, hirsute, and abused that a hobbit would suggest a pedicure.

So why do certain homely straight men worry that gay men are even re-motely interested in sexually harassing their concave asses? If strange women don't amass in large numbers to jump your bones, then why would packs of gay men hunger for you?

And, hey, I don't mean to punish those folks who are not hot, hot, hot. The plain and the lovely deserve equal amounts of love. I am only talking about sexual objectification.

So how do these dynamics change when it comes to the relationship between gay men and beautiful straight men? Does it mean gay men might sexually harass beautiful straight men?

I've never been beautiful, but gay men have hit on me, especially at gay film festivals where my movie *The Business of Fancydancing* played to slightly interested audiences. More than one man whispered his room number to me while handing me a hotel key card, which isn't nearly as romantic as handing somebody an actual, old-fashioned key and would have also relied on me being able to remember a hotel room number. When I travel, I have to take photos of the room numbers so I can refer to them when I find my way back. If I had wanted to have a one-night stand with a gay cinema fan, I would've been forced to wander the Hyatt hallways chanting, "I'm a straight Indian filmmaker looking to explore other options," and hoping that my admirer heard me from inside his room.

Once, in a private box at a Mariners game, a dude (married to a woman, who was five feet away) stealthily pushed his crotch against my blue-jeaned butt. That guy wore his closet like it was a pair of khaki pants with an open fly.

How do I react to these sexual advances? My first thought is "Men are boundaryless animals." My second thought is "Women have to deal with this shit all the time." My third thought is "How flattering." My fourth thought is "I wish this dude hitting on me was cuter."

So who are the best-looking men in the USA? The answer, obviously, is professional athletes. I mean, Jesus, Google-Image Adrian Peterson. Study how cut, shredded, and jacked he is.

Cut. Shredded. Jacked. Those are violent straight-boy adjectives that mean "beautiful." But we straight boys aren't supposed to think of other men as beautiful. We're supposed to think of the most physically gifted men as warrior soldiers, as dangerous demigods.

And there's the rub: When we're talking about professional athletes, we are mostly talking about males passionately admiring the physical attributes and abilities of other males. It might not be homosexual, but it certainly is homoerotic.

So when Jason Collins, an NBA basketball player, announced this week that he was gay and became the first active athlete in the four major professional American sports leagues to come out of the closet, I was proud of him. And I was aroused, politically speaking.

He's the Jackie Robinson of homosexual basketball big men.

He's seven feet and 250 pounds of man-loving man.

And he's an aging center in the last days of his professional career who might not be signed by a team next season.

Homophobic basketball fans will disparage his skills, somehow equating his NBA benchwarmer status with his sexuality. But let's not forget that Collins is still one of the best 1,000 basketball players in the world. He has always been better than his modest statistics would indicate, and his teams have been dramatically more efficient with him on the court. He is better at hoops than 99.9 percent of you are at anything you do. He might not be a demigod, but he's certainly a semi-demigod. Moreover, his basketball colleagues universally praise him as a physically and mentally tough player. In his prime, he ably battled that behemoth known as Shaquille O'Neal. Most of all, Collins is widely regarded as one of the finest gentlemen to ever play the game. Generous, wise, and supportive, he's a natural leader. And he has a degree from Stanford University.

In other words, he's a highly attractive dude.

If he does play in the NBA next year, I'm sure certain teammates might feel threatened by his presence in the locker room. I imagine that homophobic fans will hurl insults at him. But I'll be a fan who will see him sitting at the end of the bench, maybe getting to play a few minutes every other game, and still be jealous of his athletic gifts.

I'll be the straight boy who'd love to have a fraction of Jason Collins's physical near-perfection. And other straight-boy fans, homophobic or not, admittedly or not, will also be jealous of Collins's status among the basketball elite.

Gay folks and straight supporters have had much to celebrate recently. I am happy that gay marriage is legal in Washington State. I am happy that an exclusively heterosexual institution is admitting my gay brethren. But I'm overjoyed that an ostensibly straight-boy activity like basketball, my greatest love, is now being recognized as the homoerotic extravaganza that it is. After all, aside from swimming, diving, and water polo—the Holy Trinity of Way Gay Sports—basketball is the sport where men wear the least clothes. When playing ball, we're essentially just in underwear. Hell, even among us pathetic hoopsters, we usually play shirts against skins. Yep, one team is always topless.

I recently saw video of my topless body jogging down the court. It was a tragic version of Bo Derek running down the beach in that movie about being a perfect 10. I look like a figure eight. So I've been eating better and exercising more because I, the basketball player who loves vaginas, want to be sexually objectified by women. And men. Truly, when it comes down to it, don't we all want to be universally desired?

Analyze

1. How does Alexie use his own body as a basis for opening the conversation about male sexuality? Why do you think that he decides to do so?
2. Why aren't straight men supposed to think that other men are "beautiful"? How does Alexie challenge that argument?
3. Why does Alexie argue that sports are much more homoerotic than one might think, and how does he use his own experience in sports to help make that argument?

Explore

1. How does Alexie offer a rebuttal to those who might be critical of Jason Collins's basketball playing skills? Why does Alexie see Collins as an "attractive dude"? How does he connect those critiques to jealousy and, potentially, to homophobia?
2. Alexie asks us to "Google-Image Adrian Peterson" to get an idea of the "straight-boy adjectives that mean 'beautiful.'" Google Peterson, as well as other male athletes, such as Colin Kaepernick, Giancarlo Stanton, and LeBron James. How do we perceive these male athletes? Do we see them, as Alexie contends, as "warrior soldiers," or do we see them as beautiful? Or, can we see them as both? What does the way that we answer these questions suggest about society's beliefs about the male body?
3. Consider Alexie's essay in the context of Frazer's quiz and Jensen's essay "The High Cost of Manliness." How might Alexie perceive the questions in Frazer's quiz, and how do we know? How might Alexie respond to Jensen's argument in his essay, and why? What conversations about masculinity seem to be emerging from these readings?

Forging Connections

1. In what ways might we see Elsie Scheel as an early participant in Nomy Lamm's revolution? How might Lamm respond to the body shaming that took place following Scheel being called the "Brooklyn Venus"?

2. aerie is a lingerie company that is a subdivision of apparel company American Eagle Outfitters. In 2014, the company launched the aerie Real ad campaign featuring all unairbrushed models. Find images from this campaign online. To what extent do the ads in this campaign challenge typical representations of women in the media? How might the authors in this section respond to this ad campaign, and why?

Looking Further

1. The ideal man is something that heterosexual women are raised to believe not only exists, but also is something they should actively pursue and fight for. We especially see this in the "princess narratives" of Disney (looking ahead to Chapter 5). How does this concept of the ideal man impact the representations of men we see in the media? Think about male celebrities who would be considered "ideal": What kinds of roles do they get (if they are in television or film), and how are they perceived by both their peers and society in general? What about male celebrities that are (to use Fridkis's word) "flawed"? How are they perceived by their peers and in society? Choose two celebrities: one ideal and one flawed. How do you compare their status, based on their bodies and their perceived masculinity? Write an essay in which you compare and contrast these celebrities' masculinity, drawing on sources you've read thus far to help guide your discussion.

2. Today, many people use plastic surgery and extreme dieting to try to attain the ideal female or male body. For instance, Valeria Lukyanova is known as the "Human Barbie" and has used drastic measures (including both dieting and plastic surgery) to attain the "ideal" Barbie figure. Justin Jedlica calls himself the "Human Ken," has had 190 surgeries, and claims he will not stop until his body is "100 percent plastic." Why do you believe that some individuals strive to achieve this kind of "perfection"? Look up images of Lukyanova and Jedlica online. How do they compare with the ideal male and female figures we've included in the color art insert (Figures 2 and 3)? How do you believe this kind of distortion of the ideal occurs? Draw from the readings in this chapter to help shape your response.

5 Gender and Popular Culture

Perhaps more so than any other form of societal influence, popular culture has a pervasive hold on our lives and on the way we see the world. With the rise of the Internet and later social media, we no longer have to turn to a newspaper, magazine, radio, or television to find out information on our latest celebrity crush or to hear music by our favorite band; if we have a smartphone, all it takes is a few swipes of a finger and we become immersed in a world of *Tonight Show* clips, music videos, and pop culture news. Pop culture has become as much a commodity as material goods; we can buy it through platforms like Hulu and Spotify, and we consume it on an almost constant basis.

Because popular culture is such a significant part of our lives, we might not realize how pop culture works to portray particular gender stereotypes and to offer heavily gendered messages. For instance, *Modern Family*, our example from Chapter 3, is one of the most popular comedy shows on television. According to the Nielsen ratings, which measure audience size for television programming, *Modern Family* averaged 10 million viewers per week (not counting those who watch the show through online platforms) and has ranked consistently in the top 20 shows since its third season. The show and its cast have won numerous awards. Although the show is laugh-out-loud funny, it also becomes a platform for messages about gender. When we watch how the characters interact with each other—how Phil and Claire communicate, for instance—we are internalizing a gendered message. For example, when Phil and Claire try to plan alone time, and they are constantly interrupted by their family, this tells us that married couples must give up their needs for the needs of their children.

All aspects of popular culture—celebrities, music, video games, and so on—promote specific messages about gender. In the readings that follow, we will examine how different genres of pop culture present us with gendered messages and how we understand and critique those messages. We will see both positive and problematic gender issues raised, and, as consumers of pop culture, we ask you, along with the writers, to interrogate those messages. First, Michelle Law's essay "'Sisters Doin' It for Themselves': *Frozen* and the Evolution of the Disney Heroine" argues that the film *Frozen* changes the narrative of the traditional Disney princess into a strong female, even feminist, story. Tasha Robinson, in "We're Losing All Our Strong Female Characters to Trinity Syndrome," contends that although we have an influx of strong women in the science fiction/fantasy film genre, many of these women are given little to do and thus retain their role as window dressings, as opposed to drivers of the film's action. In "Iggy Azalea's Post-Racial Mess," Brittney Cooper argues that Iggy Azalea—a white rap artist from Australia—has usurped the style and artistry of southern black women and that black men have participated in this appropriation to the detriment of black women. Blue Telusma's essay "Kim Kardashian Doesn't Realize She's the Butt of an Old Racial Joke" looks at the history of fetishizing nonwhite women's body parts, beginning with Saartjie Baartman, known as the Hottentot Venus, in the early 19th century. In "*Orange Is the New Black*'s Irresponsible Portrayal of Men," Noah Berlatsky asserts that men are grossly—and problematically—underrepresented on the aforementioned television show. Finally, in "Candy Girl," Emily Nussbaum offers a review of the television show *The Unbreakable Kimmy Schmidt* and advocates for the show's importance in representing television that deals with sensitive material.

Michelle Law
"Sisters Doin' It for Themselves: *Frozen* and the Evolution of the Disney Heroine"

Michelle Law is a writer, columnist, blogger, and screenwriter from Brisbane, Australia. She is the coauthor of the book *Sh*t Asian Mothers Say*, and her writing has appeared in Australian outlets such as the *Sydney Morning Herald*, *Daily Life*, and *The Drum*. She is also a screenwriter and playwright and is an artist-in-residence at La Boite Theater Company.

The following essay was published in *Screen Education*, a journal for primary and secondary school educators interested in utilizing film in the classroom, in 2014. As you read it, consider how Law draws on our prior knowledge of Disney and uses that knowledge to demonstrate how *Frozen* offers a different perspective on gender and romance than the traditional Disney animated "princess" films.

Since its US release in November 2013, Disney's latest animated offering, *Frozen* (Chris Buck & Jennifer Lee), has met with critical acclaim and extraordinary box-office success. It won this year's Academy Awards for Best Animated Feature Film and Best Original Song (for "Let It Go"), and despite being released less than six months ago, it has already grossed over US$1 billion worldwide, making it the highest-earning Disney-animated film of all time. At the time of printing, the film's soundtrack has also spent eleven non-consecutive weeks at number one on the US Billboard charts, the most held by a soundtrack since *Titanic* (James Cameron, 1997). Following the success of *Frozen*—and *Tangled* (Nathan Greno & Byron Howard, 2010), Disney's adaptation of the Rapunzel story—many are anticipating the dawn of the second Disney animation golden age. The first was what has come to be known as the Disney Renaissance, the period from the late 1980s to the late 1990s when iconic animated films such as *The Little Mermaid* (Ron Clements & John Musker, 1989) and *Aladdin* (Ron Clements & John Musker, 1992)—films that adopted the structure and style of Broadway musicals—saved the company from financial ruin. Similarly, the *Frozen* phenomenon will only continue growing and inevitably secure a reputation as one of this generation's defining feature animations for children.

Among other factors, the success of *Frozen* could arguably be attributed to its progressive portrayal of female characters and their significant life relationships. The film also adopts a modern approach to storytelling that turns the structure and outcome of the traditional fairytale on its head. With castles, princes and princesses to play with and a story centred on the attainment of true love, *Frozen* succeeds in simultaneously adhering to and challenging conventional fairytale themes, characters and gender roles. But can a fairytale ever be truly progressive in its portrayal of heroines if those heroines are princesses? Are princesses and heroines mutually exclusive concepts? And what are the messages that *Frozen* highlights about gender, love, self-discovery and acceptance?

The film kicks off by introducing us to Elsa (Idina Menzel) and Anna (Kristen Bell), two sisters and princesses who share a close friendship and bond. Elsa, the older of the two, is gifted with a magic ability that enables her to freeze objects and conjure ice and snow. It's a talent that proves entertaining until a near-fatal incident in which Elsa accidentally strikes Anna with ice. In order to be healed, Anna's memories of Elsa's powers are wiped from her mind. But Elsa, guided by her own mammoth guilt and the instructions of her parents, agrees to be locked away for most of her adolescence to protect those she loves, particularly the adoring and naive Anna. Both sisters spend their formative years isolated and lonely: Elsa, a physical and emotional prisoner in her own private nightmare, and Anna, stalking the empty chambers of the castle, desperate for human company and conversation.

When Elsa enters puberty, she becomes more fearful of herself and the wellbeing of those she may come in contact with because her powers have intensified; upon experiencing strong emotion, her physical environment freezes and becomes almost uninhabitable, a reflection of her inner turmoil. So when the girls' parents die tragically at sea, Elsa's powers become uncontrollable. She withdraws further into herself despite Anna's attempts at reconciliation, and the sisters' relationship becomes unsalvageable. It's on Coronation Day, when Elsa comes of age and becomes queen, that two instances change the course of the sisters' lives and relationship.

Anna meets and immediately becomes engaged to her "true love," Hans (Santino Fontana), a charming and understanding prince from a neighbouring kingdom who offers Anna the love and companionship that she never received from her sister. And Elsa, despite her best attempts, loses control over her emotions, revealing her magic powers to the entire kingdom. She flees to the mountains, effectively liberating herself but also banishing herself from her home, and inadvertently plunges the kingdom into a harsh and unrelenting winter. It becomes Anna's mission—and the mission of several sidekicks she encounters along the way, including Kristoff the ice salesman (Jonathan Groff), Olaf the anthropomorphic snowman (Josh Gad) and Sven the reindeer—to retrieve Elsa so they can make amends to end the deadly winter and, more significantly, repair the sisters' broken relationship.

The Traditional Disney Princess

If we examine the pantheon of iconic Disney princesses of the past century, including Snow White (Adriana Caselotti in *Snow White and the Seven Dwarfs*, William Cottrell et al., 1937), Aurora (Mary Costa in *Sleeping Beauty*, Clyde Geronimi, 1959), Cinderella (Ilene Woods in *Cinderella*, Clyde Geronimi et al., 1950) and Ariel (Jodi Benson in *The Little Mermaid*), we see that they all share key commonalities. They each fulfil and reinforce the idea that princesses are beautiful, flawless, feminine, romantic and very naive individuals. And despite being the protagonists and driving forces in each of their stories, they are ultimately victims who must be rescued by their valiant prince and his act of "true love." In short, the "heroines" are not necessarily the heroes of their own stories. They are saved, and there's a kiss, a wedding and a life lived happily ever after. However, over time the Disney princess began evolving with Jasmine (Linda Larkin in *Aladdin*) and Belle (Paige O'Hara in *Beauty and the Beast*, Gary Trousdale & Kirk Wise, 1991), who are both headstrong female characters who refuse to marry (at first) and choose to love someone based on their character rather than their looks or wealth (and in Belle's case, we see a princess with book smarts for the first time). Further along the trajectory we meet Pocahontas (Irene Bedard in *Pocahontas*, Mike Gabriel & Eric Goldberg, 1995) and Mulan (Ming-Na Wen in *Mulan*, Tony Bancroft & Barry Cook, 1998), female protagonists who are self-sufficient and clever, and harbour aspirations greater than just romantic love. However, Pocahontas and Mulan are rarely regarded or marketed as Disney princesses, if at all. They are popular characters, but they are not princess material (at least in the Disney canon), in part due to their proactive natures and warrior narratives. And, superficially speaking, in *Pocahontas* and *Mulan* there are no conventional princes or castles to be seen.

Elsa and Anna: Modern Women and Gender Politics in *Frozen*

The Bechdel test is a set of criteria introduced by graphic novelist Alison Bechdel that states that a work of fiction, particularly film, must have at least two female characters, that these female characters must talk to each other, and that their conversation(s) must be about something other than a man or men. *Frozen*, then, a film centred on the familial bond between two sisters, passes the Bechdel test with flying colours—something that can largely be attributed to the influence of screenwriter and co-director Jennifer Lee, the first ever female director of a feature-length Disney animation. Certainly, the most striking and refreshing thing about Elsa and Anna is that they are three-dimensional, complex women who grow and mature as the film progresses. They are princesses, but they are also human, and therefore possess real and relatable flaws. Elsa is cold, proud and stubborn, and Anna is goofy and socially awkward. They are also, by the film's denouement, both active, strong and fearless—characteristics typical of male heroes or princes. But this doesn't detract from their appeal; the fact that they possess "masculine" characteristics while retaining their femininity is arguably what leads to their success, and sends a strong message to audiences about what being a hero means.

The film also provides a broader commentary on gender roles and women's rights. Elsa is literally locked away and forced to hide herself and her gift from the world, highlighting that a woman with power is often perceived as threatening. There is also a subtle nod towards Elsa's burgeoning sexuality and womanhood when she chooses to embrace her new identity as the snow queen, complete with a self-directed makeover and a more confident, sassy gait. And when Elsa chooses to accept and embrace her true self, we see the gradual shift in the townspeople's responses to her: from fear, intimidation and scorn, to respect, admiration and love. Gender roles are flipped in numerous instances: Anna chooses to punch Hans herself; Kristoff becomes emotional at the sight of Elsa's ice castle; Elsa rules the kingdom successfully as queen; Anna is fearless and chooses to pursue Elsa herself; and Elsa transforms into a powerful woman who builds her own magnificent castle instead of being whisked away to one. These are all positive messages about women who are in control of their own fates and are proactive in their own journeys.

Be Yourself: Championing the Marginalised Outsider

Despite *Frozen* being a princess film, it explores universal themes relevant to both boys and girls, particularly identity and the stigma of being different. (On a demographic note, Disney has gone to great lengths to ensure young male viewers aren't deterred by *Frozen*, which accounts for why much of the marketing centres on Olaf, an asexual character, and why, like *Tangled*, which was first titled "Rapunzel," the title offers little clue to there being female protagonists.[1]) Elsa is constantly being punished by others and herself for her point of difference and the fact that she is "abnormal." She conceals her powers, which are in fact quite beautiful and special, because hiding them is preferable to being ostracised. It's only when she embraces her true self and lets go of people's judgements that she develops into a confident and happy person. "Let It Go" is itself an anthem about forgetting the past and moving towards a freer life, and Elsa's coming of age reinforces the narrative of the outsider triumphing over adversity.

Good versus Evil

During pre-production, Disney struggled to portray Elsa as anything but villainous and vindictive.[2] She was evil for no reason and this lent little depth to the story or the characters' journey. The beauty of the final rendering of Elsa is that she is an inherently good person whose life circumstances have led her to act out in harmful ways. Like all of us, she has something to lose, and unintentionally hurts people in an attempt to protect herself. In this way, the film promotes sympathy and forgiveness by showing that being "good" or "evil" isn't necessarily black and white, and instances of evil can be triggered by mistreatment and misunderstanding. The filmmakers drive this point home during the trolls' song, "Fixer Upper": "People make bad choices if they're mad or scared or stressed / Throw a little love their way and you'll bring out their best / True love brings out the best." Even the truly villainous characters, such as the Duke of Weselton (Alan Tudyk) and Prince Hans, have reasons behind their misdoings, and when they are thwarted, we pity them and understand what led to their misguided pursuit of power.

Challenging the Concept of True Love

Frozen is the first Disney princess film that doesn't revolve around the pursuit or attainment of romantic love and marriage. Certainly, those elements are referenced in Hans and Anna's engagement and the presence of Kristoff as another romantic interest, but romance is challenged, often quite overtly, in two ways. Firstly, the film repeatedly questions the notion of "love at first sight." This is a trope commonly employed in Disney princess films: Ariel spies Eric (Christopher Daniel Barnes) on a ship and becomes smitten; Snow White is resurrected by a stranger's kiss; and Cinderella falls head over heels for her prince after a waltz, not a conversation. Conversely, when Anna and Hans become engaged on the day they meet, Elsa refuses to give them her blessing. Later, Kristoff mocks Anna about her speedy engagement, grilling her about how she could commit herself to someone she knows nothing about. Anna's idealism quite self-reflexively mirrors the romanticism of the Disney princesses of the past, whereas Elsa and Kristoff represent the modern voices of reason.

Frozen also champions platonic love (such as Olaf's friendship with Anna) and familial relationships. At the film's climax, Anna, who is literally freezing to death after Elsa accidentally strikes ice into her chest, searches for an act of true love that will thaw her frozen heart. It is surprising and profoundly moving when Anna realises that the act of true love must come from herself. When faced with an impossible decision (kiss Kristoff and save herself, or protect Elsa from being slain by Hans), Anna makes two telling decisions: she chooses her sister over a man, and then she makes the selfless decision to sacrifice herself so that Elsa may live. Ultimately, it's Anna's act of love that resurrects her and saves the day. There is still a "happily ever after," but it's not prescriptive. By showing that romantic love is not the only or the most valid kind of love, *Frozen* encourages audiences to appreciate and search for instances of true love that already exist in their own lives. (The fact that Anna and Kristoff end up together by the film's conclusion, almost as a side note, reinforces this idea that you can have romantic love but also that it's not the most important kind.)

Frozen strikes a difficult balance in adhering to the conventions of the Disney-princess genre while also subverting them in subtle ways. By drawing audiences in with familiar tropes and characters, we are lulled into a false sense of expectation, but are ultimately surprised by the outcome—the most obvious example of this being Anna's sacrifice. We jump to the inevitable conclusion that true love's kiss will save Anna, and then it does not. Yes, there is a "happily ever after." Yes, it is a princess movie. Yes, it's about love. But it is not restrictive about what love is and what being a princess means. There is a greater focus on women's relationships and journeys and how girls can save the day—Anna, through her sacrifice, and Elsa, by being herself. For once, we are presented with princesses that don't need rescuing, proving what women have always known but is rarely depicted in princess and children's films: that girls can be the heroines of their own stories.

> "Girls can be the heroines of their own stories."

NOTES

1. Brooks Barnes, "Boys Don't Run Away from These Princesses," *The New York Times*, 1 December 2013, <http://www.nytimes.com/2013/12/02/movies/frozen-disneys-new-fairy-tale-is-no-2 -at-box-office.html>, accessed 5 March 2014.

2. Rob Lowman, "Unfreezing *Frozen*: The Making of the Newest Fairy Tale in 3D by Disney," *Los Angeles Daily News*, 19 November 2013, <http://www.dailynews.com/arts-and-entertainment/20131119/unfreezing-frozen-the-making-of -the-newest-fairy-tale-in-3d-by-disney>, accessed 6 March 2014.

Analyze

1. Why does Law believe that, prior to *Frozen*, the princesses in Disney films, although technically the "heroines," were not really "heroes"? What's the difference she is addressing here?

2. According to Law, how does *Frozen* offer a commentary on traditional gender roles and women's rights, especially through the characters of Elsa, Anna, Kristoff, and Hans?

3. Why was Elsa such a difficult character to create? How does the song "Let It Go" represent the complexity of her character and of the film in general?

Explore

1. Law argues in this essay that the titles of recent Disney films, like *Frozen* and *Tangled*, have moved away from the traditional notion of using the name of the female protagonist somewhere in the title of the film (e.g., *The Little Mermaid* or *Beauty and the Beast*) to appeal to both boys and girls. Look at some recent titles of popular films for children (from studios like Disney or Pixar). Do you see them following this trend of creating gender-neutral titles that will appeal to boys and girls alike? Why is that a significant shift?

2. How is Anna's quest for true love different from the Disney princesses that came before her (such as Ariel, Belle, or Cinderella)? How might this suggest a changing narrative in Disney princess films? Write an essay in which you compare *Frozen* to at least one other Disney film and in which you analyze the extent to which the narrative of *Frozen* is similar to or different from that of other Disney films, as well as the significance of those comparisons.

3. Japanese filmmaker Hayao Miyazaki is often called the "Japanese Walt Disney"; his animated films are some of the most popular and beloved in Japan. However, Miyazaki's films are known for their strong, complex female characters and lack of romance as a driving force in the narrative. One of Miyazaki's first films, *Nausicaa of the Valley of the Wind*, is also a princess story. Watch the film and compare its main character Nausicaa to Anna and Elsa. What similarities do you notice in the characters? What differences?

Tasha Robinson
"We're Losing All Our Strong Female Characters to Trinity Syndrome"

Tasha Robinson is a senior editor for the website *The Dissolve*. Her writings have appeared in *The Chicago Tribune*, the *Los Angeles Times*, and *Science Fiction Weekly*. In this article, published on *The Dissolve* in 2014, Robinson argues that although film is giving audiences more "Strong Female Characters," these characters are often not allowed to become part of the film's narrative and are instead left with "nothing to do." As you read, think about Robinson's assumptions about her audience. What does she assume that we know about film, specifically about science fiction and fantasy films? How does she use that assumed knowledge to present her argument?

DreamWorks's *How to Train Your Dragon 2* considerably expands the world introduced in the first film, and that expansion includes a significant new presence: Valka, the long-lost mother of dragon-riding protagonist Hiccup, voiced by Cate Blanchett. The film devotes much of its sweet, sensitive middle act to introducing her and building her up into a complicated, nuanced character. She's mysterious and formidable, capable of taking Hiccup and his dragon partner Toothless out of the sky with casual ease. She's knowledgable: two decades of studying dragons means she knows Toothless's anatomy better than he does. She's wise. She's principled. She's joyous. She's divided. She's damaged. She's vulnerable. She's something female characters so often aren't in action/adventure films with male protagonists: she's *interesting*.

Too bad the story gives her absolutely nothing to do.

There's been a cultural push going on for years now to get female characters in mainstream films some agency, self-respect, confidence, and capability, to make them more than the cringing victims and eventual trophies of 1980s action films or the grunting, glowering, sexless-yet-sexualized types that followed, modeled on the groundbreaking badass Vasquez in *Aliens*. The idea of the Strong Female Character—someone with her own identity, agenda, and story purpose—has thoroughly pervaded the conversation about what's wrong with the way women are often perceived and portrayed today, in comics, videogames, and film especially. Sophia McDougall has intelligently dissected and dismissed the phrase, and artists Kate Beaton, Carly Monardo, Meredith Gran have hilariously lampooned what it often becomes in comics. "Strong Female Character" is just as often used derisively as descriptively, because it's such a simplistic, low bar to vault, and it's more a marketing term than a meaningful goal. But just as it remains frustratingly uncommon for films to pass the simple, low-bar Bechdel Test, it's still rare to see films in the mainstream action/horror/science-fiction/fantasy realm introduce women with any kind of meaningful strength, or women who go past a few simple stereotypes.

And even when they do, the writers often seem lost after that point. Bringing in a Strong Female Character™ isn't actually a feminist statement, or an inclusionary statement, or even a basic equality statement, if the character doesn't have any reason to be in the story except to let filmmakers point at her on the poster and say "See? This film totally respects strong women!"

Valka is just the latest example of the Superfluous, Flimsy Character disguised as a Strong Female Character. And possibly she's the most depressing, considering *Dragon 2*'s other fine qualities, and considering how impressive she is in the abstract. The film spends so much time on making her first awe-inducing, then sympathetic, and just a little heartbreakingly pathetic in her isolation and awkwardness at meeting another human being. But once the introductions are finally done, and the battle starts, she immediately becomes useless, both to the rest of the cast and to the rapidly moving narrative. She faces the villain (the villain she's apparently been successfully resisting alone for years!) and she's instantly, summarily defeated. Her husband and son utterly overshadow her; they need to rescue her twice in maybe five minutes. Her biggest contribution to the narrative is in giving Hiccup a brief, rote "You are the Chosen One" pep talk. Then she all but disappears from the film, raising the question of why the story spent so much time on her in the first place. It may be because writer-director Dean DeBlois originally planned for her to be the film's villain, then discarded that idea in later drafts. But those later drafts give her the setup of a complicated antagonist . . . and the resolution of no one at all. (Meanwhile, the actual villain gets virtually no backstory—which is fine, in a way—but it leaves the film unbalanced.)

And Valka's type—the Strong Female Character With Nothing To Do—is becoming more and more common. *The Lego Movie* is the year's other most egregious and frustrating example. It introduces its female lead, Elizabeth Banks' Wyldstyle, as a beautiful, super-powered, super-smart, ultra-confident heroine who's appalled by how dumb and hapless protagonist Emmet is. Then the rest of the movie laughs at her and marginalizes her as she turns into a sullen, disapproving nag and a wet blanket. One joke has Emmet tuning her out entirely when she tries to catch him up on her group's fate-of-the-world struggle; he replaces her words with "Blah blah blah, I'm so pretty." Her only post-introduction story purpose is to be rescued, repeatedly, and to eventually confer the cool-girl approval that seals Emmet's transformation from loser to winner. After a terrific story and a powerful ending, the movie undermines its triumph with a tag where WyldStyle actually *turns to her current boyfriend for permission to dump him* so she can give herself to Emmet as a reward for his success. For the ordinary dude to be triumphant, the Strong Female Character has to entirely disappear into Subservient Trophy Character mode. This is Trinity Syndrome à la *The Matrix*: the hugely capable woman who never once becomes as independent, significant, and exciting as she is in her introductory scene. (Director Chris McKay sorta-acknowledged the problem in a *DailyMail* interview presented as "*The Lego Movie* filmmaker promises more 'strong females' in the sequel," though his actual quotes do nothing of the sort.)

And even when strong, confident female characters do manage to contribute to a male-led action story, their contributions are still more likely to be marginal, or relegated entirely to nurturer roles, or victim roles, or romantic roles. Consider Tauriel in *The Hobbit: The Desolation Of Smaug*, a wholly invented Strong Female Character ostensibly created to add a little gender balance to an all-male adventure. She's capable of killing approximately a billion spiders and orcs with elven archery kung-fu, but she only shows any actual personality when she's swooning over the dwarf Kili, and being swooned over in return by Legolas, in a wearyingly familiar *Twilight*-esque love triangle. Consider Katee Sackhoff's Dahl in *Riddick*, introduced as a tough second-in-command who proclaims early on that she's no man's sexual object—unlike the movie's only other woman, a brutalized, chained rape victim, casually killed to make a point—but given no particular plot relevance. Despite what Dahl says, she's just sexual spice for the film: She strips for the camera, fights off a rape attempt, smirks through the antihero's graphically crude come-ons, then decides at the end that she *would* like to be his sexual object. Consider Alice Eve's Carol Marcus in *Star Trek: Into Darkness*, introduced as a defiant, iconoclastic rules-breaker exactly like James Kirk, but ultimately winding up in the story largely so she can strip onscreen and present herself as an embarrassingly ineffectual hostage. Rinko Kikuchi's Mako Mori in *Pacific Rim* is weak next to Charlie Hunnam's Raleigh—her past trauma blocks her from being effective in mecha combat, and endangers everyone around her—but even when she proves her strength, he still has to assert himself by knocking her out and dumping her limp body as he heads off to save the day at the end. Ditto with Tom Cruise's Jack in *Oblivion*, who pulls the same move on Julia (Olga Kurylenko), his capable partner.

It's hard for any action movie to have two or more equal heroes, and the ensemble approach doesn't work for every story. It's understandable that for a Hero's Journey plot to entirely resolve, the hero sometimes has to take the last steps alone. For male heroes, that often means putting independence and self-sacrifice before any other consideration. But for decades, action movies have found ways to let male sidekicks drop back at the climax of a story without dying, disappearing, or waiting at home to offer themselves to the hero to celebrate his victory. Female characters don't have to dominate the story to come across as self-reliant, but they do have to have some sense of purpose. Valka's is, apparently, to deliver some heartening information and a little inspiration to Hiccup, and nothing else. It's a bafflingly piddly role for someone whom the narrative seems to care about passionately . . . until it's time for her to *do* something.

So here's a quick questionnaire for filmmakers who've created a female character who isn't a dishrag, a harpy, a McGuffin to be passed around, or a sex toy. Congratulations, you have a Strong Female Character. That's a great start! But now what? Screenwriters, producers, directors, consider this:

- After being introduced, does your Strong Female Character then fail to do anything fundamentally significant to the outcome of the plot? Anything at all?
- If she does accomplish something plot-significant, is it primarily getting raped, beaten, or killed to motivate a male hero? Or deciding to have sex with/not have sex with/agreeing to date/deciding to break up with a male hero? Or nagging a male hero into growing up, or nagging

him to stop being so heroic? Basically, does she only exist to service the male hero's needs, development, or motivations?

- Could your Strong Female Character be seamlessly replaced with a floor lamp with some useful information written on it to help a male hero?
- Is a fundamental point of your plot that your Strong Female Character is the strongest, smartest, meanest, toughest, or most experienced character in the story—until the protagonist arrives?
- . . . or worse, does he enter the story as a bumbling fuck-up, but spend the whole movie rapidly evolving past her, while she stays entirely static, and even cheers him on? Does your Strong Female Character exist primarily so the protagonist can impress her?
- It's nice if she's hyper-cool, but does she only start off that way so a male hero will look even cooler by comparison when he rescues or surpasses her?
- Is she so strong and capable that she's never needed rescuing before now, but once the plot kicks into gear, she's suddenly captured or threatened by the villain, and needs the hero's intervention? Is breaking down her pride a fundamental part of the story?
- Does she disappear entirely for the second half/third act of the film, for any reason other than because she's doing something significant to the plot (besides being a hostage, or dying)?

If you can honestly answer "no" to every one of these questions, you might actually have a Strong Female Character worthy of the name. Congratulations!

But there are exceptions to every rule. *Edge Of Tomorrow* features Emily Blunt as Rita, an ultra-tough female character who dies to motivate the male protagonist. (Repeatedly!) She starts off as the biggest bad-ass in her world, but is eventually surpassed by hero William Cage (Tom Cruise), who starts off as a bumbling fuck-up. She mostly exists in the story to provide Cage with information and cheer him on, and eventually validates him with a brief romantic moment. And yet the story doesn't degrade, devalue, weaken, or dismiss her. It sends the hero on without her at the end— but only at the very end, after she's proved her worth again and again. She's tough. She's confident. She's desperate. She's funny. In short, she's aspirational and inspirational, and just as exciting at the end of the movie as she is at the beginning.

So maybe all the questions can boil down to this: Looking at a so-called Strong Female Character, would you—the writer, the director, the actor, the viewer—*want to be her*? Not want to prove you're better than her, or to have her praise you or acknowledge your superiority. Action movies are all about wish-fulfillment. Does she fulfill any wishes for herself, rather than for other characters? When female characters are routinely "strong" enough to manage that, maybe they'll make the "Strong Female Characters" term meaningful enough that it isn't so often said sarcastically.

Analyze

1. What is the "Trinity Syndrome"? Why does Robinson believe that this syndrome is so problematic for female characters in science fiction and fantasy films?

2. What examples does Robinson use to demonstrate her theory? In what ways are these women "Strong Female Characters with Nothing to Do"?

3. Why does Robinson include a checklist of qualities for a Strong Female Character? What happens if we answer "yes" to any of the questions she asks, and why?

4. What, ultimately, does Robinson believe is the significance of Strong Female Characters in cinema, and why are they important characters for both female *and* male audience members?

5. Why is the term "Strong Female Characters" capitalized and trademarked?

Explore

1. How might Robinson perceive the characters of Anna and Elsa in *Frozen*, and why? How would her analysis of the characters be similar to or different from the perspective Law presents in the preceding essay?

2. How does Robinson's essay address Bordo's discussion of how women are perceived by society in "The Body and the Reproduction of Femininity"?

3. Consider Robinson's checklist for knowing whether we have a Strong Female Character in a film. Think about an example of a character you would typically characterize as one and apply Robinson's checklist to that character. Does she emerge still Strong? Why or why not?

Brittney Cooper
"Iggy Azalea's Post-Racial Mess: America's Oldest Race Tale, Remixed"

Brittney Cooper is a professor of women's and gender studies and Africana studies at Rutgers University. She is a scholar of black women's intellectual history, black feminist thought, and race and gender in popular culture, and has written for *The New York Times*, *NPR*, and *Al-Jazeera America*, among others. Cooper is also a cofounder of the Crunk Feminist Collective, a feminist-of-color scholar-activist group, and identifies as a hip-hop-generation feminist. In the article included here, published on *Salon*'s website in 2014, Cooper examines Iggy Azalea's appropriation of "the sonic Blackness of Southern Black women," as well as black men's participation in this appropriation—to the detriment of black women in hip-hop. Consider how Cooper's discussion of Iggy Azalea and hip-hop also reveals a broader cultural critique.

Recently, my nine-year-old nephew came running into the room, eager to find a seat to watch a performance by Iggy Azalea on an awards show. He sat, enraptured by her performance, yelling, "Iggy!" utterly oblivious to the look of chagrin and dismay on my face, as I, too, tuned in to watch this white girl from Australia, turned ATL-style rapper, caricature everything I love about Southern Hip Hop.

The look and feeling of chagrin has stayed with me each time I turn on my radio and hear Iggy's hit song, "Fancy" coming through my speakers. And some of the dismay I feel is at myself, because almost without fail, I immediately start bobbing my head to the beat.

Iggy is a protégé of T.I., one of my all-time favorite rappers. Though T.I. is known for Atlanta-style, crunk Southern bravado that is a hallmark of Black culture in that city, according to journalist/blogger Bené Viera, T.I. recently expressed disappointment that "we're at a place in America where we still see color." Apparently, color is only relevant when he's talking about racist acts against Black men, but not when he has to think through his complicity in white appropriation of Hip Hop music.

As a born-and-raised Southern girl, who believes that lazy summer evenings are best spent with your top back or your sun roof open, bass-heavy music booming through nice speakers, while you slowly make a few blocks through the neighborhood, to see who's out and what's poppin', I resent Iggy Azalea for her co-optation and appropriation of sonic Southern Blackness, particularly the sonic Blackness of Southern Black women. Everytime she raps the line "tell me how you luv dat," in her song "Fancy," I want to scream "I don't love dat!" I hate it. The line is offensive because this Australian born-and-raised white girl almost convincingly mimics the sonic register of a downhome Atlanta girl.

The question is why? Why is her mimicry of sonic Blackness okay? Though rap music is a Black and Brown art form, one does not need to mimic Blackness to be good at it. Ask the Beastie Boys, or Eminem, or Macklemore. These are just a smattering of the white men who've been successful in rap in the last 30 years and generally they don't have to appropriate Blackness to do it. In the case of Southern rappers like Bubba Sparxx or Paul Wall, who do "sound Black" as it were, at least it is clear that they also have the accents of the places and communities in which they grew up.

Not so with Iggy Azalea, who left Australia at age 16. To be clear, I know *all* of the problems with the phrases "sound Black" and "sonic Blackness." As a kid, I was mercilessly teased for and accused of "talking white," "acting white" and basically attempting to "be white." I learned during those difficult days to dissent from social norms that suggested that the only English for Black people is a vernacular English that stands adjacent to "corporate," "standard," or white English. I balked at such suggestions and reveled in my ability to master "standard" English.

Still I knew that at home, around my family and especially around my Grandmother, my tongue got lazier, as I spoke of things I was "fin (fixing) to do," as I yelled at my cousins about how "nary a one of them" (which sounded more like "nair one") treated me right, as "th" sounds at the beginning of words easily became "d" sounds, and as the "g" sounds fell off the end of -ing words. At home, in the safety, comfort and cocoon of my Southern Black family, I talked how my people talked.

In the predominantly white classrooms of my school days though, proficient use of "standard" English showed those white folks that I had every right to be there, that I was just as good if not better. What I'm describing is what communications scholars have called for decades "code switching." The kind of literacies necessary to master communicating with different communities of people is a hallmark of what it means to grow up as a minority subject with the U.S. and any other country with a history of colonization and slavery.

Iggy Azalea interlopes on this finely honed soundscape of Southern Blackness to tell us "how fancy" she is, and ask "how we love dat." Her recklessness makes clear that she does not understand the difference between code-switching and appropriation. She may get the science of it, but not the artistry. Appropriation is taking something that doesn't belong to you and wasn't made for you, that is not endemic to your experience, that is not necessary for your survival and using it to sound cool and make money. Code-switching is a tool for navigating a world hostile to Blackness and all things non-white. It allows one to move at will through all kinds of communities with as minimal damage as possible.

But it is also rooted in a love and respect for one's culture and for the struggle. That kind of love and respect for sonic Southern Blackness made Zora Neale Hurston one of the greats. Hell, it made Mark Twain one of the greats. But Iggy is more like the Joel Chandler Harris of Hip Hop.

Even though I have taken issue with the way that hip hop fans stand for Macklemore, I appreciate that he has a vocal critique of white privilege and the way it operates in his own life and career.

Not so, with Iggy. More than one blogger has ferreted out her problematic tweets about race, which suggests that while she may love hip hop, she has very little appreciation of Black culture or the problematic ways that white privilege can colonize that culture to the tune of millions of dollars.

That Black men have no sustained critique of the politics of caping for white women in hip-hop is lamentable. That their race politics don't extend far enough to include Black women in any substantive way is downright unacceptable. Forty years ago, Black male race leaders told us that race was the only thing that mattered, feminism be damned. Now in this political moment of My Brother's Keeper, in the cultural arena, rap crews like Lil Wayne's Young Money Cash Money and T.I.'s Grand Hustle Entertainment throw their weight behind white women rappers without a second thought. From this, Black women are supposed to conclude two things: 1) race does not matter, except if you are a Black man and 2) if Black men do anything for any woman, it's the same as being hospitable and/or progressive to every woman.

By riding for white female rappers to the exclusion of Black women, Black men collude with the system against Black women, by demonstrating that our needs, aspirations and feelings do not matter and are not worthy of having a hearing.

Black men keep on proving that when given access to power, money and influence, be it political or cultural, it is not Black women they ride or die for. They want our unwavering devotion, even as they make choices that contribute to the silencing of women of color in a culture we helped to build. And young, oblivious white women, caught up in fanciful ideas about a post-racial universe, climb on board, taking my unsuspecting nephew and his friends for the ride of their lives.

In all cases, Black women remain relegated to being what poet Jessica Care Moore calls "hip hop cheerleaders," "cheering from the sidelines of a stage we built."

The ability of Blackness to travel to and be performed by non-Black bodies is supposed to be a triumph of post-racial politics, a feat that proves once and for all that race is not biological. Race does not have any biological basis, but I maintain that there is no triumph and no celebration when we embrace a white girl who deliberately attempts to sound like a Black girl, in a culture where Black girls can't get no love.

How can I "love dat," when this culture ain't never loved us?

Iggy profits from the cultural performativity and forms of survival that Black women have perfected, without having to encounter and deal with the social problem that is the Black female body, with its perceived excesses, unruliness, loudness and lewdness. If she existed in hip hop at a moment when Black women could still get play, where it would take more than one hand to count all the mainstream Black women rap artists, I would have no problem. Iggy would be one among the many. But in this moment, she represents a problem of co-optation. She represents the ways in which hip hop is on a crash course to take exactly the path that rock 'n roll took such that 20 years from now, people my nephew's age, will look at the Macklemores and Iggys of the world as representative of Hip Hop Culture, with nary a Black soul making their top ten list of hip hop greats.

This kind of cultural appropriation of Black women's labor and creativity for white women's gain, white men's gain and Black men's gain, is not new at all. It is the oldest race tale on American soil, remixed for a new era. And I ain't got no love for that.

Analyze

1. Why does Cooper want to scream every time she hears Iggy Azalea rap "tell me how you luv dat"?

2. What is code-switching? How does mentioning this and contrasting it with the term "appropriation" contribute to Cooper's overall argument?
3. Cooper finds the ways that "white privilege can colonize that [black] culture to the tune of millions of dollars" to be problematic. What are the implications of her use of the word "colonize"?

Explore

1. What issues of gender are revealed in Cooper's piece, and how are these tied to issues of race?
2. Cooper claims that you can count all of the mainstream black women rap artists on one hand. She's obviously exaggerating, but how much? With what black female rap artists are you familiar? How many can you name? Examine *Complex Magazine*'s list "The Best Rapper Alive, Every Year Since 1979" (found easily online). How many women earned the distinction of Best Rapper Alive? How many women earned honorable mentions? Does this list reinforce or challenge Cooper's claim? How so?
3. Watch Jessica Care Moore's Def Jam Poetry performance of "I'm a Hip Hop Cheerleader" (available on YouTube). How does Moore add to the conversation begun by Cooper?

Blue Telusma
"Kim Kardashian Doesn't Realize She's the Butt of an Old Racial Joke"

Blue Telusma is a writer, filmmaker, and founder of the production company BlueCentric. She contributes regularly to media outlets like *The Grio* and *CNN*. In "Kim Kardashian Doesn't Realize She's the Butt of an Old Racial Joke," published on *The Grio* website in 2014, Telusma critiques Kim Kardashian's cover image for *Paper* magazine, linking it to images of Saartjie Baartman and centuries of racism, oppression, and misogyny. Before you read, look at Kardashian's cover photo, as well as Jean-Paul Goude's photo entitled "Champagne Incident," both of which are available online.

Last night, social media was flooded with images of *Paper Magazine*'s Winter 2014 cover featuring Kim Kardashian's glistening posterior. The response was both explosive and polarizing. Some rolled their eyes and complained "*I'm so tired of seeing her naked. She's a mother! Put some clothes on*" while others applauded her boldness and sex appeal.

Regardless of how you felt about the spread or the Kardashians in general, one thing was very clear: *Paper Magazine* set out to break the Internet, a fact they proudly declared from the jump. And they may have very well succeeded, but at what cost?

First off, those of you declaring that these pictures are "history-making" need to chill out. There is nothing new or even original about this spread. Renowned French photographer Jean-Paul Goude just dug into his archives, pulled out some of his old favorites and recreated them with reality TV's reigning It Girl.

That's it.

At best, these pictures are recycled art, and at worst, they are lazy sensationalism—but innovative they are not.

On the flip side—those of you saying that Kim Kardashian *needs to put on some clothes* simply because she is a mother *also* need to sip a big champagne glass of "Girl, Bye!" Because this antiquated idea that mothers are not allowed to celebrate their sexuality is ridiculous and naive. How exactly do you think women become mothers? Immaculate conception? I've never been a fan of policing other women's bodies, and I'm not about to start now. Ya'll can have that.

So last night while everyone *else* was arguing over Kim K's right to show her butt, my focus was on something else entirely. When I looked at the spread all I saw was a not so subtle reincarnation of Saartjie Baartman—imagery that is steeped in centuries of racism, oppression and misogyny. For those who don't know who she is, here's an excerpt from Wikipedia:

> Sarah "Saartjie" Baartman (before 1790–29 December 1815 (also spelled Bartman, Bartmann, Baartmen) was the most famous of at least two Khoikhoi women who were exhibited as **freak show attractions** in 19th-century Europe under the name Hottentot Venus—"Hottentot" as the then-current name for the Khoi people, now considered an offensive term, and "Venus" in reference to the Roman goddess of love.

Saartjie was a woman whose large buttocks brought her questionable fame and caused her to spend much of her life being poked and prodded as a sexual object in a freak show.

Sound familiar?

But something tells me Kim probably has no clue about the cultural and historic significance of what she's done. Instead, she probably just thought it would be cool to do an edgy photo shoot with a famous photographer. And many of you have fallen for that oversimplified stance as well.

I'm the first to admit that some of the work that Jean-Paul Goude has done over the past 30 years has become iconic, particularly his work with his (then-girlfriend) Grace Jones. But the one he chose to recreate for *Paper Magazine* is problematic for several reasons.

The original shot is of a black woman standing in front of a blue wall while she pops champagne into a glass placed on her rear end. And it's from a book entitled: *Jungle Fever*.

Let that soak in for a second. **Jungle. Fever.**

According to a *People Magazine* article written about the couple in 1979:

> Jean-Paul has been fascinated with women like Grace since his youth. The son of a French engineer and an American-born dancer, he grew up in a Paris suburb. From the moment he saw *West Side Story* and the Alvin Ailey dance troupe, he found himself captivated by "ethnic minorities—black girls, PRs. I had jungle fever." He now says, "Blacks are the premise of my work."

This is a man who boldly told news reporters that his black girlfriend was a "*schizo . . . outrageous bitch*" and that at times he would get hysterical and explode in violence during their arguments.

Back in 1982 (before shows like *Law & Order: SVU* taught folks how to identify the subtleties of abuse), when this book came out, many were dazzled by his pictures of Grace Jones and, since she and Goude were lovers, assumed that when he took shots of her in a cage, on all fours bearing her teeth like a caged animal—it was ok.

Because lovers don't ever disrespect each other right?

Right.

All of a sudden, my correlation between these images and Saartjie's treatment as a sideshow animal don't seem so far-fetched, do they? The parallels are so literal and un-nuanced you'd have to *willfully* ignore what's right in front of your face. This idea that "black equals erotic" is fetishism in its purest form; it mocks "otherness" while pretending to celebrate it and defines human beings by their genitals instead of seeing them as whole people.

Yes—I recognize that Kim Kardashian has found a way to work the system and quite literally use what her mama gave her to build an empire—but in this instance, she's being pimped by a paradigm much larger than anything she or her momager Kris Jenner could ever fathom. Kim herself has admitted that until she gave birth to a black child, she never even gave much thought to race or what it means to be a person of color in this world.

This came out of her own mouth. I couldn't make this stuff up if I wanted to, folks.

In a cultural landscape that continues to appropriate all things black, it looks like Mrs. West has just Columbused several hundred years of black female exploitation and most likely has no friggin idea.

The joke is on her—and anyone else who thinks this is just a sexy picture on the cover of a magazine.

If only it were really that simple.

Author's note: I encourage you all to look up the life and times of Saartjie Baartman and draw your own conclusions. This mess runs deep.

Analyze

1. Describe Telusma's tone in this piece. How does her tone help her make her point? Or does it?

2. Why does Telusma insert a quote from *People Magazine*'s 1979 article about Goude and Grace Jones? What does it help to illustrate?

3. Near the end of the essay, Telusma writes, "In a cultural landscape that continues to appropriate all things black, it looks like Mrs. West has just Columbused several hundred years of black female exploitation and most likely has no friggin idea." What does she mean by "Columbused"?

Explore

1. What do you think about the fact that Telusma quotes directly from Wikipedia, considering that Wikipedia is generally considered best for presearching, but not as a source? Does this limit her ethos (credibility) in any way? Why or why not?

2. Do some research on Saartjie Baartman (beyond Wikipedia). How "deep" does "this mess" run? How could you expand on Telusma's argument based on a deeper understanding of Baartman and her historical significance?

3. What do you think about the debate surrounding the responses to Kim Kardashian that suggest that she *"needs to put on some clothes* simply because she is a mother"? What does this suggest about cultural conceptions of sexuality and motherhood? Are the two opposed?

Noah Berlatsky
"Orange Is the New Black's Irresponsible Portrayal of Men"

Author of *Wonder Woman: Bondage and Feminism in the Marston/Peter Comics, 1941–1948*, **Noah Berlatsky** also edits the online comics-and-culture website *The Hooded Utilitarian.* He's also a regular contributor to *The Atlantic*, where this essay was originally published in 2014. In *"Orange Is the New Black*'s Irresponsible Portrayal of Men," Berlatsky argues that Neflix's hit show "reinforces old stereotypes that hurt both genders." As you read, consider whether Berlatsky's praise of the show complements his critique.

Orange Is the New Black has been justly praised for its representation of groups who are often either marginalized or completely invisible in most mainstream media. The show has prominent, complex roles for black women, Latinas, lesbian and bisexual women, and perhaps the first major role for a trans woman played by a trans woman, the wonderful Laverne Cox. There remains, however, one important group that the show barely, and inadequately, represents.

That group is men.

This may seem like a silly complaint. Men, after all, are amply represented in the media, in major and minor roles, whether on *Game of Thrones* or *Mad Men* or *Breaking Bad* or *The Wire*. For that matter, there are in fact a number of male characters on *OITNB*, such as counselor Sam Healey (Michael Harney) who gets a typical guy-plot about struggling against disillusionment and prejudice to be a good man. Why should *OITNB*, unique in being devoted to women, bother with more men?

The reason: While media is full of men, real-life prisons are even more so. Men are incarcerated at more than 10 times the rate of women. In 2012, there were 109,000 women in prison. That's a high number—but it's dwarfed by a male prison population that in 2012 reached just over 1,462,000. In 2011, men made up about 93 percent of prisoners.

Of course, *Orange Is the New Black* is under no obligation to accurately represent prison demographics, and just because they're a minority in prison doesn't mean that women's stories there aren't important. The problem is that the ways in which *OITNB* focuses on women rather than men seem to be linked to stereotypically gendered ideas about who can be a victim and who can't.

The few male prisoners who are shown on *OITNB* are presented in almost aggressively stereotypical ways. Early in the second season, when Piper (Taylor Schilling) is being moved to Chicago to testify in a drug trial, we're shown a number of male inmates being transported as well. They are presented as a threatening, uniform mass. The one prisoner who is given a more substantial role is a black man who makes frightening sexual verbal advances towards Piper; he's a contract killer and refers to himself, apparently without irony, as a "super-predator." He eventually delivers a message for Piper in exchange for her dirty panties. The one male prisoner we meet, then, is violent and abusive, with a sexual kink that is presented as laughable and repulsive. He[is] deviant, dangerous, and the show seems to think that he is exactly where he belongs—behind bars.

Female prisoners on the show are treated very differently. They may be violent and may be queer, but they are, for the most part, presented as sympathetic. This seems like a feminist move, on the surface. But the inability to extend that sympathy to male inmates raises a disturbing possibility: that the show is condescending to women while reinforcing old and destructive attitudes about men.

Adam Jones argues in his book *Gender Inclusive* that empathy for victims is often, in our culture, dependent on the victim being a woman. As he says, "We live in a culture that is trained to view the violent victimization of women as a much more serious offense than the violent victimization of men."

Jones includes a wide range of supportive evidence. Male victims of domestic violence are almost entirely ignored, though domestic violence is perpetrated by men and women at about equal rates (though, Jones points out, violence by men is disproportionately more serious because of strength and weight difference.) In Bosnia, human-rights organizations focused on the (horrible, important) suffering of women rape victims and refugees, while largely ignoring the mass, gender-targeted killing of "battle-age" men. Similarly, violent attacks on women receive much more media attention than violent attacks on men, though men are substantially more likely to be attacked.

In other words, male victimization is seen as natural, or not worth commenting on. As a result, Jones argues, it is difficult to see that "the most severe and institutionalized human rights abuses in the United States are overwhelmingly inflicted upon men, especially—though far from exclusively—younger, poorer, and minority men."

I don't know that I agree that men are the victims of the worst human rights abuses in this country, nor am I sure that ranking abuses in that way is helpful. But I think Jones is absolutely right that part of the reason we see our violent, abusive prison system as acceptable is because we have trouble seeing violence against young, black men as violence. That's why, Jones argues, men are 17 percent more likely to be put in prison than women for similar crimes, and serve an additional year in prison when they are incarcerated.

According to *Orange Is the New Black*, though, men in prison are "super-predators" while women in prison are, often, innocent victims, doomed by circumstances and their own painful but touching character flaws. *OITNB* underlines this most clearly in its flashbacks, where we see each inmate's life-story as a tragic melodrama (a significantly gendered genre) leading to prison.

Though there are a couple of exceptions (like cancer-victim Rosa, a former bank-robbing adrenaline junkie, or sociopathic new villain Vee (Lorraine Toussaint)) for the most part the characters land behind bars because of a tragic lack of love. Taystee (Danielle Brooks) is a foster-child who craves a mother; Suzanne (Uzo Aduba) is a black adoptee of a white family hungry for affection and acceptance; Morello (Yael Stone) is a stalker fixated on romantic love; even Sister Ingalls (Beth Fowler), the nun, has a story framed around her failure to connect with Jesus in her heart. The backstories don't really focus on systemic injustices. Instead, they show how individual weaknesses lead the women to prison. A woman in *OITNB* goes to the bad when her impulse for love is thwarted.

In contrast, a former prisoner reviewing the series at the *Washington City Paper* said, "I get the need for drama and stories, but if the lady who runs this show wanted to be realistic, most of these flashbacks would be about 8 seconds long." She adds:

> I mean that a lot of the girls I knew in prison were in there for really uncomplicated and undramatic reasons. Like, an accurate flashback scene would be a black girl sitting on the couch watching TV, and her boyfriend . . . says "Hey, baby, do you mind if I leave this shit here for my cousin to pick up?" And she says "OK," without even looking up from QVC. And then, boom, cut to her serving 10 years.

The prison pipeline is routine—and, just as significantly, it's a routine involving, and closely connected, to men.

As Yasmin Nair points out, heroin in *OITNB* is presented as some sort of absolute, corrupting, verboten evil—precisely the attitude that has created our decades-old incarceration binge. Minority, marginalized men, often deliberately segregated and barred from most employment, turn to the drug trade. The state typically uses moral panic around drug use as an opportunity to police, harass, and imprison them.

Occasionally, women—especially minority women—end up getting caught in the gears too. That doesn't make for a dramatic, personal story about victimized individuals who want love. It's just the boring, soul-crushing, everyday grind of institutional oppression, mostly aimed at controlling minority men who are perceived, by virtue of their race and gender, as a violent threat just for existing. Destroying the lives of minority women is, in that context, mostly an accidental bonus oppression.

This isn't to say that minority women aren't discriminated against in many, many ways. The fact that *Orange Is the New Black* has been able to attract such a range of phenomenally talented women actors of color speaks loudly about the shamefully limited opportunities for black and Latina women in television and film. But despite its path-breaking representation of minority women, the show remains trapped by gender preconceptions that aren't path-breaking at all. *OITNB* is so eager to sympathize with broken-hearted women and their individual sadnesses that it has no time to consider the institutional machinery of injustice that, in this case, has little directly to do with either individuals or women. It's hard to see how such a distorted view of incarceration helps prisoners of any gender.

Analyze

1. After noting the inadequate representation of men in *Orange Is the New Black*, Berlatzky acknowledges, "This may seem like a silly complaint." Is he hedging here, or does his admission serve another purpose?

2. How, according to Berlatsky, are the male prisoners depicted on the show "presented in almost aggressively stereotypical ways"? How, then, is this linked to "stereotypically gendered ideas about who can be a victim and who can't"?

3. Why does Berlatsky say, "I don't know that I agree that men are the victims of the worst human rights abuses in this country, nor am I sure that ranking abuses in that way is helpful," in response to his quote from Adam Jones? Because Berlatsky questions one of his sources, does this weaken the source's ability to support Berlatsky's argument? Why or why not?

Explore

1. Berlatsky claims that "we have trouble seeing violence against young, black men as violence." Do you agree with this claim?

2. Put Berlatsky's essay in conversation with Jade Chong-Smith's argument about men and the prison industrial complex. In particular, compare and contrast how these two authors discuss stereotypes of men within the prison system. Where do they agree or disagree, and why?

3. Berlatsky rightly notes that "*Orange Is the New Black* has been justly praised for its representation of groups who are often either marginalized or completely invisible in most mainstream media." Do some research on Hollywood's history of whitewashing, as well as its criticism of under- or misrepresentation of minority actors and characters. Then write an argument that explains why it is significant that *Orange Is the New Black* features "prominent, complex roles for black women, Latinas, lesbian and bisexual woman, and perhaps the first major role for a trans woman played by a trans woman."

Emily Nussbaum
"Candy Girl: The Bright Pink Resilience of *Unbreakable Kimmy Schmidt*"

Emily Nussbaum is the television critic for *The New Yorker*. She has written about shows such as *The Good Wife* and *Mad Men* and has previously written for *New York* magazine. This essay, a review of the television show *The Unbreakable Kimmy Schmidt*, was published in *The New Yorker* in 2015. *The Unbreakable Kimmy Schmidt* follows its main character, a young woman trapped in a bunker by a cult leader for fifteen years, as she chooses to leave her home in Indiana and move to New York. How does Nussbaum discuss the way in which the show uses comedy to deal with the very real violence perpetrated on Kimmy by her captor, a violence reflected in contemporary society?

The credit sequence for "Unbreakable Kimmy Schmidt" is a variation on a familiar viral meme: an excitable trailer-park resident gets interviewed on local TV, only to have his words Auto-Tuned into a catchy jingle. The witness describes a bizarre rescue: four women emerge from a concealed bunker where they've been held captive for years by the "weird old white dude" next door—the leader of a doomsday cult. "Unbreakable!" the resident shouts, waving his arms, flooded with emotion. "They *alive*, dammit. But *females*. Are *strong as hell*."

At once crude and affecting (and impossible to get out of your head), the clip operates as shorthand for the show itself, the first post–*30 Rock* series to be produced by Tina Fey and Robert Carlock. Like its opening credits, *Kimmy Schmidt* is a peculiar, propulsive mashup of tabloid obsessions, a sitcom about one of the "Indiana mole women," Kimmy Schmidt, who was kidnapped by the Reverend Richard Wayne Gary Wayne in eighth grade. She then endured—the show strongly implies—pretty much what you'd imagine. When Kimmy escapes, however, she doesn't look wrecked: instead, her expression is pure sunshine, a toothy grin of astonishment and delight. In her intractable optimism, she shares something with another Indiana native, Leslie Knope, from *Parks and Recreation*, except that this is a Leslie Knope who has been to Hell.

In the first episode, Kimmy and her fellow-captives appear on the *Today* show, where they're offered an "ambush makeover" and gift bags, then sent off with a cry of "Thank you, victims!" As the van heads out, Kimmy makes a run for it. Rather than go back to her hometown, she decides, she'll reinvent herself in Manhattan: she'll get a job, an apartment, and a life in which no one sees her as damaged goods. She finds a batty landlady, played by Carol Kane, and an outrageous roommate, Titus Andromedon (played by Tituss Burgess, who played D'Fwan on "30 Rock"'s "Real Housewives" parody, "Queen of Jordan"); she also finds a boss, Jacqueline Voorhees (Jane Krakowski), an Upper East Side trophy wife, whom Kimmy initially mistakes for another captive—because, after a face peel, Jacqueline isn't allowed to step outside her gated townhouse. "Is that your reverend?" Kimmy asks, seeing a portrait of Jacqueline's husband. "Did he peel your face? Do you need help?" She does need help, actually: Kimmy becomes her assistant.

Fey and Carlock sold the show to NBC, under the title "Tooken," but the network eventually passed—at which point Netflix stepped in, committing to two seasons. In the context of cable comedy, "Kimmy Schmidt" is a very odd bird. Plenty of ambitious series do dark material, but they match their insides to their outsides: they're dramedies, like "Getting On," or indie-inflected auteurist shows, like "Louie" and "Girls"; sometimes they're caustic satires, in the tradition of the original British version of "The Office." "Kimmy Schmidt," on the other hand, is network bright. It's all neon pink and Peeps yellow, energized by the Muppet-like intensity of Ellie Kemper's performance as Kimmy and packed, like "30 Rock," with surreal zingers. At times, it resembles a Nickelodeon tween show—which is just how its heroine might imagine her own life. Yet, without any contradiction, it's also a sitcom about a rape survivor.

The show doesn't address sexual violence head on; it's possible to watch without dwelling on the details. But Kimmy's ugly history comes through, in inference and in sly, unsettling jokes about trauma, jagged bits that puncture what is a colorful fish-out-of-water comedy. The backstory that emerges combines elements from a number of familiar tabloid stories: those of Katie Beers (abducted from her abusive family, kept in an underground bunker), Elizabeth Smart (snatched from her bedroom by a self-styled messiah), Jaycee Dugard (abducted from her front yard), and the three women who were rescued two years ago in Cleveland, after having been beaten and raped for years by Ariel Castro. At times, the story feels inspired by Michelle Knight, one of Castro's victims, who wrote a memoir called "Finding Me." Like Kimmy,

Knight had no family to go back to; her upbringing was a horror. But, to judge from newspaper profiles, she has not merely survived the abuse—she's resilient and downright giggly, a fan of karaoke and dancing, angels and affirmations. It's a powerfully girlish model of human toughness.

Kimmy's vision of the good life has exactly that vibe: she wants to enjoy what she's missed out on. Roaming around New York, she binges on candy, like a crazed toddler. She buys sparkly sneakers. Peppy and curious to the point of naïveté, she acts as if she'd learned about life from sitcoms—she gets into a love triangle, she goes back to school, she's eager for every party. But there's also something tense and over-chipper about Kimmy's zest, an artificial quality that even the cartoonish characters around her can sense is "off." Yes, there was "weird sex stuff" in the bunker, she blurts out to her roommate. She has an unexplained Velcro phobia. At night, she wakes up from a fugue state and finds herself rinsing off a knife in the shower or attacking her roommate. ("This isn't the Chinatown bus!" Titus tells her. "You can't just choke people who are sleeping.") When Kimmy decides to take things to "the next level" with her new boyfriend, she mashes his face with the heel of her palm and tries to overpower him. She marvels, "All the stuff I thought I knew was way wrong."

This is rare material for a sitcom. But it's not unusual for modern television, which has been experiencing an uptick in stories about sexual violence—a subject once reserved for Lifetime and "Law & Order." Here's a partial list of dramas in which at least one central character has been raped: "Game of Thrones," "House of Cards," "Mad Men," "American Horror Story," "Outlander," "The Americans," "The Fall," "The Fosters," "Scandal," "Top of the Lake," "How to Get Away with Murder," and "Switched at Birth." You could call this a copycat phenomenon, but I'd argue that better roles for actresses made it happen: when women's lives are taken seriously, sexual violence is going to be part of the drama.

For some critics, these recurrent rape stories seem cheap and exploitative—a way to show violent sex in the guise of social commentary or, in other cases, to insert a sad backstory to justify a woman's harshness. There are definitely examples of this: a scene on "Game of Thrones" last season in which an evil brother overpowered his evil sister (who was also his evil lover—this is "Game of Thrones" we're talking about) was so incoherently conceived that it couldn't separate kink from assault. But what's striking is that most such plots, in genres from camp melodrama to domestic fiction, are skillfully handled. Well-drawn characters like Mellie Grant, on

"Scandal," Elizabeth Jennings, on "The Americans," and Callie Jacob, on "The Fosters," may be rape survivors, but that's not where their stories stop. They're more than their worst day.

In Kimmy's sparkliest dreams, that's how she hopes the world will see her, too. Like many newbie sitcoms, "Kimmy Schmidt" stumbles, at times, to find its tone—and, with thirteen episodes launched at once, it doesn't have the freedom to rejigger itself. A few characters flop, such as Kimmy's Gomer Pyle-ish stepdad. While jokes about race were a strength of "30 Rock," in "Kimmy Schmidt" they have a lower hit rate. Titus, an effervescently gay, black failed actor from Mississippi, pulls off every daring gag. (He also gets the best subplots, including a truly silly music video called "Pinot Noir," meaning "black penis.") But Kimmy's Vietnamese boyfriend, Dong, is bland, and one of her fellow-hostages, a Latina maid, is a cipher. As Arthur Chu wrote in a sharp essay for Slate, the problem isn't that the show's hackier ethnic jokes are rude; it's that they're not rude enough—they don't explode stereotypes with real daring and specificity.

When it comes to jokes about trauma, however, the show takes more risks. Kimmy buries her P.T.S.D. attacks in a SoulCycle-like class, only to find that she has submitted to another cult. She dates a Second World War veteran, since he's the perfect shrink: he's too senile to remember what she tells him. In one of the show's funniest episodes, Kimmy and Jacqueline bond over their desire to hide any sign of sadness—an "outside in" philosophy. When Kimmy is disturbed by seeing her first selfie, Jacqueline takes her to her plastic surgeon, played by a deranged Martin Short, his face perverted into gargoyle features. Dr. Grant (pronounced Franff) is fascinated by Kimmy's appearance: "Absolutely no sun damage, but you've clearly experienced a tremendous amount of stress. Are you a coal miner? Submarine captain? Because you have very distinct scream lines. Where did those come from, I wonder."

In the pilot, Titus tells Kimmy to go home to Indiana; he's trying to protect her. "Protect me from what?" she snorts. "The worst thing that ever happened to me happened in my own front yard." The line echoes an incident from Fey's life: at five, in her family's yard, she was slashed by a mentally ill stranger, leaving her with a scar—a distinctive but not defining feature. It's not the type of experience that you'd think would inspire comedy, but that's the key to "Kimmy Schmidt"'s ambition: by making horrible things funny, it suggests that surviving could be more than just living on. It could be a kind of freedom, too.

Analyze

1. According to Nussbaum, what makes *Kimmy Schmidt* stand out against other comedies and against other shows that deal with such difficult subject material?

2. Where does Nussbaum argue that the show stumbles, and why? On what subject does she believe the show does its best work, and why?

3. How does the show deal with the horrors that Kimmy faced while trapped in the bunker by her abductor? To what extent does Nussbaum believe this is effective, and why?

Explore

1. Think about the structure of this essay as a review of a television show. How does Nussbaum ultimately feel about the show, and why? How do we know? Look at the content of the paragraphs of the essay to figure out how Nussbaum sets up her critique of the show, and why.

2. If you haven't seen *Kimmy Schmidt* and don't have access to the show itself, watch the opening theme song online. How does the song present Kimmy and her fellow "Indiana Mole Women"? What do you think about the style of the opening—the autotuned interview with the reverend's neighbor? How does your interpretation of the opening compare to Nussbaum's argument?

3. Read some additional reviews of *Kimmy Schmidt* online—in particular, Arthur Chu's review on *Slate* (which Nussbaum references here). How do other critics perceive the show? How does Nussbaum's review fit with the other critiques?

4. Based on Nussbaum's review (and perhaps the other reviews you read), would you be interested in watching *Kimmy Schmidt*? Why or why not? If you have already seen the show, how did Nussbaum's review inform your interpretation of the show? To what extent do reviews like Nussbaum's have persuasive power over our desire to do something (or not)?

Forging Connections

1. How do both *The Unbreakable Kimmy Schmidt* and the concept of Trinity Syndrome offer a commentary on the way that women are both perceived by and presented in the media? In what ways are these commentaries similar, and in what ways are they different?

2. How might scholars like Adrienne Rich and Susan Bordo respond to Law's argument that *Frozen* is a positive shift in Disney's princess narrative? Why? Come up with specific examples from their essays to support your point.

Looking Further

1. In this chapter, we have looked at examples that present both positive and problematic representations of gender. Sometimes, the popular culture we consume is more complex. For example, Megan Trainor's song "All about That Bass" was hailed as a feminist anthem when it was released in 2014; however, the lyrics are fraught with conflicting ideas of women's bodies and how they should be perceived. Take a closer look at the lyrics to "All about That Bass," as well as her song "Dear Future Husband" (both of which are available online); how could we read these songs as feminist, and how might we read them as dubious? What message do Trainor's songs ultimately send girls? Imagine that you have a younger female friend who is obsessed with Trainor's music. Based on what you have learned in this chapter (and the preceding chapters) about the impact of popular culture on women's perceptions of their bodies, what would you tell her to enjoy about it, and what would you ask her to look at more carefully? Write a letter to your friend, citing specific lyrics from Trainor's music, as well as evidence from the readings.

2. Tasha Robinson's essay looks specifically at science fiction/fantasy films; to what extent is all cinema falling victim to the Trinity Syndrome? Look at two recent films from a specific genre (romance, comedy, drama, horror, etc.) and apply Robinson's checklist; do those genres also utilize the "Strong Female Character with Nothing to Do" trope? Why? To what extent, then, can we claim that cinema is including more Strong Female Characters? Write an essay applying Robinson's checklist to your films and demonstrating your answer to the previous question.

6 Gender and Work

Congratulations! You have just graduated from college and landed your first job. You're working as a junior copywriter for a publishing company; the pay is low, but the opportunity for promotion is high. You're excited to see where this job takes you in the coming years.

After the first three years at your job, you apply for a promotion to be an assistant editor. You have plenty of experience and the drive and initiative to bring new life to the team. Your dual degrees in English and marketing should also help, you think. However, you're turned down in favor of a younger (male) junior copywriter, who has only been at the company for one year.

No big deal, you think. I'll apply again next year.

It takes you three more years to get that promotion.

When you join your new team and meet the other assistant editor, he asks if you are pleased with the "big bump in pay." You're confused. You did get a pay raise, but it was only 2%. What percentage does this promotion entail? you ask, feigning ignorance. When he tells you 4%, you can't help but get a little angry. You and he will be doing the same job, the same hours, the same everything, yet he got a 4% wage increase. Why should he be paid more than you?

Later, when you are married and expecting a child, you learn that there is no paid family leave at the company. You hope for a healthy pregnancy and delivery so you won't have to take much time off.

When your child is two years old, you're given another promotion—this time to senior editor. It's a big jump, but with this promotion comes extended work hours during the week, some weekend work, and less time for vacation. You want this promotion, but worry that you won't have time to be a good employee, a good partner, and a good parent. Then, you find out you're expecting another child. The cost of two children in daycare is prohibitive. You and your partner begin discussing stay-at-home parenting as an option.

This narrative is one that could be applied to many careers throughout the United States. It demonstrates that gender plays a significant role in how Americans approach the workplace and that it impacts both men and women. In this chapter, we will examine issues such as the ones described in the scenario about pay, family leave, the idea of "having it all," and stay-at-home parenting. In this chapter, we ask you to consider both the advancements that women have made in the workforce and the elements that continue to hold them back. First, Judy Brady's essay "I Want a Wife" parodies the idea of being a "Wife" to show how much work women actually do in that role. In "Why Women Still Can't Have It All," Anne-Marie Slaughter claims that women can't be powerful career women, partners, and mothers, no matter how badly they want to be. Stephanie Coontz responds to Slaughter's essay in "Why Is 'Having It All' Just a Women's Issue?" by countering that the issue at stake in Slaughter's essay is not feminism or women's rights, but a systemic problem in the American workplace. In his essay "'Daddy Makes Books and Sammies': The Stay-at-Home Dad in the 21st Century" Damien Cowger explores the way that masculinity ties to work and how it is impacted when the father is the one who is the stay-at-home parent. Megan H. MacKenzie argues in "Let Women Fight" that preventing women from fighting on the front lines of combat continues discriminatory gender stereotypes based on dated perceptions of women's—and men's—abilities. Finally, the World Bank's "Taking Stock" demonstrates that gender equality in the workplace is still a global issue.

Judy Brady
"I Want a Wife"

Judy Brady (then Syfers) wrote her now-iconic essay "I Want a Wife" for a fiftieth anniversary celebration of the Nineteenth Amendment, which gave women the right to vote. As she read it, she was heckled by the men in the audience. It was first published in the premier issue of *Ms.* magazine in 1972 and has been anthologized many times since. Using wit and irony, Brady points out not only the mostly unrecognized work of housewives and the privileges it affords their husbands, but also the difficulty a woman without a wife (or perhaps a husband who would take on a wife's duties—which was mostly unheard of when this essay was written) would have in doing something as simple as going to school. Consider how the repetition of the phrase "I want a wife" emphasizes what she lacks as a woman without one.

I belong to that classification of people known as wives. I am A Wife. And, not altogether incidentally, I am a mother. Not too long ago a male friend of mine appeared on the scene fresh from a recent divorce. He had one child, who is, of course, with his ex-wife. He is looking for another wife. As I thought about him while I was ironing one evening, it suddenly occurred to me that I, too, would like to have a wife. Why do I want a wife?

I would like to go back to school so that I can become economically independent, support myself, and, if need be, support those dependent upon me. I want a wife who will work and send me to school. And while I am going to school, I want a wife to take care of my children. I want a wife to keep track of the children's doctor and dentist appointments. And to keep track of mine, too. I want a wife to make sure my children eat properly and are kept clean. I want a wife who will wash the children's clothes and keep them mended. I want a wife who is a good nurturant attendant to my children, who arranges for their schooling, makes sure that they have an adequate social life with their peers, takes them to the park, the zoo, etc. I want a wife who takes care of the children when they are sick, a wife who arranges to be around when the children need special care, because, of course, I cannot miss classes at school. My wife must arrange to lose time at work and not lose the job. It may mean a small cut in my wife's income from time to time, but I guess I can tolerate that. Needless to say, my wife will arrange and pay for the care of the children while my wife is working.

I want a wife who will take care of my physical needs. I want a wife who will keep my house clean. A wife who will pick up after my children, a wife who will pick up after me. I want a wife who will keep my clothes clean, ironed, mended, replaced when need be, and who will see to it that my personal things are kept in their proper place so that I can find what I need the minute I need it. I want a wife who cooks the meals, a wife who is a good cook. I want a wife who will plan the menus, do the necessary grocery shopping, prepare the meals, serve them pleasantly, and then do the cleaning up while I do my studying. I want a wife who will care for me when I am sick and sympathize with my pain and loss of time from school. I want a wife to go along when our family takes a vacation so that someone can continue to care for me and my children when I need a rest and change of scene.

"I want a wife who will not bother me with rambling complaints about a wife's duties." I want a wife who will not bother me with rambling complaints about a wife's duties. But I want a wife who will listen to me when I feel the need to explain a rather difficult point I have come across in my course studies. And I want a wife who will type my papers for me when I have written them.

I want a wife who will take care of the details of my social life. When my wife and I are invited out by my friends, I want a wife who will take care of the baby-sitting arrangements. When I meet *people* at school that I like and want to entertain, I want a wife who will have the house clean, will prepare a special meal, *serve* it to me and my friends, and not interrupt when I talk about things that interest me and my friends. I want a wife who will have arranged that the children are fed and ready for bed before my guests arrive so that the children do not bother us. I want a wife who takes care of the needs of my guests so that they feel comfortable, who makes sure that they have an ashtray, that they are passed the hors d'oeuvres, that they are offered a second helping of the food, that their wine glasses are replenished when necessary, that their coffee is served to them as they like it.

And I want a wife who knows that sometimes I need a night out by myself.

I want a wife who is sensitive to my sexual needs, a wife who makes love passionately and eagerly when I feel like it, a wife who makes sure that I am satisfied. And, of course, I want a wife who will not demand sexual attention when I am not in the mood for it. I want a wife who assumes the complete responsibility for birth control, because I do not want more children. I want a wife who will remain sexually faithful to me so that I do not have to clutter up my intellectual life with jealousies. And I want a wife who understands that my sexual needs may entail more than strict adherence to monogamy. I must, after all, be able to relate to people as fully as possible.

If, by chance, I find another person more suitable as a wife than the wife I already have, I want the liberty to replace my present wife with another one. Naturally, I will expect a fresh, new life; my wife will take the children and be solely responsible for them so that I am left free.

When I am through with school and have a job, I want my wife to quit working and remain at home so that my wife can more fully and completely take care of a wife's duties. My God, who wouldn't want a wife?

Analyze

1. What does Brady's essay reveal about the roles men and women were expected to perform at the time it was written? How does the essay reveal this?

2. What is Brady's purpose in repeating the phrase "I want a wife" throughout the essay? Is this an effective rhetorical strategy? Why or why not?

3. Why does she end the essay with the question, "My God, who wouldn't want a wife?"? What effect is this meant to have on the reader?

Explore

1. To truly understand Brady's piece, you must put it into an accurate sociohistorical context. What was going on in the late 1960s and early

1970s that may have influenced Brady to write this essay? What was the typical division of domestic labor at that time? How common was divorce? How common was it for women to pursue a college education? With these questions in mind, go to the library and see what kind of sources you can find to help you answer them. Once you've done a little digging, consider the following: Has your understanding of Brady's argument changed based on your research? If so, how? Write an essay that describes the sociohistorical context of the essay and then reflect on how this research has impacted your understanding of Brady's claim.

2. Based on Brady's description of wifely duties and the expectations placed on her, how would you describe the characteristics of the hypothetical husband attached to this wife?

3. Has the status of women improved since this essay was published in 1972? Why or why not? Provide evidence from your own life to support your answer.

Anne-Marie Slaughter
"Why Women Still Can't Have It All"

Anne-Marie Slaughter is currently the president and chief executive officer of the New America Foundation, a nonprofit, nonpartisan organization dedicated to the "renewal of American politics, prosperity, and purpose in the digital age." Previously, she was the Bert G. Kerstetter '66 University Professor of Politics and International Affairs at Princeton University and dean of its Woodrow Wilson School of Public and International Affairs. She also served as director of policy planning for the U.S. State Department under Secretary of State Hillary Clinton. In "Why Women Still Can't Have It All," Slaughter details the difficult balancing act that occurs when women in high-powered jobs are raising children at the same time. As you read, consider how Slaughter uses her personal experience as evidence, but how this experience is not necessarily universal.

Eighteen months into my job as the first woman director of policy planning at the State Department, a foreign-policy dream job that traces its origins back to George Kennan, I found myself in New York, at the United Nations' annual assemblage of every foreign minister and head of state in the world. On a Wednesday evening, President and Mrs. Obama hosted a glamorous reception at the American Museum of Natural History. I sipped champagne, greeted foreign dignitaries, and mingled. But I could not stop thinking about my 14-year-old son, who had started eighth grade three weeks earlier and was already resuming what had become his pattern of skipping homework, disrupting classes, failing math, and tuning out any adult who tried to reach him. Over the summer, we had barely spoken to each other—or, more accurately, he had barely spoken to me. And the previous spring I had received several urgent phone calls—invariably on the day of an important meeting—that required me to take the first train from Washington, D.C., where I worked, back to Princeton, New Jersey, where he lived. My husband, who has always done everything possible to support my career, took care of him and his 12-year-old brother during the week; outside of those midweek emergencies, I came home only on weekends.

As the evening wore on, I ran into a colleague who held a senior position in the White House. She has two sons exactly my sons' ages, but she had chosen to move them from California to D.C. when she got her job, which meant her husband commuted back to California regularly. I told her how difficult I was finding it to be away from my son when he clearly needed me. Then I said, "When this is over, I'm going to write an op-ed titled 'Women Can't Have It All.'"

She was horrified. "You *can't* write that," she said. "You, of all people." What she meant was that such a statement, coming from a high-profile career woman—a role model—would be a terrible signal to younger generations of women. By the end of the evening, she had talked me out of it, but for the remainder of my stint in Washington, I was increasingly aware that the feminist beliefs on which I had built my entire career were shifting under my feet. I had always assumed that if I could get a foreign-policy job in the State Department or the White House while my party was in power, I would stay the course as long as I had the opportunity to do work I loved. But in January 2011, when my two-year public-service leave from Princeton University was up, I hurried home as fast as I could.

A rude epiphany hit me soon after I got there. When people asked why I had left government, I explained that I'd come home not only because of Princeton's rules (after two years of leave, you lose your tenure), but also because of my desire to be with my family and my conclusion that juggling high-level government work with the needs of two teenage boys was not possible. I have not exactly left the ranks of full-time career women: I teach a full course load; write regular print and online columns on foreign policy; give 40 to 50 speeches a year; appear regularly on TV and radio; and am working on a new academic book. But I routinely got reactions from other women my age or older that ranged from disappointed ("It's such a pity that you had to leave Washington") to condescending ("I wouldn't generalize from your experience. *I've* never had to compromise, and *my* kids turned out great").

The first set of reactions, with the underlying assumption that my choice was somehow sad or unfortunate, was irksome enough. But it was the second set of reactions—those implying that my parenting and/or my commitment to my profession were somehow substandard—that triggered a blind fury. Suddenly, finally, the penny dropped. All my life, I'd been on the other side of this exchange. I'd been the woman smiling the faintly superior smile while another woman told me she had decided to take some time out or pursue a less competitive career track so that she could spend more time with her family. I'd been the woman congratulating herself on her unswerving commitment to the feminist cause, chatting smugly with her dwindling number of college or law-school friends who had reached and maintained their place on the highest rungs of their profession. I'd been the one telling young women at my lectures that you *can* have it all and do it all, regardless of what field you are in. Which means I'd been part, albeit unwittingly, of making millions of women feel that *they* are to blame if they cannot manage to rise up the ladder as fast as men and also have a family and an active home life (and be thin and beautiful to boot).

Last spring, I flew to Oxford to give a public lecture. At the request of a young Rhodes Scholar I know, I'd agreed to talk to the Rhodes community about "work–family balance." I ended up speaking to a group of about 40 men and women in their mid-20s. What poured out of me was a set of very frank reflections on how unexpectedly hard it was to do the kind of job I wanted to do as a high government official and be the kind of parent I wanted to be, at a demanding time for my children (even though my husband, an academic, was willing to take on the lion's share of parenting for the two years I was in Washington). I concluded by saying that my time in office had convinced me that further government service would be very un-likely while my sons were still at home. The audience was rapt, and asked many thoughtful questions. One of the first was from a young woman who began by thanking me for "not giving just one more fatuous 'You can have it all' talk." Just about all of the women in that room planned to combine careers and family in some way. But almost all assumed and accepted that they would have to make compromises that the men in their lives were far less likely to have to make.

The striking gap between the responses I heard from those young women (and others like them) and the responses I heard from my peers and associ-ates prompted me to write this article. Women of my generation have clung to the feminist credo we were raised with, even as our ranks have been steadily thinned by unresolvable tensions between family and career, be-cause we are determined not to drop the flag for the next generation. But when many members of the younger generation have stopped listening, on the grounds that glibly repeating "you can have it all" is simply airbrushing reality, it is time to talk.

I still strongly believe that women can "have it all" (and that men can too). I believe that we can "have it all at the same time." But not today, not with the way America's economy and society are currently structured. My experiences over the past three years have forced me to confront a number of uncomfortable facts that need to be widely acknowledged—and quickly changed.

Before my service in government, I'd spent my career in academia: as a law professor and then as the dean of Princeton's Woodrow Wilson School of Public and International Affairs. Both were demanding jobs, but I had the ability to set my own schedule most of the time. I could be with my kids when I needed to be, and still get the work done. I had to travel frequently, but I found I could make up for that with an extended period at home or a family vacation.

I knew that I was lucky in my career choice, but I had no idea how lucky until I spent two years in Washington within a rigid bureaucracy, even with bosses as understanding as Hillary Clinton and her chief of staff, Cheryl Mills. My workweek started at 4:20 on Monday morning, when I got up to get the 5:30 train from Trenton to Washington. It ended late on Friday, with the train home. In between, the days were crammed with meetings, and when the meetings stopped, the writing work began—a never-ending stream of memos, reports, and comments on other people's drafts. For two years, I never left the office early enough to go to any stores other than those open 24 hours, which meant that everything from dry cleaning to hair appointments to Christmas shopping had to be done on weekends, amid children's sporting events, music lessons, family meals, and conference calls. I was entitled to four hours of vacation per pay period, which came to one day of vacation a month. And I had it better than many of my peers in D.C.; Secretary Clinton deliberately came in around 8 a.m. and left around 7 p.m., to allow her close staff to have morning and evening time with their families (although of course she worked earlier and later, from home).

In short, the minute I found myself in a job that is typical for the vast majority of working women (and men), working long hours on someone else's schedule, I could no longer be both the parent and the professional I wanted to be—at least not with a child experiencing a rocky adolescence. I realized what should have perhaps been obvious: having it all, at least for me, depended almost entirely on what type of job I had. The flip side is the harder truth: having it all was not possible in many types of jobs, including high government office—at least not for very long.

I am hardly alone in this realization. Michèle Flournoy stepped down after three years as undersecretary of defense for policy, the third-highest job in the department, to spend more time at home with her three children, two of whom are teenagers. Karen Hughes left her position as the counselor to President George W. Bush after a year and a half in Washington to go home to Texas for the sake of her family. Mary Matalin, who spent two years as an assistant to Bush and the counselor to Vice President Dick Cheney before stepping down to spend more time with her daughters, wrote: "Having control over your schedule is the only way that women who want to have a career and a family can make it work."

Yet the decision to step down from a position of power—to value family over professional advancement, even for a time—is directly at odds with the prevailing social pressures on career professionals in the United States. One phrase says it all about current attitudes toward work and family, particularly among elites. In Washington, "leaving to spend time with your family" is a euphemism for being fired. This understanding is so ingrained that when Flournoy announced her resignation last December, *The New York Times* covered her decision as follows:

> Ms. Flournoy's announcement surprised friends and a number of
> Pentagon officials, but all said they took her reason for resignation

at face value and not as a standard Washington excuse for an official who has in reality been forced out. "I can absolutely and unequivocally state that her decision to step down has nothing to do with anything other than her commitment to her family," said Doug Wilson, a top Pentagon spokesman. "She has loved this job and people here love her."

Think about what this "standard Washington excuse" implies: it is so unthinkable that an official would *actually* step down to spend time with his or her family that this must be a cover for something else. How could anyone voluntarily leave the circles of power for the responsibilities of parenthood? Depending on one's vantage point, it is either ironic or maddening that this view abides in the nation's capital, despite the ritual commitments to "family values" that are part of every political campaign. Regardless, this sentiment makes true work–life balance exceptionally difficult. But it cannot change unless top women speak out.

Only recently have I begun to appreciate the extent to which many young professional women feel under assault by women my age and older. After I gave a recent speech in New York, several women in their late 60s or early 70s came up to tell me how glad and proud they were to see me speaking as a foreign-policy expert. A couple of them went on, however, to contrast my career with the path being traveled by "younger women today." One expressed dismay that many younger women "are just not willing to get out there and do it." Said another, unaware of the circumstances of my recent job change: "They think they have to choose between having a career and having a family."

A similar assumption underlies Facebook Chief Operating Officer Sheryl Sandberg's widely publicized 2011 commencement speech at Barnard, and her earlier TED talk, in which she lamented the dismally small number of women at the top and advised young women not to "leave before you leave." When a woman starts thinking about having children, Sandberg said, "she doesn't raise her hand anymore . . . She starts leaning back." Although couched in terms of encouragement, Sandberg's exhortation contains more than a note of reproach. We who have made it to the top, or are striving to get there, are essentially saying to the women in the generation behind us: "What's the matter with you?"

They have an answer that we don't want to hear. After the speech I gave in New York, I went to dinner with a group of 30-somethings. I sat across from two vibrant women, one of whom worked at the UN and the other at a big New York law firm. As nearly always happens in these situations, they soon began asking me about work–life balance. When I told them I was writing this article, the lawyer said, "I look for role models and can't find any." She said the women in her firm who had become partners and taken on management positions had made tremendous sacrifices, "many of which they don't even seem to realize . . . They take two years off when their kids are young but then work like crazy to get back on track professionally, which means that they see their kids when they are toddlers but not teenagers, or really barely at all." Her friend nodded, mentioning the top professional women she knew, all of whom essentially relied on round-the-clock nannies. Both were very clear that they did not want that life, but could not figure out how to combine professional success and satisfaction with a real commitment to family.

I realize that I am blessed to have been born in the late 1950s instead of the early 1930s, as my mother was, or the beginning of the 20th century, as my grandmothers were. My mother built a successful and rewarding career as a professional artist largely in the years after my brothers and I left home—and after being told in her 20s that she could not go to medical school, as her father had done and her brother would go on to do, because, of course, she was going to get married. I owe my own freedoms and opportunities to the pioneering generation of women ahead of me—the women now in their 60s, 70s, and 80s who faced overt sexism of a kind I see only when watching *Mad Men*, and who knew that the only way to make it as a woman was to act exactly like a man. To admit to, much less act on, maternal longings would have been fatal to their careers.

But precisely thanks to their progress, a different kind of conversation is now possible. It is time for women in leadership positions to recognize that although we are still blazing trails and breaking ceilings, many of us are also reinforcing a falsehood: that "having it all" is, more than anything, a function of personal determination. As Kerry Rubin and Lia Macko, the authors of *Midlife Crisis at 30*, their cri de coeur for Gen-X and Gen-Y women, put it:

> What we discovered in our research is that while the empowerment part of the equation has been loudly celebrated, there has been very little honest discussion among women of our age about the real barriers and flaws that still exist in the system despite the opportunities we inherited.

I am well aware that the majority of American women face problems far greater than any discussed in this article. I am writing for my demographic— highly educated, well-off women who are privileged enough to have choices in the first place. We may not have choices about whether to do paid work, as dual incomes have become indispensable. But we have choices about the type and tempo of the work we do. We are the women who could be leading, and who should be equally represented in the leadership ranks.

Millions of other working women face much more difficult life circumstances. Some are single mothers; many struggle to find any job; others support husbands who cannot find jobs. Many cope with a work life in which good day care is either unavailable or very expensive; school schedules do not match work schedules; and schools themselves are failing to educate their children. Many of these women are worrying not about having it all, but rather about holding on to what they do have. And although women as a group have made substantial gains in wages, educational attainment, and prestige over the past three decades, the economists Justin Wolfers and Betsey Stevenson have shown that women are less happy today than their predecessors were in 1972, both in absolute terms and relative to men.

The best hope for improving the lot of all women, and for closing what Wolfers and Stevenson call a "new gender gap"—measured by well-being rather than wages—is to close the leadership gap: to elect a woman president and 50 women senators; to ensure that women are equally represented in the ranks of corporate executives and judicial leaders. Only when women wield power in sufficient numbers will we create a society that genuinely works for all women. That will be a society that works for everyone.

[. . .]

Innovation Nation

A s I write this, I can hear the reaction of some readers to many of the proposals in this essay: It's all fine and well for a tenured professor to write about flexible working hours, investment intervals, and family-comes-first management. But what about the real world? Most American women cannot demand these things, particularly in a bad economy, and their employers have little incentive to grant them voluntarily. Indeed, the most frequent reaction I get in putting forth these ideas is that when the choice is whether to hire a man who will work whenever and wherever needed, or a woman who needs more flexibility, choosing the man will add more value to the company.

In fact, while many of these issues are hard to quantify and measure precisely, the statistics seem to tell a different story. A seminal study of 527 U.S. companies, published in the *Academy of Management Journal* in 2000, suggests that "organizations with more extensive work–family policies have higher perceived firm-level performance" among their industry peers. These findings accorded with a 2003 study conducted by Michelle Arthur at the University of New Mexico. Examining 130 announcements of family-friendly policies in *The Wall Street Journal*, Arthur found that the announcements alone significantly improved share prices. In 2011, a study on flexibility in the workplace by Ellen Galinsky, Kelly Sakai, and Tyler Wigton of the Families and Work Institute showed that increased flexibility correlates positively with job engagement, job satisfaction, employee retention, and employee health.

This is only a small sampling from a large and growing literature trying to pin down the relationship between family-friendly policies and economic performance. Other scholars have concluded that good family policies attract better talent, which in turn raises productivity, but that the policies themselves have no impact on productivity. Still others argue that results attributed to these policies are actually a function of good management overall. What is evident, however, is that many firms that recruit and train well-educated professional women are aware that when a woman leaves because of bad work–family balance, they are losing the money and time they invested in her.

Even the legal industry, built around the billable hour, is taking notice. Deborah Epstein Henry, a former big-firm litigator, is now the president of Flex-Time Lawyers, a national consulting firm focused partly on strategies for the retention of female attorneys. In her book *Law and Reorder*, published by the American Bar Association in 2010, she describes a legal profession "where the billable hour no longer works"; where attorneys, judges, recruiters, and academics all agree that this system of compensation has perverted the industry, leading to brutal work hours, massive inefficiency, and highly inflated costs. The answer—already being deployed in different corners of the industry—is a combination of alternative fee structures, virtual firms, women-owned firms, and the outsourcing of discrete legal jobs to other jurisdictions. Women, and Generation X and Y lawyers more generally, are pushing for these changes on the supply side; clients determined to reduce legal fees and increase flexible service are pulling on the demand side. Slowly, change is happening.

At the core of all this is self-interest. Losing smart and motivated women not only diminishes a company's talent pool; it also reduces the return on its investment in training and mentoring. In trying to address these issues, some firms are finding out that women's ways of working may just be better ways of working, for employees and clients alike.

Experts on creativity and innovation emphasize the value of encouraging nonlinear thinking and cultivating randomness by taking long walks or looking at your environment from unusual angles. In their new book, *A New Culture of Learning: Cultivating the Imagination for a World of Constant Change*, the innovation gurus John Seely Brown and Douglas Thomas write, "We believe that connecting play and imagination may be the single most important step in unleashing the new culture of learning."

Space for play and imagination is exactly what emerges when rigid work schedules and hierarchies loosen up. Skeptics should consider the "California effect." California is the cradle of American innovation—in technology, entertainment, sports, food, and lifestyles. It is also a place where people take leisure as seriously as they take work; where companies like Google deliberately encourage play, with Ping-Pong tables, light sabers, and policies that require employees to spend one day a week working on whatever they wish. Charles Baudelaire wrote: "Genius is nothing more nor less than childhood recovered at will." Google apparently has taken note.

No parent would mistake child care for childhood. Still, seeing the world anew through a child's eyes can be a powerful source of stimulation. When the Nobel laureate Thomas Schelling wrote *The Strategy of Conflict*, a classic text applying game theory to conflicts among nations, he frequently drew on child-rearing for examples of when deterrence might succeed or fail. "It may be easier to articulate the peculiar difficulty of constraining [a ruler] by the use of threats," he wrote, "when one is fresh from a vain attempt at using threats to keep a small child from hurting a dog or a small dog from hurting a child."

The books I've read with my children, the silly movies I've watched, the games I've played, questions I've answered, and people I've met while parenting have broadened my world. Another axiom of the literature on innovation is that the more often people with different perspectives come together, the more likely creative ideas are to emerge. Giving workers the ability to integrate their non-work lives with their work—whether they spend that time mothering or marathoning—will open the door to a much wider range of influences and ideas.

Enlisting Men

Perhaps the most encouraging news of all for achieving the sorts of changes that I have proposed is that men are joining the cause. In commenting on a draft of this article, Martha Minow, the dean of the Harvard Law School, wrote me that one change she has observed during 30 years of teaching law at Harvard is that today many young men are asking questions about how they can manage a work–life balance. And more systematic research on Generation Y confirms that many more men than in the past are asking questions about how they are going to integrate active parenthood with their professional lives.

Abstract aspirations are easier than concrete trade-offs, of course. These young men have not yet faced the question of whether they are prepared to give up that more prestigious clerkship or fellowship, decline a promotion, or delay their professional goals to spend more time with their children and to support their partner's career.

Yet once work practices and work culture begin to evolve, those changes are likely to carry their own momentum. Kara Owen, the British foreign-service officer who worked a London job from Dublin, wrote me in an e-mail:

> I think the culture on flexible working started to change the minute the Board of Management (who were all men at the time) started to work flexibly—quite a few of them started working one day a week from home.

Men have, of course, become much more involved parents over the past couple of decades, and that, too, suggests broad support for big changes in the way we balance work and family. It is noteworthy that both James Steinberg, deputy secretary of state, and William Lynn, deputy secretary of defense, stepped down two years into the Obama administration so that they could spend more time with their children (for real).

Going forward, women would do well to frame work–family balance in terms of the broader social and economic issues that affect both women and men. After all, we have a new generation of young men who have been raised by full-time working mothers. Let us presume, as I do with my sons, that they will understand "supporting their families" to mean more than earning money.

I have been blessed to work with and be mentored by some extraordinary women. Watching Hillary Clinton in action makes me incredibly proud—of her intelligence, expertise, professionalism, charisma, and command of any audience. I get a similar rush when I see a front-page picture of Christine Lagarde, the managing director of the International Monetary Fund, and Angela Merkel, the chancellor of Germany, deep in conversation about some of the most important issues on the world stage; or of Susan Rice, the U.S. ambassador to the United Nations, standing up forcefully for the Syrian people in the Security Council.

These women are extraordinary role models. If I had a daughter, I would encourage her to look to them, and I want a world in which they are extraordinary but not unusual. Yet I also want a world in which, in Lisa Jackson's words, "to be a strong woman, you don't have to give up on the things that define you as a woman." That means respecting, enabling, and indeed celebrating the full range of women's choices. "Empowering yourself," Jackson said in her speech at Princeton, "doesn't have to mean rejecting motherhood, or eliminating the nurturing or feminine aspects of who you are."

I gave a speech at Vassar last November and arrived in time to wander the campus on a lovely fall afternoon. It is a place infused with a spirit of community and generosity, filled with benches, walkways, public art, and quiet places donated by alumnae seeking to encourage contemplation and connection. Turning the pages of the alumni magazine (Vassar is now co-ed), I was struck by the entries of older alumnae, who greeted their classmates with *Salve* (Latin for "hello") and wrote witty remembrances sprinkled with literary allusions. Theirs was a world in which women wore their learning lightly; their news is mostly of their children's accomplishments. Many of us look back on that earlier era as a time when it was fine to joke that women went to college to get an "M.R.S." And many women of my generation abandoned the Seven Sisters as soon as the formerly all-male Ivy League universities became coed. I would never return to the world of segregated sexes and rampant discrimination. But now is the time to revisit the assumption that women must rush to adapt to the "man's world" that our mothers and mentors warned us about.

I continually push the young women in my classes to speak more. They must gain the confidence to value their own insights and questions, and to present them readily. My husband agrees, but he actually tries to get the young men in his classes to act more like the women—to speak less and listen more. If women are ever to achieve real equality as leaders, then we have to stop accepting male behavior and male choices as the default and the ideal. We must insist on changing social policies and bending career tracks to accommodate *our* choices, too. We have the power to do it if we decide to, and we have many men standing beside us.

We'll create a better society in the process, for *all* women. We may need to put a woman in the White House before we are able to change the conditions of the women working at Wal-Mart. But when we do, we will stop talking about whether women can have it all. We will properly focus on how we can help all Americans have healthy, happy, productive lives, valuing the people they love as much as the success they seek.

Analyze

1. Slaughter argues, "I still strongly believe that women can 'have it all' (and that men can too). I believe that we can 'have it all at the same time.' But not today, not with the way America's economy and society are currently structured." Why does she include men in this statement, and why "not today"? Do you agree?

2. Slaughter clearly identifies her audience. For whom does she write this piece? Who, then, does she leave out?

3. What is the "new gender gap" as defined by Wolfers and Stevenson? How does Slaughter use their idea to further her own argument?

Explore

1. Slaughter writes, "Going forward, women would do well to frame work–family balance in terms of the broader social and economic issues that affect both women and men." Why does she assert that men must be included when addressing the issue of work–family balance? Why does she feel it necessary to then add, "Let us presume, as I do with my sons, that they will understand 'supporting their

families' to mean more than earning money"? According to Slaughter, then, what support must men provide? Do you see men in your life already providing this kind of support? If so, how? And if not, why don't they?

2. Slaughter acknowledges the criticism that she knows she will receive: "As I write this, I can hear the reaction of some readers to many of the proposals in this essay: It's all fine and well for a tenured professor to write about flexible working hours, investment intervals, and family-comes-first management." She follows this with the question, "But what about the real world?" Are the examples that follow truly representative of the "real world"? Why or why not? What additional real-world examples would you include?

3. Consider Slaughter's text as a continuation of the conversation started by Judy Brady in her essay "I Want a Wife." Based on this, in what ways have conditions for women in the workforce improved? In what ways have women's professional opportunities remained limited? Write an essay that responds to these questions, drawing evidence from both texts to illustrate your answer.

Stephanie Coontz
"Why Is 'Having It All' Just a Women's Issue?"

Stephanie Coontz is an author and historian whose work primarily focuses on the history of marriage and the family. She teaches history and family studies at Evergreen State College, and her work has been featured in periodicals such as *The New York Times, Time* magazine, and scholarly journals such as the *Journal of Marriage and the Family*. Her books include *A Strange Stirring: The Feminine Mystique and American Women at the Dawn of the 1960s* (2011) and *Marriage: A History* (1995). This essay, published on CNN's opinion page online in 2012, is a response to Anne-Marie Slaughter's essay "Why Women Still Can't Have It All." How does Coontz both summarize Slaughter's argument and use Slaughter's ideas to craft a response?

The July/August cover story of *The Atlantic*, "Why Women Still Can't Have It All" by Anne-Marie Slaughter, has ignited a firestorm.

One side accepts the author's argument: that feminism has set women up to fail by pretending they can have a high-powered career and still be an involved mother. The other side accuses Slaughter, who left her job as the first female director of policy planning at the State Department, of setting women back by telling them to "rediscover the pursuit of happiness," starting at home.

Slaughter's article contains a powerful critique of the insanely rigid workplace culture that produces higher levels of career–family conflict among Americans—among men and women—than among any of our Western European counterparts, without measurably increasing our productivity or gross national product. And she makes sensible suggestions about how to reorganize workplaces and individual career paths to lessen that conflict.

Unfortunately, the way the discussion is framed perpetuates two myths: that feminism is to blame for raising unrealistic expectations about "having it all" and that work–family dilemmas are primarily an issue for women.

Let's start by recognizing that the women's movement never told anybody that they could "have it all." That concept was the brainchild of advertising executives, not feminist activists. Feminism insists on women's right to make choices—about whether to marry, whether to have children, whether to combine work and family or to focus on one over the other. It also urges men and women to share the joys and burdens of family life and calls on society to place a higher priority on supporting caregiving work.

Second, we should distinguish between high-powered careers that really are incompatible with active involvement in family life and those that force people to choose between work and family only because of misguided employment requirements and inadequate work–family policies.

By her account, Slaughter had one of the former. Before she "dropped out" merely to become a full-time professor, write books and make 40 to 50 speeches each year, Slaughter left Trenton, New Jersey, every Monday on the 5:30 a.m. train to Washington and didn't get back until late Friday night. Such a job is incompatible with family obligations and pleasures for men as well as for women. The real question is not why so many women feel compelled to walk away from these jobs but why so few men feel the same way.

The teaser at the top of the *Atlantic* article claims that "women who have managed to be both mothers and top professionals are superhuman, rich or self-employed." But that sentence is missing an adjective. What it really means is that women who manage simultaneously to be involved mothers and top professionals in the United States are a rare and privileged group. Men who manage to be involved fathers and top professionals are equally rare and privileged.

The irony is that most jobs, even top professional positions, do not actually require as much absenteeism from family as employers often impose. University of Texas sociologist Jennifer Glass, a senior fellow at the Council on Contemporary Families, points out that corporate and government professionals in the United States put in much longer workweeks than their counterparts in Europe, where limits on work hours are common, workplace flexibility is more widespread, and workers are entitled to far more vacation days per year than most Americans—and actually use them.

U.S. companies generally penalize workers who try to cut back on hours, reducing their hourly wages even when their hourly productivity remains the same or increases. The European Union, by contrast, forbids employers to pay less per hour for the same work when it is done part time than when it is done full time.

"In a system where work hours are encouraged to spiral out of control at the highest positions," Glass notes, "the people who make it to the top—male or female—have little time for family or community commitments, and little patience for the family commitments of the people they supervise."

Slaughter ultimately suggests some excellent reforms that would allow both men and women to meet their work and family commitments more successfully, although she inexplicably describes them as "solutions to the problems of professional women." Later she acknowledges that work–family issues plague all American workers, regardless of their sex, income level, occupational niche or even parental status since many childless workers have responsibilities to aging parents or ill partners. In fact, according to the New York–based Families and Work Institute, men now report even higher levels of work–family conflict than women do.

It was a great victory for gender equality when people finally stopped routinely saying "she's awfully good at her job—for a woman." The next big step forward will be when people stop saying, "It's awfully tough to balance work and family—for a woman." It's tough for men and women. We need to push for work–family practices and policies that allow individuals to customize their work lives according to their changing individual preferences and family obligations, not just their traditional gender roles.

Analyze

1. How does Coontz set up the controversy surrounding Slaughter's essay for us? Why does she say that this controversy exists?

2. What's Coontz's take on Slaughter's essay? How does she situate herself within the controversy about the text?

3. What, ultimately, does Coontz believe needs to change in the conversation about women "having it all"? Why?

Explore

1. An important aspect of responding to a written text is using specific examples from that text as part of your argument. What specific examples from Slaughter's essay does Coontz use in her response, and why?

2. Consult the paid maternity leave graphic (Figure 1 in the color art insert). Based on your interpretation of the graphic, to what extent do you agree with Coontz's argument in this essay? Why?

3. Although Slaughter and Coontz's articles were written in 2012, work–family practices have been a topic of conversation in the United States and around the world for a number of years. What are current paid family leave practices in the United States? What is the current debate on paid family leave in the United States? How would Slaughter and Coontz respond to that debate? How do you respond to the debate? Write an essay in which you articulate your point of view on family leave, incorporating Slaughter and Coontz as part of your evidence.

Damien Cowger
"'Daddy Makes Books and Sammies': The Stay-at-Home Dad in the 21st Century"

Damien Cowger's work has appeared in various journals including *The South-east Review* and *The Rumpus*. He is a Pushcart Prize and Best New Poets nom-inee and lives in Harrisburg, Pennsylvania. Visit him at www.damiencowger.com. In this essay, how does Cowger represent the "Stay-at-Home Dad," and how does he wrestle with issues of masculinity and male and female gender roles?

It's late Sunday afternoon in the Keystone State. Snow is falling heavy outside our window. My wife, Ashley, is hammering away on her laptop, working on lesson plans for her college English classes. Our two-year-old, Amalie, is sitting beside me, defiantly barefoot despite the season, happily sucking her fingers and watching Disney cartoons from a time before she or her parents existed. She's snuggled in tight with me and I'm maybe not as focused as I should be, because of her soft, warm skin, and because I'm continually checking my work email for news about an upcoming business trip. The weekends are the best time for me to work because my wife is home to offer a much needed helping hand with our little ball of girly rowdiness. Amalie decides when daddy time is, and daddy time seems to often come when there is a computer on my lap. Regardless, the work must be done. I am a Stay-At-Home dad in the 21st century, not necessarily a frowned upon position to be in these days, but still somewhat of a rarity in the parental world.

Movies and television, of course, aren't always the truest representations of real life, and sometimes give viewers extreme portrayals of the Stay-At-Home dad. He is often made to be a bumbling goof who runs around the house putting out small fires while wearing his wife's apron. He represents a comical figure to highlight the "absurd" situation that he finds himself in: not being the breadwinner, often because of a mistake that was made, be it a firing, or layoff due to economic downturn. Things are, of course, different from the movies, not so comical, and most of the time, not so dramatic.

This past August, my wife was offered a full-time job, itself a rarity in the English world, teaching at a college here in Pennsylvania. It was a no-brainer for our family, but one that required us to move away from Ohio. This also meant that I'd give up going to a physical office, with employees and desks, and work completely online. This is not necessarily a bad thing, just an odd situation for someone who has been used to mostly having a designated space for working. For the first time since Amalie's birth, Ashley would be working full-time, away from home. This now involves her teaching four classes per semester, holding office hours, and attending mandatory faculty meetings on a weekly basis. Primary caregiver, or Stay-At-Home Dad, quickly became a new part of my identity.

My official work title is Managing Editor of the nationally distributed literary journal, *New Ohio Review*. It is technically a part-time job, with sometimes full-time hours, that I'm lucky enough to do online from my Pennsylvania townhouse. I can usually lock myself in my upstairs office when Ashley is home, or I can open up my laptop when Amalie finally goes to sleep at 11 p.m. (she's a fighter), or when she is sitting on my lap and we are embroiled in an epic tickle-fight. I've mostly had no trouble getting my work completed, in spite of her drawing my attention away to play with trains or to read, but these are minor distractions. I'm able to have my career *and* be a good father for Amalie. I don't mind changing grotesque diapers, or sometimes wiping mucus from her angel face with the back of my hand when I can't get to tissues fast enough. What most surprises me about this double role is my own sensitivity to the world around me, and my interpretation of their perception of me as a Stay-At-Home Dad. It's not that I think that this is "woman's work," nor do I think that I am less of a man for not being the main "breadwinner," but I am continually amazed by how sensitive my reactions are to innocent, though odd comments from both friends and strangers, when reacting to a man in his thirties, out with his daughter at 11 a.m. during a weekday.

Every few visits to the grocery store, when it's just Amalie and me, a check-out person will say, in a charming Pennsylvania lilt, "Are you with Daddy today?" assuming that this were a special Daddy–Daughter scenario, or perhaps a darker I-get-her-on-MWF-and-my-ex-gets-her-TThSa-and-on-alternating-Sundays. The clerk's question is very innocent, when I really step back and consider the situation, so I'm surprised that my response is almost always, "Yep, almost *every* day!" with a slightly terse tone. My gut reaction is to want to defend that this isn't an odd occasion for a bumbling father, but my daily, proud lot. A moment that, although special to me, is standard for me. Is it fair to the clerk? Of course not. What I *should* do is let Amalie do the talking, and worry about getting gas points on my grocery card, but instead, I find the comment to be a shallow dig at my identity, and get defensive. A completely reactionary move.

On her first day at toddler swimming lessons, essentially a litany of splashing and faux jumping, Amalie's teacher came up to her and Ashley and asked some basic get-to-know-you questions, including whether or not Amalie goes to daycare. The question was meant to get a gauge on Amalie's social skills. Ashley answered "no, not until next year," and the teacher immediately said, "Oh! You get to stay home with Mama!" As with the grocery store clerk, the comment doesn't inherently make the woman a fool or a rude person, it simply shows the presumptions that we sometimes have about the world around us. The foolish part of this story is the weird feeling that I now have when I'm around this teacher, whom I see every week or two when I accompany Amalie and Ashley to swimming lessons. I'm always nice to her, but I also feel disappointed that her comment was her gut response. Disappointed that we still live in a world of presumptions about gender.

At a dinner with friends and family one night, Ashley fielded questions about her new job and our transition. When she was done, someone turned to me and said, "So you're the Stay-At-Home parent?" As with my other examples, the question is fair. One posed to get more information, to be nice, to reach out to a fellow man. My brain, my isolated and paranoid companion, hears that question with the word "just" inserted, in italics: So you're *just* the Stay-At-Home parent? This instance is the most troubling one to me. In my other examples, I felt sensitive to presumptions. In this case I went so far as to change the wording. In fact, for months, I've believed that the man *had* said "*just*." It wasn't until I sat down to write this essay that I realized he really hadn't. Suddenly, the danger of perception lies with me, and not the people that I interact with.

Above all, the main source of my angst and disappointment is my wondering why I feel defensive. I've never snapped at anyone, but my reactions to these well-meaning comments beg the question then: what's my deal? Doesn't the real issue lie with me? While it seems that the world around me still has a somewhat antiquated ideal of the parental world, I'm afraid that I'm part of this world, too, struggling with my own ideals. Do I wish that I could have a more machismo place among other men in my life? Not necessarily, and certainly not as a parent. I love the time that I have at home with my daughter, getting hugs, making peanut-butter sammies, giving stuffed animals personalities, and practicing capital letters. I relish being the only daddy at public library story time (even if I do wonder why the moms won't talk to me), and having a little person rely on me when she is scared and needy.

I sometimes wonder if people around my age are in a generation gap with lots of gender role issues. People in their early to mid-thirties were born and raised at the tail end of a time where our mothers stayed at home and raised us, but we became adults at a time when hard and fast gender roles were less enforced and expected, a glorious time when women are breadwinners more than ever, and men can be the Stay-At-Home parent. The problem lies a bit with the older crowd, who can't help but have their expectations for their kids, creating that anxiety that only parents can inflict. *My* generation carries some of the blame, too, because we have difficulty reconciling the respective views of our parents with our own ideas and an ever-changing world. My mom, save for a couple years during my childhood, was a Stay-At-Home parent. She saw us off to school, made a huge percentage of our meals, and cleaned the parts of our house that my sister and I weren't responsible for. My dad worked a difficult, and often smelly job with lousy hours for nearly the first half of my life, and even now, as he gets older, takes on part-time jobs from time to time to get ahead on bills. I have a ton of respect for my father and what he did and does for his family. Parents can be easy to idolize, especially when they have a certain amount of success. As children we model ourselves after them first, before anyone, and the modeling sticks when we enter our teens and early adulthood. My ideas about being a good father are shaped by the way that I saw my dad. Just like any dad, I try to do things for Amalie that I thought worked for me. I also do my best to avoid the things that I thought didn't work, or that I feel affected me in a negative way. There were so many more positives, though, that I may forever use my father as a measuring stick for parental greatness. Not always the smart move, but the ingrained move.

As I'm wrapping up this essay, Amalie is again sitting next to me, still in jammies, fingers yet again in her mouth. She's touching one of my hands as I type and she wonders what my wrist bone is. I explain to her about skeletons inside of us, and she starts asking me if I can show her my skeleton. It's a weird and wildly fortunate situation to be in. I get to work hard on a job that I love, and I also get to work hard at raising Amalie to ask bizarre, but pertinent questions. She's asking me to show her what is inside of me, what holds her daddy up, essentially what makes me, me. Even if my gut reactions are unfair to me, and some of the people around me, it is ultimately up to me to proudly be one of the missing links between an obsolete idea of marriage and gender roles, and focusing solely on the child's needs. It doesn't matter who is at home, or who is at work. It shouldn't matter what *other* people's ideals are. It matters that our sons and daughters have someone to answer beautifully crafted questions with poetic undertones. It is up to us to take the positives from our parents, and apply them to the positives of us as parents, and the changing world around us. For me, it might just take looking a little closer at my skeleton and realizing that I don't have to be my dad, or my dad's dad. I just need to be Amalie's dad, and do what is best for her.

Analyze

1. According to Cowger, what is the stereotypical "Stay-at-Home Dad" image, and how is this image problematic for real stay-at-home dads like him?

2. How do people perceive Cowger and his wife when they are each out with their daughter? How does Cowger believe these perceptions fit with expected gender roles for men and women?

3. How does Cowger believe that his generation is uniquely positioned to feel the tension between staying at home with one's children and being a working parent? Why?

Explore

1. In his essay, Cowger argues that parents try to model their parenting skills off their own parents—both what worked and what didn't. However, what is his ultimate conclusion at the end of the essay about masculinity and parenting? How does he use his daughter's questions about his skeleton to arrive at this concluding thought?

2. How might Cowger respond to Jensen's argument in "The High Cost of Manliness" that it's time to reshape our definition of masculinity? What might that revised definition look like?

3. To what extent are Cowger's concerns about masculinity and father-hood reflected in society? As a class, in a small group, or on your own, come up with a list of questions that you might ask a variety of individuals to gauge their perceptions of stay-at-home dads. Think about Cowger's discussion of both the stereotype and the reality as you craft your questions. Then, interview a series of individuals of different ages and genders and analyze their answers. What do you notice about how different individuals answer these questions? What seems to be the prevailing perception of stay-at-home dads in society, and why? Write an essay that addresses this question.

Megan H. MacKenzie
"Let Women Fight"

Megan H. MacKenzie is a lecturer in government and international relations at the University of Sydney. She is also the author of the book *Female Soldiers in Sierra Leone: Sex, Security, and Post-Conflict Development.* She has published widely on the issue of women in combat, which she addresses in "Let Women Fight," published in the November/December 2012 issue of *Foreign Affairs* magazine. As you read, consider how MacKenzie not only acknowledges the opposition to women in combat roles, but also what rhetorical strategies she uses to refute this opposing view. Is she successful?

Ending the U.S. Military's Female Combat Ban

Today, 214,098 women serve in the U.S. military, representing 14.6 percent of total service members. Around 280,000 women have worn American uniforms in Afghanistan and Iraq, where 144 have died and over 600 have been injured. Hundreds of female soldiers have received a Combat Action Badge, awarded for actively engaging with a hostile enemy. Two women, Sergeant Leigh Ann Hester and Specialist Monica Lin Brown, have been awarded Silver Stars—one of the highest military decorations awarded for valor in combat—for their service in Afghanistan and Iraq.

Yet the U.S. military, at least officially, still bans women from serving in direct combat positions. As irregular warfare has become increasingly common in the last few decades, the difference on the ground between the frontline and support roles is no longer clear. Numerous policy changes have also eroded the division between combat and noncombat positions. More and more military officials recognize the contributions made by female soldiers, and politicians, veterans, and military experts have all begun actively lobbying Washington to drop the ban. But Congress has not budged.

Proponents of the policy, who include Duncan Hunter (R-Calif.), former chair of the House Armed Services Committee, and former Senator Rick Santorum (R-Pa.), rely on three central arguments: that women cannot meet the physical requirements necessary to fight, that they simply don't belong in combat, and that their inclusion in fighting units would disrupt those units' cohesion and battle readiness. Yet these arguments do not stand up to current data on women's performance in combat or their impact on troop dynamics. Banning women from combat does not ensure military effectiveness. It only perpetuates counterproductive gender stereotypes and biases. It is time for the U.S. military to get over its hang-ups and acknowledge women's rightful place on the battlefield.

Women in a Man's World

Women have long served in various auxiliary military roles during wars. Further, the 1948 Women's Armed Services Integration Act created a permanent corps of women in all the military departments. This was considered a step forward at the time, but it is also the origin of the current combat ban. The act limited women's number to two percent of total service members and formally excluded them from combat duties. The exclusion policy was reinforced in 1981, when the U.S. Supreme Court ruled that the all-male draft did not constitute gender-based discrimination since it was intended to increase combat troops and women were already restricted from combat.

Despite this restriction, the share of women in the U.S. armed forces increased in the 1980s and 1990s, from 8.5 percent to 11.1 percent, as a result of the transition to an all-volunteer force in 1973 and high demand for troops. Today, the air force is the most open service for women. Women have been flying in combat aircrafts since 1993, and they now make up 70 of the 3,700 fighter pilots in the service.

In the rest of the military, restrictions on women have also been slipping for some time, albeit more slowly, due to an increase in female enlistment and the public's growing sensitivity to equal labor rights. In January 1994, a memorandum from then Secretary of Defense Les Aspin rescinded the "risk rule" barring women from any positions that could expose them to direct combat, hostile fire, or capture; the rule was replaced by the "direct ground combat assignment rule," which more narrowly tailored the restriction to frontline combat positions.

Recent policy changes have also blurred the distinction between combat and support roles. In 2003, the army began reorganizing units and increasing the number of brigades within each division. Under this system, forward support companies, which provide logistical support, transportation, and maintenance to battalions, are now grouped together on the same bases as combat units. Since women are permitted to serve in such support units, a major barrier designed to keep them away from combat has almost vanished.

The assignment of women to combat-related tasks has further undermined the strength of the ban. Beginning in 2003, for example, so-called Lioness teams were deployed to assist combat units in Iraq searching women for weapons and explosives. Drawing from this model, the military created several other female-only units in 2009, including "female engagement teams." In their first year of operation, these teams conducted over 70 short-term search-and-engagement missions in Afghanistan. Paying lip service to the exclusion policy, the military specified that these units could not contribute to hunt-and-kill foot patrols and should stay at combat bases only temporarily. In practice, however, this meant that female soldiers were required to leave their combat bases for one night every six weeks before immediately returning. Not only did this practice put women at risk with unnecessary travel in an insecure environment; it also exemplifies the waste and hardship that the preservation of the formal ban imposes on the military.

Meanwhile, the U.S. military is finding different ways to recognize the fact that women now fight in the country's wars. Members of forward support companies and female engagement teams now receive combat pay, also known as "hostile fire" or "imminent danger" pay, acknowledging the threats women regularly face. And 78 percent of the deaths of female U.S. service members in Iraq were categorized as hostile, yet another sign of how American women in uniform regularly put their lives at risk.

In light of all these changes, in 2011 the Military Leadership Diversity Commission recommended that the Department of Defense remove all combat restrictions on women. Although the total number of jobs closed to women is now relatively low, at 7.3 percent, the commission found that "exclusion from these occupations has a considerable influence on advancement to higher positions" and that eliminating the exclusion is essential "to create a level playing field for all service members who meet the qualifications." Echoing this sentiment, Senator Kirsten Gillibrand (D-N.Y.) introduced the Gender Equality in Combat Act in 2012, which seeks the termination of the ground combat exclusion policy. In addition, Command Sergeant Major Jane Baldwin and Colonel Ellen Haring, both of the Army Reserve, filed a lawsuit in May against the secretary of defense and the army's secretary, assistant secretary, and deputy chief of staff claiming that the exclusion policy violates their constitutional rights.

Responding to growing scrutiny, the Pentagon's press secretary, George Little, announced on February 9, 2012, that the Department of Defense would continue to remove restrictions on women's roles. Since then, the military has made a slew of policy revisions and commissioned a series of reviews. In May 2012, for example, the army opened up more than 14,000 combat-related jobs to women. Much of this increase, however, came from officially recognizing the combat-related nature of the jobs conducted by medics and intelligence officers, among others, positions that are already open to women. More substantially, the Marine Corps announced in April 2012 that for the first time, women can enroll and train, but not yet serve, as infantry combat officers. The army has also opened six new combat-related occupational specialties to women. In June 2012, Cicely Verstein became the first woman to serve in one of these newly opened combat support roles when she enlisted as a Bradley Fighting Vehicle systems maintainer. Women such as Verstein can now operate with combat arms units in select positions, yet they are still technically restricted from infantry and special operations roles.

Although the ban still exists on paper, the military is finding various ways to lift it in practice, and so the complete repeal of the policy would not constitute a radical change in operational terms. But it would be an acknowledgment of the contributions that women are already making to U.S. military operations. As Anu Bhagwati, a former Marine captain and now executive director of the Service Women's Action Network, explained in a BBC News interview, "Women are being shot at, are being killed overseas, are being attached to all of these combat arms units. . . . The [combat exclusion] policy has to catch up to reality." Indeed, all soldiers, female as well as male, have been given extensive combat training since 2003, when the army altered its basic training procedures in response to the growth of irregular warfare in Afghanistan and Iraq. The main obstacle that remains for women who want to serve their country is an outmoded set of biased assumptions about their capabilities and place in society.

Why Women Can Keep Up

The argument that women are not physically fit for combat is perhaps the most publicized and well-researched justification for their exclusion from fighting units. In her 2000 book, *The Kinder, Gentler Military*, the journalist Stephanie Gutmann summarized the position this way: "When butts drop onto seats, and feet grope for foot pedals, and girls of five feet one (not an uncommon height in the ranks) put on great bowl-like Kevlar helmets over a full head of long hair done up in a French braid, there are problems of fit—and those picayune fit problems ripple outward, eventually affecting performance, morale, and readiness."

This argument continues to receive a significant amount of attention in the United States, despite the fact that other militaries across the world have found that with proper training and necessary adaptations, women can complete the same physical tasks as men. In the 1970s, the Canadian military conducted trials that tested women's physical, psychological, and social capacity for combat roles. The results informed the final decision of the Canadian Human Rights Tribunal to remove Canada's female combat exclusion. After similar tests, Denmark also lifted its combat ban in the late 1980s.

The physical fitness argument, which tends to focus on differences between average male and female bodies, is also undermined by the fact that women who join the military tend to be more fit than the average American. Additional training and conditioning further decrease the gap between female and male service members, and evidence indicates that women usually benefit substantially from fitness-training programs. More to the point, performance is not necessarily determined by gender; it is determined by other attributes and by an individual's determination to reach physical prowess. To put it bluntly, there are physically fit, tough women who are suitable for combat, and weak, feeble men who are not.

The U.S. armed services would do a better job recognizing this were it not for the fact that, as critics have pointed out, the military's physical standards were created to measure male fitness, not job effectiveness. As Matthew Brown, a U.S. Army colonel and director of the Arizona Army National Guard, found in a U.S. Army War College study, "There is no conclusive evidence that all military members, regardless of occupational specialty, unit assignment, age or gender, should acquire the same level of physical fitness." The U.S. General Accounting Office (now the Government Accountability Office) also admitted in a 1998 report that physical fitness tests are not necessarily a useful gauge of operational effectiveness, explaining, "fitness testing is not aimed at assessing the capability to perform specific missions or military jobs." To be sure, men and women have different types of bodies, but growing research points to the limitations of having a single male-centered standard for fitness and equipment. Recently, for example, the army has moved to design body armor for women rather than force them to continue wearing equipment that restricts their movement and cuts into their legs because it was designed for men. With proper training and equipment, women can contribute to missions just as well as men.

Breaking Up the Band of Brothers

Even though the physical argument does not hold up to scrutiny, many in the military establishment continue to instinctively oppose the idea of women serving in combat roles. In a 1993 *New York Times* article, General Merrill McPeak, former chief of staff of the air force, admitted that he had "a culturally based hang-up." "I can't get over this image of old men ordering young women into combat," he said. "I have a gut-based hang-up there. And it doesn't make a lot of sense in every way. I apologize for it." This belief had earlier been spelled out in the 1992 report of the Presidential Commission on the Assignment of Women in the Armed Forces, which was established by George H. W. Bush to review the combat exclusion. The commission identified several factors related to having women serve in combat roles that could negatively impact troop dynamics, including the "real or perceived inability of women to carry their weight without male assistance, a 'zero privacy' environment on the battlefield, interference with male bonding, cultural values and the desire of men to protect women, inappropriate male/female relationships, and pregnancy— particularly when perceived as a way to escape from combat duty."

While campaigning for the Republican presidential nomination this year, Santorum, the former senator, echoed these concerns, arguing that "instead of focus[ing] on the mission, [male soldiers] may be more concerned about protecting . . . a [female solider] in a vulnerable position." Others fear that men will not be able to restrain themselves sexually if forced to fight and work in close proximity to women. The conservative Independent Women's Forum strongly supports the ban because of the "power of the sex drive when young women and men, under considerable stress, are mixed together in close quarters."

Even as these false assumptions about the inherent nature of men and women persist, many in the military and the general public have changed their minds. In 2010, Admiral Mike Mullen, then chairman of the U.S. Joint Chiefs of Staff, said, "I know what the law says and I know what it requires, but I'd be hard pressed to say that any woman who serves in Afghanistan today or who's served in Iraq over the last few years did so without facing the same risks as their male counterparts." Similarly, Bhagwati contends that "as proven by ten years of leading troops in combat in Iraq and Afghanistan, there are women that are physically and mentally qualified to succeed . . . and lead infantry platoons." Meanwhile, a 2011 survey conducted by ABC News and *The Washington Post* found that 73 percent of Americans support allowing women in combat.

Despite such shifts in opinion, defenders of the status quo argue that lifting the ban would disrupt male bonding and unit cohesion, which is thought to build soldiers' confidence and thereby increase combat readiness and effectiveness. In 2007, Kingsley Browne, a former U.S. Supreme Court clerk and the author of "Co-ed Combat: The New Evidence That Women Shouldn't Fight the Nation's Wars," argued that "men fight for many reasons, but probably the most powerful one is the bonding—'male bonding'—with their comrades. . . . Perhaps for very fundamental reasons, women do not evoke in men the same feelings of comradeship and 'followership' that men do." These comments betray the widely held fear that women would feminize and therefore reduce the fighting potential of the military. The Israeli military historian Martin van Creveld has echoed this sentiment, writing, "As women enter them, the armed forces in question will become both less willing to fight and less capable of doing so." And as Anita Blair, former assistant secretary of the navy, warned, "The objective for many who advocate a greater female influence in the armed services is not so much to conquer the military as conquer manhood: they aim to make the most quintessentially masculine of our institutions more feminine." By such lights, women fundamentally threaten the unified masculine identity of the military and could never properly fill combat roles because they are inherently incapable of embodying the manly qualities of a soldier.

This argument is intuitive and plausible. It is also dead wrong. It assumes that a key objective of the military is enhancing masculinity rather than national security and that unit bonding leads to better task performance. In fact, a 1995 study conducted by the U.S. Army Research Institute for the Behavioral and Social Sciences found that "the relation between cohesiveness and performance is due primarily to the 'commitment to the task' component of cohesiveness, and not the 'interpersonal attraction' or 'group pride' components of cohesiveness." Similarly, a 2006 study in *Armed Forces and Society*, written by the scholars Robert MacCoun, Elizabeth Kier, and Aaron Belkin, concluded that "all of the evidence indicates that military performance depends on whether service members are committed to the same professional goals, not on whether they like one another."

There is significant evidence that not only male bonding but any sort of closeness can actually hinder group performance. In a 1998 study on demographics and leadership, the group management experts Andrew Kakabadse and Nada Kakabadse found that "excessive cohesion may create a harmful insularity from external forces," and they linked high cohesion to "high conformity, high commitment to prior courses of actions, [and a] lack of openness." In her analysis of gender integration in the military, Erin Solaro, a researcher and journalist who was embedded with combat troops in Afghanistan and Iraq, pointed out that male bonding often depended on the exclusion or denigration of women and concluded that "cohesion is not the same as combat effectiveness, and indeed can undercut it. Supposedly 'cohesive' units can also kill their officers, mutiny, evade combat, and surrender as groups."

The mechanisms for achieving troop cohesion can also be problematic. In addition to denigrating women, illegal activities, including war crimes, have sometimes been used as a means for soldiers to "let off steam" and foster group unity. In sum, there is very little basis on which to link group cohesion to national security.

Strength in Diversity

Over the last century, the military has been strengthened when attitudes have been challenged and changed. Despite claims in the 1940s that mixed-race units would be ineffective and that white and black service members would not be able to trust one another, for example, integration proceeded without any major hiccups. A 2011 study of the impacts of racial integration on combat effectiveness during the Korean War found that integration "resulted in improvements in cohesion, leadership and command, fighting spirit, personnel resources and sustainment that increased the combat effectiveness." Initial research indicates that mixed-gender units could provide similar benefits.

Leora Rosen, a former senior analyst at the National Institute of Justice, found that when women were accepted into mixed-gender units, the groups' effectiveness actually increased. Similarly, a 1993 RAND Corporation paper summarizing research on sexual orientation and the U.S. military's personnel policy found that diversity "can enhance the quality of group problem-solving and decision-making, and it broadens the group's collective array of skills and knowledge." These conclusions are supported by a 1993 report by the General Accounting Office, which found that "members of gender-integrated units develop brother–sister bonds rather than sexual ones. . . . Experience has shown that actual integration diminishes prejudice and fosters group cohesiveness more effectively than any other factor." The same report also found that gender homogeneity was not perceived by soldiers to be a requirement for effective unit operations.

It should come as no surprise that elements of the military want uniformity in the ranks. The integration of new groups always ruffles feathers. But the U.S. military has been ahead of the curve in terms of the inclusion of most minority groups. It was the first federal organization to integrate African Americans. And with the repeal of the "don't ask, don't tell" (DADT) policy, the military now has more progressive policies toward gay employees than many other U.S. agencies. In fact, DADT was repealed despite the fact that there are no federal laws preventing employment discrimination on the basis of sexual orientation.

In September 2012, one year after the repeal of DADT, a study published by the Palm Center found that the change "has had no overall negative impact on military readiness or its component dimensions, including cohesion, recruitment, retention, assaults, harassment or morale." The research also found that overall, DADT's "repeal has enhanced the military's ability to pursue its mission." Previous claims about the negative impact that gay service members might have on troop cohesion mirror those currently used to support the female combat exclusion.

Unlike the military's treatment of other groups, its current policies toward women are much more conservative than those of other federal and state government bodies. Women who choose military service confront not only restricted career options but also a higher chance of harassment, discrimination, and sexual violence than in almost any other profession. The weak record on addressing these issues gives the impression that the military is an unwelcome place and an unsafe career choice for women. In an interview with National Public Radio in 2011, Sergeant Kayla Williams, who served in Iraq, explicitly linked the combat exclusion and harassment: "I believe that the combat exclusion actually exacerbates gender tensions and problems within the military because the fact that women can't be in combat arms jobs allows us to be portrayed as less than fully soldiers." Fully integrating women could therefore begin to address two major issues for the U.S. military: enhancing diversity and equality and also weakening the masculine culture that may contribute to harassment.

Unsubstantiated claims about the distracting nature of women, the perils of feminine qualities, and the inherent manliness of war hardly provide a solid foundation on which to construct policy. Presumably, some levels of racism and homophobia also persist within the military, yet it would be absurd, not to mention unconstitutional, for the U.S. government to officially sanction such prejudices. The U.S. military should ensure that it is as effective as possible, but it must not bend to biases, bigotry, and false stereotypes.

Just as when African Americans were fully integrated into the military and DADT was repealed, lifting the combat ban on women would not threaten national security or the cohesiveness of military units; rather, it would bring formal policies in line with current practices and allow the armed forces to overcome their misogynistic past. In a modern military, women should have the right to fight.

Analyze

1. Why does MacKenzie begin her article by noting the number of women who have died or been injured in Afghanistan and Iraq, as well as by noting the awards women have received "for actively engaging with a hostile enemy"? How does this set up her position on the issue?

2. Why does MacKenzie point out that many female members of forward support companies and female engagement teams already receive combat pay?

3. In the section titled "Strength in Diversity," MacKenzie recalls the military's historic move to racially integrate units after 1940, as well as the repeal of the "don't ask, don't tell" policy. How do these further her argument?

Explore

1. Summarize the arguments of those who oppose lifting the ban on women in combat. How does MacKenzie refute these arguments, and what kind of evidence does she use to do so? Is her evidence effective? Why or why not? Additionally, MacKenzie argues that the central argument of proponents of the female combat ban policy "perpetuates counterproductive gender stereotypes and biases." How does the opposition, then, reinforce negative stereotypes of women?

2. MacKenzie quotes Sergeant Kayla Williams, who argues that the "combat exclusion actually exacerbates gender tensions." How does

MacKenzie then link this claim to the "masculine culture" of the military and problems of harassment? Is she right to make this link? Why or why not? Do some research on the issues of sexual harassment and sexual assault in the military. Does your research support MacKenzie's claim? Why or why not?

3. Do some research on the Lioness teams to which MacKenzie refers. If possible, view Meg McLagan and Daria Sommer's documentary *Lioness*, which tells the personal stories of the first women sent into direct ground combat as a part of a "Lioness" team. Does your research and/or these stories support or challenge MacKenzie's argument? What other issues faced by women serving in combat does your research reveal?

World Bank
"Taking Stock: Stylized Facts about Gender at Work"

The **World Bank** is an international financial institution that offers low-interest loans, credits, and grants to developing countries. Its primary goals are to "end extreme poverty by decreasing the percentage of people living on less than $1.25 a day to no more than 3%" and "promote shared prosperity by fostering the income growth of the bottom 40% for every country." "Taking Stock" describes the disparities between men and women in the "world of work," comparing and contrasting developing and high-income countries in the areas of employment status and quality, earnings, entrepreneurship and farming, and labor force participation. As you read, consider how the World Bank is able to present an expansive amount of data while still making pointed, simple claims.

The gender differences in the world of work are striking, extensive and enduring. They exist in multiple dimensions. Although the most obvious gap is in labor force participation rates, there are other persistent gender gaps—in earnings and types of jobs, particularly—that affect the extent to which paid work expands well-being, agency, and future economic opportunities.

One-dimensional pictures are limited, if not misleading. Often the focus is too narrowly on labor force participation, for example. In some of the world's poorest countries, such as Rwanda and Tanzania, women's rate of labor force participation is close to 90 percent.[1] However, this does not mean that women are employed in good jobs, farming productive crops, running profitable enterprises, or earning as much as their male counterparts. On the contrary, much of the work done by the world's poor is subsistence-based, insecure, and lacking in basic protections.

A multidimensional perspective [is important] for the 10 most populous developing countries for which we have data, representing one-third of the world's population. In all cases, women are less likely to be in the labor force, earn less than men, and, in all but Brazil, working women are less likely than working men to be employed in wage jobs. In Turkey, while gender wage gaps appear to be small, there are large disparities in labor force participation and employment in wage jobs. And a deeper analysis of Turkey's wage differences reveals that the gap widens when one controls for basic characteristics such as age, education, and tenure.[2] This underscores the importance of multidimensional appraisals of gender equality in the world of work. Box 2.1 offers an empirical picture, highlighting some key facts that are not widely known.

Employment Status and Quality

Women are less likely than men to have full-time wage jobs with an employer. Women in developing countries are underrepresented in every type of employment and are more than twice as likely to be out of the labor force altogether. Significant, though less extreme, gaps persist in high income countries as well. Globally, Gallup finds that men are nearly twice as likely as women to be in full-time employment for an employer, and people in this type of work report the highest levels of well-being.[3] These jobs are more likely to come with a higher and more dependable wage, benefits, and protections. There are also regional differences between men and women that work full time for an employer. In the Middle East and North Africa and South Asia for example, among the entire working age population, men are about four times as likely as women to have full-time jobs for an employer.[4]

Women's jobs are consistently more likely than men's to be part-time.[5] Part-time work can provide increased flexibility and bring more women into the labor force. But it tends to involve lower earnings, fewer benefits and protections, and less career mobility.[6] Notably, part-time work among women is highest in the Netherlands, who benefit from policies that extend social protection and entitlements to part-time workers.[7]

Gender inequality is perpetuated in the informal economy.

The informal economy includes workers in informal sectors—all jobs in unregistered and small-scale private unincorporated enterprises—as well as informal jobs in formal sector firms—such as unpaid family enterprise workers and casual, short-term, and seasonal workers without contracts or legal status.[8] Although men outnumber women in absolute terms in the informal economy in all regions but Sub-Saharan Africa, in developing countries working women tend to be more concentrated into informal work.[9] Recent analysis of 41 developing countries with gender-disaggregated data found that women were more likely than male counterparts to be in non-agricultural informal employment in 30 countries,[10] including 56 versus 48 percent in Peru, and 62 versus 55 percent in Uganda.[11]

As informal workers, women generally earn less than men and sort into different types of jobs.[12] Women are particularly concentrated into the more "invisible" activities, such as domestic labor and unpaid work.[13] Recent data indicate that over a quarter (27 percent) of all female wage workers in Latin America and the Caribbean, and 14 percent in Africa are domestic workers.[14] Women represent an estimated 83 percent of domestic workers worldwide.[15] Many of these workers are not covered by labor laws, including those guaranteeing maximum weekly working hours, minimum wages, and maternity leave.

BOX 2.1 TO BETTER UNDERSTAND GENDER AT WORK[16, 17]

Ten global facts everyone should know

- Women's labor force participation has stagnated, in fact decreasing from 57 percent in 1990 to 55 percent in 2012.
- Women on average earn between 10 and 30 percent less than working men.
- Women are only half as likely as men to have full-time wage jobs for an employer.

- In only five of the 114 countries for which data are available have women reached or surpassed gender parity with men in such occupations as legislators, senior officials, and managers; namely, Colombia, Fiji, Jamaica, Lesotho, and the Philippines.
- Women spend at least twice as much time as men on unpaid domestic work such as caring and housework.
- A total of 128 countries have at least one sex-based legal differentiation, meaning women and men cannot function in the world of work in the same way; in 54 countries, women face five or more legal differences.
- Across developing countries, there is a nine percentage point gap between women and men in having an account at a formal financial institution.
- More than one in three women has experienced either physical or sexual violence by a partner or non-partner sexual violence.
- In 2010–12, 42 countries reported gender gaps in secondary school enrollment rates exceeding 10 percent.
- One in three girls in developing countries is married before reaching her 18th birthday.

. . . and some signs of progress

- Women's labor force participation in Latin America and the Caribbean rose by 33 percent since 1990.
- Half of the legal constraints documented in 100 countries in 1960 on access to and control over assets, ability to sign legal documents, and fair treatment under the constitution had been removed by 2010.
- Seventy-five countries have enacted domestic violence legislation since the adoption of CEDAW in 1979.
- The global ratio of female to male primary education enrollment increased from 92 percent in 2000 to 97 percent in 2011.
- The share of people agreeing that men should have the priority over jobs fell from 48 percent in 1999–2004 to 41 percent in 2008–2012 in the 23 developed and developing countries with data.
- International commitments to gender equality are increasing. The World Bank documents nearly US$31 billion of gender-informed lending in fiscal year 2013, and, in 2011, OECD countries contributed about US$20.5 billion toward gender equality and women's empowerment projects.

Women also do most of the world's unpaid work—usually for family enterprises, as well as in the home. It is estimated that women account for 58 percent of all unpaid contributing family work, and about one out of every four women in the labor force globally is an unpaid contributing family worker—someone who works in a market orientated business owned by a related household member but is not a partner in the business (compared to one in ten men).[17] This does not include housework and childcare, which is mainly done by women as well. The unpaid contributing family worker gap is largest in South Asia (51 percent of women compared to 14 percent of men).[18] Household survey data suggest that in Latin America and the Caribbean, East Asia and the Pacific, and Sub-Saharan Africa, women are about twice as likely as men to be non-paid employees.[19] Interestingly, gender wage gaps tend to be larger in the informal than the formal sector.[20] Because the informal economy is a source of both job creation and gender inequality in the world of work, a long-term approach in the context of overall jobs creation is needed (Box 2.2).

Workers, especially women, are concentrated in farming and self-employment in low-income countries where only 9 percent of women have wage jobs, compared to 21 percent of men. The data clearly illustrate that formal-sector jobs strategies alone would not address the needs of the vast majority of women and men in developing contexts.

In terms of wage employment, men tend to dominate manufacturing, construction, transport and communications whereas women are concentrated in health, social work, and education. Differences in education, training, preferences for job security, and the need for flexible working hours help explain this segregation, alongside gender stereotyping. ILO analysis shows that in both developed and developing economies women's employment is most heavily concentrated in occupations such as clerks and service and retail sales workers. In contrast, men's employment dominates in crafts, trades, plant and machine operations, and managerial and legislative occupations.[21]

BOX 2.2 GENDER AND INFORMALITY: NUANCED PERSPECTIVES ARE NEEDED

The informal economy is an important job source for women and men in developing countries, and a major contributor to national economies. Estimates show that informal employment comprises one-half to three-quarters of non-agricultural employment in developing countries.[22] Yet gender gaps in earnings and opportunities tend to be particularly stark within the informal economy. Gender sorting into different types of work reinforces disparities in earnings and vulnerability and responds to multiple constraints.[23] For example, women's lack of access to property and financial services poses barriers to formal firm creation. Government corruption, time-intensive bureaucracy, high tax rates, and lack of flexibility in the formal sector can push women into the informal economy.[24] Domestic responsibilities and restricted mobility also limit women's ability to participate in higher paying activities farther from home. Gender differences in levels of literacy, education, skills, and aspirations further contribute to gaps.

Given women's concentration into lower-paying and more vulnerable work, gender-sensitive policies are often needed to extend social protection to those in the informal economy—both to mitigate vulnerability and to ensure that safety nets, public works, and other social services benefit vulnerable women.[25] Collective action plays a particularly important role in filling voids in voice, representation, and support where formal organizing structures and protections are otherwise lacking.[26] Groups like Women in Informal Employment Globalizing and Organizing (WIEGO, a global action-research-policy network), the Self Employed Women's Association (SEWA, an India-based organization of poor, self-employed women), HomeNet Southeast Asia (a network of home-based workers), and StreetNet International (an alliance of organizations of informal vendors and hawkers) have been critical mobilizers of rights-based action.

While movement toward formalization is one aspect of a comprehensive jobs strategy, it is necessarily longer-term in nature.[27] Overly hasty policies toward formalization could disproportionately affect women by reducing an accessible source of economic opportunity without removing barriers to entry in the formal economy.[28] WIEGO suggests a comprehensive four-tier approach that involves: (1) creating more jobs, preferably formal jobs; (2) registering informal enterprises and regulating informal jobs; (3) extending state protection (social and legal) to the informal workforce; and (4) increasing productivity of informal enterprises and incomes of the informal workforce.[29]

In some cases, strategic investments can help women enter the formal economy. For example, where Special Economic Zones exist, as in Costa Rica, Egypt, and the Philippines, these can provide women with a gateway into formal sector employment and opportunities for higher pay when they include gender-sensitive practices, such as extending health education programs, family-friendly policies, and childcare options.[30] In other cases, initiatives create jobs for women within the informal economy. For example, public–private partnerships that engage non-governmental organizations have extended opportunities through "bottom-of-the-pyramid" models, which extend distribution channels through micro-franchises selling a variety of goods, like shampoos and SIM cards, providing jobs for very poor women in countries like Bangladesh and Kenya, and helping companies penetrate hard-to-reach markets.[31] The partnerships help link services to address gendered constraints and vulnerabilities.

Women are especially underrepresented in science, technology, engineering, and math (STEM) fields. Out of 102 economies for which there are recent data, only two had at least as many female as male graduates in engineering, manufacturing, and construction, and only 30 (29 percent) had attained gender parity in science in tertiary enrolment.[32] Women's share of the information and communication technology (ICT) workforce is less than one-third in Jordan and only around one-fifth in South Africa, Sri Lanka, and the United Kingdom.[33]

Glass ceilings remain: at the top of the business ladder, corporate boards and CEO roles are dominated by men. A range of facts illustrates this basic point:

- A 2013 survey of 4,322 companies from 34 industrialized and emerging market countries found that, in aggregate, only 11 percent of board members are women.[34]
- Among Fortune 500 companies in the United States, only 4 percent of CEOs, 14 percent of executive officers, and 17 percent of board members were female in 2012.[35]
- Our analysis of survey data from 13,000 firms in 135 countries found that fewer than one in five firms (18 percent) have a female top manager, and only 10 percent of large firms have female management.[36] In South Asia, women manage about one in 16 firms.[37]
- In only five of the 114 countries for which data are available have women reached or surpassed gender parity with men in occupations as legislators, senior officials, and managers; namely, Colombia, Fiji, Jamaica, Lesotho, and the Philippines.[38]

This in turn may reflect biased expectations about leadership capacity. In 30 out of 66 developed and developing countries covered by the World Values Survey from 2005–2012, the majority of men felt that men make better executives than women.[39] While higher percentages of men than women generally subscribe to this belief, differences between countries tend to be larger than differences between sexes. In other words, where biased views against women's leadership capabilities are strong, women also internalize these views.

Earnings

Women consistently earn less than men and no country has reached gender wage parity.[40] While comparable data is a challenge, the stylized fact is clear. Evidence from 83 developed and developing countries shows that women in paid work earn 10–30 percent less than men on average.[41] Another recent analysis of gender pay gaps across 43 countries estimated the average at around 18 percent.[42] Additionally, earlier progress in reducing gender pay gaps appears to have stagnated over the last decade.[43]

Most of the pay gap in wage work is due to differing jobs and hours. Women and men earn different wages primarily because of different types of work. The ILO, for example, documents substantial earnings differences between male-dominated and female-dominated occupations.[44] The implication is that labor policies, such as minimum wages and anti-discrimination regulations, may help in some cases but will not be enough to erase gaps, and longer-term strategies are needed to reduce gender sorting into different types of jobs and firms.

Nonetheless, women earn less than men even when controlling for industry and occupation. In 2010, controlling for these factors, women earned 86 percent of what men earned in Chile, 69 percent in Estonia, and only 36 percent in Pakistan.[45] In the United States, full-time female secretaries earned 14 percent less than male secretaries in 2011, and full-time first-line women retail sales supervisors earned 21 percent less than men in the same position.[46]

Unexplained earnings gaps are largest among part-time workers and those with low levels of education. Analysis of 64 developing countries reveals that women in part-time work (20 hours or fewer per week) and with low levels of education (less than complete primary) are significantly more likely to earn less than men with similar profiles.[47] We also know that women are heavily concentrated into part-time work and, in developing countries, are more likely to have lower levels of education.

Women's earnings often decline when they have children. Across 28 developed and developing countries, 71 percent of women under the age of 30 experienced lower earnings after having children, compared to 43 percent of men.[48] Women aged 30–39 with children are twice as likely as men with children to have reduced earnings (88 versus 43 percent). Men of all ages with children are more likely to have higher earnings than men without children, which is not the case for women in any age group.

Differences in Entrepreneurship and Farming

Entrepreneurship is critical to gender at work. Micro, small, and medium enterprises (MSMEs)[49] comprise 90 percent of all jobs in developing countries,[50] and over the past decade their growth rate in low-income countries has been triple that of MSMEs in high-income countries.[51] Agricultural employment remains the primary source of livelihood for about 38 percent of the population in developing countries.[52] Women comprise about 43 percent of the agricultural labor force in developing countries overall, and about half in East Asia and Sub-Saharan Africa.[53] The "feminization of agriculture" has been documented in developing countries as men migrate farther away and for longer for off-farm employment while women, more constrained in terms of time and mobility, are more likely to continue agricultural work.[54] Women are generally concentrated into low levels of agricultural value chains, performing mostly basic smallholder farming activities.[55] Some key areas of female disadvantage are well established, although data tend to be weak.

Female-owned businesses are generally smaller and employ fewer people. The Global Entrepreneurship Monitor indicates that women are more likely than men to run single-person businesses without any employees. In Latin America and the Caribbean, for example, half of established businesses owned by women have no employees, compared to 38 percent for men, and in Sub-Saharan Africa, the respective figures are 44 and 30 percent.[56] Likewise, analysis of unregistered firms across six African countries found that women's firms were significantly smaller than men's.[57]

Female entrepreneurs in developing countries are more likely than their male counterparts to be concentrated into small and informal firms and retail sectors.[58] Most non-agricultural entrepreneurs in developing countries, especially women, operate in the retail sector. Men dominate construction and business-oriented services whereas women are more likely found in retail and manufacturing. About 18 percent of non-agricultural self-employed males work in business-oriented services, compared to only 5 percent of females.[59]

Because of differences in human capital and productive inputs, female farmers achieve lower productivity than male farmers—20 to 30 percent less, due largely to differences in human capital and access to productive inputs.[60] As a result of gender-specific constraints, female farmers tend to have lower output per unit of land and are much less likely to be active in commercial farming than men.[61] In western Kenya, the 23 percent gap in yields between male- and female-headed households has been explained largely by female-headed households having less-secure access to land and lower levels of education.[62]

When firm size, sector, and capital intensity are controlled for, gender gaps in firm productivity diminish or disappear.[63] Because women and men sort into different types of enterprises, simply comparing productivity or profitability by gender is misleading. When key firm characteristics are controlled for, Hallward-Dreimeier (2013) finds that gender gaps in productivity virtually disappear.

Women typically farm less profitable crops and smaller plots than men. Women farm both cash and subsistence crops, though social norms often result in men's farming concentrating more on the former and women's more on the latter.[64] For example, in Ghana, cocoa is grown more by male farmers, while cocoyam, a staple crop often consumed at home, is disproportionately grown by women.[65] In all 14 countries for which there are data, the farm sizes of male-headed households are larger than those of female-headed households, and in some countries the gaps are particularly wide—in Ecuador and Pakistan, for instance, farms of male-headed households are more than twice as large.[66]

Women entrepreneurs and farmers tend to have less access than men to capital, financial services, equipment, land, agricultural technologies, hired labor, and market information.[67] Women in Latin America and the Caribbean, for example, consistently have assets of lower value than men, and yet prospective female entrepreneurs are generally required to put up significantly more collateral than prospective male entrepreneurs to access capital.[68] These asset gaps are costly. According to a recent Food and Agriculture Organization (FAO) report, reducing gender inequalities in access to productive resources and services could produce an increase in yields on women's farms of between 20 percent and 30 percent, which could raise agricultural output in developing countries by 2.5 percent to 4 percent (based on data from 52 countries).[69] In some countries, the gains could be even larger. In Zambia, if women farmers had the same capital as their male counterparts, national output could rise by up to 15 percent.[70]

There are well documented disparities in access to and control of financial and physical capital—particularly credit and land.[71] For many women, this gender bias extends to non-land assets, such as livestock—especially more valuable livestock, such as cattle.[72] Sex-disaggregated data on livestock ownership are rare[73] but available data consistently shows gaps. A study of men's and women's livestock ownership in Northeastern Uganda found that 62 percent of men, compared to only 14 percent of women, owned cattle.[74]

Women have less access than men to financial services. The Global Findex database measures how people in 148 countries—including the poor, women, and rural residents—save, borrow, make payments, and manage risk.[75] The data document significant gender gaps:

- Only 47 percent of women globally have opened an account at a formal financial institution compared to 55 percent of men.
- The gap is wider in developing countries—37 percent of women compared to 46 percent of men. South Asia and the Middle East and North Africa have the largest gender gap: women are about 40 percent less likely than men to have a formal account.

The gender gap extends to access to credit as well.

Having an account at a formal financial institution has multiple benefits in the world of work and beyond. It provides a reliable payment channel for employers and government programs, it opens more opportunities for financial credit that can be used in business start-up and growth, and it provides protection for workers' earnings.[76] Access to finance affects both women as individuals and women-owned firms.[77] The IFC (2011) estimates that while women-owned entities represent over 30 percent of registered businesses worldwide, on average, only 5 to 10 percent of women-owned entities have access to commercial bank loans.

Women—especially poor women—still trail men in terms of access to information and communication technology. In 2012, 200 million fewer girls and women than boys and men were online in developing countries, a gap of 23 percent. And this gap is much higher in Sub-Saharan Africa, the Middle East and North Africa, and South Asia.[78] Women are also less likely than men to own or have access to a mobile phone in developing countries—reportedly as much as 21 percent less likely.[79] In India, only 44 percent of women own cell phones (compared to 66 percent of men), and a meager 4 percent of women use the internet regularly (compared to 9 percent of men).[80]

Labor Force Participation

Of the roughly 3.3 billion people who are part of the global labor force, 40 percent—1.3 billion—are women. Globally, in 2012, the labor force participation rate (ages 15–64) was 82 percent for men compared to 55 percent for women.[81]

Women's labor force participation has stagnated, and has actually fallen two percentage points (to 55 percent) since 1990. While the gender gap has narrowed slightly from 27 to 26 percentage points since 1990, this is entirely due to falling male labor force participation. Regional patterns vary: Sub-Saharan Africa and Latin America and the Caribbean have seen increases in female labor force participation, while female participation has declined in South Asia—particularly in India, though this case is complex.[82] Further, women's labor force participation in developing countries is often lower in urban areas. In Turkey, for example, recent declines have been attributed largely to migration out of rural areas—where a large share of women participate as unpaid family workers and subsistence farmers, and where women tend to have greater extended family networks to support childcare and household functions.[83]

Gender gaps in labor force participation occur across all regions and age groups to varying extents. In most regions, the steepest increase in gaps occurs in the 15–24 and 25–34 age groups, with the onset of childcare responsibilities. Europe and Central Asia is the exception, where the gap widens later on. In most regions, the largest gender gaps are found after age 55, suggesting that women leave the labor force earlier. The largest regional gender gap in labor force participation—62 percentage points for the age group 35–54—is found in the Middle East and North Africa.

All around the world women spend more time on unpaid domestic work—that is, child and elderly care and housework—than men.[84] Focus group discussions in 18 developing countries found that women on average report spending about three hours more per day on housework and childcare and about 2.5 hours less per day on market activities compared to men.[85]

The burden of childcare responsibilities creates a "motherhood penalty."[86] One study of panel data across 97 countries estimated that, on average, a birth reduces a woman's labor supply by almost two years during her reproductive years.[87] The gender differences in the effects of having children on caring responsibilities and work are substantial. In Australia, for example, when men have one child under five, their full-time employment on average *increases* by about 27 percent; when women have one child under five, their full-time employment *drops* by 20 percent.[88]

Women's labor force participation tends to fall as country incomes rise and some women move out of subsistence-based agricultural work. At the same [time], the nature of women's labor force participation tends to change with development. Namely, self-employment, which in developing countries is often subsistence-based, tends to decline, while the share of women in wage work increases. Notably, the share of women as employers remains constant with countries' income.[89]

In sum, gender gaps in the world of work are both extensive and multidimensional. These gaps reflect the persistence of gender-specific constraints across the lifecycle, which are explored in the next chapter. The relative magnitude and importance of different disparities depends on the country context, and it is useful to compare performance across countries. Further, while inequality in the world of work is a global phenomenon, it is clearly more extensive in particular countries and regions. It is often helpful for policy-makers, donors, and other stakeholders to start with an understanding of how a particular country of concern fares relative to others with respect to gender equality in the world of work and more broadly. Resource Box 2.1 summarizes common indices that capture aggregate outcomes and practices related to gender equality.

RESOURCE BOX 2.1 **WHERE DO COUNTRIES STAND?**
GLOBAL AND REGIONAL RANKINGS ON GENDER EQUALITY
AND WOMEN'S ECONOMIC EMPOWERMENT

Indices can provide powerful benchmarking tools for evaluating where a particular country or region stands relative to others, or to itself over time, on critical outcomes and practices related to gender equality in the world of work (see notes for Website links):

- **Gender Inequality Index** (UNDP): The index reflects women's disadvantage in three dimensions—reproductive health, empowerment and the labor market—for as many countries as data of reasonable quality allow. The index shows the loss in human development due to inequality between female and male achievements in these dimensions.[90]
- **Global Gender Gap Index** (World Economic Forum): Introduced in 2006, the index provides a framework for capturing the magnitude and scope of gender-based disparities around the world. The index benchmarks national gender gaps on economic, political, education and health-based criteria and provides country rankings that allow for comparison across regions and income groups and over time.[91]
- **Gender Equality Index** (European Institute for Gender Equality): The index, specific to the European Union, is a measurement tool that combines gender indicators, according to a conceptual framework, into a single summary measure. Core domains include: work, money, knowledge, time, power, health and two satellite domains (intersecting inequalities and violence).[92]
- **Gender GEDI Index** (Global Entrepreneurship and Development Institute): Based so far on a 17-country pilot analysis, the index measures the development of high-potential female entrepreneurship worldwide.[93]
- **Social Institutions and Gender Index** (OECD): The index is a measure of underlying discrimination against women for over 100 countries. SIGI captures and quantifies discriminatory social institutions—these include, among others, early marriage, discriminatory inheritance practices, violence against women, son bias, and restricted access to productive resources.[94]
- **WEVentureScope** (The Economist Intelligence Unit and the Multilateral Investment Fund): The tool assesses the environment for supporting and growing women's micro, small, and medium-sized businesses in Latin America and the Caribbean. It measures business operating risks, access

to finance, capacity and skill-building opportunities, and the presence of social services.[95]

• **Women's Economic Opportunity Index** (The Economist Intelligence Unit): The index is a pilot effort funded by the World Bank to assess the laws, regulations, practices, and attitudes that affect women workers and entrepreneurs. It uses 26 indicators, selected and validated by a panel of gender experts, to evaluate every aspect of the economic and social value chain for women.[96]

NOTES

1. World Development Indicators. Washington, DC: World Bank.
2. Aktas, A. and G. Uysal. 2012. "Explaining the Gender Wage Gap in Turkey Using the Wage Structure Survey." BETAM Working Paper Series #005. Istanbul, Bahçeşehir University.
3. Marlar, J. and E. Mendes. 2013. "Globally, Men Twice as Likely as Women to Have a Good Job." http://www.gallup.com/poll /164666/globally-men-twice-likely-women-good-job.aspx; Clifton, J., and J. Marlar. 2011. "World-wide, Good Jobs Linked to Higher Wellbeing." http://www.gallup.com/poll/146639/worldwide-good-jobs-linked-higher-wellbeing.aspx.
4. Team analysis of Gallup World Poll data.
5. Gender at Work team's calculations based on UN Statistics Division figures accessed on September 7, 2013, available at http://unstats.un.org/unsd/demo-graphic/products/indwm.
6. Chioda, L. 2011. *Work & Family: Latin American and Caribbean Women in Search of a New Balance.* Washington, DC: World Bank.
7. ILO. 2010. *Women in Labour Markets: Measuring Progress and Identifying Challenges.* Geneva: ILO.
8. ILO. 2013. "KILM 7th Edition Manuscript." Retrieved August 15, 2013, from http://kilm.ilo.org/manuscript/kilm08.asp.
9. Charmes, J. 2012. "The Informal Economy Worldwide: Trends and Char-acteristics." *Margin: The Journal of Applied Economic Research* 6 (2): 103–32.
10. ILO. 2012. "Statistical Update on Employment in the Informal Economy." Geneva: ILO. http://laborsta.ilo.org/applv8/data/INFORMAL_ECONOMY/2012–06-Statistical%20update%20-%20v2.pdf.
11. Authors, based on International Labor Organisation 2009 data retrieved April 14, 2013, from the *Key Indicators of the Labour Market* (7th edition) database.

12. Chen, M. A. 2001. "Women and Informality: A Global Picture, the Global Movement." *SAIS Review* 21 (1): 71–82.

13. Chant, S. and C. Pedwell. 2008. "Women, Gender and the Informal Economy: An Assessment of ILO Research and Suggested Ways Forward." Discussion Paper. Geneva: ILO.

14. ILO. 2013. *Ending Child Labour in Domestic Work and Protecting Young Workers from Abusive Working Conditions.* Geneva: ILO. http://www.ilo.org/ipecinfo/product/download.do?type=document&id=21515.

15. ILO. 2013. *Domestic Workers across the World: Global and Regional Statistics and the Extent* of *Legal Protection.* Geneva: ILO. http://www.ilo.org/travail/Whatsnew/WCMS_173363/lang--en/index.htm.

16. Boxes have retained the numbering as noted in the original work.

17. Facts come from the following sources.

For Global Facts:
1. Team analyses of ILO data.
2. World Economic Forum. 2013. "Gender Parity Task Forces." Retrieved December 1, 2013, from http://www.weforum.org/issues/gender-parity-task-forces.
3. ILO. 2008. *Global Wage Report 2008–09: Minimum Wages and Collective Bargaining, Towards Policy Coherence.* Geneva: ILO.
4. Marlar, J. and E. Mendes. 2013. "Globally, Men Twice as Likely as Women to Have a Good Job." Retrieved October 10, 2013, from http://www.gallup.com/poll/164666/globally-men-twice-likely-women-good-job.aspx.
5. World Bank Group. *Women, Business and the Law 2014.* Washington, DC: World Bank.
6. United Nations. *The World's Women 2010: Trends and Statistics.* New York: United Nations.
7. Team analyses of Gallup World data.
8. World Health Organization (WHO). 2013. *Global and Regional Estimates of Violence against Women: Prevalence and Health Effects of Intimate Partner Violence and Non-Partner Sexual Violence.* Geneva: WHO.
9. Team analyses of World Development Indicators data.
10. UNICEF. 2011. *The State of the World's Children 2011, Adolescence: An Age of Opportunity.* New York: UNICEF. (Figure excludes China).

For Signs of Progress:
1. Team analyses of World Development Indicators.
2. Team analyses of World Values Survey data.
3. Hallward-Driemeier, Mary, Tazeen Hasan, and Anca Bogdana Rusu (2013). "Women's Legal Rights over 50 Years: Progress, Stagnation or Regression?" Policy Research Working Paper No. WPS 6616. Washington, DC: World

Bank. http://documents.worldbank.org/curated/en/2013/09/18287629/women%C2%92s-legal-rights-over-50-years-progress-stagnation-or-regression.

4. World Bank Group "Women Business and the Law" team analyses.

5. Team analyses of World Development Indicators data.

6. World Bank. 2013. *Update on Implementation of the Gender Equality Agenda at the World Bank Group: Report to the Board.* Washington, DC: World Bank; and OECD. 2013. *Aid in Support of Gender Equality and Women's Empowerment.* Geneva: OECD.

17. ILO. 2010. *Women in Labour Markets: Measuring Progress and Identifying Challenges.* Geneva: ILO.

18. Ibid.

19. Gindling, T. H. and D. Newhouse. 2013. *Self-Employment in the Developing World.* Background Paper for the *World Development Report 2013.* Washington, DC: World Bank.

20. Chen, M. A. 2001. "Women and Informality: A Global Picture, the Global Movement." *SAIS Review,* 21 (1), 71–82.

21. ILO. 2012. *Global Employment Trends for Women.* Geneva: ILO.

22. ILO. 2002. *Women and Men in the Informal Economy: A Statistical Picture.* Geneva: ILO; Charmes, J. 2012. "The Informal Economy Worldwide: Trends and Characteristics." *Margin: The Journal of Applied Economic Research* 6 (2): 103–132.

23. Chen, M. A. 2012. "The Informal Economy: Definitions, Theories and Policies." Working Paper No. 1. Cambridge, Mass.: Women in Informal Employment Globalizing and Organizing (WIEGO); Ramani, S. V., A. Thutupalli, et al. 2013. "Women Entrepreneurs in the Informal Economy: Is Formalization the Only Solution for Business Sustainability?" UNU-MERIT Working Paper Series. New York: United Nations University.

24. Ramani et al. 2013. "Women entrepreneurs in the informal economy."

25. Kabeer, N. 2008. *Mainstreaming Gender in Social Protection for the Informal Economy.* London: Commonwealth Secretariat.

26. Kapoor, A. 2007. "The SEWA Way: Shaping Another Future for Informal Labour." *Futures* 39 (5): 554–68; Kabeer, N. 2008. *Mainstreaming Gender in Social Protection for the Informal Economy.* London: Commonwealth Secretariat.

27. McKenzie, D. and Y. S. Sakho. 2009. "Does It Pay Firms to Register for Taxes? The Impact of Formality on Firm Profitability." Policy Research Working Paper 4449. Washington, DC: World Bank; de Mel, S., D. McKenzie, et al. 2012. *The Demand for, and Consequences of Formalization among Informal Firms in Sri Lanka.* Impact Evaluation Series No. 52. Washington, DC: World Bank.

28. Ramani et al. 2013. "Women Entrepreneurs in the Informal Economy."

29. Chen, M. A. 2012. The Informal Economy: Definitions, Theories and Policies. Working Paper No. 1. Cambridge, Mass.: Women in Informal Employment Globalizing and Organizing (WIEGO).

30. IFC. 2011. *Fostering Women's Economic Empowerment through Special Economic Zones.* Washington, DC: IFC.

31. Dolan, C., M. Johnstone-Louis, et al. 2012. "Shampoo, Saris and SIM Cards: Seeking Entrepreneurial Futures at the Bottom of the Pyramid." *Gender & Development* 20 (1): 33–47.

32. Team analyses of data from UNESCO Institute for Statistics.

33. Information and Communications Technology Association—Jordan (int@j). 2012. *ICT & ITES Industry Statistics & Yearbook.* Amman, Jordan: int@j and Ministry of Information and Communications Technology; MG Consultants. 2010. *National ICT Workforce Survey.* e-Sri Lanka Development Project, Cr : 3986-CE, ICTA/CON/QCBS/P1/248, ICT Agency of Sri Lanka; Sanders, J. 2005. "Women and IT: Fast Facts." Presented at International Symposium of Women and ICT "Women and ICT: Creating Global Transformation," June 2005, Baltimore, USA; Griffiths, M. and K. Moore. 2006. "Issues Raised by the WINIT Project." In E. Trauth (ed.), *Encyclopedia of Gender and Information Technology.* Hershey, Penn.: Idea Group Inc.

34. Gladman, K. and M. Lamb. 2013. *GMI Ratings' 2013 Women on Boards Survey.* GMI Ratings. http://info.gmiratings.com/Portals/30022/docs/gmi-ratings_wob_042013.pdf?submissionGuid=05f4980d-638e-428a-b45c-695 17342345c.

35. Catalyst. 2013. *Catalyst Pyramid: U.S. Women in Business.* New York: Catalyst.

36. Authors. Data retrieved April 14, 2013, from the Enterprise Surveys database.

37. Ibid.

38. World Economic Forum. 2013. "Gender Parity Task Forces." Retrieved December 1, 2013, from http://www.weforum.org/issues/gender-parity-task-forces.

39. Team analysis of WVS data.

40. Hausman, R., L. D. Tyson, et al. 2012. *The Global Gender Gap Index 2012 Report* (Davos: World Economic Forum), 46. This statement uses actual estimated earned income figures, rather than those based on US$40,000 cut-offs.

41. ILO. 2008. *Global Wage Report 2008/09: Minimum Wages and Collective Bargaining, Towards Policy Coherence.* ILO: Geneva.

42. Tijdens, K. G. and M. Van Klaveren. 2012. *Frozen in Time: Gender Pay Gap Unchanged for 10 Years.* Brussels: ITUC.

43. Ibid.

44. ILO. 2010. *Women in Labour Markets: Measuring Progress and Identifying Challenges.* Geneva: ILO.

45. WDR 2013, 358–9. Note: Wage earnings for women relative to the wage earnings of men having the same characteristics; as a ratio. The estimate is based on a country-specific regression of the logarithm of monthly earnings in local currency on years of education and potential years of experience (and its square), controlling for industry, occupation, urban residence and gender. The methodology

is described by Claudio E. Montenegro and Harry Anthony Patrinos (2012) in "Returns to Schooling around the World," a background paper for the *World Development Report 2013*. Data sources: see table 9 in the WDR 2013, p. 379.

46. Institute for Women's Policy Research (IWPR). 2012. *Fact Sheet: The Gender Wage Gap by Occupation*. Washington, DC: IWPR.

47. Hugo Ñopo, Nancy Daza, and Johanna Ramos. 2012. "Gender Earning Gaps around the World: A Study of 64 Countries." *International Journal of Manpower* 33 (5): 464–513.

48. Tijdens, K. G. and M. Van Klaveren. 2012. *Frozen in Time: Gender Pay Gap Unchanged for 10 Years*. Brussels: ITUC.

49. The World Bank defines MSMEs as follows: micro: 1–9 employees, small: 10–49 employees, and medium: 50–249 employees.

50. Page, J. and S. Söderbom. 2012. Is Small Beautiful? Small Enterprise, Aid and Employment in Africa. UNU-WIDER.

51. Kushnir, K., M. L. Mirmulstein, et al. 2010. *Micro, Small, and Medium Enterprises around the World: How Many Are There, and What Affects the Count?* Washington, DC: World Bank and IMF.

52. World Development Indicators, Employment in Agriculture (% of total employment), 2010.

53. UN Food and Agriculture Organization (2011). *The State of Food and Agriculture 2010–2011*. Rome, FAO.

54. de Schutter, O. 2013. *The Agrarian Transition and the "Feminization" of Agriculture. Food Sovereignty: A Critical Dialogue*. New Haven, Conn.: Yale University.

55. World Bank (2011). *Afghanistan: Understanding Gender in Agricultural Value Chains: The Cases of Grapes/Raisins, Almonds and Saffron in Afghanistan*. Washington, DC: World Bank; World Bank (2010). *Liberia: Gender-Aware Programs and Women's Roles in Agricultural Value Chains*. Washington, DC: World Bank.

56. Kelley, D. J., et al. 2013. *Global Entrepreneurship Monitor's 2012 Women's Report*. http://www.gemconsortium.org/docs/2825/gem-2012-womens-report.

57. Amin, M. 2010. *Gender and Firm Size: Evidence from Africa*. Washington, DC: World Bank.

58. Hallward-Driemeier, M. 2013. *Enterprising Women: Expanding Economic Opportunities in Africa*. Washington, DC: World Bank.

59. Authors' calculations based on I2D2 data.

60. UN Food and Agriculture Organization (2011). *The State of Food and Agriculture 2010–2011*. Rome: FAO.

61. Croppenstedt, A., M. Goldstein, et al. 2013. "Gender and Agriculture: Inefficiencies, Segregation, and Low Productivity Traps." *World Bank Research Observer* 28 (1): 79–109.

62. Alene, A. D., et al. 2008. "Economic Efficiency and Supply Response of Women as Farm Managers: Comparative Evidence from Western Kenya." *World Development* 36 (7): 1247–60.

63. Hallward-Driemeier, M. 2013. *Enterprising Women: Expanding Economic Opportunities in Africa*. Washington, DC: World Bank.

64. Peterman, A., et al. 2011. "Understanding the Complexities Surrounding Gender Differences in Agricultural Productivity in Nigeria and Uganda." *Journal of Development Studies* 47 (10): 1482–1509; Doss, C. R. 2002. "Men's Crops? Women's Crops? The Gender Patterns of Cropping in Ghana." *World Development* 30 (11): 1987–2000.

65. Doss, C. R. 2002. "Men's Crops? Women's Crops? The Gender Patterns of Cropping in Ghana." *World Development* 30 (11): 1987–2000.

66. UN Food and Agriculture Organization (2011). *The State of Food and Agriculture 2010–2011*. Rome, FAO.

67. Mehra, R. and M. Rojas. 2008. *Women, Food Security and Agriculture in a Global Marketplace*. International Center for Research on Women. http://www.icrw.org/publications/women-food-security-and-agriculture-global-marketplace; IFC. 2013. *Assessing Private Sector Contributions to Job Creation and Poverty Reduction*. IFC Jobs Study. Washington, DC: IFC.

68. GTZ, et al. 2010. *Women's Economic Opportunities in the Formal Private Sector in Latin America and the Caribbean: A Focus on Entrepreneurship*. Washington, DC: Inter-American Development Bank.

69. UN Food and Agriculture Organization. 2011. *The State of Food and Agriculture 2010–2011*. Rome: FAO.

70. World Bank. 2009. *Gender in Agriculture Sourcebook*. Washington, DC: World Bank.

71. World Bank (2011). *World Development Report 2012: Gender Equality and Development*. Washington, DC: World Bank; ICRW. 2005. *Property Ownership for Women Enriches, Empowers and Protects: Toward Achieving the Third Millenium Development Goal to Promote Gender Equality and Empower Women*. Washington, DC: ICRW; Doss, C., et al. Forthcoming. "Gender Inequalities in Ownership and Control of Land in Africa: Myth and Reality."

72. Oladele, O. I., and M. Monkhei. 2008. "Gender Ownership Patterns of Livestock in Botswana." *Livestock Research for Rural Development* 20 (10).

73. World Bank et al. 2013. "What Does Sex-Disaggregated Data Say about Livestock and Gender in Niger?" *Livestock Data Innovation in Africa Brief*. Washington, DC: World Bank.

74. Oluka, J. et al. "Small Stock and Women in Livestock Production in the Teso Farming System Region of Uganda." *Small Stock in Development*. 2005: 151; Deere, C. D. and J. Twyman. 2010. "Poverty, Headship, and Gender Inequality in Asset Ownership in Latin America." Working Paper #296. East Lansing, Mich.: Center for Gender in Global Context, Michigan State University.

75. Demirguc-Kunt, A., L. Klapper, et al. Forthcoming. "Measuring Financial Inclusion: The Global Findex Database." Brookings Papers on Economic Activity. The database is available at: http://econ.worldbank.org/WBSITE/EXTERNAL/EXTDEC/EXTRESEARCH/EXTPROGRAMS/EXTFINRES/EXTGLOBALFIN/0,,contentMDK:23147627-pagePK:64168176-piPK:64168140~theSitePK:8519639,00.html, accessed on January 20, 2014.

76. Demirguc-Kunt, A., L. Klapper, et al. 2013. *Women and Financial Inclusion.* FINDEX Notes. Washington, DC: World Bank.

77. International Finance Corporation (IFC). 2011. *Strengthening Access to Finance for Women-Owned SMEs in Developing Countries.* Washington, DC: IFC.

78. Intel and Dalberg. 2012. *Women and the Web.* Santa Clara, Calif.: Intel Corporation.

79. GSMA 2010. *Women & Mobile: A Global Opportunity.* London: GSMA.

80. Pew Research Center. Spring 2012 Survey Data from PewResearch Global Attitudes Project. http://www.pewglobal.org/2012/04/20/spring-2012-survey-data.

81. World Development Indicators, accessed on January 15, 2014.

82. Much of the recent decline in female labor force participation in India may reflect the fact that more young women are in school. From 2005 to 2010, female labor force participation (ages 15–64) declined by 9 percent. However, during the same time period, gross female school enrollment increased by 12 percent for secondary education and by 6 percent for tertiary education. Some research projects a substantial rebound in women's labor force participation in the decade ahead as dividends from increased education begin to materialize. Nonetheless, overall labor force participation rates would still remain low, even relative to other countries in the region. For further analysis, see S. Bhalla and R. Kaur (2011), "Labour Force Participation of Women in India: Some Facts, Some Queries," Asia Research Centre Working Paper 40 (London: London School of Economics).

83. Uraz, A., M. Aran, et al. 2010. "Recent Trends in Female Labor Force Participation in Turkey." Working Paper No. 2. Ankara: State Planning Organization of the Republic of Turkey and World Bank.

84. United Nations. *The World's Women 2010: Trends and Statistics.* New York: United Nations.

85. WDR 2012, 221.

86. De Silva De Alwis, R. 2011. "Examining Gender Stereotypes in New Work/Family Reconciliation Policies: The Creation of a New Paradigm for Egalitarian Legislation." *Duke Journal of Gender Law & Policy* 18:305. http://scholarship.law.duke.edu/cgi/viewcontent.cgi?article=1190&context=djglp.

87. Bloom, D., D. Canning, G. Fink, and J. Finlay. 2009. "Fertility, Female Labor Force Participation, and the Demographic Dividend." *Journal of Economic Growth* 14 (2): 79–101. doi: 10.1007/s10887-009-9039-9.

88. Australia Human Rights Commission. 2013. "Investing in Care: Recognising and Valuing Those Who Care." Vol. 2, Technical Papers.

89. Hallward-Driemeier, M. 2013. *Enterprising Women: Expanding Economic Opportunities in Africa.* Washington, DC: World Bank.
90. http://hdr.undp.org/en/statistics/gii.
91. http://www.weforum.org/issues/global-gender-gap.
92. http://eige.europa.eu/content/gender-equality-index.
93. http://www.thegedi.org/research/womens-entrepreneurship-index.
94. http://genderindex.org.
95. http://www.weventurescope.com.
96. http://www.eiu.com/site_info.asp?info_name=womens_economic_opportunity&page=noads.

Analyze

1. Define "informal work." How does it differ from wage employment?
2. The World Bank claims that "[w]omen also do most of the world's unpaid work." What kind of work does this entail, and why is it unpaid?
3. Why do women tend to work in the fields of health, social work, and education as opposed to science, technology, engineering, and math?

Explore

1. Included within the article is "an empirical picture, highlighting some key facts that are not widely known" (Box 2.1). What makes these facts "empirical"? And why does the World Bank assert that they are "global facts that everyone should know"? Are you familiar with any of these statistics? Which ones?
2. Look at the ad series for UN Women by Memac Ogilvy and Mather Dubai (Figure 4 of the color art insert). How do the Google searches imposed over the women's mouths reinforce the World Bank's global findings on women and work?
3. One of the few references to the United States is made in the discussion of the glass ceiling. Based on this, what do you think the major differences are between women who work in the United States and those who work in developing countries?

Forging Connections

1. Consider the World Bank's data on women with children—loss of earnings, the "motherhood penalty," and so on. How does the paid

maternity leave graphic (Figure 1 in the color art insert) support the World Bank's findings? Think about both of these in conjunction with Anne-Marie Slaughter's essay "Why Women Still Can't Have It All." Do the World Bank's findings and the paid maternity leave graphic support her argument? If so, how?

2. In 2013, the United Nations published a series of ads to promote the fight against sexism on a global scale. We've included two of those ads for you in the color art insert (Figure 4). What is the message about sexism presented by those ads? How does it use an Internet search bar to convey that message? How do you think this issue of sexism continues to be pervasive in women's (and men's) work? Draw from any of the readings as you craft a response.

Looking Further

1. In 2010, Facebook chief operating officer Sheryl Sandberg gave a TED talk titled "Why We Have Too Few Women Leaders." In this now-famous talk (one that inspired her book *Lean In: Women, Work, and the Will to Lead*), Sandberg laments that too few women hold leadership positions globally and offers three pieces of advice to help women stay in the workforce: "sit at the table"; "make your partner a real partner"; and "don't leave before you leave." Watch Sandberg's talk and offer an assessment: Is her discussion of why women leave the workforce sound? What are the strengths of her argument, and what are the weaknesses? Place Sandberg's TED talk, as well as your assessment of her talk, in the context of the conversation on work in this chapter. What you do think are some of the biggest hurdles for women in the workplace, and why? Using Sandberg and the readings in the chapter, write an essay that articulates your response to the above question.

2. After reading "Taking Stock," choose a country featured in that text that is of interest to you to learn more about women's relationship to work in that country. Research that country further, and write an essay that details that relationship. For example, what jobs do women tend to hold, and why? What family leave laws are in place, and how do they enable women to maintain (or prevent them from maintaining) a work–family balance?

7 Gender and Globalization

Throughout most of this book, we have focused on gender from a Western perspective; we have read essays by Western writers about Western issues. However, as writers like Blue Telusma have suggested, and as we have seen in the World Bank's report "Taking Stock," gender inequality is pervasive on a worldwide scale. As our world grows closer, through trade, international business, and even platforms like social media, we become more cognizant of the ways in which different countries and cultures construct gender. For example, you might have a friend who travels to Africa for a summer to do work for a nongovernmental organization as part of an internship. Thanks to the rise of information technology, you can follow the details of her trip through social

325

media and read her reflections on her experience as a woman in a new culture. This is an experience that you would have had to view through letters as recently as five years ago, and it would have taken weeks for the communication to go back and forth. Now you can follow her experiences almost as quickly as she has them. The world has never seemed so small.

This process of interaction and integration among peoples from different countries and cultures is called *globalization*. Although the term "globalization" has its origins in the interactions among international businesses, with increasingly advanced information technology, it has also come to mean the interactions among the world's many peoples. We take the term "globalization" here as a means to think about the connections between how different countries and cultures construct and enact gender and gender identities. As you read, we hope that you will draw links between the ideas presented in the readings in this chapter and the readings we have studied in previous chapters.

We begin with Hillary Clinton's "Remarks at the UN Commission on the Status of Women," in which she reflects on the extent to which women have been able to initiate change from within their own countries. In Iver Arnegard's essay "The Fourth World," he recounts his experience teaching English to Palestinian refugee women in Lebanon. In "The Day I Saw 248 Girls Suffering Genital Mutilation," Abigail Haworth reports on the practice of female genital mutilation in Indonesia. Although China has traditionally been a society that privileges male children, Clarissa Sebag-Montefiore asserts in "Daughters Are More Caring" that some Chinese parents are beginning to favor female children and explains why. Last, Leila Ahmed's "The Discourse of the Veil" asserts that a Western perspective of the veil as oppressive has been appropriated into Muslim discourse with negative connotations for Muslim feminism.

Hillary Rodham Clinton
"Remarks at the UN Commission on the Status of Women"

Hillary Rodham Clinton is a U.S. politician who, after serving as First Lady during the presidency of her husband, Bill Clinton, was elected to the U.S. Senate in 2000. She then went on to serve as U.S. secretary of state in President Barack Obama's administration from 2009 to 2013. Additionally, she was a leading candidate for the Democratic Party's 2008 presidential nomination in 2008, and on 12 April 2015 she announced her candidacy for the nomination in the 2016 presidential election. Clinton delivered the following speech to the 54th session of the UN Commission on the Status of Women on 12 March 2010, during her term as secretary of state. As you read, consider the evidence Clinton uses to show that "women's progress is human progress."

Thank you very much. Thank you. Thank you to Ambassador Alex Wolff and to our U.S. Mission here at the United Nations. And it's wonderful to be back at the United Nations for this occasion.

I want to thank the deputy secretary general for being with us. I'm very pleased that my friend and someone who once represented the United States here before becoming Secretary of State, Madeleine Albright, could join us; members of the diplomatic corps and representatives to the United Nations Commission on the Status of Women; many of my friends, elected officials from New York, including Congresswoman Carolyn Maloney, who has been recognized and who is a great champion of women's rights and responsibilities—(applause)—and to all of you. This final day of the 54th session of the UN Commission brings to a close a week of a lot of activity, and it reminds us of the work that still lies ahead.

Fifteen years ago, delegates from 189 countries met in Beijing for the Fourth World Conference on Women. It was a call to action—a call to the global community to work for the laws, reforms, and social changes necessary to ensure that women and girls everywhere finally have the opportunities they deserve to fulfill their own God-given potentials and contribute fully to the progress and prosperity of their societies.

For many of us in this room today, that was a call to action that we have heeded. I know some of you have made it the cause of your life. You have worked tirelessly, day in and day out, to translate those words into realities. And we have seen the evidence of such efforts everywhere.

In South Africa, women living in shanty towns came together to build a housing development outside Cape Town all on their own, brick by brick. And today, their community has grown to more than 50,000 homes for low-income families, most of them female-headed.

In Liberia, a group of church women began a prayer movement to stop their country's brutal civil war. It grew to include thousands of women who helped force the two sides to negotiate a peace agreement. And then, those women helped elect Ellen Johnson Sirleaf president, the first woman to lead an African nation. (Applause.)

In the United States, a young woman had an idea for a website where anyone could help a small business on the other side of the world get off the ground. And today, the organization she co-founded, Kiva, has given more than $120 million in microloans to entrepreneurs in developing countries, 80 percent of them women. (Applause.)

So as we meet here in New York, women worldwide are working hard to do their part to improve the status of women and girls. And in so doing, they are also improving the status of families, communities, and countries. They are running domestic violence shelters and fighting human trafficking. They are rescuing girls from brothels in Cambodia and campaigning for public office in Kuwait. They are healing women injured in childbirth in Ethiopia, providing legal aid to women in China, and running schools for refugees from Burma. They are rebuilding homes and re-stitching communities in the aftermath of the earthquakes in Haiti and Chile. And they are literally leaving their marks on the world. For example, thanks to the environmental movement started by Nobel Laureate Wangari Maathai, 45 million trees are now standing tall across Kenya, most of them planted by women. (Applause.)

And even young girls have been empowered to stand up for their rights in ways that were once unthinkable. In Yemen, a 10-year-old girl forced to marry a much older man made headlines around the world by marching into court and demanding that she be granted a divorce, which she received. And her courage helped to shine a spotlight on the continuing practice of child marriage in that country and elsewhere.

Now, these are just a few of the stories, and everyone here could stand up and tell even more. These are the stories of what women around the world do every day to confront injustice, to solve crises, propel economies, improve living conditions, and promote peace. Women have shown time and again that they will seize opportunities to improve their own and their families' lives. And even when it seems that no opportunity exists, they still find a way. And thanks to the hard work and persistence of women and men, we have made real gains toward meeting the goals set in Beijing.

Today, more girls are in school. More women hold jobs and serve in public office. And as women have gained the chance to work, learn, and participate in their societies, their economic, political, and social contributions have multiplied. In many countries, laws that once permitted the unequal treatment of women have been replaced by laws that recognize their equality, although for too many, laws that exist on the books are not yet borne out in their daily lives.

But the progress we have made in the past 15 years is by no means the end of the story. It is, maybe, if we're really lucky, the end of the beginning. There is still so much more to be done. We have to write the next chapter to fully realize the dreams and potential that we set forth in Beijing. Because for too many millions and millions of girls and women, opportunity remains out of reach. Women are still the majority of the world's poor, the uneducated, the unhealthy, the unfed. In too many places, women are treated not as full and equal human beings with their own rights and aspirations, but as lesser creatures undeserving of the treatment and respect accorded to their husbands, their fathers, and their sons.

Women are the majority of the world's farmers, but are often forbidden from owning the land they tend to every day, or accessing the credit they need to invest in those farms and make them productive.

Women care for the world's sick, but women and girls are less likely to get treatment when they are sick.

Women raise the world's children, but too often receive inadequate care when they give birth. And as a result, childbirth remains a leading cause of death and injury to women worldwide.

Women rarely cause armed conflicts, but they always suffer their consequences. And when warring sides sit at one table to negotiate peace, women are often excluded, even though it is their future and their children's future that is being decided.

Though many countries have passed laws to deter violence against women, it remains a global pandemic. Women and girls are bought and sold to settle debts and resolve disputes. They are raped as both a tactic and a prize of armed conflict. They are beaten as punishment for disobedience and as a warning to other women who might assert their rights. And millions of women and girls are enslaved in brothels, forced to work as prostitutes, while police officers pocket bribes and look the other way.

Women may be particularly vulnerable to human rights violations like these. But we also know that in many places, women now are leading the fight to protect and promote human rights for everyone. With us today are several women I was proud to honor earlier this week at this year's United States State Department's International Women of Courage Awards. They have endured isolation and intimidation, violence and imprisonment, and even risked their lives to advance justice and freedom for others. And though they may work in lonely circumstances, these women, and those like them around the world, are not alone. Let them know that every one of us and the many others whom we represent are standing with them as they wage their lonely but essential efforts on behalf of us all. (Applause.)

The status of the world's women is not only a matter of morality and justice. It is also a political, economic, and social imperative. Put simply, the world cannot make lasting progress if women and girls in the 21st century are denied their rights and left behind.

The other day I heard *The New York Times* columnist Nick Kristof, who has done so much to bring to a wide audience the stories of individual women who are working and suffering because of conditions under which they are oppressed. And he said, you know, in the 19th century, the great moral imperative was the fight against slavery. And in the 20th century, it was the fight against totalitarianism. And in the 21st century, it is the fight for women's equality. He was right, and we must accept—(applause)—and promote that fundamental truth. (Applause.)

Now, I know there are those—hard to believe—but there are those who still dispute the importance of women to local, national, and global progress. But the evidence is irrefutable. When women are free to develop their talents, all people benefit: women and men, girls and boys. When women are free to vote and run for public office, governments are more effective and responsive to their people. When women are free to earn a living and start small businesses, the data is clear: they become key drivers of economic growth across regions and sectors. When women are given the opportunity of education and access to health care, their families and communities prosper. And when women have equal rights, nations are more stable, peaceful, and secure.

In 1995, in one voice, the world declared human rights are women's rights and women's rights are human rights. And for many, those words have translated into concrete actions. But for others they remain a distant aspiration. Change on a global scale cannot and does not happen overnight. It takes time, patience, and persistence. And as hard as we have worked these past 15 years, we have more work to do.

So today, let us renew our commitment to finishing the job. And let us intensify our efforts because it is both the right thing to do and it is the smart thing as well. We must declare with one voice that women's progress is human progress, and human progress is women's progress once and for all. (Applause.)

This principle was enshrined 10 years ago in Millennium Development Goal Number 3, the promotion of gender equality and the empowerment of women. And that goal is essential for the realization of every other goal. Today, this principle is also at the heart of the foreign policy of the United States. We believe that women are critical to solving virtually every challenge we face as individual nations and as a community of nations. Strategies that ignore the lives and contributions of women have little chance of succeeding. So in the Obama Administration, we are integrating women throughout our work around the world.

> "Women's progress is human progress, and human progress is women's progress once and for all."

We are consulting with women as we design and implement our policies. We are taking into greater account how those policies will impact women and girls. And we are working to identify women leaders and potential leaders around the world to make them our partners and to help support their work. And we are measuring progress, in part, by how much we improve the conditions of the lives of women and girls.

This isn't window dressing, and it's not just good politics. President Obama and I believe that the subjugation of women is a threat to the national security of the United States. (Applause.) It is also a threat to the common security of our world, because the suffering and denial of the rights of women and the instability of nations go hand in hand.

The United States is implementing this approach in our strategy in Afghanistan. As I said in London in January at the International Conference on Afghanistan, the women of Afghanistan have to be involved at every step in securing and rebuilding their country. Our stabilization strategy for both Afghanistan and Pakistan includes a Women's Action Plan that promotes women's leadership in both the public and private sectors; increases their access to education, health, and justice; and generates jobs for women, especially in agriculture.

This focus on women has even been embraced by the United States Military. All-women teams of Marines will be meeting with Afghan women in their homes to assess their needs. Congress has joined this focus as well. The Senate Foreign Relations Committee, under Chairman John Kerry, empowered a subcommittee charged with global women's issues that recently held hearings on promoting opportunity for Afghan women and girls.

History has taught us that any peace not built by and for women is far less likely to deliver real and lasting benefits. As we have seen from Guatemala to Northern Ireland to Bosnia, women can be powerful peacemakers, willing to reach across deep divides to find common ground. United Nations Security Council Resolution 1325 reflects this principle. Now, we must work together to render it into action and achieve the full participation of women as equal partners in peace. And as women continue to advocate for peace, even risking their lives to achieve it, many are praying that we will keep the promise we made in Resolution 1888 to take significant steps to end sexual violence against women and children in conflict.

We have begun the process laid out in the resolution. Secretary General Ban Ki-moon has appointed a special representative. Now we must press ahead to end forever the evil of rape in conflict, which has caused suffering beyond imagination for victims and their families.

For the United States, women are also central to our ongoing work to elevate development as a key pillar of our foreign policy alongside diplomacy and defense. As those who grow the world's food, collect the water, gather the firewood, wash the clothes, and increasingly, work in the factories, run the shops, launch the businesses, and create jobs, women are powerful forces for any country's economic growth and social progress. So our development strategies must reflect their roles and the benefits they bring.

Three major foreign policy initiatives illustrate our commitment. The first is our Global Health Initiative, a $63 billion commitment to improve health and strengthen health systems worldwide. Improving global health is an enormous undertaking, so we are focusing first on those people whose health has the biggest impact on families and communities—women and girls. We aim to reduce maternal and child mortality and increase access to family planning. And we especially commend the commission and the UN's adoption by consensus of the resolution on maternal mortality.

We also—(applause)—intend to further reduce the numbers of new HIV infections. AIDS has now become a woman's disease, passed from men to women and too often, to children. Through our Global Health Initiative and our continued work through PEPFAR, we hope to stop that deadly progression by giving women and girls the tools and knowledge they need to protect themselves, and by treating HIV-positive mothers so they are less likely to pass on the disease to their children.

Our global food security program, which I previewed here at the United Nations last September, is a $3.5 billion commitment to strengthen the world's food supply, so farmers can earn enough to support their families and food can be available more broadly. And women are integral to this mission. Most of the world's food is grown, harvested, stored, and prepared by women, often in extremely difficult conditions. They face droughts, floods, storms, pests without the fertilizers or enriched seeds that farmers in wealthy countries use. Many consider themselves lucky if they can scratch out a harvest sufficient to feed their children. Giving these women the tools and the training to grow more food and the opportunity to get that food to a market where it can be sold will have a transformative impact on their lives and it will grow the economies of so many countries.

I have to confess that when we started our Food Security Initiative, I did not know that most food was grown by women. I remember once driving through Africa with a group of distinguished experts. And I saw women working in the fields and I saw women working in the markets and I saw women with wood on their heads and water on their heads and children on their backs. And I remarked that women just seem to be working all the time. And one of the economists said, "But it doesn't count." I said, "How can you say that?" He said, "Well, it's not part of the formal economy." I said, "Well, if every woman who did all that work stopped tomorrow, the formal economy would collapse." (Applause.)

A third initiative is our government's response to the challenge of climate change. In Copenhagen in December, I announced that the United States would work with other countries to mobilize $100 billion a year by 2020 to address the climate needs of developing countries.

The effects of climate change will be felt by us all, but women in developing countries will be particularly hard hit, because as all of the changes of weather go on to produce more drought conditions and more storms and more floods, the women will have to work even harder to produce food and walk even farther to find water safe for drinking. They are on the front lines of this crisis, which makes them key partners and problem solvers. So we believe we must increase women's access to adaptation and mitigation technologies and programs so they can protect their families and help us all meet this global challenge.

These initiatives amount to more than an assortment of programs designed with women in mind. They reflect a fundamental shift in U.S. policy, one that is taking place in offices across Washington and in our embassies around the globe. But we are still called to do more—every single one of us. The Obama Administration will continue to work for the ratification of CEDAW. (Applause.)

Now, I don't have to tell those of you who are Americans how hard this is. But we are determined, because we believe it is past time, to take this step for women in our country and in all countries. Here at the United Nations, a single, vibrant agency dedicated to women—(applause)—run by a strong leader with a seat at the secretary general's table, would help galvanize the greater levels of coordination and commitment that the women of the world deserve. (Applause.)

And as the United Nations strives to better support the world's women, it would benefit from having more women in more of its leadership positions. (Applause.) Just as there are talented women working unnoticed in every corner of the world, there are women with great talent and experience whose potential leadership is still largely untapped, and they deserve the chance to serve and lead.

The Beijing Declaration and the Platform for Action was not only a pledge to help women in other lands, it was also a promise by all countries to do more to advance opportunity and equality for our own citizens. Because in every country on earth, talent is universal, but opportunity is not. In my travels across the United States, I've met women for whom higher education is a distant dream. They have the talent, they have the drive, but they don't have the money. I've met mothers trapped in abusive relationships desperate to escape with their children, but with no means of support. I've met too many women who cannot afford necessary healthcare for themselves and their children. And I've met girls who have heard their whole lives that they were less than—less talented, less worthy of respect— until they eventually came to believe it was true.

So whether we live in New York or New Delhi, Lagos or La Paz, women and girls share many of the same struggles and aspirations. The principle of women's equality is a simple, self-evident truth, but the work of turning that principle into practice is rarely simple. It takes years and even generations of patient, persistent work, not only to change a country's laws, but to change its people's minds, to weave throughout culture and tradition in public discourse and private views the unassailable fact of women's worth and women's rights.

Some of you may have seen the cover of the most recent issue of *The Economist*. If you haven't, I commend it to you. And like me, you may do a double-take. Because I looked quickly at it and I thought it said "genocide." And then I looked more carefully at it, and it said "gendercide." Because it was pointing out the uncomfortable fact that there are approximately 100 million fewer girls than there should be, if one looked at all the population data. I was so struck by that. A word that I had never heard before, but which so tragically describes what has gone on, what we have let go on, in our world.

My daughter is here with me today—(applause)—and being the mother of a daughter is a great inspiration and motivation for caring about the girls of the world. (Applause.) And I would hope that we would want not only for our own daughters the opportunities that we know would give them the chance to make the most of their lives, to fulfill that God-given potential that resides within each of us, but that we would recognize doing the same for other daughters of mothers and fathers everywhere would make the world a safer and better place for our own children.

So we must measure our progress not by what we say in great venues like this, but in how well we are able to improve the condition of women's lives, some near at hand who deserve the opportunities many of us take for granted, some in far distant cities and remote villages—women we are not likely ever to meet but whose lives will be shaped by our actions.

Let us recommit ourselves, as individuals, as nations, as the United Nations, to build upon the progress of the past and achieve once and for all that principle that we all believe in, or we would not be here today. The rights and opportunities of all women and girls deserve our attention and our support because as they make progress, then the progress that should be the birthright of future generations will be more likely, and the 21st century will fulfill the promise that we hold out today. So let's go forth and be reenergized in the work that lies ahead.

Thank you all very much. (Applause.)

Analyze

1. Just after beginning her speech, Clinton provides examples of progress that have occurred in women's lives, citing examples in South Africa, Liberia, the United States, and Yemen. Why does she choose these specific examples, and how do they provide context for what follows?

2. How is "women's progress" also "human progress"? What evidence does Clinton use to show the connection between the two? Is her evidence effective? Why or why not?

3. As you read, you are made aware of those places where Clinton pauses for applause. How does knowing when Clinton received applause during her speech impact you as a reader?

Explore

1. Consider Clinton's argument in relation to the World Bank's "Taking Stock: Stylized Facts about Gender at Work." How could you use the World Bank's findings to support Clinton's claims? Take a specific finding from "Taking Stock" and write a paragraph that reiterates one of Clinton's claims, integrating a quote from "Taking Stock" as evidence for that claim.

2. At several places during her speech, Clinton asserts that women are central to making progress. In September 2014, Emma Watson, actress and UN Women Goodwill Ambassador, suggested that men haven't been invited to the conversation about gender equality and asked, "How can we affect change in the world when only half of it is invited or feel welcome to participate in the conversation? Men—I would like to take this opportunity to extend your formal invitation. Gender equality is your issue too." Are these ideas contradictory? Why or why not?

3. Look at the ad series for UN Women by Memac Ogilvy and Mather Dubai (Figure 4 of the color art insert). Ogilvy and Dubai use genuine Google searches from March 2013 to reveal the pervasiveness of sexism and discrimination against women from a global perspective. Ogilvy and Dubai also created a video for UN Women to accompany these ads titled "The Autocomplete Truth." Watch the video on YouTube. How do the images of women presented in the video work to counter the "truths" revealed by the Google search highlighted in their ads? And how do both the ads and the video further Clinton's argument about gender equality?

Iver Arnegard
"The Fourth World"

Iver Arnegard is a professor in the Department of English at Colorado State University–Pueblo, where he teaches creative writing. He has had fiction, nonfiction, and poetry published in several journals, and Gold Line Press recently published his short fiction collection *Whip and Spur*. In "The Fourth World," originally published by the creative writing journal *High Contrast Review* in 2012, Arnegard describes his experience teaching English in a Palestinian refugee camp in Beirut, Lebanon. As you read, consider how his personal narrative exposes both the reality of the lives of the refugees and Arnegard's own fears about being an American male in the camp.

They call Borj al Barajneh the fourth world but that doesn't begin to describe the place. From a distance this Palestinian refugee camp could be another rundown part of Beirut, but as we draw near I see that Borj makes even the poorest parts of the city look wealthy. I am visiting this camp with my new friend, Nick, whom I just met a few hours ago. I told him I'd help him teach his English class. After the last bus stop it was almost a full kilometer's walk down the Airport Road where we took a left beneath an overpass. There, we began our trek down a nameless street bordered on one side by a razor wire fence and on the other by an empty lot that's been converted to an impromptu dump. Men and women in ragged clothing dig through trash for anything they can salvage.

The entrance to Borj al Barajneh leads into a labyrinth of concrete, plywood and twisted metal, and now I see why Nick calls it "The Maze." Alleyways shoot off in all directions, and as we pass the threshold of this walled-in camp the intense sunlight of the day fades to a dim, dusky hue, as if we've entered some kind of otherworldly canyon. Refugees have built skeletal wooden shacks on top of cracked concrete dwellings. In places, above the wooden shacks, faded canvas tents have been propped up with two by fours, branches or sticks.

The stench is overwhelming and I wonder how much shit is mixed in with the dirt and grime everywhere. Bundles of exposed wires sag between buildings and at times we have to walk around them or duck underneath.

Nick sighs and scratches his thick white beard. "Last week a boy was electrocuted here."

I turn to him. "Really?" I am trying to imagine a worse death.

"Yeah." Nick looks around. His voice is softer since we entered the camp. "It happened in another part of Borj. They lose a couple kids a year that way. All over the camp."

Arabic graffiti covers many of the walls here. In places posters of Arafat and Kadafy hang loosely from tacks and as we weave our way through the refugees I avoid eye contact though I feel the hard stares. They know I'm Western and probably sense that I'm American at that. I hope that dirty looks are all I'm met with today. When I told friends I was coming, most of them tried to talk me out of it. Camps are known for violence and some refugees blame their problems on the West. The Lebanese government lets Palestinians carry guns for protection and most of them do. This might be why Nick keeps his head down now and has scarcely said a word to me since we entered Borj.

I follow him through alleys, narrow as hallways, turning right, then left, then right again. Corridors without names or landmarks. Sometimes it feels like our path is just looping back on itself. Other times side alleys shoot off in different directions and dead end for no apparent reason. Earlier Nick told me that on his first visit he had to draw himself a map and bring it with him for weeks before remembering his way. And now I understand why.

We take one more left and reach a twisted set of concrete stairs. I follow Nick upward and through a sagging wooden doorway. There, at a cluttered desk, sits a beautiful veiled woman with olive skin and pale green eyes.

"Marhaba, Mariam," Nick says. He tells her something in Arabic and gestures toward me. "Iver," he explains.

Mariam turns and puts her palm across her chest to let me know she's orthodox and does not shake hands.

I smile. "Nice to meet you."

This has to be the center Nick described to me. Funded by the U.N., the place is run mostly by Mariam, who organizes classes and events here. As Nick speaks with her I look around the room to see Palestinian flags, beadwork and art hanging from the walls. In the corner sits a bookshelf littered with artifacts and knickknacks, carvings and colorful embroidery. I don't understand the meaning behind the art or the symbols on the flags and think how impossible it is to process everything I've seen in the last half an hour.

"Well," Nick says, turning to me. "We better get ready for class."

I've almost forgotten the reason I came and suddenly feel nervous to meet twenty Palestinian teenagers whose language I still don't understand.

"Follow me," Nick says. "It's down here."

We leave Mariam's office through a door on the left and walk along a tight corridor until we come to another threshold. Nick turns the knob and there are his students, waiting for him around a cluster of small, dilapidated tables.

As we enter the room they all turn to me and stare. Nick fires a few phrases at them in Arabic, points at me and yells: "Iver!"

Before moving to Lebanon to teach Creative Writing at the American University of Beirut I didn't realize how widespread these refugee camps were. I thought they all lay west of the Jordan. But actually camps stretch across the Middle East. Syria, Lebanon, Iraq. Over three million refugees struggling to live without citizenship or a country of their own.

I told Nick I came to help teach and that I was interested in doing some volunteer work of my own. But I'm mostly here to learn. I've only heard of these camps on TV or in newspapers and I want to try to understand the Palestinian condition for myself.

My friend, Jeff, from the university, used to volunteer at Borj and a week ago I asked if he could help get me in to see the camp. He made some calls and later said his friend Nick would bring me. Three days ago I talked briefly with Nick on the phone, and he told me to meet him at Younes—a Beirut coffee shop—at 8:45 on Saturday.

It was only four blocks from the café to the bus stop. And a forty minute ride, criss-crossing Beirut, while my new friend explained how he'd come to work at Borj.

The son of diplomats, he'd spent a few of his formative years in Lebanon, though growing up he'd moved all over the world from China to Brazil. After earning a college degree at Berkeley and a Masters in History from UVA, he'd spent much of his time in the Peace Corps, though he's quick to point out that not all of his motives were altruistic. "It was that," he told me. "Or get my head blown off in Viet Nam."

After the Peace Corps Nick spent most of his time in Vermont where he taught at various universities and eventually met his wife, Mary, a Unitarian minister. By the passionate way he talks about the problems of the Middle East, flinging around his wild mane of white hair with each gesture, it's clear that he's never lost the idealism of youth. Or his sense of adventure.

After the war of 2006 Nick and his wife decided to move back to Beirut where he would teach English and she would try to start a church. Nick took a job at the American Community School of Beirut, and began volunteering at Borj al Barajneh on weekends.

We both gaze out the window for a moment. Since the bus left Hamra ten minutes ago the passing neighborhoods have gradually deteriorated and some of the worst living conditions I've ever seen reel by in a blur: A block of gray apartment buildings riddled with bullet holes. Another block piled high with concrete rubble and twisted rebar. Then suddenly a beautiful blue mosque. Looming above the rundown cityscape. Rich, ornate designs completely out of place amidst the squalor.

Nick turns back to me. "You know, the political implications of what we do at these camps are huge." He scratches his beard. "Refugees see that some Westerners actually do care and, who knows, maybe one of them won't grow up to be a suicide bomber. Maybe years from now an embassy will be spared an attack." He shrugs. "There's no way to know. And on the other hand, you should take some time to seriously consider whether or not you want to come back and volunteer on your own. What we do here can be extremely dangerous. A lot of these kids' parents don't want them learning English—the language of the evil doers."

Over the phone Nick had briefly explained that he teaches a class of about twenty teenage Palestinian girls who dream of becoming secretaries. "The sad thing is," he told me, "probably none of them will ever get the chance. They're not allowed to work in Lebanon, so any job they get is never on record and their employers can pay them as little as they want. Or nothing at all. That's if they even get a job to begin with. Most of them will be married off by their parents, and they can only hope their husbands turn out to be somewhat decent men." Nick sighs. "These will probably be the poorest people you ever meet. But still, they're just *girls*. Some are popular. Some are socially awkward. I even have class clowns. Like Sarwat. When anyone from the outside comes in to try to teach them anything, those are some of the few moments in their lives that they actually have hope. And some of the few times that they can simply be themselves. *Girls*."

That's all I knew about Nick's students or what he does at this camp before today. And now here I am. Fidgeting in front of his class. Awkward. Out of place. I look around the room, smiling, and the girls smile back. Some wear shawls and veils, traditional Palestinian robes. But just as many are dressed like modern Lebanese teenagers. Jeans. T-shirts. One girl's top says, "I Love New York."

"Take a seat over there." Nick points to the far end of one of the tables, and I walk over and sit down. I try to get comfortable and pull out my notebook as Nick shuffles through some papers. He spouts a few Arabic phrases and passes his handouts around.

All Nick has as a textbook is an American travel guide to Lebanon, which he bought last minute before his first class this fall. The book mostly translates phrases between English and Arabic. And vice versa. Expressions that might come in handy for an American tourist in a coffee shop or restaurant.

The irony is not lost on Nick. These are situations his Palestinian students will probably never be fortunate enough to find themselves in. The refugees of Borj worry all the time about whether or not enough drinking water will reach their camp from week to week. For them, going to a restaurant would be like going to the moon. Even most of the vocabulary on household items is completely foreign and abstract to them.

And this is the first lesson Nick hands out. A photocopy from the travel guide, listing things you would find in your house. A picture of a sink with the English word beside it, next to the Arabic word, *majla*. An image of a door with the word *bab* beside it. There are about twenty terms in the list. Telephone, television, washer, dryer, microwave, window . . . He goes around the circle of girls.

"Okay, Mona, repeat after me. In my house I have a TV, a couch and a bed. Pick three things in your house and say, 'In my house I have . . .' Just choose three so you can practice."

It's obvious the girls aren't catching every word, but they're quick to imitate. Mona, a tall and slender Palestinian speaks the words slowly and with a heavy Arab accent: "In my house," she says. "I have a door, a window and a bed."

"Excellent Mona. Lina? Your turn." He nods to the next girl and she peers down at the handout.

"In mine house," she says. "I have a sink, a couch and a cupboard."

Eventually Nick goes around the entire circle, asking each girl to practice the phrase. None of them ever uses words like *television, microwave, washer* or *dryer*.

Nick's next exercise is called *At The Coffee Shop* and lists phrases you would use to order coffee. There are translations for basic terms like *cream* and *sugar*. This time, instead of circling the room in order, Nick picks students at random. "Sara," he says, pointing to an especially young-looking Palestinian. "What do you want in your coffee?"

She shakes her head and frowns.

Nick says, "In my coffee I want . . ."

And Sara mimics him, but she's obviously confused. "In my coffee I want . . ." There's a long pause and Nick gestures with his hands while pointing at the list.

Sara starts again. "In my coffee I want . . ." She looks down at the handout. "Sugar and bread."

Half the girls laugh. They know what bread means. The other girls are just as lost as Sara and look around nervously, wondering if they should also giggle. "La," Nick says. *No.* "Bread is . . ." He pretends to eat something with his hands and more of the girls laugh. "Okay," he says. "Sara. What do you want in your coffee?" Nick pulls an imaginary notebook and pencil out of his pocket and gets ready to write. A couple of the girls cover their mouths and snicker.

"In my coffee," Sara says, "I want cream and sugar."

"Bravo," Nick tells her. "Tamem." *Perfect.* He pretends to scribble something down on the palm of his hand. Then looks to Sarwat. "What do you want in *your* coffee?" he says.

She glances around at the rest of the class and smiles. "In my coffee," she says. "I want a washer, a dryer and a microwave."

The class cracks up, and Nick pretends he's been shot, clutching his chest and falling back in his chair. The girls laugh even harder.

"Okay," Nick says, standing up again. "Last exercise. We've done this one before. *Manager and secretary.* Mona and I will start. I'll be the manager."

Nick bends his three middle fingers and keeps his pinky and thumb pointed out to create an imaginary phone with his right hand. He dials a few numbers on his palm and puts his thumb to his ear, his pinky finger in front of his mouth. "Brrrrrring, brrrrrrring." He rolls his r's and though the girls giggle Nick remains serious, looking intently at Mona, who makes her own pretend phone and answers.

"Hello?"

"Hi, Mona. Has anyone called for me today?"

She pauses. "Yes. Mr. Abdul."

"Oh," Nick says. "What did he want?"

Mona is at a loss, but Sara whispers something in her ear. I can tell from the girl's new expression that she now remembers what she's supposed to say. "Ah. He wants you fax him paperwork."

"Great," Nick says. "I'll do that. Thank you so much, Mona. Bye." He pretends to hang up.

"Bye," Mona says, her hand dropping back down by her side. She's clearly proud that she could carry out the conversation and I am in awe of Nick as he continues around the circle, sometimes pretending to be manager, other times he's the secretary and the girls ask him about calls they've received from imaginary clients or business partners. Later, after his class is finished for the week, I'll follow him out of the camp, trying to remember my own way back to the Center for when I decide to return. I'll try to keep up with Nick as he hustles down the Airport Road toward our bus stop, gesturing wildly with his hands while he wonders aloud over the Palestinian problem. Strategizing possible solutions, though like *The Maze*, all paths seem to loop back on themselves. Or simply lead to dead ends.

For now I just sit and watch Nick teach. Amazed. As captivated as his students, I can't believe a man in his mid-sixties has three times the energy I could ever muster.

Nick finishes class with a pretend phone call to Sarwat. The only refugee who hasn't participated in the *Manager and Secretary* exercise.

"Okay," Nick says. "I'll be the manager, Sarwat. You be the secretary."

She looks around the room. All the faces of her Palestinian friends waiting for her next joke. But this time she doesn't smile.

"La," she says. *No.* "Today, I'll be the manager."

Analyze

1. How does Arnegard "show" his readers what this refugee camp looks like?
2. What is the effect of comparing the different appearances of the female students—some wearing "shawls and veils, traditional Palestinian robes," whereas others are "dressed like modern Lebanese teenagers. Jeans. T-shirts. One girl's top says 'I Love New York'"? What do these descriptions tell us about these students?
3. Arnegard ends his narrative with Sarwat, who refuses to be the secretary and instead says, "Today, I'll be the manager." What are the implications of ending the narrative in this way?

Explore

1. What does the story reveal about the position of women in the refugee camp? Is the fact that the class is composed of "teenage Palestinian girls who dream of becoming secretaries" surprising to you? If so, why?
2. What do you know about the situation of Palestinian refugees? Visit the website for the United Nations Relief and Works Agency for Palestinian Refugees in the Near East (UNRWA). What does this agency do, and how does it describe the realities of Palestinian refugees? How does understanding more about this crisis help you better understand Arnegard's narrative?
3. Arnegard writes, "They know I'm Western and probably sense that I'm American at that. I hope that dirty looks are all I'm met with today. When I told friends I was coming, most of them tried to talk me out of it. Camps are known for violence and some refugees blame their problems on the West." What accounts for these attitudes? How would you go about finding out? Create a researchable question and a list of keywords to find out why Arnegard is met with dirty looks.

Abigail Haworth
"The Day I Saw 248 Girls Suffering Genital Mutilation"

Abigail Haworth is a senior international editor for *Marie Claire USA* who is based in Asia but was born in the United Kingdom. She writes on global women's issues and human rights and has had articles published in *The Guardian* and *The Observer Magazine*. Here, in an extremely personal essay, published in *The Guardian* in 2012, she describes the Indonesian practice of female circumcision and explores its complicated history. As you read, consider the careful interplay between narrative and argument and its effect.

It's 9.30am on a Sunday, and the mood inside the school building in Bandung, Indonesia, is festive. Mothers in headscarves and bright lipstick chat and eat coconut cakes. Javanese music thumps from an assembly hall. There are 400 people crammed into the primary school's ground floor. It's hot, noisy and chaotic, and almost everyone is smiling.

Twelve-year-old Suminah is not. She looks like she wants to punch somebody. Under her white hijab, which she has yanked down over her brow like a hoodie, her eyes have the livid, bewildered expression of a child who has been wronged by people she trusted. She sits on a plastic chair, swatting away her mother's efforts to placate her with a party cup of milk and a biscuit. Suminah is in severe pain. An hour earlier, her genitals were mutilated with scissors as she lay on a school desk.

During the morning, 248 Indonesian girls undergo the same ordeal. Suminah is the oldest, the youngest is just five months. It is April 2006 and the occasion is a mass ceremony to perform *sunat perempuan* or "female circumcision" that has been held annually since 1958 by the Bandung-based Yayasan Assalaam, an Islamic foundation that runs a mosque and several schools. The foundation holds the event in the lunar month of the Prophet Muhammad's birthday, and pays parents 80,000 rupiah (£6) and a bag of food for each daughter they bring to be cut.

It is well established that female genital mutilation (FGM) is not required in Muslim law. It is an ancient cultural practice that existed before Islam, Christianity and Judaism. It is also agreed across large swathes of the world that it is barbaric. At the mass ceremony, I ask the foundation's social welfare secretary, Lukman Hakim, why they do it. His answer not only predates the dawn of religion, it predates human evolution: "It is necessary to control women's sexual urges," says Hakim, a stern, bespectacled man in a fez. "They must be chaste to preserve their beauty."

I have not written about the 2006 mass ceremony until now. I went there with an Indonesian activist organisation that worked within communities to eradicate FGM. Their job was difficult and highly sensitive. Afterwards, in fraught exchanges with the organisation's staff, it emerged that it was impossible for me to write a journalistic account of the event for the western media without compromising their efforts. It would destroy the trust they had forged with local leaders, the activists argued, and jeopardise their access to the people they needed to reach. I shelved my article; to sabotage the people working on the ground to stop the abuse would defeat the purpose of whatever I wrote. Such is the tricky partnership of journalism and activism at times.

Yet far from scaling down, the problem of FGM in Indonesia has escalated sharply. The mass ceremonies in Bandung have grown bigger and more popular every year. This year, the gathering took place in February.

Hundreds of girls were cut. The Assalaam foundation's website described it as "a celebration." Anti-FGM campaigners have proved ineffective against a rising tide of conservatism. Today, the issue is more that I can't not write about that day.

By geopolitical standards, modern Indonesia is an Asian superstar. The world's fourth-largest country and most populous Muslim nation of 240 million people, it is beloved by foreign investors for its buoyant economy and stable democracy. It is feted as a model of tolerant Islam. Last month, President Susilo Bambang Yudhoyono visited London to receive an honorary knighthood from the Queen in recognition of Indonesia's "remarkable transformation." Yet, as befitting an archipelago of 17,000 islands, it's a complicated place, too. Corruption and superstition often rule by stealth. Patriarchy runs deep. Abortion is illegal, and hardline edicts controlling what women wear and do are steadily creeping into local by-laws.

Although Indonesia is not a country where FGM is widely reported, the practice is endemic. Two nationwide studies carried out by population researchers in 2003 and 2010 found that between 86 and 100% of households surveyed subjected their daughters to genital cutting, usually before the age of five. More than 90% of adults said they wanted the practice to continue.

In late 2006, a breakthrough towards ending FGM in Indonesia occurred when the Ministry of Health banned doctors from performing it on the grounds that it was "potentially harmful." The authorities, however, did not enforce the ruling. Hospitals continued to offer sunat perempuan for baby girls, often as part of discount birth packages that also included vaccinations and ear piercing. In the countryside, it was performed mainly by traditional midwives—women thought to have shamanic healing skills known as *dukun*—as it had been for centuries. The Indonesian method commonly involves cutting off part of the hood and/or tip of the clitoris with scissors, a blade or a piece of sharpened bamboo.

Last year, the situation regressed further. In early 2011, Indonesia's parliament effectively reversed the ban on FGM by approving guidelines for trained doctors on how to perform it. The rationale was that, since the ban had failed, issuing guidelines would "safeguard the female reproductive system," officials said. Indonesia's largest Muslim organisation, the Nahdlatul Ulama, also issued an edict telling its 30 million followers that it approved of female genital cutting, but that doctors "should not cut too much."

The combined effect was to legitimise the practice all over again.

It is impossible to second-guess what kind of place holds mass ceremonies to mutilate girl children, with the aim of forever curbing their sexual pleasure. Bandung is Indonesia's third largest city, 180km east of the capital Jakarta. I had been there twice before my visit in 2006. It was like any provincial hub in booming southeast Asia: a cheerful, frenzied collision of homespun commerce and cut-price globalisation. Cheap jeans and T-shirts spilled out of shops. On the roof of a factory outlet there was a giant model of Spider-Man doing the splits.

Bandung's rampant commercialism had also reinvigorated its moral extremists. While most of Indonesia's 214 million Muslims are moderate, the 1998 fall of the Suharto regime had seen the resurgence of radical strains of Islam. Local clerics were condemning the city's "western-style spiritual pollution." Members of the Islamic Defenders Front, a hardline vigilante group, were smashing up nightclubs and harassing unmarried couples.

The stricter moral climate had a devastating effect on efforts to eradicate FGM. The Qur'an does not mention the practice, and it is outlawed in most Islamic countries. Yet leading Indonesian clerics were growing ever more insistent that it was a sacred duty.

A week before I attended the Assalaam foundation's *khitanan massal* or mass circumcision ceremony, the chairman of the Majelis Ulama Indonesia, the nation's most powerful council of Islamic leaders, issued this statement: "Circumcision is a requirement for every Muslim woman," said Amidhan, who like many Indonesians goes by a single name. "It not only cleans the filth from her genitals, it also contributes to a girl's growth."

It was early, before 8am, when we arrived at a school painted hospital green in a Bandung suburb on the day of the ceremony. Women and girls clad in long tunics were lining up outside to register. It was a female-only affair (men and boys had their own circumcision gathering upstairs), and the mood was relaxed and sisterly. From their sun-lined faces and battered sandals, some of the mothers looked quite poor—poor enough, possibly, to make the foundation's 80,000 rupiah cash handout as much of an enticement as the promise of spiritual purity.

Inside, I was greeted by Hdjella, 57, a teacher and midwife who would supervise the cutting. She was wearing a pink floral apron with a frilly pocket. She had been a traditional midwife for 32 years, she said, although, like most dukun, she had no formal training.

"Boy or girl?" she asked me, brightly. I was almost six months pregnant at the time.

"Boy," I told her.

"Praise Allah."

Hdjella insisted that the form of FGM they practised is "helpful to girls' health." She explained that they clean the genitals and then use sterilised scissors to cut off part of the hood, or prepuce, and the tip of the clitoris.

"How is this helpful to girls' health?" I asked. "It balances their emotions so they don't get sexually over-stimulated," she said, enunciating in schoolmistress fashion. "It also helps them to urinate more easily and reduces the bad smell."

Any other benefits? "Oh yes," she said, with a tinkling laugh. "My grandmother always said that circumcised women cook more delicious rice."

FGM in Indonesia is laden with superstition and confusion. A common myth is that it is largely "symbolic," involving no genital damage. A study published in 2010 by Yarsi University in Jakarta found this is true only rarely, in a few animist communities where the ritual involves rubbing the clitoris with turmeric or bamboo. While Indonesia doesn't practise the severest forms of mutilation found in parts of Africa and the Middle East, such as infibulation (removing the clitoris and labia and sewing up the genital area) or complete clitoral excision, the study found the Indonesian procedure "involves pain and actual cutting of the clitoris" in more than 80% of cases.

Hdjella took me to the classroom where the cutting would soon begin. The curtains were closed. Desks had been covered in sheets and towels to form about eight beds. Around each one, three middle-aged women wearing headscarves waited in readiness. Their faces were lit from underneath by cheap desk lamps, giving them a ghoulish glow. There were children's drawings and multiplication tables on the walls.

The room filled up with noise and people. Girls started to cry and protest as soon as their mothers hustled them inside. Rapidly, the mood turned business-like. "We have many girls to circumcise this morning, about 300," Hdjella shouted above the escalating din. As children were hoisted on to desks I realised with a jolt: this is an assembly line.

Hdjella led me to a four-year-old girl who was lying down. As the girl squirmed, two midwives put their faces close to hers. They smiled at her, making soft noises, but their hands took an arm and a leg each in a claw-like grip. "Look, look," Hdjella commanded, as a third woman leant in and steadily snipped off part of the girl's clitoris with what looked like a pair of nail scissors. "It's nothing, you see? There is not much blood. All done!" The girl's scream was a long guttural rattle, which got louder as the midwife dabbed at her genitals with antiseptic.

In the dingy, crowded room, her cries merged with the sobs and screeches of other girls lying on desks, the grating sing-song clucking of the midwives, the surreally casual conversational hum of waiting mothers. There was no air.

Outside in the courtyard, the festive atmosphere grew as girls and their mothers emerged from the classroom. There were snacks and music, and later, prayers.

Ety, 40, was elated. She had brought her two daughters, aged seven and three, to be cut. "I want them to be teachers. Being circumcised will bring them good luck," she said. Ety was a farmer who came from a village outside Bandung. "Daughters should be pure and obey their parents."

Neng Apip, 28, was smiling radiantly. She said she was happy her newly cut daughter Rima would now grow up into "a good Muslim girl." Rima, whose enormous brown eyes were oozing tears, was nine months old. Apip kissed her and gave her a rice cracker to suck. "Shh, shh, all better now," she cooed.

Tradition is usually about remembering. In the case of FGM in Indonesia it seems to be a cycle of forgetting. The act of cutting is a hidden business perpetrated by mothers and midwives, nearly all of whom underwent FGM themselves as young children. The women I met had little memory of being cut, so they had few qualms about subjecting their daughters to the same fate. "It's just what we do," I heard over and over again.

When the pain subsides, it is far from all better. The girls in the classroom don't know that removing part of their clitoris not only endangers their health but reflects deep-rooted attitudes that women do not have the right to control their own sexuality. The physical risks alone include infection, haemorrhage, scarring, urinary and reproductive problems, and death. When Yarsi University researchers interviewed girls aged 15–18 for their 2010 study, they found many were traumatised when they learned their genitals had been cut during childhood. They experienced problems such as depression, self-loathing, loss of interest in sex and a compulsive need to urinate.

I saw my interpreter, Widiana, speaking to Suminah, the 12-year-old who was the oldest girl there, and went to join them. Suminah said she didn't want to come. "I was shaking and crying last night. I was so scared I couldn't sleep." It was a "very bad, sharp pain" when she was cut, she said, and she still felt sore and angry. Widiana asked what she planned to do in the evening. "We will have a special meal at home and then read the Qur'an," said Suminah. "Then I will listen to my Britney Spears CD."

Back in Jakarta, an Indonesian friend, Rino, agreed to help me find out about the newborn-girl "package deals" at city hospitals. Rino phoned around Jakarta's hospitals. They told him he must see a doctor to discuss the matter. So we decided that is what we would do: since I was visibly pregnant, we'd visit the hospitals as husband and wife expecting our first baby. ("It's not necessary to bring your wife," Rino was told repeatedly when he rang back to book the appointments.)

We visited seven hospitals chosen at random. Only one, Hermina, a specialist maternity hospital, said it did not perform sunat perempuan. The other six all gave package prices, varying from 300,000 rupiah to 550,000 rupiah (£20–£36), for infant vaccinations, ear piercing and genital cutting within two months of birth.

Interestingly, the only doctor who argued against the procedure was a female gynaecologist from the largest Islamic government hospital, the Rumah Sakit Islam Jakarta. "You can have it done here if you wish," the doctor said with a sigh. "But I don't recommend it. It's not mandatory in Islam. It's painful and it's a great pity for girls."

Last month I spoke to Andy Yentriyani, a commissioner at Indonesia's National Commission on Violence Against Women. Yentriyani told me the problem is now worse than ever. Since the government's guidelines on FGM came into effect last year, more hospitals have started offering the procedure.

"Doctors see the guidelines as a licence to make money," she says. "Hospitals are even offering female circumcision in parts of Sumatra where there has never been a strong tradition of cutting girls."

"They are creating new demand purely for profit?"

"Yes. They're including it in birth packages. People don't really understand what they're signing up for." Nor do some medical staff, she adds. The new guidelines say doctors should "make a small cut on the frontal part of the clitoris, without harming the clitoris." But Yentriyani says that most doctors are trained only in male circumcision, so they follow the same principle of slicing off flesh.

Moreover, according to *The Jakarta Post*, the guidelines were rushed through partly in response to the deaths of several infant girls from botched FGM procedures at hospitals.

Likewise, Yentriyani says, the recent endorsement of FGM by some Islamic leaders has vindicated those carrying out mass cutting ceremonies, such as the Assalaam foundation. "Women are caught in a power struggle between religion and state as Indonesia finds a new identity," the activist explains. "Clamping down on morality, enforcing chastity, returning to so-called traditions such as female circumcision—these things help religious leaders to win hearts and minds."

Yentriyani and other Indonesian supporters of women's rights believe FGM can never be justified as a religious or cultural tradition. "Our government and religious leaders must condemn it outright as an act of violence, otherwise it will never end," she says. Her view is supported by organisations such as Amnesty International, which has called on Indonesia to repeal its guidelines allowing FGM. US Secretary of State Hillary Clinton has also weighed in, saying in February this year that, although many cultural traditions must be respected, female genital cutting is not one of them. "It is, plain and simply, a human rights violation," Clinton declared.

Suminah will be 18 now; a grown woman. She could well be married, or at least betrothed. Soon enough she will probably have her own kids. I hope she's forgotten her pain, but held on to her rage.

Analyze

1. Haworth's narrative is incredibly descriptive. What is the effect of "showing" her reader the room inside the school building where the mass ceremony to perform sunat perempuan takes place?
2. Why does Haworth inform her reader, "I have not written about the 2006 ceremony until now"? What is the implication of this?
3. Within the essay, Haworth describes Hdjella, a "teacher and midwife" who was "wearing a pink floral apron with a frilly pocket" and had a "tinkling laugh." This image is in stark contrast to the act being performed. Why does Haworth create this contrast?

Explore

1. Haworth describes the newborn-girl "package deals" offered by many of the hospitals she visited. Having read her essay, does this practice surprise you? Why or why not?

2. The practice of female genital mutilation (FGM) is still common in parts of Africa and the Middle East. Why is it practiced? Who is at risk? What are the different ways it is performed? And what are the health risks involved? Visit the websites for the United Nations Children's Fund and the World Health Organization. What do these tell you about FGM, and how do they suggest resolving the issue?
3. Look up the phrase "vacation cutting." What does this reveal about the practice of FGM in the United States? Does this surprise you? Why or why not?

Clarissa Sebag-Montefiore
"Daughters Are More Caring"

Clarissa Sebag-Montefiore is a freelance journalist who has written for *The Economist*, the *Los Angeles Times*, and the *Wall Street Journal*. She is a former books editor for *Time Out Beijing* and arts editor for *Time Out Shanghai* and currently lives in Sydney, Australia. In "Daughters Are More Caring," published by the *New Internationalist* in 2013, Sebag-Montefiore examines the extent to which China is changing its perspective on the value of daughters versus that of sons. Chinese culture, like other cultures around the world, has traditionally tended to favor male over female children, and this had led to problems like sex-selective abortions and female infanticide. As you read, assess the reasons Sebag-Montefiore offers for this changing cultural attitude.

Twenty-six year old Hong Hong married last year and is now ready to have a baby. But contrary to centuries-old Confucian tradition Hong does not want a boy. She wants a girl.

"My father's generation wants to have boys due to the old view which values male children only. No matter how poor they are, they want boys," says Hong, who grew up in eastern Anhui province but now works for an international company in Shanghai. "[But] I would definitely prefer to have a baby girl."

She is not alone. Beijing-based Zhao Hui, 27, had a baby daughter this year. He is delighted. "Girls are usually emotionally closer to fathers than sons," reasons Zhao. "Daughters are more caring about parents, which should be one important reason that more parents want a girl."

China has the worst birth sex ratio in the world—it has hovered at around 120 for nearly a decade. While the introduction of the one-child policy in 1979 seemed to help raise the status of women (forcing parents to pool all their resources into their one girl child) it has also led to millions of missing girls. The discovery of pre-birth sex-selection technologies in the early 1980s led couples to choose boys over girls in the womb. Sex ratios began to rise dramatically that decade as baby girls were abandoned, aborted or, in extreme cases, murdered.

Health and Happiness

Today, however, it seems that attitudes are changing. For the fourth consecutive year the sex ratio has shown a slight decline, according to the National Population and Family Planning Commission. And a recent study has found that China's younger generation is beginning to reject son-preference, stating a desire instead to have daughters.

"Girls are seen as easier to look after, easier to manage, and have got a better chance of getting married. People are beginning to realize that there is a sex ratio problem so if you want your child to get married in the future, women have got a much better chance," explains Therese Hesketh, a professor at University College London's Centre for International Health and Development and a co-author of the study *Changing Gender Preference in China Today: Implications for the Sex Ratio.* "Most people [in our study] wanted a boy and a girl. And if they could only have one, more people are now saying they would want a girl."

Of the 212 individuals from both rural and urban areas interviewed for *Changing Gender Preference* 79 per cent said they wanted both a son and daughter. When asked what gender they would choose if they could only have one child, 63 per cent said that the baby's health and happiness, rather than their sex, mattered to them the most. Of those who had a preference, 13 per cent said they wanted a son and 21 per cent a daughter.

This is not universal. Sex selection in the womb is still ongoing in many parts of China (in six provinces sex ratios at birth are over 130). Many rural families are allowed two children under the one-child policy if their first-born is a girl; but this has led to sex selection being most common for second children as parents become desperate to secure an heir.

Hesketh is careful to point out that there is "often a bit of a gap between what people say and what they do." Yet it is more than just anecdotal evidence that points to shifting perspectives. Sex ratios peaked across the country around 2004, with 121 boys born to 100 girls. In the 2010 census this dropped to 118. According to Hesketh, it is estimated to come down still further in the upcoming 2015 census.

Dramatic Role Change

Son-preference has been most prominent in China's poverty-stricken rural hinterlands where sons are expected to help till the land; it is also usually the men who inherit family property. While women in the past have typically been married off to live with their husband's family, where they must care for their in-laws, men have stayed with their own parents to help look after them in old age. (Crucial in a country with a scant free healthcare or pension system.)

But in recent years, in part due to the one-child policy, filial roles have changed dramatically. In imperial China women occupied an inferior position in society. During the Maoist era they were largely emancipated into the workforce (Mao Zedong famously declared that "women hold up half the sky"). Women's education and rights continued to improve in the three decades following China's opening-up and reform.

Today, as the country has witnessed the largest rural to urban migration in world history, many women have abandoned tending farms to work in cities. They now make up 48 per cent of China's labour force, 47 per cent of university graduates, and 39 per cent of leaders in industry. In 2012 seven of the world's top 10 wealthiest self-made female billionaires were Chinese. Such success has helped wear down the preference for sons.

"Daughters are increasingly providing not only emotional but also heavy financial support for their parents," explains Leta Hong Fincher, author of a forthcoming book on gender inequality in China. "The daughter is seen as more likely to take better care of the parents in their old age."

And while daughters were once considered a financial burden the opposite is now true. This largely comes down to property. With millions of men looking for but unable to find partners, owning a house and a car is often viewed as crucial criteria in a competitive marriage market.

Yet with price-to-income ratios for housing ranging from 11.6 in Beijing to 15.6 in the southern city of Shenzhen (with a level of 7 seen as reasonable in a fast-developing country) many are locked out of the housing boom. Fincher explains: "Older parents whose sons are of marrying age often complain that it is very expensive to have a son because they feel obliged to buy him an apartment. But if they have a daughter they don't feel obliged to buy her anything."

Hong agrees. She wants a girl to look after her and her husband in old age and believes that having a baby girl will avoid her having to pour money into property. "Girls are more considerate than boys when they have grown up and we become old," muses Hong. "Traditionally, when your son wants to get married, you need to buy a new house for them, so it must be a big pressure. I think more parents living in cities prefer baby girls because the real estate price is too high to bear for most families."

There remain opposing views, particularly from the older generation. Yang Shoufu, a government worker in Beijing in his 40s, is aware that "many young parents want girls due to the high prices of houses." But he still believes boys are better. "Men are more likely to succeed," he says simply.

Views like this have helped lead to the skewed birth rates. One consequence is that tens of millions of men will never be able to find a wife; by 2020 it is estimated that there will be 24 million surplus bachelors in China. Some say this has led to an increase in human trafficking with women kidnapped from poor regions of the country, or other Asian countries such as Vietnam, to be sold as wives to rural families.

These bachelors are known in China as "bare branches." In 2007 the economist Lena Edlund argued that the rise in the country's sex ratio coincided with a dramatic increase in crime. The state-run *China Daily* has stated that the presence of too many young unmarried men has led to "gambling, alcohol and drug abuse, kidnapping and trafficking of women," all of which, it says, are "rising steeply in China." (Hesketh's research, however, shows that many single men without prospects of marriage are depressed or have mental-health problems; social unrest and violence are less common.)

Efforts, Bribes and Tip-Offs

Meanwhile, child abduction remains an issue born from son-preference. Earlier this year state media reported the case of a baby boy who was kidnapped by a doctor in Shaanxi province; the boy was then sold to a Henan farmer for 60,000 yuan (around $9,800). Police rescued 15,458 women from human trafficking and 8,660 abducted children in 2011, according to the state-run news agency *Xinhua*.

The government has played its part in attempting to correct the imbalance. Sex selective abortions are technically illegal. In southern Guangdong province, for example, the public can receive 5,000 yuan ($800) to tip off authorities on couples using ultrasound to determine the sex of their unborn baby. Other initiatives have included a poster crusade in 24 provinces called the Care for Girls Campaign. And since 2005, parents of girls in the countryside have been given a government stipend of 600 yuan ($100) a month.

Such efforts have been partially successful. But often the legislation against sex selective abortion is not enforced, largely because doctors can receive lucrative bribes for letting a baby's sex slip. "It would be quite easy for them to enforce this legislation. [But] it is corruption. A lot of people are making money out of it," explains Hesketh.

Despite such problems the future, particularly in cities, does look brighter. The government wants to bring the sex ratio down to 115 boys born for every 100 girls by 2015. There are also signs that the one-child policy will be significantly relaxed within the next five years. But for now, at least, Hesketh believes that "in urban areas most people are quite accepting of having a girl."

Analyze

1. According to Sebag-Montefiore, what are some of the reasons that boys are preferred over girls in Chinese culture? What is the government's role in that reasoning? How has that reasoning become increasingly problematic for daughters in China?

2. How is Chinese culture starting to change the attitude that male children are preferable? What reasons for preferring a male child are being challenged?

3. What are some of the consequences of China's "one-child rule," for both men and women?

Explore

1. Although Sebag-Montefiore is focusing on Chinese culture, the idea of sex preference for a child is common all over the world. As a class, on your own, or in small groups, come up with a list of benefits and drawbacks to

having a male versus a female child in the United States. How do these benefits and drawbacks compare to what you've learned about having a son or a daughter in China?

2. Both Arnegard and Haworth discuss the significance of gender inequality for women on a global scale. To what extent do you think that Sebag-Montefiore offers a different perspective on gender inequality, and why?

3. In the essay, Sebag-Montefiore calls Chinese bachelors "bare branches." Look up this term; what does it mean? What is its significance? Is China the only society that has these kind of "bare branches" men?

Leila Ahmed
"The Discourse of the Veil"

Leila Ahmed is the Victor S. Thomas Professor of Divinity at Harvard Divinity School. Her research examines Islam and gender in America and issues of race, class, and gender in the Middle East during the late Colonial period. Ahmed's most recent book, *A Quiet Revolution: The Veil's Resurgence, from the Middle East to America* (2011), won the Grawemeyer Award in Religion for 2012.

This essay, "The Discourse of the Veil," is from Ahmed's book *Women and Gender in Islam: The Historical Roots of a Modern Debate* (1993). Ahmed argues that the "discourse of the veil," or the debate on the extent to which the veil should be seen as "oppressive" to Muslim women, is a Western colonialist discourse that has been appropriated into Islamic discourse. She advocates for examining how the veil as a symbol is tied to empowering women. As you read this essay, consider how Ahmed presents her argument. What is the structure of her essay, and how does that structure help you gain a better understanding of her ideas?

Qassim Amin's *Tahrir Al-Mar'a* (The Liberation of Woman), published in 1899, during a time of visible social change and lively intellectual ferment, caused intense and furious debate. Analyses of the debate and of the barrage of opposition the book provoked have generally assumed that it was the radicalness of Amin's proposals with respect to women that caused the furore. Yet the principal substantive recommendations that Amin advocated for women—giving them a primary-school education and reforming the laws on polygamy and divorce—could scarcely be described as innovatory. As we saw in the last chapter, Muslim intellectuals such as al-Tahtawi and 'Abdu had argued for women's education and called for reforms in matters of polygamy and divorce in the 1870s and 1880s and even earlier without provoking violent controversy. Indeed, by the 1890s the issue of educating women not only to the primary level but beyond was so uncontroversial that both state and Muslim benevolent societies had established girls' schools.

The anger and passion Amin's work provoked become intelligible only when one considers not the substantive reforms for women that he advocated but rather, first, the symbolic reform—the abolition of the veil—that he passionately urged and, second, the reforms, indeed the fundamental changes in culture and society, that he urged upon society as a whole and that he contended it was essential for the Egyptian nation, and Muslim countries generally, to make. The need for a general cultural and social transformation is the central thesis of the book, and it is within this thesis that the arguments regarding women are embedded: changing customs regarding women and changing their costume, abolishing the veil in particular, were key, in the author's thesis, to bringing about the desired general social transformation. Examining how Amin's recommendations regarding women formed part of his general thesis and how and why he believed that unveiling was the key to social transformation is essential to unraveling the significance of the debate that his book provoked.

Amin's work has traditionally been regarded as marking the beginning of feminism in Arab culture. Its publication and the ensuing debate certainly constitute an important moment in the history of Arab women: the first battle of the veil to agitate the Arab press. The battle inaugurated a new discourse in which the veil came to comprehend significations far broader than merely the position of women. Its connotations now encompassed issues of class and culture—the widening cultural gulf between the different classes in society and the interconnected conflict between the culture of the colonizers and that of the colonized. It was in this discourse, too, that the issues of women and culture first appeared as inextricably fused in Arabic discourse. Both the key features of this new discourse, the greatly expanded signification of the veil and the fusion of the issues of women and culture, that made their formal entry into Arab discourse with the publication of Amin's work had their provenance in the discourses of European societies. In Egypt the British colonial presence and discursive input constituted critical components in the situation that witnessed the emergence of the new discourse of the veil.

The British occupation, which began in Egypt in 1882, did not bring about any fundamental change in the economic direction in which Egypt had already embarked—the production of raw material, chiefly cotton, to be worked in European, mainly British, factories. British interests lay in Egypt's continuing to serve as a supplier of raw materials for British factories; and the agricultural projects and administrative reforms pursued by the British administration were those designed to make the country a more efficient producer of raw materials. Such reforms and the country's progressively deeper implication in European capitalism brought increased prosperity and benefits for some classes but worse conditions for others. The principal beneficiaries of the British reform measures and the increased involvement in European capitalism were the European residents of Egypt, the Egyptian upper classes, and the new middle class of rural notables and men educated in Western-type secular schools who became the civil servants and the new intellectual elite. Whether trained in the West or in the Western-type institutions established in Egypt, these new "modern" men with their new knowledges displaced the traditionally and religiously trained ʿulama as administrators and servants of the state, educators, and keepers of the valued knowledges of society. Traditional knowledge itself became devalued as antiquated, mired in the old "backward" ways. The ʿulama class was adversely affected by other developments as well: land-reform measures enacted in the nineteenth century led to a loss of revenue for the ʿulama, and legal and judicial reforms in the late nineteenth century took many matters out of the jurisdiction of the shariʿa courts, over which the ʿulama presided as legislators and judges, and transferred them to the civil courts, presided over by the "new men."

The law reforms, under way before the British occupation, did not affect the position of women. The primary object of the reforms had been to address the palpable injustice of the Capitulary system, whereby Europeans were under the jurisdiction of their consular powers and could not be tried in Egyptian courts. (The Capitulations were concessions gained by European powers, prior to colonialism, which regulated the activities of their merchants and which, with the growing influence of their consuls and ambassadors in the nineteenth century, were turned into a system by which European residents were virtually outside the law.) The reforms accordingly established Mixed Courts and promulgated civil and penal codes applicable to all communities. The new codes, which were largely based on French law, bypassed rather than reformed shariʿa law, although occasionally, concerning homicide, for instance, shariʿa law, too, was reformed by following an Islamic legal opinion other than the dominant opinion of the Hanafi school, the school followed in Egypt. This method of reforming the shariʿa, modifying it by reference to another Islamic legal opinion, was followed in Turkey and, later in the twentieth century, in Iraq, Syria, and Tunisia—but not Egypt—in order to introduce measures critically redefining and amending the law on polygamy and divorce in ways that fundamentally curtailed male license.[1]

Other groups besides the ʿulama were adversely affected by Western penetration and the local entrenchment of Western power. Artisans and small merchants were unable to compete with Western products or were displaced by the agents of Western interests. Others whose circumstances deteriorated or whose economic advancement was blocked by British administrative policies were rural workers who, as a result of peasant dispossession, flocked to the cities, where they swelled the ranks of urban casual laborers. A growing lower-middle class of men who had received a Western-type secular education up to primary level and who filled the lower ranks of the administration were unable to progress beyond these positions because educational facilities for further training were not available. The British administration not only failed to provide more advanced facilities but responded to the problem by increasing fees at primary level to cut enrollment. Measures such as these, which clearly discriminated in favor of the well-to-do and frustrated the hopes and ambitions of others, accentuated class divisions.[2]

The British administration pursued its educational policy in the teeth of both a popular demand for education for boys and for girls and the urgings of intellectuals of all political and ideological complexions that the administration give priority to providing more educational facilities because of the importance of education to national development. The British administration espoused its restrictive policy partly for political reasons. Cromer, the British consul general, believed that providing subsidized education was not the province of government, and he also believed that education could foster dangerous nationalist sentiments.[3]

Even this brief outline of the consequences of the increasing economic importance of the West and of British colonial domination suggests how issues of culture and attitudes toward Western ways were intertwined with issues of class and access to economic resources, position, and status. The lower-middle and lower classes, who were generally adversely affected by or experienced no benefits from the economic and political presence of the West had a different perspective on the colonizer's culture and ways than did the upper classes and the new middle-class intellectuals trained in Western ways, whose interests were advanced by affiliation with Western culture and who benefited economically from the British presence. Just as the latter group was disposed by economic interests as well as training to be receptive to Western culture, the less prosperous classes were disposed, also on economic grounds, to reject and feel hostile toward it. That attitude was exacerbated by the blatant unfairness of the economic and legal privileges enjoyed by the Europeans in Egypt. The Capitulations—referred to earlier— not only exempted Europeans from the jurisdiction of Egyptian law but also virtually exempted them from paying taxes; Europeans consequently engaged in commerce on terms more favorable than those applied to their native counterparts, and they became very prosperous.

Conflicting class and economic interests thus underlay the political and ideological divisions that began ever more insistently to characterize the intellectual and political scene—divisions between those eager to adopt European ways and institutions, seeing them as the means to personal and national advancement, and those anxious to preserve the Islamic and national heritage against the onslaughts of the infidel West. This states somewhat simply the extremes of the two broad oppositional tendencies within Egyptian political thought at this time. The spectrum of political views on the highly fraught issues of colonialism, westernization, British policies, and the political future of the country, views that found expression in the extremely lively and diverse journalistic press, in fact encompassed a wide range of analyses and perspectives.

Among the dominant political groups finding voice in the press at the time Amin's work was published was a group that strongly supported the British administration and advocated the adoption of a "European outlook." Prominent among its members were a number of Syrian Christians who founded the pro-British daily *Al-muqattam*. At the other extreme was a group whose views, articulated in the newspaper *Al-mu'ayyad*, published by Sheikh 'Ali Yusuf, fiercely opposed Western encroachment in any form.

This group was also emphatic about the importance of preserving Islamic tradition in all areas. The National party (Al-hizb al-watani), a group led by Mustapha Kamil, was equally fierce in its opposition to the British and to westernization, but it espoused a position of secular rather than Islamic nationalism. This group, whose organ was the journal *Al-liwa*, held that advancement for Egypt must begin with the expulsion of the British. Other groups, including the Umma party (People's party), which was to emerge as the politically dominant party in the first decades of the twentieth century, advocated moderation and an attitude of judicious discrimination in identifying political and cultural goals. Muhammad ʿAbdu . . . was an important intellectual influence on the Umma party, though its members were more secular minded; he had advocated the acquisition of Western technology and knowledge and, simultaneously, the revivification and reform of the Islamic heritage, including reform in areas affecting women. The Umma party advocated the adoption of the European notion of the nation-state in place of religion as the basis of community. Their goals were to adopt Western political institutions and, at the same time, to gradually bring about Egypt's independence from the British.

Umma party members, unlike Mustapha Kamil's ultranationalists or the Islamic nationalists, consequently had an attitude, not of hostility to the British, but rather of measured collaboration. Among its prominent members were Ahmad Lutfi al-Sayyid and Saʿd Zaghloul.

The colonial presence and the colonizer's economic and political agenda, plus the role that cultural training and affiliation played in widening the gap between classes, provided ample ground for the emergence at this moment of the issue of culture as fraught and controversial. Why the contest over culture should center on women and the veil and why Amin fastened upon those issues as the key to cultural and social transformation only becomes intelligible, however, by reference to ideas imported into the local situation from the colonizing society. Those ideas were interjected into the native discourse as Muslim men exposed to European ideas began to reproduce and react to them and, subsequently and more pervasively and insistently, as Europeans—servants of empire and individuals resident in Egypt—introduced and actively disseminated them.

The peculiar practices of Islam with respect to women had always formed part of the Western narrative of the quintessential otherness and inferiority of Islam.[4] A detailed history of Western representations of women in Islam and of the sources of Western ideas on the subject has yet to be written, but broadly speaking it may be said that prior to the seventeenth century Western ideas about Islam derived from the tales of travelers and crusaders, augmented by the deductions of clerics from their readings of poorly understood Arabic texts. Gradually thereafter, through the seventeenth and eighteenth centuries, readings of Arabic texts became slightly less vague, and the travelers' interpretations of what they observed approximated more closely the meanings that the male members of the visited societies attached to the observed customs and phenomena. (Male travelers in Muslim societies had extremely limited access to women, and the explanations and interpretations they brought back, insofar as they represented a native perspective at all, essentially, therefore, gave the male point of view on whatever subject was discussed.)

By the eighteenth century the Western narrative of women in Islam, which was drawn from such sources, incorporated elements that certainly bore a resemblance to the bold external features of the Islamic patterns of male dominance, but at the same time it (1) often garbled and misconstrued the specific content and meaning of the customs described and (2) assumed and represented the Islam practiced in Muslim societies in the periods in which the Europeans encountered and then in some degree or other dominated those societies to be the only possible interpretation of the religion. Previous chapters have already indicated the dissent within Islam as to the different interpretations to which it was susceptible. And some sense of the kinds of distortions and garbling to which Muslim beliefs were subject as a result of Western misapprehension is suggested by the ideas that a few more perceptive Western travelers felt themselves called upon to correct in their own accounts of Muslims. The eighteenth-century writer and traveler Lady Mary Wortley Montagu, for example, attacked the widespread belief among her English contemporaries that Muslims believed that women had no souls, an idea that she explained was untrue. (Montagu believed that many of the misapprehensions of her contemporaries about Islam arose from faulty translations of the Quran made by "Greek Priests, who would not fail to falsify it with the extremity of Malice.") She also said that having herself not only observed veiled women but also used the veil, she was able to assert that it was not the oppressive custom her compatriots believed it to be and in fact it gave women a kind of liberty, for it enabled them not to be recognized.[5]

But such rebuttals left little mark on the prevailing views of Islam in the West. However, even though Islam's peculiar practices with respect to women and its "oppression" of women formed some element of the

European narrative of Islam from early on, the issue of women only emerged as the centerpiece of the Western narrative of Islam in the nineteenth century, and in particular the later nineteenth century, as Europeans established themselves as colonial powers in Muslim countries.[6]

The new prominence, indeed centrality, that the issue of women came to occupy in the Western and colonial narrative of Islam by the late nineteenth century appears to have been the result of a fusion between a number of strands of thought all developing within the Western world in the latter half of that century. Thus the reorganized narrative, with its new focus on women, appears to have been a compound created out of a coalescence between the old narrative of Islam just referred to (and which Edward Said's *Orientalism* details) and the broad, all-purpose narrative of colonial domination regarding the inferiority, in relation to the European culture, of all Other cultures and societies, a narrative that saw vigorous development over the course of the nineteenth century. And finally and somewhat ironically, combining with these to create the new centrality of the position of women in the colonial discourse of Islam was the language of feminism, which also developed with particular vigor during this period.[7]

In the colonial era the colonial powers, especially Britain (on which I will focus my discussion), developed their theories of races and cultures and of a social evolutionary sequence according to which middle-class Victorian England, and its beliefs and practices, stood at the culminating point of the evolutionary process and represented the model of ultimate civilization. In this scheme Victorian womanhood and mores with respect to women, along with other aspects of society at the colonial center, were regarded as the ideal and measure of civilization. Such theories of the superiority of Europe, legitimizing its domination of other societies, were shortly corroborated by "evidence" gathered in those societies by missionaries and others, whose observations came to form the emergent study of anthropology. This same emergent anthropology—and other sciences of man—simultaneously served the dominant British colonial and androcentric order in another and internal project of domination. They provided evidence corroborating Victorian theories of the biological inferiority of women and the naturalness of the Victorian ideal of the female role of domesticity. Such theories were politically useful to the Victorian establishment as it confronted, internally, an increasingly vocal feminism.[8]

Even as the Victorian male establishment devised theories to contest the claims of feminism, and derided and rejected the ideas of feminism and the notion of men's oppressing women with respect to itself, it captured the language of feminism and redirected it, in the service of colonialism, toward Other men and the cultures of Other men. It was here and in the combining of the languages of colonialism and feminism that the fusion between the issues of women and culture was created. More exactly, what was created was the fusion between the issues of women, their oppression, and the cultures of Other men. The idea that Other men, men in colonized societies or societies beyond the borders of the civilized West, oppressed women was to be used, in the rhetoric of colonialism, to render morally justifiable its project of undermining or eradicating the cultures of colonized peoples.

Colonized societies, in the colonial thesis, were alike in that they were inferior but differed as to their specific inferiority. Colonial feminism, or feminism as used against other cultures in the service of colonialism, was shaped into a variety of similar constructs, each tailored to fit the particular culture that was the immediate target of domination—India, the Islamic world, sub-Saharan Africa. With respect to the Islamic world, regarded as an enemy (and indeed as *the* enemy) since the Crusades, colonialism—as I have already suggested—had a rich vein of bigotry and misinformation to draw on.

Broadly speaking, the thesis of the discourse on Islam blending a colonialism committed to male dominance with feminism—the thesis of the new colonial discourse of Islam centered on women—was that Islam was innately and immutably oppressive to women, that the veil and segregation epitomized that oppression, and that these customs were the fundamental reasons for the general and comprehensive backwardness of Islamic societies. Only if these practices "intrinsic" to Islam (and therefore Islam itself) were cast off could Muslim societies begin to move forward on the path of civilization. Veiling—to *Western* eyes, the most visible marker of the differentness and inferiority of Islamic societies—became the symbol now of both the oppression of women (or, in the language of the day, Islam's degradation of women) and the backwardness of Islam, and it became the open target of colonial attack and the spearhead of the assault on Muslim societies.

The thesis just outlined—that the Victorian colonial paternalistic establishment appropriated the language of feminism in the service of its assault on the religions and cultures of Other men, and in particular on Islam, in order to give an aura of moral justification to that assault at the very same

time as it combated feminism within its own society—can easily be substantiated by reference to the conduct and rhetoric of the colonizers. The
activities of Lord Cromer are particularly illuminating on the subject, perfectly exemplifying how, when it came to the cultures of other men, white
supremacist views, androcentric and paternalistic convictions, and feminism came together in harmonious and actually entirely logical accord in
the service of the imperial idea.

Cromer had quite decided views on Islam, women in Islam, and the veil.
He believed quite simply that Islamic religion and society were inferior to
the European ones and bred inferior men. The inferiority of the men was
evident in numerous ways, which Cromer lists at length. For instance: "The
European is a close reasoner; his statements of fact are devoid of ambiguity;
he is a natural logician, albeit he may not have studied logic; he loves symmetry in all things . . . his trained intelligence works like a piece of mechanism. The mind of the Oriental on the other hand, like his picturesque
streets, is eminently wanting in symmetry. His reasoning is of the most
slipshod description."[9]

Cromer explains that the reasons "Islam as a social system has been a
complete failure are manifold." However, "first and foremost," he asserts,
was its treatment of women. In confirmation of this view he quotes the
words of the preeminent British Orientalist of his day, Stanley Lane-Poole:
"The degradation of women in the East is a canker that begins its destructive work early in childhood, and has eaten into the whole system of Islam"
(2:134, 134n).

Whereas Christianity teaches respect for women, and European men
"elevated" women because of the teachings of their religion, Islam degraded
them, Cromer wrote, and it was to this degradation, most evident in the
practices of veiling and segregation, that the inferiority of Muslim men
could be traced. Nor could it be doubted that the practices of veiling and
seclusion exercised "a baneful effect on Eastern society. The arguments in
the case are, indeed, so commonplace that it is unnecessary to dwell on
them" (2:155). It was essential that Egyptians "be persuaded or forced into
imbibing the true spirit of western civilisation" (2:538), Cromer stated, and
to achieve this, it was essential to change the position of women in Islam,
for it was Islam's degradation of women, expressed in the practices of veiling and seclusion, that was "the fatal obstacle" to the Egyptian's "attainment of that elevation of thought and character which should accompany
the introduction of Western civilisation" (2:538–39); only by abandoning

those practices might they attain "the mental and moral development which he [Cromer] desired for them."[10]

Even as he delivered himself of such views, the policies Cromer pursued were detrimental to Egyptian women. The restrictions he placed on government schools and his raising of school fees held back girls' education as well as boys'. He also discouraged the training of women doctors. Under the British, the School for Hakimas, which had given women as many years of medical training as the men received in the School of Medicine, was restricted to midwifery. On the local preference among women for being treated by women Cromer said, "I am aware that in exceptional cases women like to be attended by female doctors, but I conceive that throughout the civilised world, attendance by medical men is still the rule."[11]

However, it was in his activities in relation to women in his own country that Cromer's paternalistic convictions and his belief in the proper subordination of women most clearly declared themselves. This champion of the unveiling of Egyptian women was, in England, founding member and sometime president of the Men's League for Opposing Women's Suffrage.[12] Feminism on the home front and feminism directed against white men was to be resisted and suppressed; but taken abroad and directed against the cultures of colonized peoples, it could be promoted in ways that admirably served and furthered the project of the dominance of the white man.

Others besides the official servants of empire promoted these kinds of ideas: missionaries, for example. For them, too, the degradation of women in Islam legitimized the attack on native culture. A speaker at a missionary conference held in London in 1888 observed that Muhammad had been exemplary as a young man but took many wives in later life and set out to preach a religion whose object was "to extinguish women altogether"; and he introduced the veil, which "has had the most terrible and injurious effect upon the mental, moral and spiritual history of all Mohammedan races." Missionary women delivered themselves of the same views. One wrote that Muslim women needed to be rescued by their Christian sisters from the "ignorance and degradation" in which they existed, and converted to Christianity. Their plight was a consequence of the nature of their religion, which gave license to "lewdness." Marriage in Islam was "not founded on love but on sensuality," and a Muslim wife, "buried alive behind the veil," was regarded as "prisoner and slave rather than . . . companion and helpmeet." Missionary-school teachers actively attacked the custom of veiling by seeking to persuade girls to defy their families and not wear one. For the missionaries, as for Cromer, women were the key to converting backward Muslim societies into civilized Christian societies. One missionary openly advocated targeting women, because women molded children. Islam should be undermined subtly and indirectly among the young, and when children grew older, "the evils of Islam could be spelled out more directly." Thus a trail of "gunpowder" would be laid "into the heart of Islam."[13]

Others besides officials and missionaries similarly promoted these ideas, individuals resident in Egypt, for example. Well-meaning European feminists, such as Eugénie Le Brun (who took the young Huda Sha'rawi under her wing), earnestly inducted young Muslim women into the European understanding of the meaning of the veil and the need to cast it off as the essential first step in the struggle for female liberation.

Whether such proselytizers from the West were colonial patriarchs, then, or missionaries or feminists, all essentially insisted that Muslims had to give up their native religion, customs, and dress, or at least reform their religion and habits along the recommended lines, and for all of them the veil and customs regarding women were the prime matters requiring reform. And all assumed their right to denounce native ways, and in particular the veil, and to set about undermining the culture in the name of whatever cause they claimed to be serving—civilizing the society, or Christianizing it, or saving women from the odious culture and religion in which they had the misfortune to find themselves.

Whether in the hands of patriarchal men or feminists, the ideas of Western feminism essentially functioned to morally justify the attack on native societies and to support the notion of the comprehensive superiority of Europe. Evidently, then, whatever the disagreements of feminism with white male domination within Western societies, outside their borders feminism turned from being the critic of the system of white male dominance to being its docile servant. Anthropology, it has often been said, served as a handmaid to colonialism. Perhaps it must also be said that feminism, or the ideas of feminism, served as its other handmaid.

The ideas to which Cromer and the missionaries gave expression formed the basis of Amin's book. The rationale in which Amin, a French-educated upper-middle-class lawyer, grounded his call for changing the position of women and for abolishing the veil was essentially the same as theirs. Amin's text also assumed and declared the inherent superiority of Western civilization and the inherent backwardness of Muslim societies: he wrote that anyone familiar with "the East" had observed "the backwardness of

Muslims in the East wherever they are." There were, to be sure, local differences: "The Turk, for example, is clean, honest, brave," whereas the Egyptian is "the opposite."[14] Egyptians were "lazy and always fleeing work," left their children "covered with dirt and roaming the alleys rolling in the dust like the children of animals," and were sunk in apathy, afflicted, as he put it, "with a paralysis of nerves so that we are unmoved by anything, however beautiful or terrible" (34). Nevertheless, over and above such differences between Muslim nationals, Amin asserted, the observer would find both Turks and Egyptians "equal in ignorance, laziness and backwardness" (72).

In the hierarchy of civilizations adopted by Amin, Muslim civilization is represented as semicivilized compared to that of the West.

> European civilization advances with the speed of steam and electricity, and has even overspilled to every part of the globe so that there is not an inch that he [European man] has not trodden underfoot. Any place he goes he takes control of its resources . . . and turns them into profit . . . and if he does harm to the original inhabitants, it is only that he pursues happiness in this world and seeks it wherever he may find it. . . . For the most part he uses his intellect, but when circumstances require it, he deploys force. He does not seek glory from his possessions and colonies, for he has enough of this through his intellectual achievements and scientific inventions. What drives the Englishman to dwell in India and the French in Algeria . . . is profit and the desire to acquire resources in countries where the inhabitants do not know their value nor how to profit from them.
>
> When they encounter savages they eliminate them or drive them from the land, as happened in America . . . and is happening now in Africa. . . . When they encounter a nation like ours, with a degree of civilization, with a past, and a religion . . . and customs and . . . institutions . . . they deal with its inhabitants kindly. But they do soon acquire its most valuable resources, because they have greater wealth and intellect and knowledge and force. (69–70)

Amin said that to make Muslim society abandon its backward ways and follow the Western path to success and civilization required changing the women. "The grown man is none other than his mother shaped him in childhood," and *this is the essence of this book. . . . It is impossible to breed successful men if they do not have mothers capable of raising them to be successful.* This is the noble duty that advanced civilisation has given to women in our age and which she fulfills in advanced societies" (78; emphasis in original).

In the course of making his argument, Amin managed to express not just a generalized contempt for Muslims but also contempt for specific groups, often in lavishly abusive detail. Among the targets of his most dismissive abuse were the rulers of Egypt prior to the British, whom he called corrupt and unjust despots. Their descendants, who still constituted the nominal rulers of the country, were championed by some nationalist anti-British factions, including Mustapha Kamil's party, as the desirable alternative to British rule. Amin's abuse thus angered nationalists opposed to the British as well as the royal family. Not surprisingly, Khedive Abbas, compelled to govern as the British wished him to, refused to receive Amin after the publication of his book. And Amin's eager praise of the British also inflamed the anti-British factions: he represented British dominion in Egypt as bringing about an age of unprecedented justice and freedom, when "knowledge spread, and national bonding appeared, and security and order prevailed throughout the country, and the basis of advancement became available" (69).

In Amin's work only the British administration and European civilization receive lavish praise. Among those singled out as targets of his abuse were the 'ulama. Amin characterizes them as grossly ignorant, greedy, and lazy. He details the bleakness of their intellectual horizons and their deficiencies of character in unequivocal terms.

> Our 'ulama today . . . takes no interest in . . . the intellectual sciences; such things are of no concern to them. The object of their learning is that they know how to parse the bismillah [the phrase "in the name of God"] in no fewer than a thousand ways, and if you ask them how the thing in their hands is made, or where the nation to which they belong or a neighboring nation or the nation that occupied their country is located geographically and what its strengths and weaknesses are, or what the function of a bodily part is, they shrug their shoulders, contemptuous of the question; and if you talk with them about the organization of their government and its laws and economic and political condition, you will find they know nothing. Not only are they greedy . . . they always want to escape hard work, too. (74)

Those for whom Amin reserved his most virulent contempt—ironically, in a work ostensibly championing their cause—were Egyptian women. Amin describes the physical habits and moral qualities of Egyptian women in considerable detail. Indeed, given the segregation of society and what must have been his exceedingly limited access to women other than members of his immediate family and their retinue, and perhaps prostitutes, the degree of detail strongly suggests that Amin must have drawn on conceptions of the character and conduct of women based on his own and other European or Egyptian men's self-representations on the subject, rather than on any extensive observation of a broad-enough segment of female society to justify his tone of knowledgeable generalization.[15] Amin's generalizations about Egyptian women include the following.

> Most Egyptian women are not in the habit of combing their hair everyday ... nor do they bathe more than once a week. They do not know how to use a toothbrush and do not attend to what is attractive in clothing, though their attractiveness and cleanliness strongly influence men's inclinations. They do not know how to rouse desire in their husband, nor how to retain his desire or to increase it. . . . This is because the ignorant woman does not understand inner feelings and the promptings of attraction and aversion. . . . If she tries to rouse a man, she will usually have the opposite effect. (29)

Amin's text describes marriage among Muslims as based not on love but on ignorance and sensuality, as does the missionary discourse. In Amin's text, however, the blame has shifted from men to women. Women were the chief source of the "lewdness" and coarse sensuality and materialism characterizing Muslim marriages. Because only superior souls could experience true love, it was beyond the capacity of the Egyptian wife. She could know only whether her husband was "tall or short, white or black." His intellectual and moral qualities, his sensitive feelings, his knowledge, whatever other men might praise and respect him for, were beyond her grasp. Egyptian women "praise men that honorable men would not shake hands with, and hate others that we honor. This is because they judge according to their ignorant minds. The best man to her is he who plays with her all day and night ... and who has money ... and buys her clothes and nice things. And the worst of men is he who spends his time working in his office; whenever she sees him ... reading ... she ... curses books and knowledge" (29–30).

One further passage about Egyptian women is worth citing for its surely unwarranted tone of authority. It is also interesting for the animus against women, perhaps even paranoia, that it betrays.

> Our women do nothing of housework, and work at no skill or art, and do not engage themselves in the pursuit of knowledge, and do not read and do not worship God, so what do they do? I will tell you, and you know as I do that what occupies the wife of the rich man and the poor, the learned and the ignorant, master and servant, is one thing . . . which takes many forms and that is her relationship with her husband. Sometimes she will imagine he hates her, and then that he loves her. At times she compares him with the husbands of her neighbors. . . . Sometimes she sets herself to finding a way to change his feelings toward his relatives. . . . Nor does she fail to supervise his conduct with the servant girls and observe how he looks when women visitors call . . . she will not tolerate any maid unless the maid is hideous. . . . You see her with neighbors and friends, . . . raising her voice and relating all that occurs between herself and her husband and her husband's relatives and friends, and her sorrows and joys, and all her secrets, baring what is in her heart till no secret remains—even matters of the bed. (40)

Of course, not many women would have had the wealth to be as free of housework as Amin suggests, and even wealthy women managed homes, oversaw the care of their children, and saw to their own business affairs, as I described in an earlier chapter, or took an active part in founding and running charities, as I will discuss in the following chapter. But what is striking about Amin's account (addressed to male readers) of how he imagined that women occupied themselves is that even as he describes them as obsessed with their husband and with studying, analyzing, and discussing his every mood and as preoccupied with wondering whether he hates them and whether he is eying the maid or the guest, Amin does not have the charity to note that indeed men had all the power and women had excellent reason to study and analyze a husband's every mood and whim. On a mood or a whim, or if a maid or a guest caught his fancy, they could find themselves, at any age, divorced, and possibly destitute. To the extent, then, that Amin was right in his guess as to what women discussed when no men were present— and some women did endlessly talk about their husbands—perhaps those that did, did indeed need to be vigilant about their husbands' moods and conduct and to draw on their women friends for ideas.

On the specific measures for the "liberation" of woman that Amin called for, and even what he meant by liberation, the text is turgid and contradictory to a degree attributable variously to intellectual muddle on the part of the writer, to the intrinsic confusion and speciousness inherent in the Western narrative, which he adopted, and to the probability that the work was the fruit of discussions on the subject by several individuals, whose ideas Amin then threw together. Indeed, the contribution of other individuals to the work was apparently more than purely verbal: certain chapters, suggests Muhammad 'Amara, editor of Amin's and 'Abdu's works, were written by 'Abdu. One chapter that 'Amara argues was 'Abdu's is distinctly different in both tone and content and consequently will be discussed here separately. It may be noted in this context that one rumor in circulation when the book was published was that it had been written at Cromer's urgings. Given the book's wholehearted reproduction of views common in the writings of the colonizers, that idea was not perhaps altogether farfetched.[16]

Amin's specific recommendations regarding women, the broad rhetoric on the subject notwithstanding, are fairly limited. Among his focuses is women's education. He was "not among those who demand equality in education," he stated firmly, but a primary-school education was necessary for women (36). Women needed some education to enable them to fulfill their function and duty in life as wives. As Amin spelled it out: "It is the wife's duty to plan the household budget . . . to supervise the servants . . . to make her home attractive to her husband, so that he may find ease when he returns to it and so that he likes being there, and enjoys the food and drink and sleep and does not seek to flee from home to spend his time with neighbors or in public places, and it is her duty—and this is her first and most important duty—to raise the children, attending to them physically, mentally, and morally" (31).

Clearly there is nothing in this definition to which the most conservative of patriarchs could not readily assent. Amin's notion that women should receive a primary-school education similarly represented the conservative rather than the liberal point of view among intellectuals and bureaucrats of his day. After all, Amin's book was published in 1899, thirty years after a government commission had recommended providing government schools for both boys and girls and toward the end of a decade in which the demand for education at the primary and secondary level far exceeded capacity. In the 1890s girls, it will be recalled, were already attending schools—missionary schools and those made available by Muslim benevolent societies as well as government schools—and they flooded the teacher-training college with applications when it opened in 1900. In 1891 one journal had even published essays on the role of women by two women from the graduating class of the American College for Girls. Amin's call for a primary-school education for women was far from radical, then; no one speaking out in the debate sparked by his book contested this recommendation.

The demand that was most vehemently and widely denounced was his call for an end to segregation and veiling. Amin's arguments, like the discourse of the colonizers, are grounded in the presumption that veiling and seclusion were customs that, in Cromer's words, "exercised a baneful effect on Eastern society." The veil constituted, wrote Amin, "a huge barrier between woman and her elevation, and consequently a barrier between the nation and its advance" (54). Unfortunately, his assault on the veil represented not the result of reasoned reflection and analysis but rather the internalization and replication of the colonialist perception.

Pared of rhetoric, Amin's argument against seclusion and veiling was simply that girls would forget all they had learned if they were made to veil and observe seclusion after they were educated. The age at which girls were veiled and secluded, twelve to fourteen, was a crucial age for the development of talents and intellect, and veiling and seclusion frustrated that development; girls needed to mix freely with men, for learning came from such mixing (55–56). This position is clearly not compatible with his earlier statement that anything beyond a primary-school education was "unnecessary" for girls. If intellectual development and the acquisition of knowledge were indeed important goals for women, then the rational recommendation would be to pursue these goals directly with increased schooling, not indirectly by ending segregation and veiling so that women could associate with men.

Even more specious—as well as offensive to any who did not share Amin's uncritical and wholesale respect for European man and his presumption of the inferiority of native practices—was another argument he advanced for the abandonment of the veil. After asserting that veiling and seclusion were common to all societies in ancient times, he said: "Do Egyptians imagine that the men of Europe, who have attained such completeness of intellect and feeling that they were able to discover the force of steam and electricity . . . these souls that daily risk their lives in the pursuit of knowledge and honor above the pleasures of life, . . . these intellects and these souls that we so admire, could possibly fail to know the means of safeguarding woman and preserving her purity? Do they think that such a people would have abandoned veiling after it had been in use among them if they had seen any good in it?" (67).

In one section of the book, however, the argument against veiling is rationally made: the chapter which ʿAmara suggests was composed by ʿAbdu. ʿAbdu points out the real disadvantages to women of segregation and veiling. These customs compel them to conduct matters of law and business through an intermediary, placing poor women, who need to earn a living in trade or domestic service, in the false and impossible position of dealing with men in a society that officially bans such dealings (47–48).

The section as a whole is distinctly different in tone and ideas from the rest of the work, and not just in the humane rather than contemptuous prose in which it frames its references both to women and to the Islamic heritage. As a result, some of the views expressed there contradict or sit ill with those expressed elsewhere in the book. There is surely some discrepancy, for example, between Amin's view that women are "deficient in mind, strong in cunning" (39) and need no more than a primary-school education, on the one hand, and the sentiments as to the potential of both sexes that finds expression in the following passage, on the other: "Education is the means by which the individual may attain spiritual and material happiness. . . . Every person has the natural right to develop their talents to the limit.

"Religions address women as they do men. . . . Arts, skills, inventions, philosophy . . . all these draw women as they do men. . . . What difference is there between men and women in this desire, when we see children of both sexes equal in their curiosity about everything falling within their ken? Perhaps that desire is even more alive in girls than in boys" (22–23).

Passages suggestive of careful thought are the exception rather than the rule in this work, however.[17] More commonly the book presented strident criticism of Muslim, particularly Egyptian, culture and society. In calling for women's liberation the thoroughly patriarchal Amin was in fact calling for the transformation of Muslim society along the lines of the Western model and for the substitution of the garb of Islamic-style male dominance for that of Western-style male dominance. Under the guise of a plea for the "liberation" of woman, then, he conducted an attack that in its fundamentals reproduced the colonizer's attack on native culture and society. For Amin as for the colonizers, the veil and segregation symbolized the backwardness and inferiority of Islamic society; in his discourse as in theirs, therefore, the veil and segregation came in for the most direct attack. For Amin as for Cromer, women and their dress were important counters in the discourse concerning the relative merits of the societies and civilizations of men and their different styles of male domination; women themselves and their liberation were no more important to Amin than to Cromer.

Amin's book thus represents the rearticulation in native voice of the colonial thesis of the inferiority of the native and Muslim and the superiority of the European. Rearticulated in native upper-middle-class voice, the voice of a class economically allied with the colonizers and already adopting their life-styles, the colonialist thesis took on a classist dimension: it became in effect an attack (in addition to all the other broad and specific attacks) on the customs of the lower-middle and lower classes.

The book is reckoned to have triggered the first major controversy in the Arabic press: more than thirty books and articles appeared in response to its publication. The majority were critical, though the book did please some readers, notably members of the British administration and pro-British factions: the pro-British paper *Al-muqattam* hailed the book as the finest in years.[18] There were evidently many reasons for Muslims and Egyptians, for nationalists of all stripes, to dislike the work: Amin's adulation of the British and of European civilization, his contempt for natives and native ways, his insulting references to the reigning family and to specific groups and classes, such as the ʿulama (who were prominent among the critics of his book), and his implied and indeed explicit contempt for the customs of the lower classes. However, just as Amin had used the issue of women and the call for their unveiling to conduct his generalized assault on society, so too did the rebuttals of his work come in the form of an affirmation of the customs that he had attacked—veiling and segregation. In a way that was to become typical of the Arabic narrative of resistance, the opposition appropriated, in order to negate them, the terms set in the first place by the colonial discourse.

Analysts routinely treat the debate as one between "feminists," that is, Amin and his allies, and "antifeminists," that is, Amin's critics. They accept at face value the equation made by Amin and the originating Western narrative: that the veil signified oppression, therefore those who called for its abandonment were feminists and those opposing its abandonment were antifeminists.[19] As I have suggested, however, the fundamental and contentious premise of Amin's work was its endorsement of the Western view of Islamic civilization, peoples, and customs as inferior, whereas the author's position on women was profoundly patriarchal and even somewhat misogynist. The book merely called for the substitution of Islamic-style male dominance by Western-style male dominance. Far from being the father of Arab feminism, then, Amin might more aptly be described as the son of Cromer and colonialism.

Opponents with a nationalist perspective were therefore not necessarily any more antifeminist than Amin was feminist. Some who defended the national custom had views on women considerably more "feminist" than Amin's, but others who opposed unveiling, for nationalist and Islamist reasons, had views on women no less patriarchal than his. For example, the attacks on Amin's book published in *Al-liwa*, Mustapha Kamil's paper, declared that women had the same right to an education as men and that their education was as essential to the nation as men's—a position considerably more liberal and feminist than Amin's. The writers opposed unveiling not as antifeminists, it seems, but as cogent analysts of the current social situation. They did not argue that veiling was immutable Islamic custom, saying, on the contrary, that future generations might decree otherwise. They argued that veiling was the current practice and that Amin's call to unveil was merely part of the hasty and unconsidered rush to imitate the West in everything.[20] This perspective anticipates an incisive and genuinely feminist analysis of the issue of the veil and the accompanying debate offered a few years later by Malak Hifni Nassef....

Tal'at Harb's nationalist response to Amin, in contrast, defended and upheld Islamic practices, putting forward a view of the role and duties of women in society quite as patriarchal as Amin's; but where Amin wanted to adopt a Western-style male dominance, describing his recommendation as a call for women's liberation, Harb argued for an Islamic patriarchy, presenting his views quite simply as those of traditional, unadorned, God-ordained patriarchy. Harb invoked Christian and Muslim scriptures and Western and Muslim men of learning to affirm that the wife's duty was to attend to the physical, mental, and moral needs of her husband and children[21]—the same duty that Amin ascribed to her. Their prescriptions for women differed literally in the matter of garb: Harb's women must veil, and Amin's unveil. The argument between Harb and Amin centered not on feminism versus antifeminism

but on Western versus indigenous ways. For neither side was male dominance ever in question.

Amin's book, then, marks the entry of the colonial narrative of women
and Islam—in which the veil and the treatment of women epitomized Islamic inferiority—into mainstream Arabic discourse. And the opposition
it generated similarly marks the emergence of an Arabic narrative developed
in resistance to the colonial narrative. This narrative of resistance appropriated, in order to negate them, the symbolic terms of the originating narrative. The veil came to symbolize in the resistance narrative, not the
inferiority of the culture and the need to cast aside its customs in favor of
those of the West, but, on the contrary, the dignity and validity of all native
customs, and in particular those customs coming under fiercest colonial
attack—the customs relating to women—and the need to tenaciously
affirm them as a means of resistance to Western domination. As Frantz
Fanon was to say of a later battle of the veil, between the French and the
Algerians, the Algerians affirmed the veil because "tradition demanded the
rigid separation of the sexes" and because "*the occupier was bent on unveiling
Algeria*" (emphasis in original).[22] Standing in the relation of antithesis to
thesis, the resistance narrative thus reversed—but thereby also accepted—
the terms set in the first place by the colonizers. And therefore, ironically, it
is Western discourse that in the first place determined the new meanings of
the veil and gave rise to its emergence as a symbol of resistance.

Amin's book and the debate it generated; and the issues of class and culture with which the debate became inscribed, may be regarded as the pre-
cursor and prototype of the debate around the veil that has recurred in a
variety of forms in a number of Muslim and Arab countries since. As for
those who took up Amin's call for unveiling in Egypt (such as Huda
Sha'rawi), an upper-class or upper-middle-class background, and to some
degree or other a Western cultural affiliation, have been typical of those
who became advocates of unveiling. In Turkey, for example, Ataturk, who
introduced westernizing reforms, including laws affecting women, repeatedly denounced the veil in terms that, like Amin's, reproduced the Western
narrative and show that his concern was with how the custom reflected on
Turkish men, allowing them to appear "uncivilized" and objects of "ridicule." In one speech Ataturk declared: "In some places I have seen women
who put a piece of cloth or a towel or something like that over their heads
to hide their faces, and who turn their backs or huddle themselves on the
ground when a man passes by. What are the meaning and sense of this

behaviour? Gentlemen, can the mothers and daughters of a civilised nation adopt this strange manner, this barbarous posture? It is a spectacle that makes the nation an object of ridicule. It must be remedied at once."[23]

Similarly, in the 1920s the Iranian ruler Reza Shah, also an active reformer and westernizer, went so far as to issue a proclamation banning the veil, a move which had the support of some upper-class women as well as upper-class men. The ban, which symbolized the Westerly direction in which the ruling class intended to lead the society and signaled the eagerness of the upper classes to show themselves to be "civilized," was quite differently received by the popular classes. Even rumors of the move provoked unrest; demonstrations broke out but were ruthlessly crushed. For most Iranians, women as well as men, the veil was not, as a historian of Iranian women has observed, a "symbol of backwardness," which members of the upper classes maintained it was, but "a sign of propriety and a means of protection against the menacing eyes of male strangers." The police had instructions to deal harshly with any woman wearing anything other than a European-style hat or no headgear at all, and many women chose to stay at home rather than venture outdoors and risk having their veils pulled off by the police.[24]

In their stinging contempt for the veil and the savagery with which they attack it, these two members of the ruling class, like Amin, reveal their true motivation: they are men of the classes assimilating to European ways and smarting under the humiliation of being described as uncivilized because "their" women are veiled, and they are determined to eradicate the practice. That is to say, theirs are the words and acts of men exposed to the Western discourse who have accepted its representation of their culture, the inferiority of its practices, and the meaning of the veil. Why Muslim men should be making such statements and enacting such bans is only intelligible against the background of the global dominance of the Western world and the authority of its discourses, and also against the background of the ambiguous position of men and women of the upper classes, members of Muslim societies whose economic interests and cultural aspirations bound them to the colonizing West and who saw their own society partly through Western eyes.

The origins and history, just described, of the idea of the veil as it informs Western colonial discourse *and* twentieth-century Arabic debate have a number of implications. First, it is evident that the connection between the issues of culture and women, and more precisely between the cultures of Other men and the oppression of women, was created by Western discourse. The idea (which still often informs discussions about women in Arab and Muslim cultures and other non-Western world cultures) that improving the status of women entails abandoning native customs was the product of a particular historical moment and was constructed by an androcentric colonial establishment committed to male dominance in the service of particular political ends. Its absurdity and essential falseness become particularly apparent (at least from a feminist point of view) when one bears in mind that those who first advocated it believed that Victorian mores and dress, and Victorian Christianity, represented the ideal to which Muslim women should aspire.

Second, these historical origins explain another and, on the face of it, somewhat surprising phenomenon: namely, the peculiar resemblance to be found between the colonial and still-commonplace Western view that an innate connection exists between the issues of culture and women in Muslim societies and the similar presumption underlying the Islamist resistance position, that such a fundamental connection does indeed exist. The resemblance between the two positions is not coincidental: they are mirror images of each other. The resistance narrative contested the colonial thesis by inverting it—thereby also, ironically, grounding itself in the premises of the colonial thesis.

The preceding account of the development of a colonial narrative of women in Islam has other implications as well, including that the colonial account of Islamic oppression of women was based on misperceptions and political manipulations and was incorrect. My argument here is not that Islamic societies did not oppress women. They did and do; that is not in dispute. Rather, I am here pointing to the political uses of the idea that Islam oppressed women and noting that what patriarchal colonialists identified as the sources and main forms of women's oppression in Islamic societies was based on a vague and inaccurate understanding of Muslim societies. This means, too, that the feminist agenda for Muslim women as set by Europeans—and first devised by the likes of Cromer—was incorrect and irrelevant. It was incorrect in its broad assumptions that Muslim women needed to abandon native ways and adopt those of the West to improve their status; obviously, Arab and Muslim women need to reject (just as Western women have been trying to do) the androcentrism and misogyny of whatever culture and tradition they find themselves in, but that is not at all the same as saying they have to adopt Western culture or reject

Arab culture and Islam comprehensively. The feminist agenda as defined by Europeans was also incorrect in its particularities, including its focus on the veil. Because of this history of struggle around it, the veil is now pregnant with meanings. As item of clothing, however, the veil itself and whether it is worn are about as relevant to substantive matters of women's rights as the social prescription of one or another item of clothing is to Western women's struggles over substantive issues. When items of clothing— be it bloomers or bras—have briefly figured as focuses of contention and symbols of feminist struggle in Western societies, it was at least Western feminist women who were responsible for identifying the item in question as significant and defining it as a site of struggle and not, as has sadly been the case with respect to the veil for Muslim women, colonial and patriarchal men, like Cromer and Amin, who declared it important to feminist struggle.

That so much energy has been expended by Muslim men and then Muslim women to remove the veil and by others to affirm or restore it is frustrating and ludicrous. But even worse is the legacy of meanings and struggles over issues of culture and class with which not only the veil but also the struggle for women's rights as a whole has become inscribed as a result of this history and as a result of the cooptation by colonialism of the issue of women and the language of feminism in its attempt to undermine other cultures.

This history, and the struggles over culture and between classes, continues to live even today in the debates on the veil and on women. To a considerable extent, overtly or covertly, inadvertently or otherwise, discussions of women in Islam in academies and outside them, and in Muslim countries and outside them, continue either to reinscribe the Western narrative of Islam as oppressor and the West as liberator and native classist versions of that narrative or, conversely, to reinscribe the contentions of the Arabic narrative of resistance as to the essentialness of preserving Muslim customs, particularly with regard to women, as a sign of resistance to imperialism, whether colonial or postcolonial.[25]

Further, colonialism's use of feminism to promote the culture of the colonizers and undermine native culture has ever since imparted to feminism in non-Western societies the taint of having served as an instrument of colonial domination, rendering it suspect in Arab eyes and vulnerable to the charge of being an ally of colonial interests. That taint has undoubtedly hindered the feminist struggle within Muslim societies.

In addition, the assumption that the issues of culture and women are connected—which informed and to an extent continues to inform Western discussions of women in Islam and which, entering Arabic discourse from colonialist sources, has become ensconced there—has trapped the struggle for women's rights with struggles over culture. It has meant that an argument for women's rights is often perceived and represented by the opposing side as an argument about the innate merits of Islam and Arab culture comprehensively. And of course it is neither Islam nor Arab culture comprehensively that is the target of criticism or the objects of advocated reform but those laws and customs to be found in Muslim Arab societies that express androcentric interests, indifference to women, or misogyny. The issue is simply the humane and just treatment of women, nothing less, and nothing more—not the intrinsic merits of Islam, Arab culture, or the West.

I suggested in an earlier chapter that Western economic penetration of the Middle East and the exposure of Middle Eastern societies to Western political thought and ideas, though undoubtedly having some negative consequences for women, nonetheless did lead to the dismantling of constrictive social institutions and the opening up of new opportunities for women. In the light of the evidence reviewed in the present chapter it appears that a distinction has to be made between, on the one hand, the consequences for women following from the opening of Muslim societies to the West and the social changes and the expansion of intellectual horizons that occurred as a result of the interest within Arab societies in emulating Western technological and political accomplishments and, on the other hand, the quite different and apparently essentially negative consequences following from the construction and dissemination of a Western patriarchal discourse targeting the issue of women and coopting the language of feminism in the service of its strategies of domination.

True, reforms introduced by upper- and middle-class political leaders who had accepted and internalized the Western discourse led in some countries, and specifically Turkey, to legal reforms benefiting women. Ataturk's programs included the replacement of the shari'a family code with a code inspired by the Swiss family code, which at once outlawed polygamy, gave women equal rights to divorce, and granted child-custody rights to both parents. These reforms benefited primarily women of the urban bourgeoisie and had little impact beyond this class. Moreover, and more importantly, whether they will prove enduring remains to be seen, for even in Turkey, Islam and the veil are resurgent: militant Turkish women have staged sit-ins and hunger strikes to demand the right to veil.[26] Reforms in laws governing marriage and divorce that were introduced in Iran in the 1960s and 1970s, though not as far-reaching as Turkish reforms, have already been reversed. Possibly, reforms pursued in a native idiom and not in terms of the appropriation of the ways of other cultures would have been more intelligible and persuasive to all classes and not merely to the upper and middle classes, and possibly, therefore, they would have proved more durable.

NOTES

1. See J. N. Anderson, "Law Reform in Egypt: 1850–1950," in *Political and Social Change in Modern Egypt*, ed. P. M. Hold (London: Oxford University Press, 1969), 209–30; and Noel J. Coulson and Doreen Hinchcliffe, "Women and Law Reform in Contemporary Islam," in *Women in the Muslim World*, ed. Lois Beck and Nikki Keddie (Cambridge: Harvard University Press, 1978), 37–51.

2. Robert L. Tignor, *Modernisation and British Colonial Rule in Egypt, 1882–1914* (Princeton: Princeton University Press, 1966), 324.

3. Ibid., 324–6.

4. In Dante's *Divine Comedy*, for instance, in which Muhammad is relegated to one of the lowest circles of hell, Muhammad is associated with a figure whose transgressions similarly were in the area of what he preached with respect to women. See *The Comedy of Dante Alighieri*, trans. Dorothy Sayers (Penguin Books, 1949), Canto 28, 346–47, 251. For some accounts of early Western representations of Islam see Norman Daniel, *Islam and the West* (Edinburgh: Edinburgh University Press, 1966); and R. W. Southern, *Western Views of Islam in the Middle Ages* (Cambridge: Harvard University Press, 1962).

5. *The Complete Letters of Lady Mary Wortley Montagu*, 2 vols., ed. Robert Halsband (Oxford: Clarendon Press, 1965), 1:318. She corrects "our Vulgar Notion that they do not own women to have any Souls" but perpetuates a modified version of that error in writing, "'Tis true, they say they [women's souls] are not of so elevated a kind, and therefore must not hope to be admitted into the paradise appointed for the Men." Ibid., 1:363. For her statements on polygamy and the parallel "inconsistency" of European men see ibid., 1:329. Montagu also points out in this context that Muslim women of the upper classes owned property in their own right and thus were less at the mercy of men than their Christian sisters. For her remarks on the veil see ibid., 1:328.

6. Timothy Mitchell's *Colonising Egypt* (Cambridge: Cambridge University Press, 1988) offers an interesting and valuable exploration of the issues of colonialism and its discursive designs.

7. Edward Said, *Orientalism* (London: Routledge and Kegan Paul, 1978).

8. For discussions of the uses of anthropology to colonial theory and its uses in reinforcing sexist views of women see Mona Etienne and Eleanor Leacock, "Introduction," in *Women and Colonisation: Anthropological Perspectives*, ed. Etienne and Leacock (New York: Praeger Publishers, 1980), 1–24; Susan Carol Rogers, "Women's Place: A Critical Review of Anthropological Theory," *Comparative Studies in Society and History* 20, no. 1 (1978): 123–62; Elizabeth Fee, "The Sexual Politics of Victorian Social Anthropology," in *Clio's Consciousness Raised*, ed. M. Hartman and L. Banner (New York: Harper Torchbooks, 1974), 86–102.

9. Earl of Cromer, *Modern Egypt*, 2 vols. (New York: Macmillan, 1908), 2:146; hereafter cited in the text.

10. A. B. De Guerville, *New Egypt* (London: William Heineman, 1906), 154.

11. Cromer Papers, cited in Judith E. Tucker, *Women in Nineteenth-Century Egypt* (Cambridge: Cambridge University Press, 1985), 122.

12. Cromer was so prominent in the antisuffrage movement that it was sometimes called the Curzon–Cromer combine after Cromer and Lord Curzon, first marquis of Keddleston. See Constance Rover, *Women's Sufffrage and Party Politics in Britain, 1866–1914* (London: Routledge and Kegan Paul; Toronto: University of Toronto Press, 1967), 171–73; see also Brian Harrison, *Separate Spheres: The Opposition to Women's Suffrage in Britain* (New York: Holmes and Meier Publishers, 1978).

13. Rev. Robert Bruce, in *Report of the Centenary Conference on Protestant Missions of the World Held in Exeter Hall, London (June 9–19th)*, 2 vols., ed. James Johnston (New York: F. H. Revell, [1889]), 1:18–19; Annie van Sommer and Samuel M. Zwemer, eds., *Our Moslem Sisters: A Cry of Need from Lands of Darkness by Those Who Heard It* (New York: F. H. Revell, 1907), 27–28; van Sommer and Zwemer, eds., *Daylight in the Harem* (Edinburgh: Oliphant, Anderson and Ferrier, 1911), 149–50.

14. Qassim Amin, *Tahir al-mar'a*, in *Al-a'mal al-kamila li Qassim Amin*, 2 vols., ed. Muhammad 'Amara (Beirut: Al-mu'assasa al-'arabiyya lil-dirasat wa'lnashr, 1976), 2:71–72; hereafter cited in text. All quotations from *Tahrir al-mar'a* are from vol. 2.

15. For a discussion of Amin's family life see Mary Flounders Arnett, *Qassim Amin and the Beginnings of the Feminist Movement in Egypt* (Ph.D. diss., Dropsie College, 1965).

16. 'Amara, "Hadith 'an al'a'mal al-kamila" (Discussion of the works of Amin), in *Al-a'mal al-kamila li Qassim Amin*, ed. 'Amara, 1:133. 'Amara mentions that the work was the outcome of a gathering in Geneva in 1897 attended by Muhammad 'Abdue, Sa'd Zaghloul, Lutfi al-Sayyid, and Qassim Amin. Indeed, 'Amara points to particular sections that he believes were written by Muhammad 'Abdu. Ibid., 1:139.

17. Perhaps passages such as the above were contributed by 'Abdu or by others—Sa'd Zaghloul or Lutfi al-Sayyid—who have also been mentioned as collaborators

with Amin. See Afaf Lutfi al-Sayyid Marsot, *Egypt and Cromer* (London: John Murray, 1968), 187.

18. Mukhtar Tuhami, *Al-sahafa wa'l-fikr wa'l-thawra, thalath ma'ariq fikriyya* (Baghdad: Dar ma'mun lil-tiba'a, 1976), 28.

19. Among the more interesting pieces on the subject is Judith Gran, "Impact of the World Market on Egyptian Women," *Middle East Research and Information Report*, no. 58 (1977): 307; and Juan Ricardo Cole, "Feminism, Class, and Islam in Turn-of-the-Century Egypt," *International Journal of Middle East Studies* 13, no. 4 (1981): 394–407.

20. Tuhami, *Thalath ma'ariq fikriyya*, 42–45.

21. Tal'at Harb, *Tarbiyet al-mar'a wa'l-hijab*, 2d ed. (Cairo: Matba'at al-manar, 1905), e.g., 18, 19, 25, 29.

22. Frantz Fanon, *A Dying Colonialism*, trans. Haakon Chevalier (New York: Grove Press, 1967), 65. A useful discussion of the interconnections between thesis and antithesis and the ways in which antithesis may become locked in meaning posed by the thesis may be found in Joan W. Scott, "Deconstructing Equality-versus-Difference: Or, the Uses of Poststructuralist Theory for Feminism," *Feminist Studies* 14, no. 1 (1988): 33–49.

23. Ataturk, speech at Kastamonu, 1925, quoted in Bernard Lewis, *The Emergence of Modern Turkey* (London: Oxford University Press, 1961), 165. For further discussions of Turkish articulations of the issue see S. Mardin, *The Genesis of Young Ottoman Thought* (Princeton: Princeton University Press, 1962); and O. Ozankaya, "Reflections of Semsiddin Sami on Women in the Period before the Advent of Secularism," in *Family in Turkish Society*, ed. T. Erder (Ankara: Turkish Social Science Association, 1985).

24. Guity Nashat, "Women in Pre-Revolutionary Iran: A Historical Overview," in *Women and Revolution in Iran*, ed. Nashat (Boulder, Colo.: Westview Press, 1982), 27.

25. One problem with rebuttals of the Islamicist argument voiced by women of Muslim background (and others) generally, but not exclusively, based in the West is the extent to which they reproduce the Western narrative and its iteration in native upper-class voice without taking account of the colonialist and classist assumptions in which it is mired. This silent and surely inadvertent reinscription of racist and classist assumptions is in rebuttals offered from a "Marxist" perspective as much as in rebuttals aligned with the Western liberal position. See, for example, Mai Ghoussoub, "Feminism—or the Eternal Masculine—in the Arab World," *New Left Review* 161 (January–February 1987): 3–18; and Azar Tabari, "The Women's Movement in Iran: A Hopeful Prognosis," *Feminist Studies* 12, no. 2 (1986): 343–60. The topic of Orientalism and the study of Arab women is addressed with particular acumen in Rosemary Sayigh, "Roles and Functions of Arab Women: A Reappraisal of Orientalism and Arab Women," *Arab Studies Quarterly* 3, no. 3 (1981): 258–74.

26. See Deniz Kandiyoti, "Women and the Turkish State: Political Actors or Symbolic Pawns?" in *Women—Nation—State*, ed. Nira Yuval-Davis (London: Macmillan, 1989), 126.

Analyze

1. How did the discourse surrounding the veil change from before the 17th century, through the 17th and 18th centuries, and finally to the 19th century? How did these changes reflect gender politics in Muslim countries?

2. How did colonial powers view the veil? How did this view become a signifier for Islam? What did abolishing the veil come to mean for Western colonists?

3. Why have Muslim leaders felt compelled to conform to Western ideals, especially of the veil? What does this mean for the women who wear the veil, and why?

Explore

1. Ahmed doesn't clearly articulate her thesis until several pages into her essay. Why do you think she decides to place the thesis there, instead of at the end of the first or second paragraph? How does the information she provides leading up to her thesis help establish the background for her argument?

2. How has the discourse the West shaped on the veil impacted Muslim culture's perspective on feminism? Why?

3. "The Discourse of the Veil" was written in 1993, seventeen years before Hillary Clinton's "Remarks at the UN Commission on the Status of Women." What would Ahmed think of the women's accomplishments that Clinton cites? Would she agree with Clinton that there has been some real progress for women, and are there additional issues Ahmed would address (or urge Clinton to address)? If so, what would those be?

Forging Connections

1. In this chapter we include several narratives that present "rebellious" women. How might we compare the situations of Sumiyah from

Haworth's essay and Sarwat from Arnegard's? Why is it important that these essays end with their stories?

2. Feminism takes many different forms. What do the feminisms directly discussed in this chapter reveal about the status of feminism as a global concept? What have we learned about feminism, and how might we define it? Why?

Looking Further

1. In "The Discourse of the Veil," Leila Ahmed argues that "colonialism's use of feminism to promote the culture of the colonizers and undermine native cultures has ever since imparted to feminism in non-Western societies the taint of having served as an instrument of colonial domination, rendering it suspect in Arab eyes and vulnerable to the charge of being an ally of colonial interests. This taint has undoubtedly hindered the feminist struggle within Muslim societies." Are there other places in our readings where you have seen Western feminism as a hindrance, rather than a help, for women's rights, either in a Western or in a global context? If so, where? In what ways does Western feminism perhaps need to change to meet the needs of a global feminism, and why? Write a thesis-driven essay that articulates your assessment of Western feminism, drawing from the readings in this book to support your argument.

2. Do some research into your online habits. To what extent do you have access to global representations of gender? For example, do you have friends living in other countries whom you stay in touch with via social media? Do you follow individuals from other countries on Twitter? Do you watch media from other countries online? How has globalization affected your own understanding of gender?

appendix

Researching and Writing About Gender

Megan L. Titus and Wendy L. Walker with Barbara
Rockenbach and Aaron Ritzenberg

Research-based writing lies at the heart of the mission of higher education:
to discover, transform, and share ideas. As a college student, it is through
writing and research that you will become an active participant in an intellectual community. Doing research in college involves not only searching
for information but also digesting, analyzing, and synthesizing what you
find to create new knowledge. Your most successful efforts as a college
writer will report on the latest and most important ideas in a field as well as
make new arguments and offer fresh insights.

It may seem daunting to be asked to contribute new ideas to a field in
which you are a novice. After all, creating new knowledge seems to be the
realm of experts. In this guide, we offer strategies that demystify the research
and writing process, breaking down some of the fundamental steps that
scholars take when they do research and make arguments. You'll see that contributing to scholarship involves strategies that can be learned and practiced.

Throughout this guide we imagine doing research and writing as engaging
in a scholarly conversation. When you read academic writing, you'll see that
scholars reference the studies that came before them and allude to the studies

Barbara Rockenbach, Director of Humanities & History Libraries, Columbia University. Aaron
Ritzenberg, Associate Director of First-Year Writing, Columbia University.

that will grow out of their research. When you think of research as engaging in a conversation, you quickly realize that scholarship always has a social aspect. Even if you like to find books in the darkest corners of the library, even if you like to draft your essays in deep solitude, you will always be awake to the voices that helped you form your ideas and to the audience who will receive your ideas. As if in a conversation at a party, scholars mingle: they listen to others and share their most recent ideas, learning and teaching at the same time. Strong scholars, like good conversationalists, will listen and speak with an open mind, letting their own thoughts evolve as they encounter new ideas.

You may be wondering, "What does it mean to have an open mind when I'm doing research? After all, aren't I supposed to find evidence that supports my thesis?" We'll be returning to this question soon, but the quick answer is: to have an open mind when you're doing research means that you'll be involved in the research process well before you have a thesis. We realize this may be a big change from the way you think about research. The fact is, however, that scholars do research well before they know any of the arguments they'll be making in their papers. Indeed, scholars do research even before they know what specific topic they'll be addressing and what questions they'll be asking.

When scholars do research they may not know exactly what they are hunting for, but they have techniques that help them define projects, identify strong interlocutors, and ask important questions. This guide will help you move through the various kinds of research that you'll need at the different stages of your project. If writing a paper involves orchestrating a conversation within a scholarly community, there are a number of important questions you'll need to answer: How do I choose what to write about? How do I find a scholarly community? How do I orchestrate a conversation that involves this community? Whose voices should be most prominent? How do I enter the conversation? How do I use evidence to make a persuasive claim? How do I make sure that my claim is not only interesting but also important?

GETTING STARTED

You have been asked to write a research paper. This may be your first research paper at the college level. Where do you start? The important thing when embarking on any kind of writing project that involves research is to find something that you are interested in learning more about. Writing and research is easier if you care about your topic. Your instructor may have given you a topic, but you can make that topic your own by finding something that appeals to you within the scope of the assignment.

Academic writing begins from a place of deep inquiry. When you are sincerely interested in a problem, researching can be a pleasure, since it will satisfy your own intellectual curiosity. More important, the intellectual problems that seem most difficult—the questions that appear to resist obvious answers—are the very problems that will often yield the most surprising and most rewarding results.

PRESEARCHING TO GENERATE IDEAS

When faced with a research project, your first instinct might be to go to Google or Wikipedia or even to a social media site. This is not a bad instinct. In fact, Google, Wikipedia, and social media can be great places to start. Using Google, Wikipedia, and social media to help you discover a topic is what we call *presearch*—it is what you do to warm up before the more rigorous work of academic research. Academic research and writing will require you to go beyond these sites to find resources that will make the work of researching and writing both easier and more appropriate to an academic context.

Google

Let's start with Google. You use Google because you know you are going to find a simple search interface and that your search will produce many results. These results may not be completely relevant to your topic, but Google helps in the discovery phase of your work. For instance, suppose that you are asked to write about gender and work.

Figure A.1   Google. Results of a Google search for "gender and work."

This Google search will produce articles from many diverse sources—magazines, government sites, and corporate reports among them. It's not a bad start. Use these results to begin to hone in on a topic you are interested in pursuing. A quick look through these results may yield a more focused topic, such as how globalization is impacting gender and work around the world. In this case, you may find a particular source that mentions this impact in the context of world development and another that examines why gender equality stalled in the United States as women's labor-force participation leveled off in the 1990s.

Wikipedia

A Wikipedia search on gender and work will lead you to several articles that address both concepts. The great thing about Wikipedia is that it is an easy way to gain access to a wealth of information about thousands of topics. However, it is crucial to realize that Wikipedia itself is not an authoritative source in a scholarly context. Although you may see Wikipedia cited in mainstream newspapers and popular magazines, academic researchers do not consider Wikipedia a reliable source and do not consult or cite it in their own research. Wikipedia itself says that "Wikipedia is not considered a credible source. . . . This is especially true considering that anyone can edit the information given at any time." For research papers in college, you should use Wikipedia only to find basic information about your topic and to point you toward scholarly sources. Wikipedia may be a great starting point for presearch, but it is not an adequate ending point for research. Use the References section at the bottom of the Wikipedia article to find other, more substantive and authoritative resources about your topic.

References [edit]

1. ^ OECD *OECD*. 🗎 Retrieved on November 11, 2013.[dead link]
2. ^ European Commission. Tackling the *Gender Pay Gap in the European Union*. 🗎 Retrieved on May 28, 2015, "The gender pay gap is the difference between men's and women's pay, based on the average difference in gross hourly earnings of all employees."
3. ^ O'Brien, Sara Ashley (April 14, 2015). "78 cents on the dollar: The facts about the gender wage gap" 🔗. *CNN Money* (New York). Retrieved 28 May 2015.
4. ^ http://social.dol.gov/blog/myth-busting-the-pay-gap/ 🔗
5. ^ *a b* "An Analysis of Reasons for the Disparity in Wages Between Men and Women" 🗎 (PDF). Consad.com. Retrieved 2014-03-12.

Figure A.2   Wikipedia. List of references from a Wikipedia search on the gender pay gap. Use these links to further your research.

Using Social Media

Social media such as Facebook and Twitter can be useful in the presearch phase of your project, but you must start thinking about these tools in new ways. You may have a Facebook or Twitter account and use it to keep in touch with friends, family, and colleagues. These social networks are valuable, and you may already use them to gather information to help you make decisions in your personal life and your workplace. Although social media is not generally useful to your academic research, both Facebook and Twitter have powerful search functions that can lead you to resources and help you refine your ideas.

After you log in to Facebook, use the "Search for people, places, and things" bar at the top of the page to begin. When you type search terms into this bar, Facebook will first search your own social network. To extend beyond your own network, try adding the word "research" after your search terms. For instance, a search on Facebook for "gender research" will lead you to the Facebook page for San Francisco State University's Center for Research and Education on Gender and Sexuality. The posts on this page link to current news stories on gender, to other similar research centers, and to topics of interest in the field of gender research. You can use these search results as a way to see part of the conversation about a variety of topics. You can also do an additional search on a particular topic on which you'd like to focus. For example, a search for "women's health United States" will lead you to the Facebook page for the U.S. Department of Health and Human Services Office on Women's Health. The posts on this page reveal the health issues faced by women in the United States and in many cases link to the web pages of the government programs that address them. This is not necessarily the scholarly conversation we referred to at the start of this guide, but it is a social conversation that can still be useful in helping you determine what you want to focus on in the research process.

Twitter is an information network in which users can post short messages (or "tweets"). Although many people use Twitter simply to update their friends ("I'm going to the mall" or "Can't believe it's snowing!"), more and more individuals and organizations are using Twitter to comment on noteworthy events or link to interesting articles. You can use Twitter as a presearch tool because it aggregates links to sites, people in a field of research, and noteworthy sources. Communities, sometimes even scholarly communities, form around topics on Twitter. Users group posts together using hashtags—words or phrases that follow the "#" sign. Users

Figure A.3 Facebook. Facebook page for the Office on Women's Health—U.S. Department of Health and Human Services.

can respond to other users using the @ sign followed by a user's twitter name. When searching for specific individuals or organizations on Twitter, you search using their handle (such as @HillaryClinton or @UN_Women). You will retrieve either tweets that were created by the person or organization or tweets that mention the person or organization. When searching for a topic to find discussions, you search using the hashtag symbol, #. For instance, a search on #gender will take you to tweets and threaded discussions on the topic of gender. Once you retrieve results, you can search again by clicking on any of the words that are hyperlinked within your results, such as #sweden.

If you consider a hashtag (the # sign) an entry point into a community, you will begin to discover a conversation around topics. For instance, a search on Twitter for #gender leads you to the World Economic Forum (@wef), a Swiss nonprofit organization "committed to improving the state of the world by engaging business, political, academic, and other leaders of society to shape global, regional, and industry agendas." News agencies such as Reuters are also active on Twitter, so an article from a Reuters publication will also be retrieved in a search. Evaluating information and sources found in social media is similar to how you evaluate any information you encounter during the research process. And, as with Wikipedia and Google searches, this is just a starting point to help you get a sense of the spectrum of topics. This is no substitute for using library resources. Do not cite Facebook, Twitter, or Wikipedia in a research paper; use them to find more credible, authoritative sources. We'll talk about evaluating sources in the sections that follow.

CREATE A CONCEPT MAP

Once you have settled on a topic that you find exciting and interesting, the next step is to generate search terms, or keywords, for effective searching. Keywords are the crucial terms or phrases that signal the content of any given source. Keywords are the building blocks of your search for information. We have already seen a few basic keywords such as "gender" and "work." One way to generate keywords is to tell a friend or classmate what you are interested in. What words are you using to describe your research project? You may not have a fully formed idea or claim, but you have a vague sense of your interest. A concept map exercise can help you generate more keywords and, in many cases, narrow your topic to make it more manageable.

A concept map is a way to visualize the relationship between concepts or ideas. You can create a concept map on paper, or there are many free programs online that can help you do this (see, for instance, http://vue.tufts .edu/, http://wisemapping.org/, or http://freeplane.sourceforge.net/). There are many concept mapping applications available for mobile devices; the concept map here was created using the app SimpleMind.

Here is a guide to using a concept map. First, begin with a term like "gender." Put that term in the first box. Then think of synonyms or related words to describe gender and work such as "jobs," "inequality," "pay gap," "glass ceiling," and "motherhood penalty." This brainstorming process will help you develop keywords for searching. Note that keywords can also be short phrases.

After some practice, you'll discover that some phrases make for excellent keywords and others make for less effective search tools. The best keywords are precise enough to narrow your topic so that all of your results are relevant, but are not so specific that you might miss helpful results. Concept maps created using apps such as SimpleMind allow you to use templates, embed hyperlinks, and attach notes, among other useful functions.

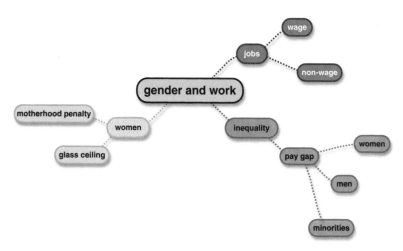

Figure A.4   Concept map. A concept map about gender and work.

KEYWORD SEARCH

One of the hardest parts of writing is coming up with something to write about. Too often, we make the mistake of waiting until we have a fully formed idea before we start writing. The process of writing can actually help you discover what your idea is and, most important, what is interesting about your idea.

Keyword searches are most effective at the beginning stages of your research. They generally produce the greatest number of results and can help you determine how much has been written on your topic. You want to use keyword searches to help you achieve a manageable number of results. However, what is a "manageable number of results"? This is a key question when beginning research. Our keyword search in Google on gender and work produced more than 700 million results. The same search in JSTOR. org produces more than 400,000 results. These are not "manageable" results sets. Let's see how we can narrow our search.

Keyword searches, in library resources or on Google, are most effective if you employ a few search strategies that will focus your results. These strategies are frequently recommended by librarians and are called "Boolean operators" in library-speak. If you and your class visit your school library and have a lesson in research from a librarian, he/she will most likely refer to these strategies by the above name.

1. Use AND when you are combining multiple keywords. We have used this search construction previously:

gender AND work

The AND ensures that all your results will contain both the term "gender" and the term "work." Many search engines and databases will assume an AND search, meaning if you type:

gender work

the search will automatically look for both terms. However, in some cases the AND will not be assumed and "gender work" will be treated as a phrase. This means that "gender" will have to be next to the word "work" to return results. Worse yet, sometimes the search automatically assumes an OR. That would mean that all your results would come back with either "gender" or "work." This will produce a large and mostly irrelevant set of results. Therefore, use AND whenever you want two or more words to appear in a result.

2. Use quotation marks when looking for a phrase. For instance, if you are looking for information on gender and nonwage work you can ensure that the search results will include all of these concepts and increase the relevance using the following search construction:

gender AND "wage gap"

This phrasing will return results that contain both the word "gender" and the phrase "wage gap."

3. Using OR can be effective when you want to use several terms to describe a concept such as

inequality OR "wage gap" OR "pay gap"

A search on gender and work can be broadened to include particular kinds of inequality. The following search casts a broader net because results will come back with gender and either inequality, or wage gap, or pay gap:

gender AND work AND (inequality OR "wage gap" OR "pay gap")

Not all of these words or phrases will appear in each record. Note also that the parentheses set off the OR search, indicating that gender and work must appear in each record and then inequality, wage gap, or pay gap needs to appear along with gender and work.

4. Use NOT to exclude terms that will make your search less relevant. You may find that a term keeps appearing in your search that is not useful. Try this:

gender AND work NOT "glass ceiling"

If you are interested in the wage gap side of this debate, getting a lot of results that discuss the glass ceiling may be distracting. By excluding the keyword "glass ceiling," you will retrieve far fewer sources and hopefully more relevant results.

RESEARCHABLE QUESTION

In a college research paper, it is important that you make an argument, not just offer a report. In high school you may have found some success by merely listing or cataloging the data and information you found; you might have offered a series of findings to show your teacher that you investigated your topic. In college, however, your readers will not be interested in data or information merely for its own sake; your readers will want to know what you make of these data and why they should care.

To satisfy the requirements of a college paper, you'll need to distinguish between a topic and a research question. You will likely begin with a topic, but it is only when you move from a topic to a question that your research will begin to feel motivated and purposeful. A topic refers only to the general subject area that you'll be investigating. A researchable question, on the other hand, points toward a specific problem in the subject area that you'll be attempting to answer by making a claim about the evidence you examine.

"Gender and work" is a topic, but not a researchable question. It is important that you ask yourself, "What aspect of the topic is most interesting to me?" It is even more important that you ask, "What aspect of the topic is it most important that I illuminate for my audience?" Ideally, your presearch phase of the project will yield questions about globalization and language that you'd like to investigate.

A strong researchable question will not lead to an easy answer, but rather into a scholarly conversation in which there are many competing claims.

For instance, the question, "Are men more likely than women to have full-time jobs?" is not a strong researchable question, because there is only one correct answer and thus there is no scholarly debate surrounding the topic. It is an interesting question (the answer is yes: Gallup estimates that, globally, men are almost twice as likely as women to have full-time jobs), but it will not lead you into a scholarly conversation.

When you are interested in finding a scholarly debate, try using the words "why" and "how" rather than "what." Instead of leading to a definitive answer, the words "why" and "how" will often lead to complex, nuanced answers for which you'll need to marshal evidence to be convincing. "How do social norms affect women's ability to succeed in the workforce?" is a question that has a number of complex and competing answers that might draw from a number of different disciplines (political science, history, economics, psychology, and sociology, among others). If you can imagine scholars having an interesting debate about your researchable question, it is likely that you've picked a good one.

Once you have come up with an interesting researchable question, your first task as a researcher is to figure out how scholars are discussing your question. Many novice writers think that the first thing they should do when beginning a research project is to articulate an argument and then find sources that confirm their argument. This is not how experienced scholars work. Instead, strong writers know that they cannot possibly come up with a strong central argument until they have done sufficient research. So, instead of looking for sources that confirm a preliminary claim you might want to make, look for the scholarly conversation.

Looking at the scholarly conversation is a smart way to figure out if you've found a research question that is suitable in scope for the kind of paper you're writing. Put another way, reading the scholarly conversation can tell you whether your research question is too broad or too narrow. Most novice writers begin with research questions that are overly broad. If your question is so broad that there are thousands of books and articles participating in the scholarly conversation, it's a good idea to focus your question so that you are asking something more specific. If, on the other hand, you are asking a research question that is so obscure that you cannot find a corresponding scholarly conversation, you will want to broaden the scope of your project by asking a slightly less specific question.

Rhetoric scholar Kenneth Burke created the metaphor of the parlor for scholarly, or academic, conversation in his book *The Philosophy of Literary*

Form: Studies in Symbolic Action (1941). In that book, he describes the conversation as such:

> Imagine that you enter a parlor. You come late. When you arrive, others have long preceded you, and they are engaged in a heated discussion, a discussion too heated for them to pause and tell you exactly what it is about. In fact, the discussion had already begun long before any of them got there, so that no one present is qualified to retrace for you all the steps that had gone before. You listen for a while, until you decide that you have caught the tenor of the argument; then you put in your oar. Someone answers; you answer him; another comes to your defense; another aligns himself against you, to either the embarrassment or gratification of your opponent, depending upon the quality of your ally's assistance. However, the discussion is interminable. The hour grows late, you must depart. And you do depart, with the discussion still vigorously in progress. (Burke 110)

In this metaphor, Burke describes the conversation as one that has "long preceded" us, and thus, to contribute properly, we must listen to the current conversation to get the gist of the argument. We need to have an understanding of different perspectives to shape our own point of view on the topic of conversation. It's also important to note that, in Burke's parlor, the conversation is ongoing; it started long before we reached the party and will continue long after we leave. We become part of that conversation; we become part of the knowledge that will be imparted to future partygoers. Thus, we want to be sure that we have a clearly articulated point of view that is uniquely ours.

Let's bring the concept of the "Burkean parlor" to a conversation about gender. If you walk into a room and people are talking about gender and the wage gap, it would be out of place for you to begin immediately by making a huge, vague claim, such as "The wage gap exists because of motherhood." It would be equally out of place for you to begin immediately by making an overly specific claim, such as "Motherhood makes it impossible for women to succeed in the workforce because having children forces a career interruption." Rather, you would gauge the scope of the conversation and figure out what seems like a reasonable contribution.

Your contribution to the conversation, at this point, will likely be a focused research question. This is the question you take with you to the library. In the next section, we'll discuss how best to make use of the library. Later, we'll explore how to turn your research question into an argument for your essay.

YOUR CAMPUS LIBRARY

You have probably used libraries all your life, checking out books from your local public library and studying in your high school library. The difference between your previous library experiences and your college library experience is one of scale. Your college library has more stuff. It may be tangible stuff like books, journals, and videos, or it may be virtual stuff, like online articles, e-books, and streaming video. Your library pays a lot of money every year to buy or license content for you to use for your research. By extension, your tuition dollars are buying a lot of really good research material. Resorting to using only Google and Wikipedia means you are not getting all you can out of your college experience.

Not only will your college library have a much larger collection, but also it will have a more up-to-date and relevant collection than your high school or community public library. Academic librarians spend considerable time acquiring research materials based on classes being taught at your institution. You may not know it, but librarians carefully monitor what courses are being taught each year and are constantly trying to find research materials appropriate to those courses and your professor's research interests. In many cases, you will find that the librarians will know about your assignment and will already have ideas about the types of sources that will make you most successful.

Get to Know Your Librarians!

The most important thing to know during the research process is that there are people to help you. Although you may not yet be in the habit of going to the library, there are still many ways in which librarians and library staff can be helpful. Most libraries now have an email or chat service set up so you can ask questions without even setting foot in a library. No question is too basic or too specific. It's a librarian's job to help you find answers, and all questions are welcome. The librarian can even help you discover the right question to ask given the task you are trying to complete.

Help can also come in the form of consultations. Librarians will often make appointments to meet one-on-one with students to offer in-depth help on a research paper or project. Chances are you will find a link on your library website for scheduling a consultation.

Among the many questions fielded by reference librarians, three stand out as the most often asked. Because librarians hear these questions with such regularity, we suggest that students ask these questions when they begin their research. You can go to the library and ask these questions in person, or you can ask via email or online chat.

1. How do I find a book relevant to my topic?

The answer to this question will vary from place to place, but the thing to remember is that finding a book can be either a physical process or a virtual process. Your library will have books on shelves somewhere, and the complexity of how those shelves are organized and accessed depends on factors of size, number of libraries, and the system of organization your library uses. You will find books by using your library's online catalog and carefully noting the call number and location of a book.

Your library is also increasingly likely to offer electronic books, or e-books. These books are discoverable in your library's online catalog as well. When looking at the location of a book you will frequently see a link for e-book versions. You will not find an e-book in every search, but when you do, the advantage is that e-book content is searchable, making your job of finding relevant material in the book easier.

If you find one book on your topic, use it as a jumping-off point for finding more books or articles on that topic. Most books will have bibliographies, either at the end of each chapter or at the end of the book, in which the author has compiled all the sources he or she used. Consult these bibliographies to find other materials on your topic that will help support your claim.

Another efficient way to find more sources once you've identified a particularly authoritative and credible book is to go back to the book's listing in your library's online catalog. Once you find the book, look carefully at the record for links to subjects. By clicking on a subject link, you are finding other items in your library on the same subject. For instance, a subject search on

gender AND work

will link you to items with subjects such as

Equal pay for equal work

Sex discrimination in employment

Sexual division of labor

2. **What sources can I use as evidence in my paper?**

There are many types of resources to use as you orchestrate a scholarly conversation and support your paper's argument. Books, which we discussed earlier, are great sources if you can find them on your topic, but often your research question will be something that is either too new or too specific for a book to cover. Books are good for historical questions and overviews of large topics. For current topics, you will want to explore articles from magazines, journals, and newspapers.

Magazines or periodicals (you will hear these terms used interchangeably) are published on a weekly or monthly schedule and contain articles of popular interest. These sources can cover broad topics like the news in magazines such as *Newsweek, Time,* and *U.S. News and World Report.* They can also be more focused for particular groups like feminists—(*Ms.*)—or photographers (*Creative Photography*). Articles in magazines or periodicals are by professional writers who may or may not be experts. Magazines typically are not considered scholarly and generally do not contain articles with bibliographies, endnotes, or footnotes. This does not mean they are not good sources for your research. In fact, there may be good reasons to use a magazine article to help support your argument. Magazines capture the point of view of a

Figure A.5   Online catalog. Library catalog search return for books about gender and work.

particular group on a subject, such as how farmers feel about increased globalization of food production. This point of view may offer support for your claim or an opposing viewpoint to counter. Additionally, magazines can also highlight aspects of a topic at a particular point in time. Comparing a *Newsweek* article from 1989 on women and the workforce with an article on the same topic in 2009 allows you to draw conclusions about the changing relationship between women and work over that twenty-year period.

Journals are intended for a scholarly audience of researchers, specialists, or students of a particular field. Journals such as *Frontiers: A Journal of Women's Studies, Signs: Journal of Women in Culture and Society,* or *Women's Studies Quarterly* are all examples of scholarly journals focused on a particular field or research topic. You may hear the term "peer-reviewed" or "referred" in reference to scholarly journals. This means that the articles contained in a journal have been reviewed by a group of scholars in the same field before being published in the journal, ensuring that the research has been vetted by a group of peers. Articles from scholarly journals can help provide some authority to your argument. By citing experts in a field, you are bolstering your argument and entering into the scholarly conversation we talked about at the beginning of this guide.

Newspaper articles are found in newspapers that are generally published daily. There is a broad range of content in newspapers, from articles written by staff reporters, to editorials written by scholars, experts, and general readers, to reviews and commentary written by experts. Newspapers are published more frequently and locally than magazines or journals, making them excellent sources for recent topics and events as well as those with regional significance. Newspaper articles can provide you with a point of view from a particular part of the country or world (how the wage gap in the United States differs from that in Sweden) or a strong opinion on a topic from an expert (a journalist writing an editorial on the wage gap's toll on families).

A good argument uses evidence from a variety of sources. Do not assume you have done a good job if your paper only cites newspaper articles. You need a broad range of sources to fill out your argument. Your instructor will provide you with guidelines about the number of sources you need, but it will be up to you to find a variety of sources. Finding two to three sources in each of the categories above will help you begin to build a strong argument.

3. Where should I look for articles on my topic?

The best way to locate journal, magazine, or newspaper articles is to use a database. A database is an online resource that organizes research material of a particular type or content area. For example, *PsycINFO* is a psychology database where you would look for journal articles (as well as other kinds of sources) in the discipline of psychology. Your library licenses or subscribes to databases on your behalf. Finding the right database for your topic will depend on what is available at your college or university because every institution has a different set of resources. Many libraries will provide subject or research guides that can help you determine what database would be best for your topic. Look for these guides on your library website. Your library's website will have a way to search databases. Look for a section of the library website on databases, and look for a search box in that section. For instance, if you type "gender" in a database search box, you may find that your library licenses a database called *GenderWatch*. A search for "history" in the database search box may yield *American History and Life* or *Historical Abstracts*. In most instances, your best bet is to ask a librarian which database or databases are most relevant to your research.

When using the databases that your library provides for you, you will know that you are starting to sufficiently narrow or broaden your topic when you begin to retrieve thirty to fifty sources during a search. This kind of narrow result field will rarely occur in Google, which is one of the reasons why using library databases is preferable to using Google when doing academic research. Databases will help you determine when you have begun to ask a manageable question.

When you have gotten down to thirty to fifty sources in your results list, begin to look through those results to see what aspects of your topic are being written about. Are there lots of articles on work, motherhood, and gender inequality? If so, that might be a topic worth investigating since there is a lot of information for you to read. This is where you begin to discover where your voice might add to the ongoing conversation on the topic.

USING EVIDENCE

The quality of evidence and how you deploy the evidence are ultimately what will make your claims persuasive. You may think of evidence as what will help prove your claim. But if you look at any scholarly book or article, you'll see that evidence can be used in a number of different ways. Evidence can be used to provide readers with crucial background information. It can be used to tell readers what scholars have commonly thought about a topic (with which you may disagree). It can offer a theory that you use as a lens. It can offer a methodology or an approach that you would like to use. And, finally, evidence can be used to back up the claim that you'll be making in your paper.

Novice researchers begin with a thesis and try to find all the evidence that will prove that their claim is valid or true. What if you come across evidence that doesn't help with the validity of your claim? A novice researcher might decide not to take this complicating evidence into account. Indeed, when you come across complicating evidence, you might be tempted to pretend you never saw it! But rather than sweeping imperfect evidence under the rug, you should figure out how to use this evidence to complicate your own ideas.

The best scholarly conversations take into account a wide array of evidence, carefully considering all sides of a topic. As you probably know, often the most fruitful and productive conversations occur not only when you are talking to people who already agree with you, but also when you are fully engaging with the people who might disagree with you.

Coming across unexpected, surprising, and contradictory evidence, then, is a good thing! It will force you to make a complex, nuanced argument and will ultimately allow you to write a more persuasive paper.

OTHER FORMS OF EVIDENCE

We've talked about finding evidence in books, magazines, journals, and newspapers. Here are a few other kinds of evidence you may want to use.

Interviews

Interviews can be a powerful form of evidence, especially if the person you are interviewing is an expert in the field that you're investigating. Interviewing can be intimidating, but it might help to know that many people (even experts!) will feel flattered when you ask them for an interview. Most scholars are deeply interested in spreading knowledge, so you should feel comfortable asking a scholar for his or her ideas. Even if the scholar doesn't know the specific answer to your question, he or she may be able to point you in the right direction.

Remember, of course, to be as courteous as possible when you are planning to interview someone. This means sending a polite email that fully introduces yourself and your project before you begin asking questions. Email interviews may be convenient, but an in-person interview is best, since this allows for you and the interviewee to engage in a conversation that may take surprising and helpful turns.

It's a good idea to write down a number of questions before the interview. Make sure not to just get facts (which you can likely get somewhere else). Ask the interviewee to speculate about your topic. Remember that "why" and "how" questions often yield more interesting answers than "what" questions.

If you do conduct an in-person interview, act professionally. Be on time, dress respectfully, and show sincere interest and gratitude. Bring something to record the interview. Many reporters still use a pen and a pad, since these feel unobtrusive and are portable. Write down the interviewee's name, the date, and the location of the interview and have your list of questions ready. Don't be afraid, of course, to veer from your questions. The best questions might be the follow-up questions that couldn't have occurred to you before the conversation began. You're likely to get the interviewee to talk freely and openly if you show real intellectual curiosity. If you're not a fast writer, it's certainly OK to ask the interviewee to pause for a moment while you take notes. Some people like to record their interviews. Just make sure that you ask permission if you choose to do this. It's always nice to send a brief thank you note or email after the interview. This would be a good time to ask any brief follow-up questions.

Images

Because we live in a visual age, we tend to take images for granted. We see them in magazines, on TV, and on the Internet. We don't often think about them as critically as we think about words on a page. Yet, a critical look at an image can uncover helpful evidence for a claim. Images can add depth and variety to your argument and they are generally easy to find on the Internet. Use Google Image search or flickr.com to find images using the same keywords you used to find books and articles. Ask your instructor for guidance on how to properly cite and acknowledge the source of any images you wish to use.

Multimedia

Like images, multimedia such as video, audio, and animations are increasingly easy to find on the Internet and can strengthen your claim. For instance, if you are researching gender and the wage gap, you could find audio or video news clips illustrating that women earn roughly 78 cents for every dollar men earn. There are several audio and video search engines available such as Vimeo (vimeo.com) or Blinkx (blinkx.com), a search engine featuring audio and video from the BBC, Reuters, and the Associated Press, among others. As with images, ask your instructor for guidance on how to properly cite and acknowledge the source of any multimedia you wish to use. If you want to present your research outside of a classroom project (for example, publish it on a blog or share it at a community event), ask a research librarian for guidance on avoiding any potential copyright violations.

EVALUATING SOURCES

A common problem in research isn't a lack of sources, but an overload of information. Information is more accessible than ever. How many times have you done an online search and asked yourself the question: "How do I know which information is good information?" Librarians can help. Evaluating online sources is more challenging than evaluating traditional sources because it is harder to make distinctions between good and bad online information than it is with print sources. It is easy to tell that *Newsweek* magazine is not as scholarly as an academic journal, but online everything may look the same. There are markers of credibility and authoritativeness when it comes to online information, and you can start to recognize them. We'll provide a few tips here, but be sure to ask a librarian or your professor for more guidance whenever you're uncertain about the reliability of a source.

1. **Domain**—The "domain" of a site is the last part of its URL. The domain indicates the type of website. Noting the web address can tell you a lot. A .edu site indicates that an educational organization created that content. This is not a guarantee that the information is accurate, but it does suggest less bias than a .com site, which will be commercial in nature, with a motive to sell you something, including ideas.
2. **Date**—Most websites include a date somewhere on the page. This date may indicate a copyright date, the date something was posted, or the date the site was last updated. These dates tell you when the content on the site was last changed or reviewed. Older sites might be outdated or contain information that is no longer relevant.

3. **Author or editor**—Does the online content indicate an author or editor? Like print materials, authority comes from the creator of the content. It is now easier than ever to investigate an author's credentials. A general Google search may lead you to a Wikipedia entry on the author, a LinkedIn page, or even an online résumé. If an author is affiliated with an educational institution, try visiting the institution's website for more information.

MANAGING SOURCES

Now that you've found sources, you need to think about how you are going to keep track of the sources and prepare the bibliography that will accompany your paper. Managing your sources is called "bibliographic citation management," and you will sometimes see references to bibliographic citation management on your library's website. Don't let this complicated phrase deter you—managing your citations from the start of your research will make your life much easier during the research process and especially the night before your paper is due when you are compiling your bibliography.

EndNote and RefWorks

Chances are your college library provides software, such as *EndNote* or *RefWorks*, to help you manage citations. These are two commercially available citation management software packages that are not freely available to you unless your library has paid for a license. *EndNote* or *RefWorks* enable you to organize your sources in personal libraries. These libraries help you manage your sources and create bibliographies. Both *EndNote* and *RefWorks* also enable you to insert endnotes and footnotes directly into a Microsoft Word document.

Zotero

If your library does not provide *EndNote* or *RefWorks*, a freely available software called *Zotero* (Zotero.org) will help you manage your sources. *Zotero* helps you collect, organize, cite, and share your sources, and it lives right in your web browser where you do your research. As you are searching Google, your library catalog, or your library database, *Zotero* enables you to add a book, article, or website to a personal library with one click. As you add items to your library, *Zotero* collects both the information you need for your bibliography and any full-text content. This means that the content of journal articles and e-books will be available to you right from your *Zotero* library.

To create a bibliography, simply select the items from your *Zotero* library you want to include, right click and select "Create Bibliography from Selected Items . . . ," and choose the citation style your instructor has asked you to use for the paper. To get started, go to Zotero.org and download *Zotero* for the browser of your choice.

Taking Notes

It is crucial that you take good, careful notes while you are doing your research. Careful note-taking is necessary to avoid plagiarism and can help you think through your project while you are doing research.

Whereas many researchers used to take notes on index cards, most people now use computers. If you're using your computer, open a new document for each source that you're considering using. The first step in taking notes is to make sure that you gather all the information you might need in your bibliography or works cited. If you're taking notes from a book, for instance, you'll need the author, title, place of publication, name of press, and year. Be sure to check the style guide assigned by your instructor to make sure you're gathering all the necessary information.

After you've recorded the bibliographic information, add one or two keywords that can help you sort this source. Next, write a one- or two-sentence summary of the source. Finally, have a section on your document that is reserved for specific places in the text that you might want to work with. When you write down a quote, remember to be extra careful that you are capturing the quote exactly as it is written—and that you enclose it in quotation marks. Do not use abbreviations or change the punctuation. Remember, too, to write down the exact page numbers from the source you are quoting. Being careful with small details at the beginning of your project can save you a lot of time in the long run.

WRITING ABOUT GENDER

In your writing, as in your conversations, you should always be thinking about your audience. Although your most obvious audience is the instructor, most college instructors will want you to write a paper that will be interesting and illuminating for other beginning scholars in the field. Many students are unsure of what kind of knowledge they can presume of their audience. A good rule of thumb is to write not only for your instructor but also for other students in your class and for other students in classes similar to yours. You can assume a reasonably informed audience that is curious but also skeptical.

Of course it is crucial that you keep your instructor in mind. After all, your instructor will be giving you feedback and evaluating your paper. The best way to keep your instructor in mind is to periodically reread the assignment while you are writing. Are you answering the assignment's prompt? Are you adhering to the assignment's guidelines? Are you fulfilling the assignment's purpose? If your answer to any of these questions is uncertain, it's a good idea to ask the instructor.

FROM RESEARCH QUESTION TO THESIS STATEMENT

Many students like to begin the writing process by writing an introduction. Novice writers often use an early draft of their introduction to guide the shape of their paper. Experienced scholars, however, continually return to their introduction, reshaping it and revising it as their thoughts evolve. After all, since writing is thinking, it is impossible to anticipate the full thoughts of your paper before you have written it. Many writers, in fact, only realize the actual argument they are making after they have written a draft or two of the paper. Make sure not to let your introduction trap your thinking. Think of your introduction as a guide that will help your readers down the path of discovery—a path you can only fully know after you have written your paper.

A strong introduction will welcome readers to the scholarly conversation. You'll introduce your central interlocutors and pose the question or problem that you are all interested in resolving. Most introductions contain a thesis statement, which is a sentence or two that clearly states the main argument. Some introductions, you'll notice, do not contain the argument, but merely the promise of a resolution to the intellectual problem.

Is Your Thesis an Argument?

So far, we've discussed a number of steps for you to take when you begin to write a research paper. We started by strategizing about ways to use presearch to find a topic and ask a researchable question, and then we looked at ways to find a scholarly conversation using your library's resources. Now we'll discuss a crucial step in the writing process: coming up with a thesis.

Your thesis is the central claim of your paper—the main point that you'd like to argue. You may make a number of claims throughout the paper; when you make a claim, you are offering a small argument, usually about a piece of evidence that you've found. Your thesis is your governing claim, the central argument of the whole paper. Sometimes it is difficult to know whether you have written a proper thesis. Ask yourself, "Can a reasonable person disagree with my thesis statement?" If the answer is no, then you likely have written an observation rather than an argument. For instance, the statement, "A wage gap exists between men and women in the United States" is not a thesis, since this is a true fact. A reasonable person cannot disagree with this fact, so it is not an argument. The statement, "A wage gap exists for all women in the United States, but it widens for women of color because of institutionalized racism in the workplace" is a thesis, since it is a debatable point. A reasonable person might disagree (by arguing, for instance, that "women of color earn less than white women because of a lack of access to education"). Remember to keep returning to your thesis statement while you are writing. You will be able to make sure that your writing remains on a clear path, and you'll be able to keep refining your thesis so that it becomes clearer and more precise.

Make sure, too, that your thesis is a point of persuasion rather than one of belief or taste. "Women work harder than men" is certainly an argument you could make to your friend, but it is not an adequate thesis for an academic paper, because there is no evidence that you could provide that might persuade a reader who doesn't already agree with you.

Organization

For your paper to feel organized, readers should know where they are headed and have a reasonable idea of how they are going to get there. An introduction will offer a strong sense of organization if it:

- Introduces your central intellectual problem and explains why it is important;
- Suggests who will be involved in the scholarly conversation;
- Indicates what kind of evidence you'll be investigating; and
- Offers a precise central argument.

Some readers describe well-organized papers as having a sense of flow. When readers praise a sense of flow, they mean that the argument moves easily from one sentence to the next and from one paragraph to the next. This allows your reader to follow your thoughts easily. When you begin writing a sentence, try using an idea, keyword, or phrase from the end of the previous sentence. The next sentence, then, will appear to have emerged smoothly from the previous sentence. This tip is especially important when you move between paragraphs. The beginning of a paragraph should feel like it has a clear relationship to the end of the previous paragraph.

Keep in mind, too, a sense of wholeness. A strong paragraph has a sense of flow and a sense of wholeness: this will allow your reader to trace your thoughts smoothly and you will ensure that your reader understands how all your thoughts are connected to a large, central idea. Ask yourself as you write a paragraph, what does this paragraph have to do with the central intellectual problem that I am investigating? If the relationship isn't clear to you, then your readers will likely be confused.

Novice writers often use the form of a five-paragraph essay. In this form, each paragraph offers an example that proves the validity of the central claim. The five-paragraph essay may have worked in high school, since it meets the minimum requirement for making an argument with evidence. You'll quickly notice, however, that experienced writers do not use the five-paragraph essay, and, indeed, your college instructors will expect you to move beyond it. This is because a five-paragraph essay relies on static examples rather than fully engaging new evidence. A strong essay will grow in complexity and nuance as the writer brings in new evidence. Rather than thinking of an essay as something that offers many examples to back up the same static idea, think of it as the evolution of an idea that grows ever more complex and rich as the writer engages with scholars who view the idea from various angles.

Integrating Your Research

As we have seen, doing research involves finding an intellectual community by looking for scholars who are thinking through similar problems and may be in conversation with one another. When you write your paper, you will not merely be reporting what you found; you will be orchestrating the conversation that your research has uncovered. Orchestrating a conversation involves asking a few key questions: Whose voices should be most prominent? What is the relationship between one scholar's ideas and another scholar's ideas? How do these ideas contribute to the argument that your own paper is making? Is it important that your readers hear the exact words of the conversation, or can you give them the main ideas and important points of the conversation in your own words? Your answers to these questions will determine how you go about integrating your research into your paper.

Using evidence is a way of gaining authority. Although you may not have known much about your topic before you started researching, the way you use evidence in your paper will allow you to establish a voice that is authoritative and trustworthy. You have three basic choices to decide how best you'd like to present the information from a source: summarize, paraphrase, or quote. Let's discuss each one briefly.

Summary   You should summarize a source when the source provides helpful background information for your research. Summaries do not make strong evidence, but they can be helpful if you need to chart the intellectual terrain of your project. Summaries can be an efficient way of capturing the main ideas of a source. Remember when you are summarizing to be fully sympathetic to the writer's point of view. Put yourself in the scholar's shoes. If you later disagree with the scholar's methods or conclusions, your disagreement will be convincing because your reader will know that you have given the scholar a fair hearing. A summary that is clearly biased not only is inaccurate and ethically suspect, but also will make your writing less convincing because readers will be suspicious of your rigor.

Let's say you come across the following quote that you'd like to summarize. Here's an excerpt from the electronic journal article "White Women and Women of Color at Work: Making the Relationship Work" by Jean Mavrelis:

> For white men race and gender are not things they historically have had to consider in mainstream U.S. settings. For white women in mainstream contexts, gender awareness is central to their reality. For women of color, race, ethnicity and gender are core pieces: race and ethnicity, often being of more central significance than gender. Failure to acknowledge these differences leads white women on executive tracks in engineering, law, science, finance, manufacturing, sales, and other formerly male dominated professions, to believe that the biggest challenge is breaking down gender barriers. It is for them. However, white women often overlook that women of color also need to contend with their

"different" race and ethnicity. So how can white women and women of color begin to deal with their differences? They can begin by understanding how they are different and the challenges they face trying to bridge the gap.

Consider this summary:

> In "White Women and Women of Color at Work: Making the Relationship Work," Jean Mavrelis says that white women often overlook women of color when they challenge gender barriers at work.

If you compare this summary to what Mavrelis actually said, you will see that this summary is a biased, distorted version of the actual quote. Mavrelis did not make a universal claim about whether white women overlook women of color. Rather, she made a claim about why white women need to consider race and ethnicity in addition to gender.

Now let's look at another summary:

> According to Mavrelis, white women need to acknowledge race and ethnicity, and understand the different challenges faced by women of color, when breaking down gender barriers at work.

This is a much stronger summary than the previous example. The writer shortens Mavrelis's original language, but she is fair to the writer's original meaning and intent.

Paraphrase   Paraphrasing involves putting a source's ideas into your own words. It's a good idea to paraphrase if you think you can state the idea more clearly or more directly than the original source does. Remember that if you paraphrase you need to put the entire idea into your own words. It is not enough for you to change one or two words. Indeed, if you only change a few words, you may put yourself at risk of plagiarizing.

Let's look at how we might paraphrase the Mavrelis quote that we've been discussing. Consider this paraphrase:

> For white women in mainstream situations, gender awareness is at the center of their reality. For women of color, race, ethnicity and gender are key pieces: race and ethnicity, often being more important than gender (Mavrelis).

You will notice that the writer simply replaced some of Mavrelis's original language with synonyms. Even with the parenthetical citation, this is unacceptable paraphrasing. Indeed, this is a form of plagiarism, because the writer suggests that the language is his or her own when it is in fact an only slightly modified version of Mavrelis's own phrasing.

> While an awareness of gender is of central importance to white women, for women of color, awareness of race and ethnicity is often more significant than that of gender alone (Mavrelis).

Here the writer has taken Mavrelis's message but has used his or her own language to describe what Mavrelis originally wrote. The writer offers Mavrelis's ideas with fresh syntax and new vocabulary, and the writer is sure to give Mavrelis credit for the idea in a parenthetical citation.

Quotation   The best way to show that you are in conversation with scholars is to quote them. Quoting involves capturing the exact wording and punctuation of a passage. Quotations make for powerful evidence, especially in humanities papers. If you come across evidence that you think will be helpful in your project, you should quote it. You may be tempted to quote only those passages that seem to agree with the claim you are working with. But remember to write down the quotes of scholars who may not seem to agree with you. These are precisely the thoughts that will help you build a powerful scholarly conversation. Working with fresh ideas that you may not agree with can help you revise your claim to make it even more persuasive, since it will force you to take into account potential counterarguments. When your readers see that you are grappling with an intellectual problem from all sides and that you are giving all interlocutors a fair voice, they are more likely to be persuaded by your argument.

To make sure that you are properly integrating your sources into your paper, remember the acronym ICE. ICE stands for introduce, cite, and explain. Let's imagine that you've found an idea that you'd like to incorporate into your paper. We'll use a quote from Leslie McCall's *Complex Inequality: Gender, Class and Race in the New Economy* as an example. On page 8, you find the following quote that you'd like to use: "Our challenge, then, is to conceptualize inequality as an outcome of both economic restructuring and gender and racial divisions of labor—what I will refer to as a joint economic and social analysis of inequality."

The first thing you need to do is **introduce** the quote. To introduce a quote, provide context so that your readers know where it is coming from, and you must integrate the quote into your own sentence. Here are some examples of how you might do this:

> In her book *Complex Inequality: Gender, Class and Race in the New Economy*, Leslie McCall argues . . .
> One expert on social and economic inequalities claims . . .
> Professor of sociology Leslie McCall explains that . . .
> In her recent book, McCall contends . . .

Note that each of these introduces the quote in such a way that readers are likely to recognize it as an authoritative source.

The next step is to **cite** the quote. Here is where you indicate the origin of the quotation so that your readers can easily look up the original source. Citing is a two-step process that varies slightly depending on the citation style that you're using. We'll offer an example using MLA style. The first step involves indicating the author and page number in the body of your essay. Here is an example of a parenthetical citation that gives the author and page number after the quote and before the period that ends the sentence:

> One expert on social and economic inequalities claims that the "challenge, then, is to conceptualize inequality as an outcome of both economic restructuring and gender and racial divisions of labor" (McCall 8).

Note that if it is already clear to readers which author you're quoting, you need only to give the page number:

> In her book *Complex Inequality: Gender, Class and Race in the New Economy*, Leslie McCall argues, "Our challenge, then, is to conceptualize inequality as an outcome of both economic restructuring and gender and racial divisions of labor" (8).

The second step of citing the quote is providing proper information in the works cited or bibliography of your paper. This list should include the complete bibliographical information of all the sources you have cited. An essay that includes the quote by David Harvey should also include the following entry in the Works Cited:

> McCall, Leslie. *Complex Inequality: Gender, Class and Race in the New Economy*. New York: Routledge, 2001. Print.

Finally, the most crucial part of integrating a quote is to **explain** it. This is often overlooked, but a strong explanation is the most important step to involve yourself in the scholarly conversation. Here is where you will explain how you interpret the source you are citing, what aspect of the quote is most important for your readers to understand, and how the source pertains to your own project. For example:

> Leslie McCall writes, "Our challenge, then, is to conceptualize inequality as an outcome of both economic restructuring and gender and racial divisions of labor—what I will refer to as a joint economic and social analysis of inequality" (8). As McCall explains, inequality must be understood as having both social and economic influences, and that these have gender, race, and class dimensions.

Or

> Leslie McCall writes, "Our challenge, then, is to conceptualize inequality as an outcome of both economic restructuring and gender and racial divisions of labor—what I will refer to as a joint economic and social analysis of inequality" (8). For McCall, analysis of inequality must include economic and social changes in conjunction with one another.

Novice writers are sometimes tempted to end a paragraph with a quote that they feel is especially compelling or clear. But remember that you should never leave a quote to speak for itself (even if you love it). After all, as the orchestrator of this scholarly conversation, you need to make sure that readers are receiving exactly what you'd like them to receive from each quote. Note in the above examples that the first explanation suggests that the writer quoting McCall is centrally concerned with influences on inequality, whereas the second explanation suggests that the writer is centrally concerned with how analysis of inequality is conducted. The explanation, in other words, is the crucial link between your source and the main idea of your paper.

Avoiding Plagiarism

Scholarly conversations are what drive knowledge in the world. Scholars using each other's ideas in open, honest ways form the bedrock of our intellectual communities and ensure that our contributions to the world of thought are important. It is crucial, then, that all writers do their part in maintaining the integrity and trustworthiness of scholarly conversations. It is crucial that you never claim someone else's ideas as your own and that you always are extra careful to give the proper credit to someone else's thoughts. This is what we call responsible scholarship.

The best way to avoid plagiarism is to plan ahead and keep careful notes as you read your sources. Remember the advice (above) on *Zotero* and taking notes: find the way that works best for you to keep track of what ideas are your own and what ideas come directly from the sources you are reading. Most acts of plagiarism are accidental. It is easy to lose track of where a quote or idea came from when you are drafting a paper; plan ahead and this won't happen. Here are a few tips for making sure that confusion doesn't happen to you.

1. Know what needs to be cited. You do not need to cite what is considered common knowledge such as facts (the day Lincoln was born), concepts (the earth orbits the sun), or events (the day Martin Luther King was shot). You do need to cite the ideas and words of others from the sources you are using in your paper.
2. Be conservative. If you are not sure whether you should cite something, either ask your instructor or a librarian or cite it. It is better to cite something you don't have to than not cite something you should.
3. Direct quotations from your sources need to be cited; you must also cite the source any time you paraphrase the ideas or words from your sources.
4. Finally, extensive citation not only helps you avoid plagiarism, but also boosts your credibility and enables your reader to trace your scholarship.

Citation Styles

It is crucial that you adhere to the standards of a single citation style when you write your paper. The most common styles are MLA (Modern

Language Association, generally used in the humanities), APA (American Psychological Association, generally used in the social sciences), and Chicago (*Chicago Manual of Style*). If you're not sure which style you should use, you must ask your instructor. Each style has its own guidelines regarding the format of the paper. Although proper formatting within a given style may seem arbitrary, there are important reasons behind the guidelines of each style. For instance, whereas MLA citations tend to emphasize authors' names, APA citations tend to emphasize the date of publications. This distinction makes sense, especially given that MLA standards are usually followed by departments in the humanities and APA standards are usually followed by departments in the social sciences. Whereas papers in the humanities value original thinking about arguments and texts that are canonical and often old, papers in the social sciences tend to value arguments that take into account the most current thought and the latest research.

There are a number of helpful guidebooks that will tell you all the rules you need to know to follow the standards for various citation styles. If your instructor hasn't pointed you to a specific guidebook, try the following online resources:

Purdue Online Writing Lab: http://owl.english.purdue.edu/

Internet Public Library: http://www.ipl.org/div/farq/netciteFARQ.html/

Modern Language Association (for MLA style): http://www.mla.org/style/

American Psychological Association (for APA style): http://www.apastyle.org/

The Chicago Manual of Style Online: http://www.chicagomanualofstyle.org/ tools_citationguide.html/

Sample Student Research Paper

The following essay was written by Jenna Wilush for Megan's research writing class that focused on gender. For this essay, students were asked to choose a topic related to gender that they had an interest in but knew little about. Before writing this essay, they completed a research narrative that detailed their search into the topic and ended with their point of view. The subsequent paper asked students to take the point of view from their research narrative, defend it, and discuss it in great detail. For her topic, Jenna chose women in combat. The following essay is an argument for why women should be allowed to fight alongside men on the front lines.

Jenna Wilush
May 7th, 2013

Women in Combat

To some, seeing a woman succeed at what was once considered a man's job may be mind-boggling. In reality, it's the way of the future. According to Kate Bolick's article "All the Single Ladies," she explains that in today's world, women are more likely to go to college than men. She informs "in 2010, 55 percent of all college graduates ages 25 to 29 were female" (par. 21). She also adds, "Today women outnumber men not only in college but in graduate school; they earned 60 percent of all bachelor's and master's degrees awarded in 2010, and men are now more likely than women to hold only a high-school diploma" (par. 22). These statistics show how the times are changing, from a time when women rarely went to college and it was a man's world, to women surpassing men in many areas. In today's world, it is not uncommon to see a woman surpass a man in many categories, so why should the military be any different. The world is evolving, and with this evolution comes more opportunity; women are unstoppable.

These rights for women are present in the general workforce, and now they are present in the military. With the lifting of the Pentagon ban that once restricted women from the front line, women are now officially allowed in combat. Although some may see this new right as problematic and unfair, if women are able to do the same tasks as men and surpass them in the workplace, I believe that they should be allowed in combat. Women should be allowed in front line combat based upon their ability to meet the predetermined standards for the job, their physical abilities, as well as their history serving for their country in other military positions. Meeting the requirements for combat and being both physically and psychologically ready for the position, women should be encouraged and able to enlist in the military just like a man. With their abilities and given a chance, women in combat will serve as an asset to the military protecting their country.

Not everyone feels the same way about the potential women have. One main concern many individuals have with

> Although the thesis statement of an academic essay typically appears in the first paragraph, Jenna uses this space to set up the idea that we are living in "different" times for women, and that we need to think about opportunities for women in new ways.

> Jenna's thesis is clearly stated and offers three clear reasons why women should be allowed in front-line combat.

Wilush   3

allowing women into combat is their body type. Women are known to be generally smaller, fragile, and more sensitive than men. Their smaller figures, dainty arms and fingers, and light statures may inhibit them from performing in combat, and

Jenna sets up this paragraph by pointing out how "naysayers" might respond to her thesis, which she will then address in subsequent paragraphs.

become a weakness to the army. Mackubin Thomas Owens agrees with these concerns about a women's body type. In his article, "Coed Combat Units: A Bad Idea on All Counts" he remarks how an average female is about five inches shorter than a male. A woman has less upper body strength and aerobic capacity. Owens uses aerobic capacity to compare a woman during her peak age between 20 and 30 years old to a 50-year-old male. He uses this to show that a woman is nowhere near as capable as a man when compared to aerobic capacity. Owens also states their lighter skeleton can face permanent damage if carrying equipment that is too heavy. Ultimately, Owens presents that women would serve as a nuisance in combat not being able to carry out the jobs. Therefore, a woman joining the military as a front line soldier would inhibit the force altogether. Owens points out that her body figure is just not cut out for the role of strenuous labor against individuals double her size in a life or death situation.

Owens' assumption that this physical deficiency is in every woman is putting the military at a disadvantage. In reality, everyone's body is built differently. To address this issue, gender-neutral fitness tests will be instilled before any individual enlists into combat. Therefore, women will be held to the same standards as men. By enforcing this fitness test, it will prevent any woman who is physically incapable of performing the duties of a soldier from entering into combat, rather than just discriminating against her due to common stereotypes. In the end, if a woman were to pass the designated fitness test, denying her capabilities would only hurt the military in the end.

Elisabeth Bumiller's article, "First Pull-Ups, Than Combat, Marines Say," promotes this idea of gender-neutral fitness tests before admitting an individual into combat. Bumiller asserts that by requiring this test, each individual is held to the same standard. Given this information, Bumiller proves the idea that if women are capable of reaching the same standards that men have to attain, they are ready for combat and should be able to enlist. She quotes Greg Jacob, a former commander and advocate for ending the ban on women in combat on his belief that everyone, no matter their gender, is different. "'There are lots of men who don't have the same muscle mass as other men,' he said. 'There is physical diversity regardless of gender'" (par. 17). By stating this, Bumiller proves that not only should women be held to the same standard as men, but men should also be held to the same standards as women. In reality, everyone is different and a woman might surpass a man in physicality. In one circumstance, there could be a physically capable man, and in the other, a physically capable woman.

Lisa Grossman, author of "The Right to Fight: Women at War," agrees with having gender-neutral fitness tests

> Jenna puts her sources in conversation with one another, showing where and why they might agree or disagree.

Wilush   5

to assess the ability of the individual regardless of gender. She reveals there will be predetermined standards that are required to be met before being admitted into front line combat. These standards will include tasks such as throwing a grenade a specific distance, or being able to lift a specific weight on your back for a certain amount of time. This mechanism will separate the individuals who do have the capability from those who do not. This system will benefit the military in the end as it weeds out physically incapable individuals, both men and women that inhibit the military's performance while replacing them with physically capable individuals.

All in all, gender should not be the deciding factor of who is allowed in combat. This policy limits the military from benefitting from the potential a woman adds. Instead of gender, physicality differences need to be the deciding rule. Gender-neutral fitness tests will make this possible. Physicality will separate the individuals that pass from the ones that don't, ultimately separating who is admitted into combat and who is not. This reason of admission will serve as an asset to the military and strengthen the front line, ensuring that all individuals capable of reaching the minimum standards of combat situations are included.

Physical differences aren't the only factor inhibiting women from combat in some individual's minds. Many believe women should not be allowed in combat because of the living conditions soldiers are forced to face. Since men are more

Note Jenna's use of attributive tags here. She is careful to present Boykin's point of view in a neutral tone, thus offering a solid summary of his argument.

likely to do the down and dirty types of jobs, women don't seem to fit in the harsh living conditions of combat. Jerry Boykin, author of "Women in Combat a Dangerous Experiment" believes women should not be allowed in combat for these reasons. Boykin notes the living conditions when being deployed are harsh. There is no privacy that a woman typically needs, and it is difficult to maintain personal hygiene, something women are usually very concerned with. Entering into combat would be a huge reality check for the high maintenance woman looking for the powder room on the combat field.

Wouldn't Boykin think a woman who cares about her personal hygiene and privacy more than the security of our nation purposely wouldn't enlist for combat, though? Currently, enlisting into the military is a voluntary task. The women who are concerned with their personal space and privacy would not choose to enlist into a job that sends them out into the middle of nowhere with barely any resources to live off of. Boykin makes it sound like a woman has no idea what being in the military is like, and if they are allowed in combat they will get a serious reality check. This is a false assumption though. For many years, women have been in the military, serving as a huge asset towards our fighting force. Although they have never formally been allowed to hold the title of combat soldiers, many women have seen and been in equally as dangerous situations that a combat environment brings.

"Let Women Fight," by Meghan H. MacKenzie, contends that for many years, women have been in the military risking their lives doing dangerous jobs. She also informs the reader that these brave women make up a significant amount of the military. According to her article, "Today, 214,098 women serve in the U.S. military, representing 14.6 percent of total service members" (par. 1). This proves women serve as a functional part of the military in the jobs they do. Without them, the military would be 214,098 people short. Whether they're in the medical staff, mechanics, logistical personnel or anything else, no woman knows what's going to happen at any given time. MacKenzie supports the fact of the dangers in the military by saying that "78 percent of the deaths of female U.S. service members in Iraq were categorized as hostile, yet another sign of how American women in uniform regularly put their lives at risk" (par. 9). If women are dying serving for their country without even being allowed in direct combat, they are risking their lives either way when they make the choice to enlist.

Additionally, Rebekah Havrilla mentioned in "Trauma on the Front Line" believes there is no such thing as front line, and everyone in the military is susceptible of the environment of combat. She quotes, "anywhere you are you have the potential to deal with combat related incidents. One of my friends was killed because a rocket hit the chow hall tent" (par. 3). This example proves the risk women currently take to be in the military, as there are no defined lines separating war zone, caution death, and safe zone. When you enlist, you enlist for anything and everything.

Given their background with the military, a woman who is interested in combat is clearly aware of her duties. This won't be the first time she is forced to urinate in the dirt, or go without a shower. Boykin's assumption is illogical. As a man, one has to face the same embarrassment urinating without privacy, as women will. Furthermore, if Boykin believes privacy is the main concern with being in combat, there is an even bigger issue at stake here. There are much larger concerns with being in combat than privacy.

After taking into consideration all the evidence presented, Jenna offers an assessment of Boykin's original claim that women will not be mentally prepared to deal with the conditions on the front lines.

It's valid to say that adding women to combat units could challenge unit cohesion. This doesn't mean there isn't a solution though. But, in many minds it questions the effectiveness of the military's front line. Mackubin Thomas Owens, who also challenged this topic based on women's physical abilities, believes their presence will break up the unit cohesion of the soldiers. He believes this cohesion brings success on the battlefield. Owens defines cohesion based on six factors: the share of common values, conformity to norms to ensure survival, dismissing individual identity and conforming to group identity, focus on group goals, dependence on one another, and members meet standards as not to inhibit survival. Owens compares group cohesion to brotherly love and it can otherwise be disrupted if the opposite gender is permitted. Owens concludes that men treat each other differently than they treat women and that this behavior will inhibit the performance on the front line.

Although unit cohesion is an important factor in performance, it is not the most prominent one. Obtaining the best group of people for the desired job where the individual contributes significantly to the mission takes precedence over the male bonding that forms unit cohesion. Take a group of men who work great together, but no one really contributes significantly to the group. Instead, everyone is on the same level and works together towards the same standards. Then, take a woman who dominates and can add significantly to the group, bringing it up to the next level. Acquiring the woman would be the most beneficial choice, regardless of interrupting male bonding. Dan Nagasaki and Glenn Doi, authors of "Sex, Human Nature, and Women in Combat," believe this is what strengthens an army. Instead of putting together a group of qualified soldiers and leaving them to bond and form a good group as a team, one needs to put together groups effectively. By doing so, the best person for each job is selected, rather than just anyone. Nagasaki and Doi compare applying for a job to the situation. When taking applications, the hirer looks for the individual that will work best for the position, not that will work best with the group already hired. The same goes for the military. By enforcing this rule, a woman who is significantly capable of doing the best at the task will ultimately strengthen the group. There won't be any issues of breaking up unit cohesion if she's adding her skills to the group successfully.

Finally, the last prominent issue raised as a reason to prevent women from being in combat is psychological. Lisa

Jenna's transition sentence uses what the reader already knows—unit cohesion—to connect to a new idea, women contributing to the group dynamic.

Grossman addresses in her article "The Right to Fight: Women at War" an assumption made by many that women are more likely to be traumatized than men. Their motherly psychological functions make them unable to bear the cruel images of combat and women are more susceptible to harsh memories. They then conclude women should not be allowed in the environment of combat. In fact, this may be true in some cultures, as Grossman states in her article with Israeli Defense Forces, but not so much with the United States. After conducting a study of female United States soldiers that had experienced direct combat during the wars with Iraq and Afghanistan, the results proved otherwise. The study found that women didn't feel any more threatened in the war zones than men. Also, the women were just as resilient as men to combat-related stress. They were also equally as resilient in dealing with the stress from combat after returning home from serving.

Given these facts, women should not be categorized as easily traumatized, preventing them from direct combat. The facts and study prove that men and women deal with psychological issues equally, with no one sex being better than the other. Therefore, women should not be restricted from combat because of a stereotype. By punishing women and not allowing them into combat for something not true hinders the military. While emotionally ready women are sitting out, there could be a mentally hurt and emotional man suffering and worsening the other soldiers' performance. Women are no weaker psychologically than men, and if they were, those women wouldn't be enlisting. Instead, an individual's specific psychological capabilities will help them deal with the harmful images of combat, no matter if the individual is a male or female.

Considering all of the potential women have, the assumptions causing them to be left out of combat are not supported in reality. Women are just as capable, or even more so than men. Based on their physical abilities proven by administering a gender-neutral fitness test for admissions and predetermined standards to be met, there is no reason for a woman not to participate in combat if she passes. Her physical abilities will serve as an asset to the military as she is equally physically capable of meeting the challenges required. Women's history in the military has prepared them well for the harsh conditions combat brings, and their mental capabilities shield them from being any more traumatized than a man. Furthermore, women are capable of having all of the qualities necessary for combat. Prohibiting them from serving is only hurting the military in the long run, but admitting them is strengthening the force for combat, protecting our country. The time has come for our country to proudly allow women to serve in combat on a basis consistent with men.

The conclusion clearly states Jenna's point of view again, while also indicating why this point of view is important on a larger scale.

Works Cited

Bolick, Kate. "All the Single Ladies." *The Atlantic* 30 Sept. 2011. Web. 15 April 2013.

Boykin, Jerry. "Women in Combat a Dangerous Experiment."
    CNN.com 26 January 2013. Web. 14 April 2013.

Bumiller, Elisabeth. "First Pull-Ups, Then Combat, Marines
    Say." *New York Times* 2 Feb. 2013. Web. 15 April 2013.

Grossman, Lisa. "The Right to Fight: Women at War." *New
    Scientist* 217.2902 (Feb. 2013): 6–7. Academic Search
    Premier. Web. 13 April 2013.

MacKenzie, Megan H. "Let Women Fight." *Foreign Affairs* 91.6
    (Nov./Dec. 2012): 32–42. EconLit. Web. 14 April 2013.

Nagasaki, Dan, and Glenn Doi. "Sex, Human Nature, and
    Women in Combat." *American Thinker.* 27 Jan. 2013.
    Web. 15 April 2013.

Owens, Mackubin. Thomas. "Coed Combat Units: A Bad
    Idea on All Counts." *Weekly Standard* 18.20 (4 Feb. 2013):
    31–33. LexisNexis. Web. 13 April 2013.

"Trauma on the Front Line." *New Scientist* 217.2902
    (2 Feb. 2013): 6–7. MAS Ultra. Web. 13 April 2013.

credits

Chapter 1—Introduction to Gender

Chapter 2—Gender and Identity

"What Does a Woman Need to Know?" from *Blood, Bread, and Poetry: Selected Prose 1979–1985* by Adrienne Rich. Copyright © 1986 by Adrienne Rich. Used by permission of W. W. Norton & Company, Inc.

"Guadalupe the Sex Goddess" by Sandra Cisneros from *Goddess Of The Americas/La Diosa De Las Americas: Writings on the Virgin de Guadalupe* ed. by Ana Castillo. Copyright © 1996 by Sandra Cisneros. Copyright © 1996 by Ana Castillo. Riverhead Books, New York. By permission of Susan Bergholz Literary Services, New York, NY, and Lamy, NM. All rights reserved.

"Two Spirit: The Story of a Movement Unfolds" by Zachary Pullin. Originally published in *Native Peoples* (May/June 2014). Copyright © 2014 by Zachary Pullin. Reprinted by permission of Zachary Pullin.

"Cisgender Privilege, Intersectionality, and the Criminalization of CeCe McDonald: Why Intercultural Communication Needs Transgender Studies" by Julia Johnson, *Journal of International and Intercultural Communication* (May 2013), 6.2. Copyright © 2013 by Taylor & Francis, Ltd. Reprinted by permission of Copyright Clearance Center for Taylor & Francis Group, LLC, a division of Informa plc.

"He Defies You Still: The Memoirs of a Sissy" by Tommi Avicolli, *Radical Teacher*, 100 (Fall 2014). Copyright © 2014 by Tommi Avicolli Mecca. Reprinted by permission of Tommi Avicolli Mecca.

"Why I'm Still a Butch Lesbian" by Vanessa Urquhart, *Slate*, July 25, 2014. Copyright © 2014 by Slate. Reprinted by permission of PARS for Slate.

Chapter 3—Gender and Stereotypes

Photo on p. 126: Copyright © Matt Schario. Reprinted by permission of Matt Schario.

"How Big Are Your Balls?" by Brian Frazer, *Esquire* (147.3), February 28, 2007: 200. Copyright © 2007 by Brian Frazer. Reprinted by permission of Brian Frazer.

"The High Cost of Manliness" by Robert Jensen, *Alternet*, September 7, 2006. Reprinted by permission of Robert Jensen.

"If Men Could Menstruate" by Gloria Steinem, *Ms.* magazine, 1978. Copyright © 1978 by Gloria Steinem. Reprinted by permission of East Toledo Productions.

"In Search of Our Mothers' Gardens" from *In Search Of Our Mothers' Gardens: A Womanist Prose* by Alice Walker. Copyright © 1974 by Alice Walker. Reprinted by permission of Houghton Mifflin Harcourt Publishing Company and The Joy Harris Literary Agency, Inc. All rights reserved.

"Hard Time: Lessons from a Maximum-Security Prison" by Jade Chong-Smith, *Huffington Post*, November 19, 2014. Copyright © 2014 by Jade Chong-Smith. Reprinted by permission of Jade Chong-Smith.

"The Coming Out We All Ignored" by Jonathan Zimmerman, *NY Daily News*, May 1, 2013. Copyright © 2013 by Daily News, L.P. (New York). Used by permission.

"Rape Myth Beliefs and Bystander Attitudes among Incoming College Students" by Sara McMahon, *Journal of American College Health*, (July/August 2010), Vol. 50, No. 1. Copyright © 2010 by Routledge. Reprinted by permission of Taylor & Francis Group, LLC, a division of Informa plc.

CHAPTER 4—Gender and the Body

"The Body and the Reproduction of Femininity" from *Unbearable Weight: Feminism, Western Culture and the Body* by Susan Bordo. Copyright © 1993 by The Regents

of the University of California. Reprinted by permission of The
University of California Press.

"Call Cornell Co-Ed the 'Perfect Girl.'" *The New York Times*, December 21, 1912.

"Brooklyn Venus Much Too Large Is Verdict of Physical Culturists." *New York
Herald*, December 22, 1912.

"An Exercise in Body Image" by Brooke Kantor, Helen Clark, and Lydia Federico,
Harvard Political Review, June 28, 2014. Copyright © 2014 by Brooke Kantor,
Helen Clark, and Lydia Federico. Reprinted by permission of the authors.

"It's a Big Fat Revolution" by Nomy Lamm in *Listen Up: Voices from the Next Feminist
Generation* by Barbara Findlen. Copyright © September 11, 2001 by Barbara Findlen.
Reprinted by permission of Seal Press, a member of the Perseus Books Group.

"Why I'm Hot for Peter Dinklage" by Kate Fridkis, *The Frisky*, April 25, 2012.
Copyright © 2012 by Kate Fridkis. Reprinted by permission of Kate Fridkis.

"Jason Collins Is the Envy of Straight Men Everywhere" by Sherman Alexie, *The
Stranger*, May 1, 2013. Copyright © 2013 by Sherman Alexie. Reprinted by permission of Nancy Stauffer Associates on behalf of the author.

Chapter 5—Gender and Popular Culture

"'Sisters Doin' It for Themselves': *Frozen* and the Evolution of the Disney Heroine" by
Michelle Law, *Screen Education Magazine*, 74 (June 2014), pp. 16–25. Copyright
© 2014 by Australian Teachers of Media. Reprinted by permission of the
publisher.

"We're Losing All Our Strong Female Characters to Trinity Syndrome" by Tasha
Robinson, *The Dissolve*, June 16, 2014. Copyright © 2014 by Tasha Robinson.
Reprinted by permission of the author from thedissolve.com.

"Iggy Azalea's Post-Racial Mess: America's Oldest Race Tale, Remixed" by Brittney
Cooper, *Salon.com*, July 15, 2014. This article first appeared in *Salon.com* at http://
www.salon.com/2014/07/15/iggy_azaleas_post_racial_mess_america_oldest_
race_tale_remixed/. An online version remains in the *Salon* archives. Reprinted
with permission.

"Kim Kardashian Doesn't Realize She's the Butt of an Old Racial Joke" by Blue
Telusma, *The Grio*, November 12, 2014. Copyright © 2014 by Marie Emmanuelle
Telusma. Reprinted by permission of the author.

"*Orange Is the New Black*'s Irresponsible Portrayal of Men" by Noah Berlatsky,
The Atlantic, June 30, 2014. Copyright © 2014 by The Atlantic Media Co., as first
published in *The Atlantic Magazine*. All rights reserved. Distributed by Tribune
Content Agency, LLC.

"Candy Girl: The Bright Pink Resiliency of *Unbreakable Kimmy Schmidt*" by Emily
Nussbaum, *The New Yorker*, March 30, 2015. Copyright © 2015 by Conde Nast.
Reprinted by permission of the publisher.

Chapter 6—Gender and Work

"I Want a Wife" by Judy Brady, *Ms.* magazine, July 1972. Copyright © 1972 by Judy
Brady. Reprinted by permission of the author.

Excerpted from "Why Women Still Can't Have It All" by Anne-Marie Slaughter, *The
Atlantic*, July/August 2012. Copyright © 2012 by The Atlantic Media Co., as first
published in *The Atlantic Magazine*. All rights reserved. Distributed by Tribune
Content Agency, LLC.

Chapter 7—Gender and Globalization

index